Fictionalism in Metaphysics

FICTIONALISM IN METAPHYSICS

Edited by
Mark Eli Kalderon

CLARENDON PRESS · OXFORD

OXFORD
UNIVERSITY PRESS

Great Clarendon Street, Oxford OX2 6DP

Oxford University Press is a department of the University of Oxford.
It furthers the University's objective of excellence in research, scholarship,
and education by publishing worldwide in

Oxford New York

Auckland Cape Town Dar es Salaam Hong Kong Karachi
Kuala Lumpur Madrid Melbourne Mexico City Nairobi
New Delhi Shanghai Taipei Toronto

With offices in

Argentina Austria Brazil Chile Czech Republic France Greece
Guatemala Hungary Italy Japan Poland Portugal Singapore
South Korea Switzerland Thailand Turkey Ukraine Vietnam

Oxford is a registered trade mark of Oxford University Press
in the UK and in certain other countries

Published in the United States
by Oxford University Press Inc., New York

British Library Cataloguing in Publication Data
Data available

Library of Congress Cataloging in Publication Data
Data available

Typeset by SPI Publisher Services, Pondicherry, India
Printed in Great Britain
on acid-free paper by
Biddles Ltd, King's Lynn, Norfolk

ISBN 0–19–928218–8   978–0–19–928218–0
ISBN 0–19–928219–6 (Pbk.)   978–0–19–928219–7 (Pbk.)

10 9 8 7 6 5 4 3 2 1

In memory of David Lewis

CONTENTS

Notes on Contributors

Simon Blackburn is Professor of Philosophy at the University of Cambridge. He is the author of *Spreading the Word* (1984), *Essays in Quasi-Realism* (1993), and *Ruling Passions* (1998). His research interests include metaphysics, ethics, philosophy of mind, and language.

Cian Dorr is an Assistant Professor of Philosophy at the University of Pittsburgh, specializing in metaphysics and philosophy of language. Before coming to Pittsburgh Professor Dorr was at New York University for three years.

Richard Joyce is a Research Fellow in the Philosophy Program at the Research School of Social Sciences. He is the author of *The Myth of Morality* (2001). His primary research interest is in metaethics (increasingly with a biological twist), and his philosophical interests range over philosophy of language, metaphysics, philosophy of mind, and aesthetics.

Mark Eli Kalderon is a Reader in the Philosophy Department at University College London. He is the author of *Moral Fictionalism* (2005). His research interests include the philosophy of language, philosophy of mind, philosophy of mathematics, and ethics.

Seahwa Kim is an Assistant Professor in the School of Liberal Arts at the Seoul National University of Technology. Her research interests include metaphysics, the philosophy of the emotions, and aesthetics.

Frederick Kroon is an Associate Professor in the Philosophy Department at the University of Auckland, Faculty of Arts. His research interests include logic, philosophy of language, philosophical logic, metaphysics, and epistemology.

David Lewis joined the Philosophy Department of Princeton University in 1970 and remained at Princeton for the rest of his life. He is the author of *Convention: A Philosophical Study* (1969), *Counterfactuals* (1973), and *On the Plurality of Worlds* (1986). Professor Lewis made seminal contributions to the philosophy of mind, philosophy of language, metaphysics, and epistemology.

DANIEL NOLAN is a Lecturer in the Department of Philosophy at the University of St Andrews. He works on a range of topics: primarily metaphysics, but also philosophy of science, philosophy of language, metaethics, philosophical logic... He tends to be interested in a lot of things at once.

GIDEON ROSEN is Professor of Philosophy at Princeton University. He is the author (with John P. Burgess) of *A Subject with No Object* (1997). His research interests include philosophy of mathematics, metaphysics, and epistemology.

KENDALL WALTON is the Charles Stevenson Collegiate Professor of Philosophy at the University of Michigan, Ann Arbor, and is a Fellow of the American Academy of Arts and Sciences, and the President of the American Society of Aesthetics. He is the author of *Mimesis and Make Believe: On the Foundations of the Representational Arts* (1990). Much of Professor Walton's work consists in exploring connections between theoretical questions about the arts and issues of philosophy of mind, metaphysics, and philosophy of language.

JAMES A. WOODBRIDGE is a Visiting Lecturer in the Philosophy Department at Yale University. His current research investigates logical and metaphysical problems confronting our central semantic notions and their implications in accounting for linguistic and mental content.

STEPHEN YABLO is a Professor in the Department of Linguistics and Philosophy at the Massachusetts Institute of Technology and is a founding member of the Yablangers. He works on identity, essence, causation, intrinsicness, paradox, metaphor, properties, existence, definition, conceivability, and truth.

Introduction

MARK ELI KALDERON

Modern Fictionalism

Modern fictionalism emerged in 1980 with the publication of Hartry Field's *Science Without Numbers* and Bas van Fraassen's *The Scientific Image*. Field maintained that mathematics does not have to be true to be good, and van Fraassen maintained that the aim of science is not truth but empirical adequacy. The suggestion common to each is that the aim of inquiry need not be truth, and that the acceptance of a mathematical or scientific theory need not involve belief in its content.

Field (1980, 1989) claims that mathematics has a platonist interpretation and thus involves commitment to the existence of abstract objects (i.e., objects that do not participate in the causally closed system of spatiotemporal events) such as numbers, functions, and the like. Since there are no abstract objects, mathematics, interpreted at face value, is false. However, mathematics need not be abandoned as a serious intellectual discipline—despite the error involved, mathematics is useful in mediating inferences between claims purely about concreta, and the deductive utility of mathematics does not depend on its truth.

Van Fraassen (1980) claims that scientific theories are genuine representations of unobservable structures in nature. However, the aim of science is not to discover the truth about the unobservable. Rather, given the highest aspirations of the scientific endeavor, an ideally acceptance scientific theory need only have certain non-truth-involving 'virtues' such as empirical adequacy, i.e., the representation of observable regularities. The aim of science is not truth but empirical adequacy.

Thus Field and van Fraassen each, in their own way, suggests that the aim of inquiry need not be the true representation of a putative domain of fact and that the acceptance of a theory need not involve belief in its content. Acceptance is best understood in terms of its role in inquiry. A domain of inquiry, such as biology or astronomy, is associated with a region of discourse that involves a class of public language sentences couched in the distinctive vocabulary of that discipline. Let 'acceptance' be the final state of inquiry: in accepting a sentence from the region of discourse, a person considers the matter closed in the sense that he takes himself to have no reason to inquire further. ('Acceptance' is a technical term and is explicitly stipulated to be neutral as to whether acceptance is belief in the content of the accepted sentence or is some other attitude. Here I am following van Fraassen's, 1980, usage.) The distinctive commitment of fictionalism is that acceptance in a given domain of inquiry need not be truth-normed, and that the acceptance of a sentence from the associated region of discourse need not involve belief in its content.

There is an important qualification to be made. But before it can be made, a distinction needs to be drawn between two kinds of acceptance.

Acceptance can be tentative or full (see Harman, 1986: 46–7). Thus, for example, a person who denies the axiom of choice may tentatively accept that axiom in order to work out the implications of conjoining it with a standard set theory. Such a person only has a reason to tentatively accept the axiom of choice while he has reason to inquire after its implications for a standard set theory: once the implications are discovered, he ceases to tentatively accept the axiom. In contrast to tentative acceptance, full acceptance ends inquiry. In fully accepting a sentence, the issue is closed in the sense that there is no reason to inquire further. Tentative acceptance is not limited to supposition. A person may tentatively accept General Relativity considering it to be a very good approximation of the truth but an imperfect approximation nonetheless. Such a person only has a reason to accept General Relativity while there is no significantly more accurate theoretical alternative. Tentative acceptance, while distinct from full acceptance is a matter of degree. The degree of tentative acceptance depends on the extent to which a person is prepared to rely on the acceptance of the sentence in theoretical and practical reasoning and the range of contexts in which a person does so rely. If, over time, and over a wide range of contexts, a person comes to rely sufficiently on the acceptance of the sentence in theoretical and practical reasoning, he may come to fully accept that sentence. Thus, the distinction between tentative and full acceptance is best understood as an approach to a limit.

The distinctive commitment of fictionalism—that acceptance in a given domain of inquiry is not truth-normed and does not involve belief in the content of the accepted sentence—should be understood as a claim about *full* acceptance. Suppose someone's tentative acceptance of General Relativity falls short of belief. That, by itself, would not establish that scientific acceptance is not belief in the accepted theory. It is the norms that govern full acceptance and the attitudes involved in full acceptance that are relevant to a fictionalist stance towards the given domain of inquiry (see Rosen, Chapter 1, this volume). Henceforth, by 'acceptance' I will mean full acceptance.

So the fictionalist claims of a given domain of inquiry that acceptance in the area is not truth-normed and does not involve belief in the content of the accepted sentence. Why describe such an epistemic stance as 'fictionalism?' There is an important analogy with fiction—at least on one natural understanding of fiction (see Brock, 2002; Lewis, 1978; and Walton, 1990). In *Moby Dick*, Melville writes:

Yet, when by this collision forced to turn towards home, and so for long months of days and weeks, Ahab and anguish lay stretched together in one hammock, rounding in mid winter that dreary, howling Patagonian cape; then it was, that his torn body and gashed soul bled into one another, and so interfusing made him mad.

The passage describes the onslaught of Ahab's madness in the aftermath of his initial encounter with the White Whale. Whatever point there was to writing this, Melville is not reporting the truth of some historical episode. The represented events have not transpired—a fact that is at least tacitly understood by both Melville and his reader. Melville literally asserts nothing about Ahab's madness, and the witting participants of the fiction literally believe nothing about Ahab. In a fictional context, the utterance or inscription of a sentence is not the assertion of the expressed content, and the acceptance of a sentence is not belief in that content. The acceptance and pragmatics of sentences from a fictionalist inquiry thus parallels, at least to this extent, the acceptance and pragmatics of fictional sentences on one natural understanding of fiction.

Two Contrasts: Reductionism and Nonfactualism

The fictionalist stance is further clarified by contrasting it with reductionism and nonfactualism.

As opposed to earlier nominalists, Field does not propose to interpret or reinterpret mathematics in nominalistically acceptable terms. He does not propose to reduce mathematics to claims about a domain of concreta or potential concreta. Rather mathematics is interpreted at face value as involving reference to and quantification over a domain of abstracta. In this way, Field's fictionalism avoids the controversial semantic claims of earlier nominalists.

Similarly, as opposed to earlier empiricists, van Fraassen does not propose to interpret or reinterpret scientific theories in terms that involve no reference to unobservable entities. He does not propose to reduce scientific theories to claims about the observable states of measuring devices, say. Rather, according to constructive empiricism, science is interpreted at face value as involving reference to and quantification over a domain of unobservable entities. In this way, van Fraassen's fictionalism avoids the controversial semantic claims of earlier empiricists.

Thus, fictionalism stands opposed to a certain kind of reductionism. The fictionalist claims, and the reductionist denies, that the target region of discourse is interpreted at face value.

Not only is fictionalism usefully contrasted with reductionism, it is usefully contrasted as well with nonfactualism. According to nonfactualism, the sentences of the target region of discourse do not have a truth-evaluable content—they are not genuine representations of a putative domain of fact. Thus, for example, according to Ayer (1946), ethical sentences do not represent ethical facts—facts about distinctively ethical objects (such as virtues or rights) and properties (such as goodness or being just); rather, their distinctively ethical content entirely consists in the expression of the emotional attitudes of the speaker. Ayer's nonfactualist expressivism is controversial. One obstacle to it is the so-called Frege–Geach problem (see Ross, 1939: 33–4; Geach, 1958, 1960, 1965; and Searle, 1962, 1969). The problem is that sentences can meaningfully occur in unasserted contexts (such as the antecedent of a conditional, or within the scope of a negation operator, or within propositional attitude constructions), but in such contexts they do not express the relevant attitudes. In uttering the sentence 'It is not the case that lying is wrong' a speaker does not express disapproval of lying. However, if the content of 'is wrong' is exhausted by the use of sentences containing it to express disapproval, then it lacks that content and indeed, by Ayer's lights, any ethical content in unasserted contexts. But that's implausible.

The fictionalist, however, need not claim that the target region of discourse has a nonrepresentational content and so can avoid the problems associated with a nonfactualist semantics. The fictionalist can maintain that the sentences from the region of discourse are genuine representations of a putative domain of fact. Thus Field maintains that mathematical sentences are genuine, truth-evaluable representations of abstract mathematical entities, and van Fraassen maintains that theoretical sentences are genuine, truth-evaluable representations of unobservable entities. It is just that these representations are not being put forward as true and so their contents are not the objects of belief when such representations are accepted. A central cognitive use of a representation is to put forward that representation as true. While a representation might be used in that way, it need not. A representation can be used in all sorts of ways. Using it to claim that the world is the way the representation represents it to be is but one of them. Indeed this is an important insight of Wittgenstein's (1958: section 23):

But how many kinds of sentences are there? Say assertion, question, and command? There are *countless* kinds: countless different kinds of use of what we call 'symbols', 'words', 'sentences'. . . . Review the multiplicity of language-games in the following examples, and in others:

> Giving orders, and obeying them
> Describing the appearance of an object, or giving its measurements
> Constructing an object from a description (a drawing)
> Reporting an event
> Speculating about an event
> Forming and testing a hypothesis
> Presenting the results of an experiment in tables and diagrams
> Making up a story; and reading it
> Play-acting
> Singing catches
> Guessing riddles
> Making a joke; and telling it
> Solving a problem in practical arithmetic
> Translating from one language into another
> Asking, thanking, cursing, greeting, praying.

Hermeneutic and Revolutionary Fictionalism

There are two ways to understand fictionalism. Fictionalism can be understood as a *description* of an actual domain of inquiry, or it can be understood as a *prescription* for reforming that inquiry. Following John P. Burgess' (1983) terminology, let *hermeneutic fictionalism* be a description of a domain of inquiry, and let *revolutionary fictionalism* be a prescription for reforming a domain of inquiry.

Van Fraassen's constructive empiricism might be understood as a form of hermeneutic fictionalism (but see Rosen, 1994, for an important difficulty with this interpretation). So understood, given the highest aspirations of science as it is actually conducted, the acceptance of a theory is not in fact truth-normed, it is not evaluated in terms of how accurately it represents the unobservable structure of nature; rather, the norms that actually govern acceptance are such that as long as a theory displays certain non-truth-involving virtues such as empirical adequacy, we have sufficient reason to accept that theory. On this interpretation, when a scientist accepts and utters a theory, he need not believe that theory and he need not be asserting it.

Contrast this understanding of constructive empiricism with Field's nominalism. According to Field, when people accept and utter a mathematical sentence, they believe the content expressed and assert that content. Since mathematical discourse is interpreted at face value and since, so interpreted, it involves commitment to the existence of abstract objects and there are none, our actual mathematical practice involves us in systematic and pervasive error. When Field claims that mathematics does not have to be true to be good, he is not making a claim about the norms that actually govern mathematical acceptance; rather, he is proposing a reform of mathematical inquiry. We should revise our attitudes towards the mathematical sentences we accept and utter. When we accept a mathematical sentence we should believe only that it is deductively useful in mediating inferences between purely nominalistic claims or perhaps that it is true according to standard mathematics, but this falls short of believing the content of that sentence. Field's nominalism is a kind of revolutionary fictionalism. (Field's mathematical fictionalism is thus importantly different from Stephen Yablo's, Chapter 3, 'figuralism'. Whereas Field is a revolutionary fictionalist, Yablo is a hermeneutic fictionalist.)

This contrast is revealing. For while hermeneutic fictionalism is a distinctive kind of irrealism, distinct from both nonfactualism and the error theory, revolutionary fictionalism is a kind of error theory. According to an error theory, such as Mackie's (1977) account of morality, the sentences from the associated region of discourse are genuine, truth-evaluable representations of a putative domain of fact. However, no such facts obtain, and the target sentences are systematically false. There are two attitudes one might take towards an error-ridden discourse. One might take the error involved to be a reason to abandon the domain of inquiry. Thus if we decide there are no witches or phlogiston, we might decide to stop inquiring about them. However, eliminativism is not the only option. We might decide to retain the domain of inquiry despite the error involved because it is good, or useful, or interesting to do so. Doing so involves revising the attitudes towards the sentences that we accept and utter. (On pain of incoherence. Compare Santayana's notorious remark that there is no God and Mary is his mother.) If the error theorist elects to retain the domain of inquiry despite the error involved, he is a revolutionary fictionalist. So while hermeneutic fictionalism is a distinctive kind of irrealism, revolutionary fictionalism is a distinctive kind of error theory.

This Volume

Since 1980, fictionalist accounts of science, mathematics, modality, morality, and other domains of inquiry have been developed. In metaphysical disputes, the fictionalist option is now widely regarded as an option worthy of serious consideration. It is my hope that the present volume will contribute to this trend. The contributions represent the state of the art drawn from different areas of metaphysical controversy. With the exception of Kendall Walton's (Chapter 2) 'Metaphor and Prop Oriented Make-Believe', none of the contributions has been previously published.

Gideon Rosen's (Chapter 1) 'Problems in the History of Fictionalism', is a selective survey of some of the historical precedents of modern fictionalism. While fictionalism in the modern sense emerged in 1980, there are a number of important historical precedents, notable among them are Nietzsche's remarks about errors necessary for life and Vaihinger's philosophy of 'as if'. Rosen discusses fictionalist themes in pyrrhonian skepticism, ancient and renaissance astronomy, and Bentham's theory of fictions. While no uncontroversial instances of fictionalism in the modern sense are uncovered, Rosen's fascinating survey sheds light both on the relevant intellectual history and on the commitments of modern fictionalism.

Kendall Walton's (Chapter 2) 'Metaphor and Prop Oriented Make-Believe' is an important account of a class of metaphors that has influenced writers developing fictionalist accounts in a variety of areas. Walton observes that games of make-believe sometimes involve props. So when a child plays with a doll make-believing that it is her child, the doll is a prop in this imaginative activity. Sometimes the interest in the props is purely as a guide to the content of the make-believe. Sometimes, however, the interest in the make-believe in which they participate is in understanding the props themselves. Walton calls the former kind of make-believe *content oriented make-believe* and the latter *prop oriented make-believe*. He argues that the interpretation of a class of metaphors essentially involves prop oriented make-believe. The distinction between content and prop oriented make-believe is important and reoccurs in various guises in the writing of a number of modern fictionalists. In this volume, Yablo (Chapter 3) relies on it in giving a fictionalist account of mathematical inquiry, James A. Woodbridge (Chapter 5) relies on it in developing a novel form of deflationism in the guise of a fictionalist account of truth talk, and Frederick Kroon (Chapter 6) relies on it in giving an account of what we are doing making propositional attitude ascriptions with empty names in the 'that'-clause.

Stephen Yablo's (Chapter 3) 'The Myth of the Seven' develops a fictionalist account of mathematical inquiry. In contrast to Field's fictionalism, Yablo's is a hermeneutic as opposed to a revolutionary fictionalism. According to Yablo, putative mathematical entities such as numbers, functions, and the like, start off life as representational aids in articulating certain first-order logical truths. Yablo describes this as a kind of *Kantian logicism*—*Kantian*, since the necessity of mathematics is understood in terms of its representational role; *logicist*, since the represented facts are logical facts. As the mathematical game of make-believe takes on a life of its own, mathematical entities function both as props and as representational aids helping us to describe the props (a possibility anticipated by Walton, Chapter 2—see especially, his discussion of the second way in which metaphors may be 'essential').

Seahwa Kim's (Chapter 4) 'Modal Fictionalism and Analysis' is an in-depth discussion of a kind of problem for modal fictionalism. Modal fictionalism was initiated by Rosen (1990). Talk of possible worlds has proved useful and illuminating in articulating a variety of modal ideas—a fact recognized even by those uncomfortable with David Lewis' (1986) modal realism and its ersatzist alternatives. Rosen's suggestion is that one may retain the utility of possible worlds talk without a commitment to possible worlds, if we take a fictionalist attitude towards possible worlds. Drawing on Lewis' (1978) account of fiction, Rosen proposes that in accepting, say, 'There are possible worlds in which donkeys talk' the fictionalist believes only that according to the hypothesis of the plurality of worlds, there are possible worlds in which donkeys talk—a belief that falls short of commitment to possible worlds. Kim raises modal and temporal difficulties for modal fictionalism (difficulties anticipated by Nolan, 1997) and discusses a number of resolutions of these.

James A. Woodbridge's (Chapter 5) 'Truth as a Pretense' deploys Walton's notion of prop oriented make-believe to develop a novel form of deflationism about truth. Many deflationists do grammatical violence in interpreting the apparent predicate 'true' as serving some nonpredicative logical function, say, as a device of infinite conjunction. According to Woodbridge, 'true' functions grammatically and logically as a predicate, just as it appears; however, it is essentially involved in a pretense according to which sentences and the propositions they express instantiate the (nonexistent) property of being true. Woodbridge's account of truth talk thus importantly parallels Gareth Evans' (1982) treatment of existence talk also inspired by Walton's work.

Frederick Kroon's (Chapter 6) 'Belief about Nothing in Particular' deploys Walton's notion of prop oriented make-believe to address some problems for the direct reference program in accounting for propositional attitude ascriptions with empty names occurring in the 'that'-clause. According to direct reference theorists, there is nothing more to the content of a name than the object it denotes. However, if there is nothing more to the content of a name than the object that it denotes, empty names—names lacking denotations—must lack a content. This has the apparent and implausible commitment that empty names are intersubstitutable *salva veritate* (but see Braun, 1993, for a defense of this claim). One approach to this problem might be to construe empty names as denoting no existent thing but only nonexistent things. Kroon provides an account of the role of empty names in propositional attitude constructions that avoids a commitment to an implausible pattern of substitution and the ontological profligacy of a Meinongian ontology.

Daniel Nolan's (Chapter 7) 'Fictionalist Attitudes about Fictional Matters' is in many ways complementary to Kroon's contribution. Whereas Kroon draws upon Walton's account of fiction in giving a treatment of propositional attitude reports, Nolan draws upon Lewis account of fiction. (See Walton's, 1990, account of the relation between these two approaches to fiction.) As discussed above, one advantage that certain fictionalists can claim over non-factualist rivals is the problems nonfactualists face in accounting for propositional attitude constructions (this is one aspect of the Frege–Geach problem). Nolan observes that fictionalists themselves face a similar difficulty. Suppose a person is a moral fictionalist. When he accepts, say, the sentence 'Abortion is wrong' he does not believe the moral proposition expressed by that sentence. It is natural to claim that such a person believes that abortion is wrong. But reports of moral belief are not claims of morality but claims of descriptive psychology, and so not within the scope of the moral fiction. Nolan discusses how a fictionalist can account for such propositional attitude reports by extending the fiction to include propositional attitudes about the fictional subject matter.

Cian Dorr's (Chapter 8) 'What we Disagree about when we Disagree about Ontology' discusses the nature of persistent metaphysical disagreement with mereology as the central test case. Though Dorr does not give a fictionalist account of mereology (but see Dorr and Rosen, 2002), he does draw on fictionalist themes in giving a compositional semantics for the claims of rival ontologists in order to give a reconciliationist interpretation of these claims, i.e., an interpretation according to which each is making a true claim. He argues that a reconciliationist understanding of the rival claims of ontology must ultimately fail: with respect to mereology, a reconciliationist understanding ultimately favors nihilism—the view that there are no composite things.

Richard Joyce's (Chapter 9) 'Moral Fictionalism' develops a form of moral fictionalism, albeit of the revolutionary kind. Suppose that morality stands convicted of some error such that the central claims of morality are subject to systematic and pervasive error (see Mackie, 1977). Why might moral talk not be rejected outright like talk of witches or phlogiston? How might we legitimately retain moral discourse? Joyce argues that moral discourse is useful despite the error involved and thus should be retained. Specifically, he suggests that moral talk is importantly useful as a bulwark against weakness of the will and that this utility is sufficient reason to retain the error-ridden discourse.

David Lewis' (Chapter 10) 'Quasi-Realism is Fictionalism' argues that the best interpretation of Simon Blackburn's quasi-realist program in ethics is as a kind of fictionalism. One of Blackburn's avowed aims is to earn the right to say what a 'moral realist' does: that means either being or make-believedly being a moral realist. Another of his avowed aims is to avoid the realist's errors: that means not being a realist. Taking these aims together, Lewis argues, Blackburn must aim to make-believedly be a moral realist. Like the explicit fictionalist, his apparent moral assertions are merely apparent. If that is right, quasi-realism is a variety of moral fictionalism.

In (Chapter 11) 'Quasi-Realism no Fictionalism', Simon Blackburn considers Lewis' suggestion and respectfully demurs. Like Joyce (Chapter 9), Lewis focuses on a variety of errors that morality stands convicted of. Blackburn argues that revolutionary fictionalism is not sustainable the way quasi-realism might be and so the former fails as an interpretation of the latter.

REFERENCES

Ayer, Alfred J. (1946). *Language, Truth and Logic*. London: Gollancz.
Braun, David (1993). 'Empty Names.' *Noûs*, 27: 449–69.
Brock, Stuart (2002). 'Fictionalism about Fictional Characters.' *Noûs*, 36.1: 1–21.

Burgess, John P. (1983). 'Why I Am Not a Nominalist.' *Notre Dame Journal of Formal Logic*, 24: 93–105.

Dorr, Cian, and Gideon Rosen (2002). 'Composition as Fiction.' In Richard M. Gale (ed.), *Blackwell Guide to Metaphysics*. Oxford: Basil Blackwell.

Evans, Gareth (1982). *The Varieties of Reference*. John McDowell (ed.). Oxford: Clarendon Press.

Field, Hartry (1980). *Science Without Numbers*. Princeton: Princeton University Press.

—— (1989). *Realism, Mathematics and Modality*. Oxford: Basil Blackwell.

Geach, Peter T. (1958). 'Imperative and Deontic Logic.' *Analysis*, 18: 49–56.

—— (1960). 'Ascriptivism.' *The Philosophical Review*, 69: 221–5.

—— (1965). 'Assertion.' *The Philosophical Review*, 74: 449–65.

Harman, Gilbert (1986). *Change in View: Principles of Reasoning*. Cambridge, MA: MIT Press, Bradford Books.

Lewis, David (1978). 'Truth in Fiction.' *American Philosophical Quarterly*, 15.1: 37–46.

—— (1986). *On the Plurality of Worlds*. Oxford: Basil Blackwell.

Mackie, John (1977). *Ethics: Inventing Right and Wrong*. New York: Penguin Books.

Nolan, Daniel (1997). 'Three Problems for "Strong" Modal Fictionalism.' *Philosophical Studies*, 87.3: 259–75.

Rosen, Gideon (1990) 'Modal Fictionalism.' *Mind*, 99.395: 327–54.

—— (1994). 'What is Constructive Empiricism?' *Philosophical Studies*, 74: 143–78.

Ross, David W. (1939). *Foundations of Ethics*. Oxford: Oxford University Press.

Searle, John R. (1962). 'Meaning and Speech Acts.' *The Philosophical Review*, 71: 423–32.

—— (1969). *Speech Acts, An Essay in the Philosophy of Language*. Cambridge: Cambridge University Press.

van Fraassen, Bas C. (1980). *The Scientific Image*. Oxford: Oxford University Press.

Walton, Kendall L. (1990). *Mimesis as Make-Believe*. Cambridge, MA: Harvard University Press.

Wittgenstein, Ludwig (1958). *The Philosophical Investigations*. New York: Macmillan Publishing Co., Ltd.

SUGGESTED FURTHER READING

Historical Precedents

Bentham, Jeremy (1932). *The Theory of Fictions*. In Ogden (ed.), *Bentham's Theory of Fictions*. New York: Harcourt, Brace and Company

Vaihinger, Hans (1924). *The Philosophy of 'As If'*. C. K. Ogden (trans.). London: Kegan Paul.

Existence

Dummett, Michael (1993). 'Existence.' In *The Seas of Language*. Oxford: Oxford University Press.

Kroon, Frederick (1992). 'Was Meinong Only Pretending?' *Philosophy and Phenomenological Research*, 52.3: 499–526.

—— (2000). '"Disavowal through Commitment" Theories of Negative Existentials.' In Anthony Everett and Thomas Hofweber (eds.), *Empty Names, Fiction and the Puzzles of Existence*. Stanford: CSLI Publications.

Sainsbury, Mark (1999). 'Names, Fictional Names, and "Really".' *Proceedings of the Aristotelian Society*, Supplementary Volume, 73: 243–69.

Walton, Kendall L. (2000). 'Existence as Metaphor?' In Anthony Everett and Thomas Hofweber (eds.), *Empty Names, Fiction, and the Puzzles of Existence*. Stanford: CSLI Publications.

Wiggins, David (1994). 'The Kant–Frege–Russell View of Existence.' In *Modality, Morality, and Belief: Essays in Honor of Ruth Barcan Marcus*. Cambridge: Cambridge University Press.

Fiction

Byrne, Alex (1993). 'Truth in Fiction: The Story Continued.' *Australasian Journal of Philosophy*, 71.1: 24–35.

Currie, Gregory (1990). *The Nature of Fiction*. Cambridge: Cambridge University Press.

Hills, David (1997). 'Aptness and Truth in Verbal Metaphor.' *Philosophical Topics*, 25: 117–53.

Lamarque, Peter, and Stein Haugom Olsen (1994). *Truth, Fiction, and Literature: A Philosophical Perspective*. Oxford: Oxford University Press.

Walton, Kendall L. (1997). 'Spelunking, Simulation, and Slime: On Being Moved by Fiction.' In *Emotion and the Arts*. Oxford: Oxford University Press.

Mathematics

Balaguer, Mark (2000). *Platonism and Anti-Platonism in Mathematics*. Oxford: Oxford University Press.

Henkin, Leon (1953). 'Some Notes on Nominalism.' *The Journal of Symbolic Logic*, 19.1: 19–29.

Rosen, Gideon (2001). 'Nominalism, Naturalism, Epistemic Relativism.' *Philosophical Perspectives*, 15: 69–91.

Yablo, Stephen (2000a). 'Aprioricity and Existence.' In Paul Boghossian and Christopher Peacocke (eds.), *New Essays on the A Priori*. Oxford: Oxford University Press: 197–228.

—— (2002a). 'Go Figure: A Path Through Fictionalism.' *Midwest Studies in Philosophy*, 25: 72–102.

Modality

Nolan, Daniel (2002). 'Modal Fictionalism.' In Edward N. Zalta (ed.), *The Stanford Encyclopedia of Philosophy*, Summer 2002 Edition. http://plato.stanford.edu/archives/sum2002/entries/fictionalism-modal/.

Nolan, Daniel, and John O'Leary-Hawthorne (1996). 'Reflexive Fictionalisms.' *Analysis*, 56.1: 26–32.

Yablo, Stephen (1996). 'How in the World?' *Philosophical Topics*, 24.1: 255–86.

Morality

Joyce, Richard (2002). *The Myth of Morality.* Cambridge University Press, Cambridge.

—— (Chapter 9, this volume). 'Moral Fictionalism.'

Nolan, Daniel, Gregory Restall, and Caroline West (forthcoming). 'Moral Fictionalism versus The Rest.' *Australasian Journal of Philosophy.*

Kalderon, Mark Eli (2005). *Moral Fictionalism.* Oxford: Oxford University Press.

Science

Cohen, L. Jonathan (1992). *An Essay on Belief and Acceptance.* Oxford: Clarendon Press.

van Fraassen, Bas C. (1994). 'Gideon Rosen on Constructive Empiricism.' *Philosophical Studies*, 74: 179–92.

Critics

Putnam, Hilary (1975a). 'Philosophy of Logic.' Reprinted in *Mathematics, Matter and Method: Philosophical Papers, 1.* Cambridge, MA: Harvard University Press.

Richard, Mark (2000). 'Semantic Pretense.' In Anthony Everett and Thomas Hofweber (eds.), *Empty Names, Fiction, and the Puzzles of Existence.* Stanford: CSLI Publications.

Stanley, Jason (2001). 'Hermeneutic Fictionalism.' *Midwest Studies in Philosophy*, 25: 36–71.

Szabó Zoltán Gendler (2001). 'Fictionalism and Moore's Paradox.' *Canadian Journal of Philosophy*, 31: 293–308.

van Inwagen, Peter (1985). 'Pretense and Paraphrase.' In Peter McCormick (ed.), *The Reasons of Art: Artworks and the Formations of Philosophy.* Ottowa: University of Ottowa Press.

—— (2000). 'Quantification and Fictional Discourse.' In Anthony Everett and Thomas Hofweber (eds.), *Empty Names, Fiction, and the Puzzles of Existence.* Stanford: CSLI Publications.

1

Problems in the History of Fictionalism

GIDEON ROSEN

Fictionalism, What

To a first approximation, fictionalism about a region of discourse is defined by three basic contrasts:

(a) As against the instrumentalist or the non-cognitivist, the fictionalist maintains that claims made within the discourse are genuine representations of how things stand, and that they are therefore normally capable of truth and falsity.

(b) As against one sort of reductionist, the fictionalist maintains that the language of the discourse is to be interpreted 'at face value'. Claims made within the discourse genuinely imply what they are most naturally taken to imply. So if the theory seems to say, for example, that every person has a guardian angel in heaven, then the theory is true only if the angels in heaven really exist.

(c) As against one sort of realist, the fictionalist maintains that the ultimate aim of discourse in the area is not (or need not be) to produce a true account of the domain, but rather to produce theories with certain 'virtues'—virtues a theory may possess without being true.

The distinctive commitment is the third. This is what Hartry Field has in mind when he says that in mathematics, a theory need not be true in order to be good (Field 1989: 3ff). It is what Bas van Fraassen (1980: 12) has in mind when he says that acceptance of a scientific theory need not involve the belief that it is true. It is important, however, to distinguish the fictionalist's version of this thought from certain less exciting thoughts that might be expressed by the same words.

Everyone knows that a contribution to science can be valuable even if it is not correct in every detail. Newton's mechanics is clearly good or acceptable for certain purposes. The best current theories in fundamental physics are obviously *very* good, and most physicists who take an interest in these matters in some sense accept them. And yet they will presumably acknowledge that these theories are at best imperfect approximations to the truth. Obviously enough, this sensible fallibilism does not amount to anything as bold as fictionalism about fundamental physics. That is why I characterized fictionalism (following van Fraassen) as a view about the *ultimate* aim of the discourse in question, and before we begin in earnest it may help to elaborate briefly on this formulation.

Fictionalism and its rivals (realism, instrumentalism, etc.) are theses about what we have been calling regions of discourse. But it would be more accurate to say that they are positions about domains of *inquiry*. Poets and storytellers are engaged in discourse. They produce representations—and these representations may be true or false—but these representations are not part of an on-going practice in which claims are produced, criticized, refined and revised, and then relied upon as a resource for further deliberation. You misunderstand what the storyteller is up to if you ask him to support his claims with reasons. You seriously misconceive the enterprise if you treat his claims as reasons for theoretical and practical decisions of your own. In a serious inquiry, by contrast, representations serve both as resources for and as objects of rational scrutiny.

When a claim is put forward in the course of a serious inquiry, the speaker indicates a certain distinctive commitment to it. Suppose a chemist is engaged in a discussion about how to design a new piece of equipment, and suppose that in the process of criticizing some new proposal, he says, 'That won't work, because the specific gravity of mercury is only 13.623.' His remark about the specific gravity of mercury in this context is not a guess or a speculation; it is not a suggestion to the effect that the hypothesis is worth looking into. It is put forward as a reason against a certain proposed course of action. Let us say that when a claim is put forward in this spirit, the speaker indicates his *acceptance* of it. The claims you accept are the claims you regard as legitimate resources for justification, both theoretical and practical, within the context of a certain inquiry.

Acceptance is governed by norms: that is why it is subject to criticism. Some of the norms are clearly external to the discourse in question. If you risk a visit from the Inquisition if you accept the claim that earth moves, then the astronomer who accepts it is obviously open to criticism. But this criticism, however serious, would not be scientific criticism. It might be imprudent to accept the claim under the circumstances; but it would not be unscientific. The claim might still be amply justified, as we shall say, by the standard *internal* to the inquiry of which it is a part.

These internal norms or standards determine when a claim is *acceptable* from the standpoint of the discourse in question. To criticize a scientific claim on scientific grounds is (in the first instance) to argue that it would be some sort of mistake to treat it as a resource for justifying subsequent theoretical and practical developments. A claim may be acceptable for certain purposes, or given our limited state of information, or to a limited degree without being, as we shall say, ideally acceptable. To say that S is ideally acceptable is to say that given the aims and interests of the inquiry, it wants for nothing. An acceptable claim satisfies every desideratum that the enterprise imposes on claims that are to be put forward as resources for justification.

The best fundamental theories we now possess are clearly acceptable for certain serious purposes: but they are not ideally acceptable in this sense by the standards of the disciplines that take an interest in them. Each is subject to serious unanswered criticism of various sorts, and there are clearly contexts in which it would be unacceptable by internal standards simply to put them forward without qualification. In other (less fundamental) areas, however, there is no reason to doubt that we have attained something like ideal acceptability. The claim that mercury has a specific gravity of (approximately) 13.623 at 20 degrees Fahrenheit really is settled (so far as we know). It will be part of any comprehensive ideally acceptable account in the domain.

Fictionalism and realism are opposed positions about what it takes for a representation to be ideally acceptable in this sense. Everyone agrees that a false claim can be acceptable for certain purposes. The fictionalist's distinctive claim is that a false claim can be *ideally* acceptable. For the fictionalist, literal falsity is simply not a defect and literal truth as such is not a virtue. The fictionalist thus sees the production and criticism of representations in the target domain as unconcerned, in the end, with representing things as they are.

As a corollary, the fictionalist is committed to a sharp distinction between full acceptance and belief. To accept a theory without reservations is to regard it as fully acceptable. If a theory can be fully acceptable without being true, then to accept a theory is not the same thing as to believe it. Acceptance is compatible with agnosticism, or with positive disbelief. It may (and typically will) involve beliefs of various sorts. The scientist who accepts S may be committed to believing that S has certain virtues—that S is part of an empirically adequate theory, for example. But if a theory or a claim can possess the virtues in question without being true, then there is a clear difference between accepting S and believing it.

As another corollary, the fictionalist is committed to a distinction between assertion and what is sometimes called 'quasi-assertion'. When a theorist puts a claim forward in the course of inquiry, he does it by uttering a freestanding sentence, S. He says, 'The specific gravity of mercury is 13.623,' and he says it in such a way as to make it clear that he is indicating his acceptance of it. Now ordinarily we suppose that the unqualified utterance of a freestanding sentence in the course of a serious conversation is an assertion of the proposition expressed by the sentence. But to assert that P is normally to express one's belief that P, and to believe that P is (near enough) to believe that P is true. The fictionalist must therefore reject this standard pragmatic assumption. He must say that within the discourse in question, serious unqualified assertoric utterance is not assertion but quasi-assertion, where to quasi-assert that P is to express one's acceptance of P, an attitude that is compatible with agnosticism and disbelief.

The fictionalist therefore rejects what may seem a platitude, viz., that scientific inquiry aims at knowledge. His alternative picture is that in certain domains, at any rate, the aim of inquiry—the rationally constrained production and deployment of representations—is to produce a representation of reality with certain virtues: a representation which may be wildly false, and which may therefore have no claim on our belief.

Fictionalism is now a familiar option in a number of areas. The present revival may be dated with some precision to 1980—that *annus mirabilis* which saw the publication of both *The Scientific Image* and *Science without Numbers*. Field and van Fraassen were concerned with the existential commitments of science and mathematics. But in the wake of their liberating and explicit rejection of the idea that inquiry always aims at truth, we have seen a widespread deployment of their approach. We now have moderately well worked out fictionalist accounts of moral discourse, of philosophical discourse about possible worlds and propositions, and of ordinary discourse about composite objects and fictional characters. None of these views is widely accepted. And yet it seems fair to say that in most areas of metaphysical controversy, the fictionalist gambit is now generally recognized as an option worthy, if not of respect, then at least of moderately serious consideration.

It was not ever thus. The idea that the sciences broadly construed seek to represent things as they are has been a near universal conceit in Western thought. Until recently there has never been a significant fictionalist tendency in philosophy. There is no longstanding fictionalist tradition; there has never been a fictionalist school. In most times and places one searches in vain for the merest intimation of the thought that the serious intellectual disciplines are in the end unconcerned with the literal truth of what they say.

Nonetheless, as always in the history of ideas, there are precursors. Over the years a number of more or less isolated figures have proposed views with clear affinities for modern fictionalism. The best known precursor is the philosophical system of Hans Vaihinger, whose *Philosophie des Als-Ob* (1911) defends a comprehensive fictionalist treatment of the objects of science, mathematics, ethics, law, and common sense. Vaihinger's system and its reception have recently been treated with admirable clarity by Arthur Fine, so I shall have little to say about it (Fine, 1993). For similar reasons I will ignore certain celebrated anticipations: Kant's doctrine of the ideas of reason, and Nietzsche's animadversions on 'errors' necessary for life. My main aim in this present note is to sketch some of the less well-known anticipations—and apparent anticipations—in order to stress certain relatively neglected problems of interpretation and classification. I make no claim to original scholarship or to comprehensive treatment. What follows is best conceived as a selective tour for interested amateurs of some of the darker corners in which the beast may or may not be lurking.

Pyrrhonism as Protofictionalism

As we have seen, one central feature of any fictionalist view is a contrast between acceptance and belief, where acceptance is supposed to be a form of commitment that underwrites serious reliance on claims and theories while being consistent with agnosticism and disbelief. Now this contrast, or something like it, is sometimes discerned in ancient skepticism. It may therefore be useful to begin with an examination of the question, to what extent does ancient skepticism anticipate the structural features of modern fictionalism?

The skepticism in question is pyrrhonism, the most radical species of Hellenistic skepticism, as represented, for example, in the writings of Sextus

Empiricus (*fl.* Second century, AD.). The pyrrhonist is supposed to aspire to live 'without belief' or opinion. Towards this end he cultivates a range of techniques for blocking belief in himself and others. When presented with an argument or an experience that might, if unopposed, lead him to assent to some potentially controversial view, the pyrrhonist produces an 'equipollent' argument for an incompatible view, thereby inducing suspense of judgment (*epoché*). When he finds himself inclined to believe that a tower in the distance is really round, he reminds himself that what looks round from one vantage point may look square from another. When he finds himself inclined to believe that matter is composed of atoms, he rehearses one or another compelling anti-atomist argument. The pyrrhonian sage is a master of these techniques, and so finds it possible to meet every consideration on one side with an equally powerful consideration on the other. The effect is meant to be a condition of stable suspense of judgment, cultivated not from some pathological fear of error, but rather in the interest of peace of mind (*ataraxia*) (PH I 25–30).[1]

The case for regarding the pyrrhonist as a protofictionalist begins with the following natural thought. Even the pyrrhonist must think and act; and if he is to live anything like a normal human life, he must engage in ordinary conversation. But anyone who thinks and acts and speaks will inevitably find himself articulating and acting upon claims about himself and his environment. If the skeptic does not *believe* these claims (because he has managed to suspend judgment across the board), he must still accept them in some sense. He acts on and gives voice to *these* claims and not to their negations, after all. The suggestion is that the pyrrhonist anticipates the fictionalist in placing significant weight on this distinction between acceptance and belief in his account of his own practice.

The interest of this assimilation turns on a number of vexed interpretative questions, the most important of which concern the scope of the pyrrhonist's *epoché*. In certain areas it is perfectly clear that the pyrrhonist is not fictionalist. Thus no one disputes that when it comes to controversial philosophical and scientific claims—claims about the unobservable underlying natures of things—the pyrrhonist will do his best to eschew both belief and acceptance. He will not assent in any sense to the claims of (say) Stoic physics—except perhaps when engaged in a refutation of the Stoic (PH I 18). He certainly will not treat the claims of stoicism as *perfectly acceptable* (hence quasi-assertible) for the purposes of, say, scientific explanation. At this level he is thus a simple agnostic and not a fictionalist. For the pyrrhonist, scientific questions are best passed over in silence or with a presentation of equipollent arguments on both sides; whereas for the fictionalist they may be met with direct partisan answers, albeit answers which do not express belief.

On the other hand, no one disputes that the skeptical *epoché* does not extend to claims about how things appear. The skeptic may say, 'The honey appears sweet to me now.' But when he does he will say it without qualification or reservation. Commentators disagree about whether these assertions constitute expressions of belief. It is natural to suppose that they do, especially when the claim concerns how things appear to someone else.[2] Miles Burnyeat (1980: 28ff) suggests that for Sextus propositions about how things seem—as opposed to propositions about how things are—are not possible objects of belief.[3] Amplifying this thought, Jonathan Barnes (1982: 65) suggests that they are best assimilated to Wittgensteinian avowals, so that when the skeptic says 'This honey appears sweet', he is not describing his mental state but rather *expressing* it in roughly the sense in which a cry expresses pain.[4] We need not take a stand on this issue.[5] No matter how it is resolved, the skeptic is obviously not a fictionalist about appearance claims. Either he simply believes them, or they are not candidates for belief. In either case, there is no distinction between acceptance and belief at this level.

The case for regarding the pyrrhonist as a protofictionalist must therefore come from a range of intermediate claims. I shall focus on three likely candidates: claims about the manifest properties of external bodies, certain philosophical claims, and the claims of morality. In the first two cases it will emerge that while there may be a distinction to be drawn between an attitude that might be called 'acceptance' and genuine belief, the pyrrhonist's acceptance invariably lacks certain central features of acceptance as the fictionalist understands the notion. In the third case I will suggest that given a certain speculative reconstruction of the position, the affinity between pyrrhonism and contemporary fictionalism is very close.

Let's begin with the skeptic's attitude towards everyday claims about the manifest properties of ordinary objects: 'Honey is sweet', 'That is a hammer.' The skeptic will presumably say this sort of thing as he goes about his business. The discipline does not involve a reform of ordinary speech. More importantly, he will presumably rely on thoughts of this sort all the time. If he needs a hammer, he may think to himself, 'This is a hammer', and act in light of this thought. So if he systematically disavows belief in such matters, there will be some ground for distinguishing the claims he 'accepts' as a basis for speech and action from the claims whose contents he believes.

Scholars disagree about whether the pyrrhonist aims to suspend belief at this level. Michael Frede (1979) famously maintains that there is no such ambition. For Frede, the skeptical *epoché* concerns only claims about how things *really* are insofar as such claims are supposed to be supported by reasons. Frede's skeptic is not a fictionalist in any sense. When he says, 'Honey is sweet' he simply believes what he says because he finds himself believing it; and when it comes to philosophical claims about whether honey is *really* sweet—sweet in itself, independently of us—he will simply suspend judgment and say nothing at all. The case for regarding pyrrhonism as a form of fictionalism about everyday description thus gets off the ground only if we assume (following Burnyeat) that the skeptic eschews belief about the manifest properties of external things. On this reading, when the skeptic says, 'Honey is sweet' he does not believe what he says. Rather he says, 'Honey is sweet' because honey appears sweet to him and because his speech is governed by a sort of coding scheme: For '*X* is *F*' read '*X* appears *F* to me now.' (See PH I 15, where the examples are philosophical propositions.)

Again, we need not resolve the scholarly question. Even in the most favorable case the connection between skepticism and fictionalism at this level is superficial. Let's begin by distinguishing two roles in skeptical practice for ordinary remarks of the form '*X* is *F*.' On the one hand, such remarks may serve simply to express the fact that *X* appears *F* to the speaker. Here we are tempted to picture a speaker who responds to questions about how things are—'Is *X F*?'—by unreflectively blurting out an indicative sentence with the settled understanding that such blurtings are to be understood as code for claims about appearances. We can *say* that in such a case the skeptic *accepts* '*X* is *F*' without believing it. But this sort of acceptance is clearly weaker than fictionalist's distinctive attitude. In particular, the element of *commitment* is lacking. When the fictionalist puts forward a view, he takes a stand. He commits himself both to defending it in response to internal challenges and to relying on it as a resource. When the pyrrhonist says, '*X* is *F*' simply in order to express the fact that *X* strikes him as *F*, he undertakes (for all we have said) no commitment of either sort.

On the other hand, an ordinary remark of the form '*X* is *F*' may figure in the skeptic's thinking as a sort of 'premise'. Suppose he needs a hammer and after looking around the room, sees an object says to himself 'This is a hammer, so I'll take it.' Here he relies on the claim 'This is a hammer' as a basis for action. It is somewhat unclear how the proponent of Burnyeat's reading can make sense of this aspect of skeptical practice.[6] But to the extent that he can, the view involves a more interesting conception of acceptance. The idea would be that when a skeptic accepts that *X* is *F*, he is disposed to both to say '*X* is *F*' when queried as a way of expressing how things appear to him *and* to rely on this claim as a practical premise in his everyday deliberations.

Acceptance so conceived nonetheless differs from the fictionalist's distinctive attitude in several respects. Most significantly, in accepting that this is a hammer and acting accordingly, the skeptic does not (for all we've said) take the view that this claim is *superior* to its rivals. It is *his* claim only in the sense that he is disposed to act on it for now. But in putting it forward and acting on it, he claims no special virtue for it. One way to put the point is that there is so far no sense in which the pyrrhonist who utters '*X* is *F*' and relies on it in the ordinary way thereby commits himself to the *acceptability* of '*X* is *F*'—to its *choice worthiness* given the standards that govern theory choice in the area. At best he indicates that for the present he is disposed to choose it. For the fictionalist, acceptance has a normative dimension: To accept a claim is to endorse operating with it in certain ways on the ground that it exhibits features that warrant such reliance. So far, the pyrrhonist's 'acceptance' altogether lacks this normative dimension.

Something like it may seem to figure in the skeptic's deployment of certain philosophical claims. The pyrrhonist does not accept controversial philosophical claims as matters of positive doctrine. But he does have a serious use for them in certain contexts. For example, after considering a series of arguments for the claim that everything is relative; Sextus writes:

Since we have established that everything is relative, it is clear that we shall not be able to say what each existing object is like in its own nature and purely, but only what it appears to be like relative to something. It follows that we must suspend judgment about the nature of objects.

(PH I 39)

Lest this be mistaken for the expression of a philosophical opinion, Sextus cautions us explicitly:

It should be recognized that here as elsewhere, we use 'is' loosely, in the sense of 'appears', implicitly saying 'Everything appears relative.'

(PH I 40)

The philosophical thought that everything is relative will presumably figure as a resource in the skeptic's thinking. When he is inclined to believe that honey really is sweet, he may pull himself back by running through the argument that concludes, 'Everything is relative.' When he reaches this point, and it has its intended effect of blocking belief, there is a sense in which the philosophical claim is functioning as a sort of premise. But not only does it have a certain premise-like force for him in this context; when he allows it to play this role he appears to commit himself to defending it in certain ways. It seems immensely plausible, at any rate, that when the proposition is challenged (e.g., by the absolutist who is trying to disarm the relativist challenge) the skeptic will be disposed to meet the arguments with counter-arguments in defense of the relativist position. It might therefore be said when the skeptic is immersed in this sort of argument, he treats the relativist view both as a resource for his own thinking *and as a proposition that calls for defense when it is challenged,* and hence as a proposition to which he is in some sense 'committed', even though, by hypothesis, he does not believe it. Should we say that in this sort of context, the pyrrhonist is a fictionalist about the philosophical claim?

Again, it seems to me that the assimilation is unconvincing. When the pyrrhonist says, 'Everything is relative', he is supposed to mean that every-thing *appears* relative. But what can *this* mean? As Burnyeat (1980: 47ff) points out there is no question of a sensory or perceptual appearance in this case. And if he is a genuine pyrrhonist he presumably cannot mean that relativism is likely or probable. I take it that the state of mind the pyrrhonist expresses by his remark is familiar from the following sort of experience. You have been listening to a debate on a complex issue about which you are relatively uninformed. At first, whenever some expert speaks, you find his response to the previous comment perfectly convincing. But after several iterations you begin to notice the pattern. When X gives his eighteenth rejoinder to Y's remarks, you are still in some sense inclined to find his remarks convincing: they strike you as correct; you can see nothing to object to in them. But since you are reasonably confident that Y will have an equally compelling response, you withhold judgment. At this stage the balance of the evidence *seems to you* to favor X; but you place no stock in that appear-ance. You wouldn't bet a nickel on the truth of X's view. I take it that this is the sort of condition in which the pyrrhonist finds himself after a fresh rehearsal of the case for relativism. If this is right, then the condition he expresses by saying 'Everything is relative' does not amount to a positive endorsement of the relativist view—even a temporary one. Given his larger commitment to a project of meeting arguments with counterarguments, he may indeed find himself disposed to rise to its defense when the absolutist chimes in. *But he will not be defending the view because he is committed to it.* He will be defending it in order to restore the balance of argument; and when the balance starts to tip against it he will switch sides, without having altered his underlying commitments. By contrast, when the fictionalist accepts a view and a question arises, he is under normative pressure to defend it *because in accepting it he has committed himself to its acceptability*. So far, this aspect of fictionalist acceptance has no counterpart in pyrrhonist practice.

Perhaps the best case for the assimilation of pyrrhonism to fictionalism focuses on the skeptic's attitude towards the claims of conventional religion and morality. One strand in pyrrhonism stresses the skeptic's aspiration to 'live in accordance with everyday observances, without holding opinions—for we are not to be utterly inactive'. (PH I 23) In part this involves acquiescing in feeling and instinct, as when 'hunger conducts us to food and thirst to drink'. But it also involves acquiescing in the prevailing moral view.

> By the handing down of customs and laws we accept, from an everyday point of view, that piety is good and impiety bad. . . . And we say all this without holding opinions.
>
> (PH I 23)

Now if this means that the skeptic will in some sense believe that piety is good while suspending judgment on whether it is *really* good, then the view is not a form of fictionalism. But that is certainly not the only possible reading of the passage. On one natural reading, the skeptic will adopt a *policy* of acting in accordance with prevailing laws and customs without taking a position on whether these local views are correct. He will, as Sextus says, *accept* that piety is good (acting and speaking accordingly) without holding the opinion that it is. And on one version of the view, this attitude would appear to have much in common with acceptance in the fictionalist's sense of the notion.

It is sometimes claimed that this sort of stance is incoherent on the ground that to adopt a policy of acting in accordance with a system of norms is inevitably to believe (or to commit oneself to believing) the normative claims on which one acts. But this is an ambitious theoretical claim of which the pyrrhonist would have been skeptical; and in any case it is just not plausible. Imagine a dialogue with a skeptic who has just performed some pious act. 'Why did you do it?' 'Because it was the pious thing to do, and piety is good.' 'Do you really believe what you just said?' 'Not exactly. I believe that piety is good "from an everyday point of view", i.e., according to the prevailing norms. But I have no idea whether what those norms require is really good. Still, I've got a policy of pursuing what is good by local standards and of using "*X* is good" to express the view that *X* is good by local standards.' 'But why adopt this policy if you don't believe that what is good by local standards is in fact *good*?' 'One needs to act, and it's easier to act if one has a policy. That's mine, though I might conceivably have chosen another.' Given this exchange it carries no conviction to respond with, 'Hypocrite! So you believe that piety is good after all!'[7]

It is not far fetched to imagine that the skeptic's attitude towards received morality has this character. He accepts conventional morality as a code of conduct while having no opinion as to whether its claims are true. He may immerse himself in it, engaging in moral conversation or rehearsing the moral precepts *in fore interno*. But his remarks in this sort of context will signal mere acceptance, not belief. Acceptance so conceived may involve belief. However, it will not involve moral belief, but rather only the sociological belief the claim in question is true *by local standards*. The important point however is that acceptance so conceived also involves an element of commitment to conventional morality as a framework for guiding thought and conduct. When he is thinking about what to do, the thought 'X is pious' will function in his thinking as a 'reason' to do X. At first he may have to run through the argument explicitly: 'This is pious. According to conventional morality, piety is good. I have resolved to comply with conventional morality. So I'll do it.' But we can easily imagine that with practice the transition will become habitual, so that the thought 'X is pious' will immediately strike him as a ground for doing X. He may even find himself defending the moral claims that guide his conduct when they generate a certain sort of internal challenge. If you and I both accept conventional morality in this sense, we may still find ourselves disagreeing about what conventional morality requires; and insofar as we are immersed in the ordinary standpoint, our disagreement may look for all the world like an ordinary moral disagreement. If we are both pyrrhonists of this sort, however, we will have a story to tell about what's really going on. We disagree, not about whether some particular act is in fact good, but rather about whether it is good by conventional standards.

No doubt this sketch reads more into Sextus' brief remarks than is strictly warranted. But if this is indeed the pyrrhonist stance then the view has clear affinities for fictionalism in the contemporary sense. Pyrrhonist acceptance of a moral claim involves both a commitment to rely on it as a resource and to defend it against certain (internal) challenges; but it is nonetheless clearly distinct from genuine moral belief. The attitude does lack one feature of most developed fictionalist accounts of acceptance. As I have represented the view, when the pyrrhonist accepts a moral framework—the conventional framework, or some other—he does not assert that it is in some way *good*. He does not claim any particular virtue for it. He might claim certain practical advantages: Acquiescing in conventional morality is certainly easier, safer, etc. than some alternatives.[8] But as I have described it, that is not the view.

The view is that while it is useful to have some framework or other, the choice of framework is unconstrained. Still, it is unclear whether this aspect of the fictionalist's conception of acceptance should be regarded as central. And to the extent that it is not, I see no reason not to say that given this speculative reconstruction of the pyrrhonist attitude towards morality, the view represents a form of fictionalism in the contemporary sense.

Pyrrhonism turned out to be an historical dead end. The skeptical tradition that persisted into the modern era was the tradition of a more moderate 'academic' skepticism whose dogmatic target was not belief as such, but rather claims to certainty or scientific knowledge. That tradition has no clear affinity for fictionalism. Its main contemporary manifestation is probabilism, and while probabilism may be motivated by some of the same epistemological considerations that motivate fictionalism, it is clearly a very different response to those considerations.

Astronomical Fictionalism

Another ancient tradition with fictionalist elements had a considerably longer run, or so it has been alleged by the first (and only) significant historian of the subject, Pierre Duhem (1969). This is a tradition, not within philosophy narrowly conceived, but rather within technical astronomy and the methodological discourse that surrounds it. The most famous expression of this tradition is to be found in the preface *Ad lectorem* to the first edition of Nicholas Copernicus' masterpiece, *De revolutionibus orbium coelestium* (1543):

[I]t is the job of the astronomer to use painstaking and skilled observation in gathering together the history of the celestial movements, and then—since he cannot by any line of reasoning reach the true causes of these movements—to think up or construct whatever causes or hypotheses he pleases such that, by the assumption of these causes, those same movements can be calculated from the principles of geometry for the past and for the future too. . . . It is not necessary that these hypotheses should be true, or even probable; but it is enough that they provide a calculus which fits the observations. . . . For it is sufficiently clear that this art is absolutely and profoundly ignorant of the causes of the apparent irregular movements. And if it constructs and thinks up causes—and it has certainly thought up many—nevertheless it does not think them up in order to persuade anyone of their truth but only in order that they may provide a correct basis for calculation. But since for one and the same movement varying hypotheses are proposed from time to time, as eccentricity or epicycle for the movement of the sun, the astronomer much prefers to take the one which is easiest to grasp. Maybe the philosopher demands probability instead; but neither of them will grasp anything certain or hand it on unless it has been divinely revealed to him. Therefore let us permit these new hypotheses to make a public appearance among old ones which are themselves no more probable, especially since they are wonderful and bring with them a vast storehouse of learned observations.

(Copernicus, 1995: 3–4)

This would appear to be a straightforward expression of an altogether modern fictionalist stance. It contains every crucial element. In the body of the work, the Copernican hypotheses are put forward as if they were being asserted; claims are made and once defended, treated as resources for justification. The preface, however, makes it clear that these claims are not put forward 'to persuade anyone of their truth'—though from their content it is clear that they are genuine candidates for truth. Rather, the hypotheses are put forward as a reliable basis for computing the apparent motions of the stars and planets. Virtues are claimed for them: They are 'wonderful and easy', and they 'bring with them a vast storehouse of learned observations'. It is clear that from the author's point of view, nothing more can be expected of hypotheses in astronomy, the and hence that an ideal astronomical account might fail to disclose the real motions of the stars and their true causes.

Unfortunately for the fictionalist who is looking to shore up his pedigree, the preface is not the work of the great Copernicus and it does not express his view. As was revealed only much later by Johannes Kepler, it was written by Andreas Osiander (1498–1552), a Lutheran priest who had been entrusted with seeing De revolutionibus through the press as Copernicus lay dying. Nonetheless, as we shall see, the fictionalist stance articulated in the preface was endorsed by several practitioners of and commentators on late Renaissance astronomy. Its efflorescence in the sixteenth century marks the first (and perhaps the last) significant manifestation of the fictionalist idea prior to modern times, or so I shall suggest.

Duhem's little masterpiece, To Save the Phenomena, takes a different view. Duhem's main contention is that prior to the synthesis of physics and astronomy in the seventeenth century (Kepler, Galileo, Descartes), the view that the view that theoretical astronomy aspires only 'to save the phenomena' and not to represent the true causes of the stellar motions was, if not the dominant view, then at least a significant and widely endorsed option at every stage in the history of astronomy from Plato on. Duhem's sweeping account has been the subject of significant controversy in recent years, and it is now clear that it requires significant revision and qualification. What follows is a brief review of some of the issues that arise in the assessment of Duhem's main claims.

Ancient Astronomy

Ancient Greek astronomical theory proceeded by the construction of models—systems of spheres or circles along which the stars and planets were supposed to travel. It was widely acknowledged that the principle aim of this sort of model building was 'to save the phenomena', in particular, the changing angular positions of the stars and planets as viewed from earth.[9] Following a tradition attributed to Plato, the main constraint on these models was that the planetary motions were to be compounded out of uniform circular motions.[10] This is manifestly impossible so long as the planets are required to follow simple circular paths concentric with the center of the earth. Hence, certain complications were allowed. The most important of these were combinations of eccentric circles—circles whose centers are displaced from the center of the universe—and epicycles: small circles whose centers are themselves in circular motion along a larger circle called the deferent. The main technical challenge was to find a system of eccentrics and epicycles that was capable of saving the phenomena.

The task is extraordinarily difficult, but by the time of Ptolemy (*fl.* Second century AD) it was widely regarded as nearly complete. A question then arises as to the status of these astronomical models. The models are constrained to save the phenomena; but they are not simply tables for the prediction of apparent stellar positions. They embody 'claims' that go well beyond the appearances. Thus models invariably represent the ordering of the planets, and in some cases their linear distances, whereas nothing in the appearances straightforwardly entails that (e.g.) Jupiter is closer to the earth than Saturn is. More importantly, any given model will represent the apparent motions as arising from some particular combination of circular motions. The question will then arise whether the real motions do in fact arise from such a combination, or whether instead the model manages to save the appearances only 'accidentally'. Finally, the models will suggest (and sometimes contain) a physical 'mechanism' for generating the apparent motions. Some writers assume that the circles in the models correspond real physical objects—orbs and spheres—to which the planets are somehow attached. One may therefore ask whether these aspects of the models correspond to stellar reality.

These questions were pressed in antiquity. They were pressed in part because the main devices—epicycles and eccentrics—were in apparent tension with the authoritative pronouncements of Plato and Aristotle on the motions appropriate to divine celestial beings. But the main focus for the discussion is a theorem—due perhaps to Hipparchus, perhaps to

Apollonius—according to which the apparent motion of the sun may be saved either by the hypothesis that the sun moves uniformly along an eccentric circle, or by the hypothesis that it moves along an epicycle whose deferent is a concentric with the earth. By the time of Ptolemy a general version was known. If the method of eccentrics is generalized so that the geometric center of the eccentric is allowed to travel in a circular path, then the methods of eccentrics and epicycles are equivalent: any pattern of appearances that can be generated by a system of eccentrics can be generated by a system of epicycles and versa, and indeed by indefinitely many combinations of the two.

These theorems generate the first sharp underdetermination problem in the history of science. For any model framed in terms of some combination of epicycles and eccentrics, there are distinct models which generate precisely the same apparent motions. How then is the astronomer to discover the real underlying motions? One possible answer is that while purely astronomical considerations cannot decide, the question can be resolved by appeal to physics. Another is to suppose that the 'simplest' system captures the real motions. Yet another is to say that while the astronomer *aspires* to knowledge of true causes, this knowledge is unattainable given the evidence available to him, and that we therefore have grounds for doubt or despair about the enterprise. These responses are all obviously 'realist' in spirit. Finally, it might be maintained that there is no need to decide, since the aim of astronomy is simply to save the appearances by means of a model from which accurate astronomical tables may be calculated, and for this purpose, any one of the empirically equivalent models will do in principle (though in practice some may be more tractable than others). This is the fictionalist attitude whose history Duhem is concerned to trace.

This distinction between the third view mentioned above—'pessimistic realism'—and fictionalism is subtle, but it is especially important for our purposes. The pessimistic realist holds that the aim of the enterprise is an account of the real motions and their causes, and hence that astronomical hypotheses are constrained to be consistent with the established truths of physics and theology. He despairs of the possibility of a single adequate system of this sort, and so doubts that any of the existing hypotheses is fully adequate. He may grudgingly admit that these hypotheses are nonetheless useful for practical purposes. But he will never concede, as the fictionalist will, that a false system of hypotheses may leave nothing whatsoever to be desired from the standpoint of the astronomer. As we shall see, one of the main difficulties in tracing the history of astronomical fictionalism is to distinguish pessimistic realism from fictionalism in writers who were generally less concerned with the distinction than we may be.

Duhem maintains that astronomical fictionalism was widespread in antiquity:

The hypotheses of astronomy can be viewed as mathematical fictions which the geometer combines for the purpose of making the celestial motions accessible to his calculations; or they can be viewed as a description of concrete bodies and of movements that are actually realized. In the first case *only one condition is imposed on the hypotheses, namely, that they save the appearances*; in the second the intellectual freedom of the astronomer turns out to be much more limited, for if he is an advocate of a philosophy which claims to know something about the celestial essence, he will have to reconcile his hypotheses with the teachings of that philosophy. Ptolemy and the Greek thinkers who came after him adopted the first of these two opinions.

(Duhem, 1969: 28, my emphasis.)

Duhem of course concedes that some writers—notably Aristotle and his followers—maintained that astronomy was constrained by physics and that it was ultimately concerned to represent the real motions and their causes. Nonetheless he maintains that from Ptolemy (and perhaps even from Plato) on through Proclus and Simplicius, the dominant Greek understanding of astronomy was fictionalist in spirit.

A careful review of Duhem's evidence turns up little direct support for this sweeping claim. G. E. R. Lloyd (1978) has undertaken a detailed examination. Let us consider briefly two of the most important exhibits in Duhem's case.

The first major figure to whom Duhem attributes the view is Ptolemy himself. His main proof text is from Book 3 of the *Syntaxis*:

We must, as best we can, adapt the simplest hypotheses to the heavenly movements. But if these prove insufficient we must select others that fit better...

If every apparent movement gets saved, as warranted by the hypotheses, why should anyone find it surprising that it is from such complicated motions that the movements of the heavenly bodies result?

Let no one judge the real difficulties of the hypotheses in terms of the constructions we have devised. It is not fitting to compare things human with things divine. We should not base our trust in things so high on examples drawn from what is most greatly removed from them: For is there anything that differs more from changeless beings than beings that are constantly changing?

So long as we attend to these models [tabletop models] we find the composition and succession of the motions awkward. To set them up in such a way that each motion can be freely accomplished seems hardly feasible. But when we study what happens in the sky, we are not at all disturbed by such a mixture of motions.

(*Syntaxis* 13.2, translated in Duhem, 1969: 17)

Commenting on this passage, Duhem writes:

Certainly, Ptolemy means to indicate in this passage that the many motions he compounds in the *Syntaxis* to determine the trajectory of a planet have no physical reality: only the resultant motion is actually produced in the heavens.

(Duhem, 1969: 17)

But Ptolemy says nothing of the sort. He suggests that simplicity is a reasonable basis for choice among hypotheses (without saying exactly what such choice amounts to) but that fidelity to the phenomena is more important than simplicity.[11] And he cautions against the naive assumption that what we cannot implement in our workshops in wood and metal cannot exist in the heavens. All of this is compatible with the view that the Ptolemaic model is designed to describe the real circular motions from which the resultant motions are compounded, the apparent complexity of the system and our inability to build a workable tabletop model notwithstanding.

In fact Ptolemy says little about the status of his hypotheses in the *Syntaxis*.[12] But circumstantial evidence suggests that Ptolemy is a realist about the enterprise. Consider the tone of Ptolemy's detailed refutation of models which explain the diurnal motion of the firmament by positing the rotation of the earth.

Certain thinkers . . . have concocted a scheme which they consider more acceptable, and they think that no evidence can be brought to bear against them if they suggest for the sake of argument that the heaven is motionless, but that the earth rotates about one and the same axis from west to east, completing one revolution approximately every day, or alternatively, that both the heaven and the earth have a rotation of a certain amount, whatever it is, about the same axis, as we said, but such as to maintain their relative positions.

These persons forget, however, that while, so far as appearances in the stellar world are concerned, there might, perhaps, be no objection to this theory in the simpler form, yet, to judge by the conditions affecting ourselves and those in the air about us, such a hypothesis must be seen to be quite ridiculous. Suppose we could concede to them such an unnatural thing as that the most rarefied and lightest things either do not move at all or do not move differently from those of the opposite character—when it is clear as day that things in the air and less rarefied have swifter motions than any bodies of more earthly character—and that (we could further concede that) the densest and heaviest things could have a motion of their own so swift and uniform . . . yet they must admit that the rotation of the earth would be more violent than any whatever of the movements which take place about it, if it made in such a short time such a colossal turn back to the same position again, that everything not actually standing on the earth must have seemed to make one and the same movement always in the contrary sense to the earth, and clouds and any of the things that fly or can be thrown could never be seen traveling towards the east, because the earth would always be anticipating them all and forestalling their motion towards the east.

(*Syntaxis* 1.7, in Heath, 1932: 147 ff)

Ptolemy rejects the hypothesis of the earth's rotation on two grounds. First, it is manifestly incompatible with the observed fact that clouds and birds sometimes move eastward. Second, it is 'unnatural' because it entails that lighter things (the stars)—are naturally at rest while heavier things like the earth undergo violent motion. Both arguments are incompatible with the radical fictionalist view that astronomical models are constrained simply to save the *celestial* appearances. The first is compatible with the more moderate view that while it is altogether indifferent to the truth about underlying causes, astronomy is concerned to save both the terrestrial and the celestial phenomena. The appeal to physics, on the other hand (which Ptolemy clearly regards as sufficient) is surely at odds with Duhem's suggestion. If astronomy aims only to save the phenomena, why should it matter whether a model clashes with some established principle of physics?

Finally, consider the following description of the Ptolemaic project:

Now since our problem is to demonstrate, in the case of the five planets as in the case of the sun and moon, all their apparent irregularities as produced by means of regular and circular motions (for these are proper to the nature of divine things which are strangers to disparities and disorders) the successful accomplishment of this aim as truly belonging to mathematical theory in philosophy is to be considered a great thing, very difficult and yet unattained in any reasonable way by anyone.

(*Syntaxis* 9.2, in Hutchins, 1952: 270)

This makes it indisputably clear that for Ptolemy the astronomical project is informed by physics/theology. The aim is not *simply* to save the appearances, but (at a minimum) to save them by means of models that conform to the natures of divine things. The passage does not say (and so far as I can see there is no clear statement of this view in Ptolemy) that the aim is to produce a model that is accurate in all its details. But the main point of fictionalism as Duhem conceives it is that the development of science should be *altogether unconstrained* by the authoritative deliverances of metaphysics and theology. So far as I can see, there is no hint of this attitude in Ptolemy.

The second key witness in Duhem's case for fictionalism in ancient astronomy is not himself an astronomer, but rather a late neo-platonist commentator on the astronomical tradition. In the final chapter of his *Hypotyposis*—an elementary exposition of Ptolemaic astronomy—Proclus (410–485) takes up the status of epicycles and eccentrics. In Duhem's version of the crucial passage, he writes as follows:

Either these circles are merely fictive and ideal, or they have a real existence amid the planetary spheres and are to be found inside the spheres.

According to Duhem, Proclus opts decisively for the former view, insisting that those who take up the latter view:

forget that these circles exist only in thought; they interchange natural bodies and mathematical concepts; they account for natural movements by things which have no existence in nature.

(Duhem, 1969: 19)

On its face this is a nice expression of the fictionalist distinction between what exists *according to the model* and what exists *in reality*. As Duhem reads it, the passage warns explicitly against the naive assumption that (as van Fraassen would put it) every part of a successful model must correspond to something in the world. Of course this sensible admonition is compatible with the thought that the existing astronomical models are to be regarded as stages along the way to an altogether accurate representation. As we have stressed, fictionalism requires more than the recognition that scientific theories may, at any given stage, involve idealizations or imperfections. It requires the thought that for the discipline in question, falsity *per se* is not a defect. The question, then, is not whether Proclus had doubts about the reality of epicycles and eccentrics—he clearly did; it is whether Proclus conceives of astronomy as an autonomous discipline concerned to save the appearances without regard, *even in principle*, for the truth of its hypotheses.

There are several reasons to doubt that this was Proclus' view. To begin, G. E. R. Lloyd has shown that Duhem seriously misrepresents Proclus' point in the passage just cited.[13] Duhem maintains that Proclus defends the fictionalist horn of the dilemma; but according to Lloyd the passage is ultimately aporetic. On this alternative reading, Proclus argues *against* the idea that the epicycles and eccentrics are merely fictive on the ground that on this view the astronomers have 'unwittingly gone over from physical bodies to mathematical concepts and given the physical movements from things that do not exist in nature' (Lloyd, 1978: 205). He then argues against the realist hypothesis that the epicycles and eccentrics really exist on various physical grounds, maintaining in particular that this destroys the 'continuity of the spheres' (Lloyd, 1978: 205). On Lloyd's compelling interpretation, both arguments presuppose that the astronomer seeks to provide a genuine causal account. The objection to the fictionalist horn is precisely that what has no real existence cannot serve as a genuine cause. The point of the passage is to suggest that on this assumption, there is no acceptable construal of the Ptolemaic system.

Duhem goes on to cite a passage from Proclus' commentary on the *Timaeus*.

Because of our weakness, imprecision gets introduced into the series of images by which we represent what is. To know, *we* must use imagination, sense, and a multitude of other instruments. . . . When we are dealing with sublunary things, we are content . . . to grasp what happens in most instances. But when we want to know heavenly things, we use sensibility and call upon all sorts of contrivances quite removed from likelihood. As a result, when any of these things is the subject of investigation, we who dwell, as the saying goes, at the lowest level of the universe, must be satisfied with 'the approximate'. That this is the way things stand is plainly shown by the discoveries made about these heavenly things—from different hypotheses we draw the same conclusion relative to the same objects. Among these are some which save the phenomena by means of epicycles, still others which do so by means of eccentrics, still others which save the phenomena by means of counterturning spheres devoid of planets.

Surely, the gods' judgment is more certain. But as for us, we must be satisfied to come close to those things, for we are men who speak according to what is likely and whose lectures resemble fables.

(Duhem, 1969: 20–1)

The passage clearly expresses a view about the limits of astronomical knowledge. But this is compatible both with fictionalism and with pessimistic realism. Moreover, the tone of the passage (and of others like it both in the commentary on the *Timaeus* and in other works) strongly encourages the latter reading. Note first that Proclus clearly regards our incapacity to 'represent what is' without appeal to misleading images as cause for regret, even anguish.[14] If the aim of the enterprise were simply to save the phenomena, then our epistemic infirmities would not present an obstacle. The fact that they do suggests that the real (if unattainable) aim of inquiry in astronomy is knowledge of the real stellar motions. Much more importantly, *there is no indication in Proclus' writings that the Ptolemaic invocation of epicycles and eccentrics, however absurd from the standpoint of metaphysics, is nonetheless perfectly acceptable from the standpoint of astronomy.* Proclus does commend study of the

Ptolemaic system; and he does praise its hypotheses as 'the most simple and the most fitting ones for the divine bodies'.[15] (The point here seems to be that as against some alternatives, they at least privilege the circular motion as the motion proper to the heavenly bodies.)[16] At no point, however, does Proclus give voice to the fictionalist's distinctive irenic thought that for the purposes of science *it simply does not matter* whether the hypotheses conform to reality. To the contrary, Proclus clearly holds that the Ptolemaic models were ultimately unacceptable on theological and physical grounds, and that the situation of contemporary astronomy is therefore dire.[17] His position is ultimately obscure and therefore hard to classify; but it would appear to be a form of skeptical or pessimistic realism, rather than a form of fictionalism.

Lloyd's review of Duhem's evidence suggests that fictionalism in our sense (which is also Duhem's sense) is unattested in ancient astronomy.[18] After cautioning that in most cases we are simply not in a position to pronounce on the attitude of Greek astronomers towards their hypotheses, Lloyd concludes:

> Where we do have some evidence... whether from practicing astronomers or from the major commentators, it often contradicts the line of interpretation advocated so forcefully by Duhem and thereafter echoed by others. So far from the majority of those texts supporting the thesis that Greek astronomers were in general not concerned with the truth of their hypotheses and with whether they conformed to the nature of things, those texts tend to provide evidence against the thesis. In the methodological statements of Geminus, Theon and Proclus, and in the actual practice of Ptolemy, we find support for the opposing point of view, that so far from being indifferent to physics the astronomer must take his starting points from the physicist, which include not only the general Platonic assumption that the movements of the heavenly bodies are regular, uniform and circular, but also assumptions or theories concerning which bodies are at rest and which in movement... Indeed the adverse reception of the heliocentric theory itself surely tells against the view that Greek astronomers were in general indifferent to the physical implications of the hypotheses they adopted.

> (Lloyd, 1978, 219–20.)

It should perhaps be stressed that the evidence is compatible with the attribution of a certain moderate form of fictionalism to a number of Greek authors.

Astronomy is constrained by physics. Physical considerations establish, for example, that the stellar motions are compounded from circular motions, and that the earth is at rest in the center of universe. However they underdetermine the choice of a particular combination of eccentrics and epicycles. *This* choice is a matter of convenience, and at this level astronomy does not aspire to reveal the true arrangement of circles. Insofar as the astronomer puts forward a particular system, he does not claim that it is true, but only that it saves the appearances *and that it coheres with established knowledge in other areas.*

So far as I have been able to determine, however, we have no clear basis for attributing even this limited fictionalism to any of the Greek authors cited by Duhem.

Renaissance Astronomy

Astronomical fictionalism emerges as a distinctive attitude only in the late Renaissance, around the time of Copernicus.[19] Osiander's *Ad lectorem* is its clearest and most eloquent expression, though as we shall see, there were others, some even more fervent. Duhem's main claim about this period is that:

from the time of the publication of Copernicus's book up to the time of the Gregorian reform of the calendar [1582], this view [viz., that astronomical hypotheses are 'simply devices for saving the phenomena'] was, it seems, the generally accepted opinion of astronomers and theologians.'

(Duhem, 1969: 92)

Like Duhem's account of ancient astronomy, this view has been the focus of significant criticism. Indeed it has recently been argued that it is a mistake to regard Osiander's preface as the expression of a principled fictionalism or instrumentalism in astronomy. The main alternative, which we shall have to consider, is that what Duhem regards as fictionalism in this period is really 'frustrated' realism: the view that while astronomy aspires to represent the real planetary motions and their causes, it has so far been unsuccessful and must therefore be regarded—*in its present form*—as little more than a device for calculating the appearances.

Some relevant background is in order before we take up this crucial question. The prevailing triumphalist folklore in the history of astronomy tends to paint Osiander as a meddling priest—an enemy of science whose anonymous preface was a dishonest subterfuge designed to blunt the force of Copernicus' revolutionary message. This is seriously inaccurate. Osiander was a distinguished intellectual. He was primarily a theologian, but he was also an established scholar in other areas: a professor of Hebrew, an authority on Talmud and Cabala, an educational reformer and an accomplished amateur mathematician. Kepler—a fierce opponent of Osiander's opinion—nonetheless refers to him with evident respect as 'one most experienced in these matters' (Jardine 1984: 151). In retrospect he emerges as one of the most significant editors in the history of science. Not only was he charged by Rheticus with the publication of *De revolutionibus*; he was also entrusted by his close friend, Hieronymous Cardanus (Cardan) with the publication of his masterpiece, the *Ars Magna*, a landmark in the history of algebra.[20]

Osiander was associated with a group of humanist intellectuals and educators centered around Philipp Melanchthon in Wittenberg. Melanchthon himself took an active interest in the new astronomy, and while not a serious contributor himself, managed to surround himself at the University of Wittenberg with a number of world-class mathematical astronomers, the most important of whom were Georg Rheticus, Erasmus Rheinhold and Caspar Peucer. Rheticus had studies with Copernicus, and like Copernicus he was a committed realist about the novel features of the Copernican system: heliocentrism and the now familiar ordering of the planets; the explanation of the diurnal motion of the heavens in terms of the rotation of the earth; and the attribution to the planets of compound motions derived from a complex pattern of epicycles and eccentrics. Rheinhold and Peucer, on the other hand, along with the other members of Melanchthon's circle, apparently took a more nuanced attitude towards the theory.[21]

On the one hand, they regarded the Copernican system both as more accurate than its rivals and as more satisfying on intellectual grounds. Rheinhold's *Prutenic Tables*—the first detailed astronomical tables calculated from Copernican hypotheses—were clearly superior in certain respects to the best Ptolemaic alternatives. Perhaps more importantly, Copernicus had managed this improvement while dispensing with one particularly controversial Ptolemaic device: the equant—in effect, circular motion with variable speed—thereby better approximating the ancient ideal of positing only *uniform* circular motion. On the other hand, the proponents of the 'Wittenberg interpretation' (Westman, 1975b) either rejected heliocentrism and the moving earth or simply passed over these aspects of the system in silence. They thus combined admiration for the system and reliance on its empirical predictions with significant reservations about its main cosmological innovations.

Osiander's version of this view incorporates a general thesis about the aims and limits of astronomy. He begins by asserting that the astronomer cannot 'in any way attain to the true causes' of the celestial motions. So far this is compatible with the skeptical view that astronomy nonetheless aspires to causal knowledge and is therefore constrained to be consistent with established physics and theology. As against this, Osiander makes it plain that the astronomer 'will adopt whatever suppositions enable the motions to be computed correctly', adding that these suppositions 'need not be true or even probable'. Presented with empirically equivalent hypotheses he will take as his first choice 'that which is easiest to grasp'—apparently without concern for theological or physical plausibility. Since astronomical hypotheses are not put forward 'in order to persuade anyone of their truth', they need not be true and hence need not be consistent with established truths.

It has recently been suggested that Osiander's position is nonetheless a form of skeptical realism. Peter Barker and Bernard Goldstein (1998: 251–2) maintain that for Osiander as for the Melanchthon circle more generally, 'knowledge of causes is always the goal in science', and that 'this cannot be achieved in astronomy, although the true causes are known to God and those similarly well placed'. Their discussion is marred, however, by a serious misunderstanding of the fictionalist alternative as Duhem conceives it. For example they resist the attribution of 'instrumentalism' (their name for Duhem's view) to sixteenth-century astronomers on the ground that 'the same people who are supposed to be instrumentalists about astronomy are clearly not instrumentalists about physics. Is this possible? Isn't instrument-alism supposed to apply uniformly to all scientific disciplines?' (Barker and Goldstein, 1998: 235). The answer is that there is no reason at all why it should. Astronomy may present special difficulties: the underdetermination problem, for example, or the inaccessibility of its objects. Again, they suggest that 'if the Wittenberg astronomers are consistent instrumentalists then *no* Wittenberg astronomer should ever present Copernicus's system of the world. No instrumentalist has any motivation to present the cosmology that realists believe ought to accompany mathematical models' (Barker and Goldstein, 1998: 239). But of course this is mistaken. As Barker and Goldstein themselves point out, it was a commonplace in the period that cosmological models play an indispensable pedagogical and heuristic role in making the content of a theory vivid and accessible. As van Fraassen (1980) has stressed, the antirealist need not abjure the detailed construction of such models, even when the details go beyond what is strictly necessary for calculating the appearances. If Osiander and his associates in Wittenberg were fictionalists of any sort, they were apparently fictionalists of this more sophisticated sort: fictionalists who see a value in elaborating their models as if they were presenting a true account of the real causes of the phenomena, even though they place no credence in the underlying causal claims. Barker and Goldstein's rejection of the natural reading of Osiander's preface is particularly unconvincing. Thus they note that towards the end Osiander acknowledges that 'the philosopher may perhaps seek the semblance of truth'. They take this to establish that for Osiander, 'knowledge of causes is always the goal in science' (Barker and

Goldstein, 1998: 239). But surely this misses the intended contrast between the *philosopher* (who hankers after truth) and the *astronomer* who is concerned only to provide a basis for calculation.

I thus see no reason to doubt that Osiander endorses a fictionalist construal of Copernican astronomy. It remains to be seen how widespread this attitude was among his contemporaries. It seems perfectly clear that he was not alone in endorsing it. Perhaps its most extraordinary manifestation is the *de hypothesibus astronomicis tractatus* of Nicholas Ursus (1597). Ursus was a competent mathematical astronomer who made a number of genuine contributions; but he was also an intemperate bulldog who pursued a bitter priority dispute with Tycho Brahe, among others, over the discovery of geostatic alternatives to Copernicanism. His *Tractatus* is in large part a rambling screed against his adversaries. But the ostensible topic is status of hypotheses in astronomy. Here is a representative sample:

A hypothesis or fictitious supposition is a portrayal contrived out of certain imaginary circles of an imaginary form of the world-system, designed to keep track of the celestial motions, and thought up, adopted, and introduced for the purpose of keeping track of and saving the motion of the heavenly bodies and forming a method for calculating them.... These contrived hypotheses are nothing but certain fabrications which we imagine and use to portray the world system. So it is not in the least necessary that those hypotheses correspond altogether... to the world system... provided only that they agree with and correspond to a method of calculation of the celestial motions, even if not to the motions themselves. *So hypotheses do not err in the least if they contradict the commonly held principles of other arts and disciplines, or indeed, even if they contradict the infallible and certain authority of the sacred scriptures.* And so it is permitted to astronomers, as a thing required in astronomy, that they should fabricate hypotheses, whether true or false or feigned, of such a kind as may yield the phenomena.... and produce a method for calculating them *and thus achieve the intended purpose and goal of this art.*[22]

Ursus reproduces Osiander's preface in full, calling it the work of 'an author clearly learned, but unknown', and thus establishing a small but plainly attested fictionalist 'tradition' in sixteenth-century astronomy.

How widespread was the Osiander–Ursus view? By the end of the century *availability* of the position was a commonplace. When Cardinal Bellarmine offers it to Galileo in the famous letter to Foscherini, he has only to sketch it:

I think that you and Galileo would act more prudently if you presented your opinion as a hypothesis and not as an absolute truth. To assert that the earth is really moving is a very dangerous thing, because it would irritate the philosophers and theologians. ... To prove that the hypothesis of the immobility of the sun and the moving earth saves the appearances is not at all the same thing as to demonstrate the reality of the movement of the earth. I believe that one can prove the first point, but I doubt strongly whether one can prove the second point and in the case of doubt one must not abandon the sense of the Holy Bible in which it has been interpreted by the Holy Fathers.

(Frank, 1950: 77–8)

So by the time of Galileo, at any rate, the Osiander–Ursus view was a familiar option.[23] It remains to be seen, however, whether and to what extent it was taken seriously.[24] What are we to make of Duhem's assertion that in the immediate wake of Osiander's preface, fictionalism was 'the generally accepted opinion of astronomers and theologians?'

A thorough review of the issue is obviously beyond the scope of the present chapter, but let us consider one important recent treatment of the question. According to Nicholas Jardine, the Osiander–Ursus view is one manifestation of broad current in late Renaissance astronomy which Jardine has called the 'pragmatic compromise'. The compromise antedates the rise of Copernicanism. It begins as an attempt to reconcile the appeal to Ptolemaic devices in astronomy—epicycles, eccentrics, and equants—with an increasingly purist Aristotelian natural philosophy with which they were manifestly incompatible. The compromise proceeds by adapting the Aristotelian distinction between the methods of the mathematician on the one hand and the methods of the physicist on the other (*Physics 2.2*). In Aristotle there is no suggestion that the two disciplines might conflict. Rather they are assumed to be complementary, the one (mathematics) abstracting from considerations that are the proper concern of the other. Proponents of the pragmatic compromise treat physics as a positive science that reveals the real natures and causes of natural things, and therefore hold that insofar as the Ptolemaic devices are incompatible with established physics, they must not exist in nature. Their distinctive twist is to insist that insofar as mathematical astronomy conflicts with established physics, it makes no claims whatsoever about reality but rather seeks only to save the phenomena. Here is a representative statement from the influential Spanish Jesuit Benito Pereira (1460–1553):

The astrologer [i.e., the astronomer] is not concerned to seek and posit causes that are true and agree with the nature of things, but only causes of such a kind as can universally, conveniently, and constantly give an account of all those things which appear in the heavens. That is why it happens that very often he establishes principles which appear to contradict nature and sound reason: eccentrics, epicycles and non-uniform motions . . . are thought to be of this kind.[25]

Prior to Copernicus, the conflict between astronomy and physics was restricted to recondite matters of this sort. After Copernicus it was extended to the much more urgent question of the motion of the earth. On Jardine's account, the view we find in Osiander and Ursus was an application of the pragmatic compromise to this set of issues. Not only was this response the official response of the hugely influential Melanchthon circle. By the end of the century, according to Jardine, it was the dominant view both among practitioners and commentators throughout Europe.

So far this echoes Duhem. However, Jardine rejects Duhem's suggestion that the compromise constitutes a form of fictionalism.

Sixteenth-century pronouncements on the license of astronomy to use imaginary constructions in the quest for predictive adequacy have often been assimilated, following Duhem, to modern instrumentalist accounts of the status of scientific theories. This is seriously misleading. No protagonist of the pragmatic compromise expounded the strict instrumentalist view that truth and falsity are not predicable of astronomical hypotheses. And even the more relaxed instrumentalism which claims only that predictive success rather than truth is the goal of astronomy can rarely be attributed without qualification. For the skepticism or agnosticism of these authors generally applies only to the postulation of epicycles and eccentrics, not to such basic cosmological issues as the immobility of the earth or the existence and ordering of the planetary spheres. And a number of protagonists . . . explicitly endorse the view that the heavenly bodies execute their motions harmoniously in accordance with *leges motuum* prescribed by God at the creation. If we insist on placing the pragmatic compromise in a modern category, it must, I think, be that of skeptical, but not radically skeptical realism.

(Jardine, 1984: 239–40)

Jardine's position raises a number of important issues. It is certainly true that parties to the compromise often express opinions about, for example, the immobility of the earth or the existence of the celestial spheres. But this is compatible with their being full-blooded fictionalists *about astronomy*. Jardine apparently assumes that a fictionalist in Duhem's sense must be a skeptic or an agnostic about characteristic claims of the discourse in question. But as Duhem's own case attests, this is inaccurate. The fictionalist about astronomy may believe that he has independent physical or metaphysical grounds for affirming the immobility of the earth or the perfect simplicity of the celestial motions. His fictionalism will consist in the claim that the adequacy of an astronomical model as such does not require correspondence to this reality. This liberating thought—the thought that *astronomy* is unconstrained by physics and metaphysics—*does* seem to be a central feature of the pragmatic compromise as Jardine understands it. It is clearly the view of Pereira and the Jesuit tradition he represents; and it is also the view of Osiander and Ursus. So far, then, we have seen no reason to resist Duhem's characterization of the position as a form of fictionalism.

This is to some extent a verbal matter. Let me now turn to a more substantive question. On Jardine's account (as on Duhem's) the Wittenberg astronomers were party to the pragmatic compromise *in the version endorsed by Osiander*. This is clearly plausible for some of the central figures. Thus in the next generation we find Johannes Praetorius responding to Kepler's *Mysterium Cosmographicum* in the following terms:

I started to read this book with great expectations but I must truly confess that . . . I became more and more languid until I was frustrated of all hope. And if one seeks to know the reason for this, I can reply in no other way than to say that . . . this [work] departs somewhat from the definition of Astronomy, or rather, that it pertains to Physics, which surely cannot treat Astronomy in such matters. . . . It is necessary (I think) for the astronomer to apply his teachings in the following way: such that the phenomena perceived with the eyes and sense agree with one's hypotheses *as if* such changes of motion were guided by certain causes. But that speculation of the regular solids, what, I beg, does it offer to Astronomy?

(Westman, 1975c: 303, my emphasis)

And later:

. . . the astronomer is free to devise or imagine circles, epicycles and similar devices although they might not exist in nature . . . The astronomer who endeavors to discuss the truth of the positions of these or those bodies acts as a Physicist and not as an Astronomer —and in my opinion, he arrives at nothing with certainty.

(Westman, 1975c: 303)

It is much somewhat less clear, however, whether this freewheeling fictionalism was endorsed by the first generation of Wittenberg Copernicans. Let me raise two questions about this aspect of (what might be called) the Duhem–Jardine view.

The main figure for our purposes is Erasmus Rheinhold, the main technical authority on Copernicus in Wittenberg and the author of the *Prutenic Tables* (1551). There is no doubt that after 1543 Rheinhold was in some sense a Copernican. He hailed Copernicus as a new Ptolemy, he relied on Copernican assumptions in his calculations; and he played a central role in disseminating the Copernincan system in northern Europe.[26] There is however no evidence that Rheinhold endorsed Copernican heliocentrism. Indeed, he seems to have taken no interest whatsoever in Copernican cosmology. But of course this by itself does not amount to an endorsement of Osiander's principled fictionalism about astronomy. So far as I have been able to determine, Rheinhold's work contains no explicit statement of the view that the astronomer as such is concerned only with saving the appearances, and that his hypotheses need not be true or even probable. The question then arises whether Rhenhold endorsed this sort of view.

There are at least two reasons to wonder. First, as Owen Gingerich has shown, (Gingerich, 1973; also Westman, 1975b) Rheinhold's extraordinary enthusiasm for the Copernican system was grounded in a technical achievement: the capacity of the Copernican system to dispense with equants. But this raises a question: why should an astronomer for whom the aim of the enterprise is simply to save the appearances be so concerned to dispense with this sort of technical device? It is possible, of course, that he regarded the equant as mathematically inelegant. But the tone of his remarks on the matter suggest otherwise. These remarks are contained in Rheinhold's annotations to his copy of *De revolutionibus*. On the title page Rheinhold inscribed 'in beautiful and carefully formed red letters':

Axioma Astronomicum: Motus coelestis aequalis est et circularis vel ex aequabilis et circularibus compositus. [Astronomical Axiom: Celestial motion is both uniform and circular or composed of uniform and circular motion.]

(Westman, 1975b: 176)

According to Westman (1975b: 176), 'it was precisely this axiom, or boundary condition, which Copernicus had tried to satisfy... which Rheinhold consistently singles out in his annotations'. When Rheinhold writes that:

All posterity will gratefully celebrate the name of Copernicus. The science of the celestial motions was almost in ruins; the studies and world of this author have restored it. God in his goodness kindled a great light in him so that he discovered and explained a host of things which, until our day, had not been known or veiled in darkness.

(quoted in Westman, 1975b: 177)

it is this equantless astronomy—and not heliocentric cosmology—that he has in mind. But now it is hard to believe that this hyperbolic enthusiasm was the response to a mere technical simplification. To the contrary, it seems clear that Rheinhold regards the rejection of the equant as a genuine theoretical improvement. The Copernican system conforms to the Platonic requirement that the celestial motions be composed from *uniform* circular motions—a requirement that Copernicus and Rheticus had defended on explicitly realist, metaphysical grounds. It is unclear why Rheinhold attached so much importance to this feature. But it is hard to resist the sense that he regarded this 'Astronomical Axiom' as something like a metaphysical constraint on astronomical systems. And if this is right, it puts pressure on the assimilation of Rheinhold's stance to Osiander's. If the aim is *simply* to save the phenomena, then the equant is just another potentially useful device. One is left with the impression that for Rheinhold, this is not the case, and hence that on his view astronomy is not simply an instrument for saving the phenomena.

A similar impression is generated by later developments in the Wittenberg school. Rheinhold's successor, Caspar Peucer, had suggested in passing that Copernicus' equantless system could in principle be 'transferred' to a geostatic reference frame (Westman, 1975b: 180). The next generation of Wittenberg astronomers actively undertook this project, the culmination of which was Tycho Brahe's famous system. The question then arises: why should a proponent of the Osiander–Ursus view pursue this project? He might pursue it if he thought that it would improve the predictive power of the theory, and there is some reason to believe that this was one pertinent motivation. But it seems plausible that Praetorius and Tycho were also motivated to purge the Copernican system of its manifest absurdity: the motion of earth. In defending his own initial steps in this direction Tycho writes:

In our time... Nicholas Copernicus, who has justly been called a second Ptolemy, from his own observations found out something was missing in Ptolemy. He judged the hypotheses admitted by Ptolemy admitted something [viz., the equant] unsuitable and offensive to mathematical axioms ... He therefore arranged his own hypotheses in another manner, by the admirable subtlety of his erudition, and thus restored the science of the celestial motions.... For although he holds certain [theses] contrary to physical principles, for example that the Sun rests at the center of the Universe, that the Earth, the elements associated with it, and the Moon, move around the Sun with a threefold motion, and that the eighth sphere remains unmoved, he does not, for all that admit anything absurd as far as mathematical axioms are concerned. If we inspect the Ptolemaic hypotheses in this regard, however, we notice many such absurdities. ... Everything, therefore, which we consider to be evident and well-known concerning the revolutions of the stars has been established and taught by these two masters, Ptolemy and Copernicus.

(In Westman, 1975c: 307)

Westman remarks that this passage 'could well have been written by Praetorius':

The goals of the two astronomers are identical: the restoration of Ptolemaic astronomy by the conversion of equant-less Copernican models into the old reference frame.

(Westman, 1975c: 307)

It is conceivable that the aim here was simply to produce a more tractable, more readily grasped version of the system; but again, that is hard to believe. The much more natural thought is that unlike Osiander the active Wittenberg astronomers recognized constraints on astronomical theorizing over and above conformity to the appearances, and that the systems of Ptolemy and Copernicus were regarded as imperfect *from the standpoint of mathematical astronomy* to the extent that they failed to satisfy these constraints, which included the immobility of the earth and the eschewal of the equant.

Again, this is compatible with attributing a more moderate species of fictionalism to this group. They may have held, for all we have seen, that the aim of astronomy is to produce a model that saves the appearances and conforms to certain physical or metaphysical constraints, while simultaneously allowing that false theory might perfectly well achieve this aim. Praetorius appears to have held this view: whether it was more widespread, I cannot say. In any case, we shall have to recognize a distinction between what might be called the radical fictionalism of Osiander and Ursus—according to which fidelity to the appearances is the sole constraint on astronomical hypotheses—and the moderate fictionalism of the Wittenberg astronomers, which appears to recognize substantial constraints over and above empirical adequacy. Duhem's claim is that *radical* fictionalism is the dominant view among practitioners and commentators in the immediate wake of *De revolutionibus*; and *that* claim is not clearly correct, as we have seen.

The pragmatic compromise in either form insists on a sharp distinction between mathematical astronomy, on the one hand, and natural philosophy on the other; and by the end of the sixteenth century this distinction was under considerable pressure. In practice, mathematical astronomers had often relied on physical principles. The standard explanation for the eclipses, for example, relies on assumptions not just about the positions and motions of the planets, but also about their natures—e.g., their opacity. But with the improvement in observational technique and the novel focus on 'new stars' (novae and comets) beginning in the 1570s, the temptation to mix physical and astronomical considerations was overwhelming.

The great champion of this new physico-metaphysical astronomy was Johannes Kepler. His *Apologia pro Tycho contra Ursum* (translated with commentary in Jardine, 1984) is a systematic and altogether fascinating refutation of the pragmatic compromise in the strong form represented by Osiander and Ursus. Kepler makes the historical case that in the past serious proponents of hypotheses have always sought to conform to the natures of things. He addresses the underdetermination argument, maintaining that physical considerations can legitimately break the tie between empirically equivalent hypotheses, and he maintains explicitly, against Ursus' appeal to the pessimistic metainduction, that the history of astronomy argues not for skepticism but for optimism about scientific progress. This text itself was not influential, but Kepler's attitude clearly was. It would take us too far afield to explore decline of fictionalism in astronomy. It is clear, however, that by the time of Kepler's mature work and the work of Galileo, it was in retreat. (Bellarmine's appeal in his letter to Foscherini clearly failed to strike its intended audience as a serious option.) By the time of Descartes, the idea that mathematical astronomy is part of a comprehensive effort to represent nature as it is was firmly established. Certain forms of fictionalism flourished briefly in late Renaissance astronomy: but the tradition was moribund by 1640 and it has never been revived.

Bentham's Fictionalism

The first mainstream philosopher to defend the view that something called 'fiction' plays a pervasive role in serious discourse was Jeremy Bentham (1748–1832). Bentham is best known in this connection as a ruthless critic of one sort of fiction. Throughout his career Bentham was consumed with a massive program for the reform of the law, one of the explicit aims of which was to purge the law once and for all of 'the pestilential breath of fiction'. Bentham regarded legal fictions—a central feature of both Roman and British law—as a pernicious subterfuge by means of which judges usurp the law-making power of the legislature. In the course of developing his critique of legal fictions, Bentham was led to produce a general theory of fictions. And in this context he was careful to distinguish between the judicial fictions he abhorred and the 'logical fictions' without which language—or at any rate, 'language in any form superior to the language of brute creation' would be 'impossible' (Bentham, 1843, 8: 198). 'Very different in respect of purpose and necessity, very different is this logical species of fiction from the poetical and polit-ical;—very different the fiction of the logician from the fictions of poets, priests and lawyers' (Bentham, 1843, 8: 199).

It is unclear, however, whether Bentham is a fictionalist in our sense. Our sort of fictionalist insists that the language of the discourse in question be interpreted at face value. His characteristic claim is that the theorist is not (or need not be) committed to the literal truth of the theory he accepts. He may add that when the theorist accepts some statement S, there is another statement S* whose literal content he thereby believes, and that full lucidity requires that this connection between S and S* be made explicit. But it is a distinctive feature of contemporary fictionalism that this S* is not proposed as an account of what the original statement S really means. Fictionalism is thus contrasted with the hermeneutic view that the original statement S does not really entail what it seems to entail because it is really (in some strong sense) *equivalent* to the altogether innocuous S*. The problem we face in classifying Bentham's theory is to understand his conception of the relationship between the statements he brands fictional and the 'paraphrases'— Bentham's word —he offers by way of explication.

Background Ontology

Bentham's theory of fictions is a contribution to the philosophy of language.[27] But it is developed against the background of (what appears to be) an ontological scheme. The main feature of this scheme is a four-fold classification of entities. On the one hand, says Bentham, entities are either perceptible or inferential. The paradigmatic perceptible entities are ordinary bodies: animals, vegetables, and minerals. (Bentham allows that strictly speaking the sole perceptible entities are ideas. But he is completely unconcerned with the old empiricist problems of perception, and since he is mainly concerned with the taxonomy of what he calls 'substances' he insists that 'it is to corporeal substances that the characteristic and differential attribute of perceptible' properly applies (Bentham, 1843, 8: 196–7). An inferential entity is an entity which (in this life, at any rate) we cannot perceive, but whose existence is established by probable inference from perceptible things. The paradigms here are the soul, considered as separate, God and the angels.

At right angles to this familiar contrast is Bentham's (1843, 8: 195) distinctive innovation: 'an entity, whether perceptible or inferential, is either real or fictitious'. Here are Bentham's rather careful definitions:

A real entity is an entity to which, on the occasion and for the purposes of discourse, existence is really meant to be ascribed.

A fictional entity is an entity to which, though by the grammatical form of the discourse employed in speaking of it, existence be ascribed, yet in truth and reality, existence is not meant to be ascribed.

(Bentham, 1843, 8: 195)

The taxonomy is apparently predicated on the assumption that every 'noun substantive' names something: if not something real, then something fictitious. Some uses of nouns are obviously intended to commit the speaker to the real existence of a corresponding object. But sometimes, on Bentham's view, there is no such intention and no such understanding. Take Bentham's main example: When we say that a body is either in motion or at rest, the words 'motion' and 'rest' are noun substantives in Bentham's sense, so given Bentham's semantic principle, they must both refer to entities. But no one would suggest that in making such a claim we commit ourselves to the view that in reality there exist a pair of *things*, motion and rest, which every body is either in or at. 'Here then', says Bentham, 'we have two correspondent and opposite fictitious entities...a motion and a rest' (Bentham, 1843, 8: 195).

This way of presenting the theory can give the impression that Bentham was Meinongian *avant la lettre*, and if this were so his view would not be a form of fictionalism in our sense. The Meinongian holds that some statements ('The round square is round') are about non-existent entities *and that this is no obstacle to their literal truth*. As we read on, however, it becomes tolerably clear that this is not Bentham's view, and that in general the invocation of fictitious *entities* obscures his doctrine.

Let's consider Bentham's first extended treatment of his main example.

A body is said to be in motion. This, taken in the literal sense, is as much as to say, here is a body, called a motion; in this larger body, the other body, namely the really existing body is contained:

So in regard to rest. To say this body is at rest is as much as to say, here is a body, and it will naturally be supposed to be a fixed body, which is *at* the first mentioned body, i.e., attached to it, as if the fictitious body were a stake and the real body a beast tied to it.

(Bentham, 1843, 8: 197)

These bizarre explications bring out two further principles of Bentham's theory. First, Bentham assumes, not simply that every noun substantive purports to name a thing, but more specifically that every noun purports to name a *body* or a *substance* (whether perceptible or inferential). Second, he assumes that prepositions of place:

in; on, or upon; at; above; below; round; around; out—out of; from above; from under; from

(Bentham, 1843, 8: 200)

always have their spatial meaning as their 'original, physical, archetypal significance'. The view seems to be that when we say that Fred is out of luck, we strictly mean 'in the literal sense' that Fred is spatially removed (perhaps in exile from) a certain body, Luck, in which everyone who is not out of luck is somehow ensconced.

Now it seems perfectly clear that since there is no body to which everything that is at rest is physically attached, or in which the lucky few reside, these ordinarily acceptable claims about motion, luck, and the rest must be strictly false on this allegedly literal interpretation. So unlike Meinong, Bentham appears to hold that most of our ordinary acceptable claims involving names of fictitious entities are simply false when taken literally. The theory might nonetheless be construed in a semi-Meinongian spirit. We might suppose that on Bentham's view, the claim that this body is at rest is a claim about a spatial relation between an extraordinary body a certain non-existent body, namely, rest. The claim would still be false, so construed. The ordinary body is not in fact attached to this non-existent thing. But attributions of motion and rest would still be claims about genuine entities—entities about which we might speak truly in other contexts, for example, by saying that motion is a fictional entity that does not exist.

There is no doubt that this is Bentham's dominant mode of exposition. He regularly invokes 'fictitious entities' and gives the impression that he intends his philosophical remarks to constitute a body of genuine truths about them. As we read on, however, we see that this is not Bentham's considered view:

Nothing has no properties. A fictitious entity being, as this name imports, being by the very supposition, a mere nothing, cannot of itself have any properties: no proposition by which any property is ascribed to it can therefore be, in and of itself, a true one, nor therefore, an instructive one. Whatsoever truth is capable of belonging to it cannot belong to it in any other character than that of the representative—of the intended and supposed equivalent and adequate succedaneum, of some proposition having for its subject some real entity.

(Bentham, 1843, 8: 246)

The second half of this passage is of central importance, and we will come back to it. The first half, however, is on the face of it perfectly explicit. The 'fictitious entity' has no properties, and so nothing can be truly predicated of it. It is, as Bentham says, a mere nothing.

But this is puzzling and Bentham knows it. If there are fictitious entities, surely they must at least possess the property of being fictional, and if there are many of them they must presumably differ from one another in various respects. This is a version of the old platonic riddle of non-being, and Bentham wrestles manfully with it:

Entities are either real or fictitious, what can that mean? What but that of entities there are two species or sorts: viz., one which is itself and another which is neither itself nor anything else? Instead of fictitious entity...why not here say, *non-entity*?

(Bentham, 1843, 8: 198)

Initially Bentham presents the difficulty as 'an altogether inevitable contradiction' whose root is in the nature of language. Bentham holds that as language develops it inevitably introduces *names* that do not correspond to anything real. These names figure as subjects of propositions, and those propositions are put forward for serious purposes (not just for story telling). *Sometimes* when a world of this sort is used, it is clear that the speaker intends his audience to suppose that he is referring to a real entity:

In the house designated by such a number, in such a street, in such a town, lives a being called the Devil, having a head, body and limbs like a man's—horns like a goat's—wings like a bat's, and a tail like a monkey's:—Suppose this assertion made...The averment made of it is, that an object of that description really exists. Of that averment, if seriously made, the object...cannot but be to produce in the minds to which communication is thus made, a serious persuasion of an object conformable to the description thus expressed.

(Bentham, 1843, 8: 198)

In this sort of case, the word simply fails to refer: there is no entity of any sort, real or otherwise, corresponding to its subject term, and since the speaker clearly supposes otherwise, his remark, if intended seriously, is altogether false and can serve no serious constructive purpose. In other cases, however, a word that does not correspond to anything real is employed 'without any such danger as that of producing any such persuasion as that of their possessing... any separate, or strictly speaking, any real existence. Take for instance the words motion, relation, faculty, power and the like' (Bentham,1843, 8: 198) Bentham's problem is to distinguish *mere* non-referring terms like 'the Devil' from terms like 'relation' and 'power' which fail to refer to anything real (on his view) but which have a use in serious discourse.

Bentham flirts with the view that these problematic terms refer to entities which differ from real entities in being creatures of language. 'To language, then—to language alone—it is that fictitious entities owe their existence— their impossible yet indispensable existence' (Bentham,1843, 8: 198). His preferred view, however—or at any rate, the most interesting of the views he tries on for size—is that the invocation of fictitious *entities* in the presentation of the theory is itself a sort of fiction. To present the theory correctly one should distinguish, not between real and fictitious entities, but rather between real and fictitious *names*:

> The division of entities into real and fictitious, is more properly the division of *names* of real and *names* of fictitious entities.

(Bentham, 1843, 8: 198)

> Of fictitious entities, whatsoever is predicated is not, consistently with strict truth, predicated of anything but their respective names.

(Bentham, 1843, 8: 199)

Here Bentham is groping for the thought, later developed by Carnap, Quine, and others, that ascent to the formal mode—speaking of words rather than things—clears up some (though perhaps not all) of the problems associated with non-being. Bentham's idea is that instead of saying that motion is a fictitious entity (and so apparently attempting to predicate something of nothing), one should say instead that 'motion' is a fictitious name or a name-of-a-fictitious-entity, that is,—a name whose use is not intended to convey to the hearer a commitment to the real existence of an object corresponding to it.

It would be a relatively straightforward matter to replace Bentham's theoretical claims about fictional entities with corresponding claims about fictional names. Bentham resists this procedure solely on grounds of verbal convenience.

> By reason of its length and compoundedness, the use of the compound denomination *name of a fictitious entity*, would frequently be found attended with inconvenience; for the avoidance of this inconvenience, instead of this long denomination, the less long, though, unhappily, still compound denomination *fictitious entity*, will commonly, after the above warning, be employed.

(Bentham, 1843, 8: 199)

Here then we have a small commitment to a sort of fictionalism at the meta-level. The main claims of Bentham's ontology—'Every entity is either real or fictitious', 'Quality is a fictitious entity of the second remove', etc.—are all literally false and they are not put forward as true. Rather they are put forward to indicate the author's commitment to certain genuine truths about words which it would cost too much in ink to state explicitly. For Bentham, then, discourse about fictional entities is itself a useful fiction. (See Brock, 2002, for a related view.)

Archetypation and Paraphrasis

The main interest of Bentham's theory of fictions for the historian of fictionalism comes not from this fictionalist element in his account of his own technical discourse, but rather from his account of ordinary discourse about such things as motion and rest, powers, relations, dispositions, and so on. The nouns that figure in this sort of discourse are all fictional names in Bentham's sense. As such, they do not refer to real entities, and this means that on the official view they do not refer at all. There is no doubt that Bentham regards sentences involving names of this sort as fully acceptable from the standpoint of the various sciences, ethics, metaphysics, and the rest. So the question we shall have to ask is whether Bentham regards statements involving non-referring fictitious names as literally false. And here we face an important problem of interpretation.

To illustrate the difficulty, let's consider another example—Bentham's favorite case of a useful fiction in ethics. Suppose we seek to clarify the notion of an obligation. The preferred mode of explanation for any term is definition *per genus et differentiam*. But for reasons we need not pursue, Bentham holds that in the case of *sui generis* fictitious names this is impossible.[28] Bentham's main innovations in the philosophy of language are designed to supplement the standard theory of definition with an account of clarification that is applicable when definition is impossible. Bentham's fundamental thought—a genuine anticipation of Frege and Russell—is that in the cases of interest the word can only be explained by first embedding it in a sentence. Do not ask what an obligation is; ask what it means to say, for example, that *an obligation is incumbent on a man to do this or that*. The operation of embedding the target word in a sentence is called *phraseoplerosis*.

The next step is to clarify or explain this sentence in terms that do not employ the problematic fictional word, and here there are two fundamentally different procedures. One is to expound explicitly the 'archetypal' spatial relation to an extraordinary body. This is the sort of explication we have already considered in the case of motion and rest. In this case it runs as follows:

The archetypal image is that of a man lying down with a heavy body pressing upon him, to wit, in such sort as either to prevent him from acting at all, or so ordering matters that if so it be that he does act, it cannot be in any other direction or manner than the direction or manner in question.

(Bentham, 1843, 8: 247)

Alternatively, one can offer what Bentham calls a *paraphrase*, in which a fictitious subject term is replaced by a real subject term of which a genuine attribute is predicated. In this case:

An obligation (viz., the obligation of conducting himself in a certain manner) is incumbent upon a man . . . insofar as, in the event of his failing to conduct himself in this manner, pain or loss of pleasure is considered as about to be experienced by him.

(Bentham, 1843, 8: 247)

Bentham's conception of paraphrase is (so far as can be determined) the modern conception. When a contemporary philosopher says, for example, that talk about numbers is perfectly legitimate even though strictly speaking there are no numbers, and then goes on to provide a procedure for recasting claims involving the offending idiom in terms whose literal truth is not in doubt, he is doing precisely what Bentham is doing here—whatever *that* is. Bentham does not seem to have appreciated one point that is central to contemporary discussions, viz., that one explains the term only when one has provided a *general* paraphrase procedure that covers every significant context in which it meaningfully occurs. But he clearly did appreciate the main point, that sometimes the only way to explain a term is to provide an independently intelligible paraphrase of a range of sentences in which it figures.

Our question is: what relation do the archetypation and the paraphrase bear to the original sentence on Bentham's view? We have already seen passages which suggest that the archetypation gives the literal meaning. On this reading, Bentham really is a fictionalist in the contemporary sense about discourse involving fictitious names. For the archetypation of a claim involving a fictional name will invariably be a false claim about an extraordinary body. So if the archetype gives the literal meaning, the original claim will be false strictly speaking, and yet clearly useful (indeed, fully acceptable) for serious purposes. On this view, the paraphrase may be regarded as giving, not the literal meaning of the original claim, but rather the sober truth in the vicinity which the original is typically used to convey.

The attribution of this view to Bentham cannot be decisively refuted. As we have seen, Bentham appears to endorse it explicitly in the *Ontology*;[29] and if it is correct, Bentham is a fictionalist in our sense about obligations and the rest. On the other hand, it is obviously a *mad, mad* view. It is the view that whenever we use an abstract noun as the subject of a proposition or in a prepositional phrase, our claim strictly speaking entails the existence of an enormous physical object to which real things stand in one or another spatial relation. Moreover it quickly generates absurdities. Consider the Benthamite archetypation of 'Nora is in love with Nick.' Presumably it is along the following lines: here is a body, Love,—a diaphanous pink heart-shaped body?—in which Nick and Nora are both embedded. But now if this is the literal content of the original statement, the original presumably entails that Nick is in love with Nora, since the relation mentioned in the archetypation is symmetric. But this is absurd. Betham's examples of archetypation are never worked out in systematic detail; but it is hard to believe he would have failed to notice this sort of problem. That counts against the thought that for Bentham, the archetypation gives the literal meaning of the original claim.

It is also worth noting that Bentham never says that sentences involving fictitious names are always literally false, as they would have to be if this were his view. His remarks to this effect are always qualified. Here is a passage we have already considered:

A fictitious entity being, as thing name imports, being by the very supposition, a mere nothing, cannot *of itself* have properties: no proposition by which any property is ascribed to them can therefore be, *in and of itself,* a true one, nor therefore an instructive one. Whatsoever truth is capable of belonging to it cannot belong to it in any other character than that of the representative—*of the intended and supposed equivalent and adequate succedaneum*—of some proposition having for its subject some real entity.

(Bentham, 1843, 8: 246)

When the passage is read with emphasis on the qualifications, it suggests another picture—more modern and more plausible, and yet less congenial to the contemporary fictionalist trolling the history of philosophy in search of ancestors.

On this alternative picture, the archetypation does not give the literal meaning or the truth-condition of the original: it gives the mental imagery that initially and perhaps even typically accompanies its use.

By the sort of proposition here in question, viz., a proposition which has for its subject some fictitious entity... the image of some real action or state of things, in every instance, is presented to the mind. This image may be termed the archetype, emblem, or archetypal image pertaining to the fictitious proposition.

(Bentham, 1843, 8: 246)

Bentham is enough of an empiricist to suppose that thinking and understanding typically involve entertaining mental images associated with words. He makes it clear, however, that imagery is not always strictly essential:

To a considerable extent, archetypation, i.e., the origin of the psychological, in some sense physical idea, is often in a manner lost;—its physical marks being more or less obliterated by the frequency of its use.

(Bentham, 1843, 8: 246)

So Bentham knows that when *we* say that a body is in motion, we do not normally picture it embedded in some larger body. He never says the sort of thing that Frege says in this connection, viz., that the mental image, while psychologically real, nonetheless has nothing to do with the literal meaning of the claim in question. But it is possible to read Bentham as anticipating this sort of view. On this alternative reading, the archetypation of a claim involving a fictional name does not spell out the literal content of the utterance. It spells out the semantically inessential window dressing. So from the fact that the archetypation is patently false, nothing follows about the truth or falsity of the original. This might follow if there were no other meaning for the claim to have (as for example, with claims about *natural* obligations which are not backed up by threats of punishment.) But where paraphrase is possible, there is an alternative candidate. The paraphrase of 'M is under an obligation to do A', viz., 'M will suffer pain or loss of pleasure unless he does A' is a reasonable candidate for the literal meaning. It is not implausible that on Bentham's view, the paraphrase says explicitly what must be true if the original is to be true, much as Russell's quantificational paraphrase is meant to say what it takes for a claim involving 'the present king of France' to be true. When a paraphrase is available for a claim involving a fictional name—when the claim is not simply 'nonsense upon stilts'—then the original is, as Bentham says, 'the intended and supposed equivalent' of the paraphrase, and it is true insofar as the paraphrase is true.

On this account Bentham is no more a fictionalist about ordinary claims about motion, rest, obligation, and the like than Russell is a fictionalist about claims involving definite descriptions. He is a reductionist who holds that the original claim does not have the consequences that it might naively be supposed to have: the claim that Jones is under an obligation to do A does not entail that there is an item—the obligation—under which Jones labors. That is a misconstrual of the underlying grammar of the sentence, which is better given by the paraphrase. Taken literally—though perhaps not quite at face value—the original claim will be true provided its paraphrase is true. So on this reading Bentham's theory fails to endorse the fictionalist thought that in a false claim can be perfectly acceptable.

So far as I can see there is no clear textual basis for preferring one of these accounts over the other. For all his care on certain matters, Bentham does not seem particularly interested in whether the claims that he himself accepts claims involving fictitious names are strictly true, or whether they are simply associated with truths by paraphrase. In this he resembles Quine, who is similarly nonchalant about such matters. And if this is correct then Bentham is at best a problematic protofictionalist. He is clearly some sort of fictionalist about his theoretical invocations of fictitious entities. These claims (though theoretically convenient and possibly 'indispensable') are not strictly true: the truth in the vicinity is always a statement about fictional names. What remains unclear is whether Bentham is a fictionalist about motion, rest, obligation, and the rest, and hence about the central abstract claims of science, ethics, and philosophy.

Conclusion

Where in history are the fictionalists? We have not looked everywhere, and even within its self-imposed limits our examination has been cursory. But in any case it is clear that what we find is not a well-defined tradition but rather a family of problems. In the case of pyrrhonism we find a place for a version of the acceptance/belief distinction: But apart from a certain speculative account of the pyrrhonist account of morality, we do not find a clear expression of the view that a theorist may reflectively and deliberately endorse a theory as fully *acceptable* for some serious purpose without committing himself to its truth. In the case of ancient astronomy we find a great deal of ambivalence about the status of epicycles and eccentrics, but no clear expression of the liberating thought that for the purposes of astronomy it simply does not matter whether the circles really are as the theory as they are. We *do* find this view in late Renaissance astronomy—in Osiander and in some others; but we have seen reason to doubt Duhem's claim that this was the dominant attitude. In Bentham's case we have a rather different set of problems. Bentham clearly regards a range of acceptable claims as involving non-referring 'fictitious names'. It is unclear, however, whether he regards these claims as false for failure of reference, or whether he regards them as equivalent to their paraphrases, in which case they will be acceptable only insofar as they are true.

Some historians regard it as a methodological blunder to approach the past with modern taxonomical interests in mind. No doubt there is a risk of anachronism and distortion in the procedure. But it seems to me that there is also much to be gained. The distinction between fictionalism and other alternatives to realism has only emerged with real clarity in recent years. To the extent that we find it hard to classify some historical figure in our terms, this must mean either we are uncertain about his or her view or that we are uncertain about what it is to be a fictionalist. One way to sharpen both our understanding of the past and our grasp on our own taxonomical categories is to approach the history of philosophy with these categories in mind. It seems to me that despite the difficulties we have encountered, in the case of fictionalism this strategy retains considerable promise.

NOTES

1. References to Sextus are the *Outlines of Pyrrhonism,* translated in (Sextus, 2000).
2. The pyrrhonist clearly assumes that claims about how things appear to others have the same unproblematic status as claims about how things appear to oneself. See for example (PH 1 87):

    But if the same things affect humans differently depending on the differences among them, then it is likely that suspension of judgment will be introduced in this way too, since we are no doubt able to say how each existing thing appears, with reference to each difference, but are not able to assert what it is in its nature.

    On this see Burnyeat (1980: 41, n.32).
3. References are to the reprint in Burnyeat and Frede (1997).
4. References are to the reprint in Burnyeat and Frede (1997).
5. One problem for Barnes' idea is that the Wittgensteinian account applies only to first-person present-tense appearance statements, whereas when Sextus insists that the skeptic does not deny appearances, he clearly has something much more general in mind. See note 3.
6. If the statement 'This is a hammer' merely expresses the fact that the thing appears to be a hammer—then it does not justify or rationalize the relevant course of action (picking it up). Consider a more explicit, less misleading version of the 'reasoning' in question. 'I need a hammer. This appears to be a hammer, though this appearance is fully compatible with its being a teaspoon and in no way supports the opinion that it is a hammer. So I'll pick it up.' This is hopeless. But it is a constraint on any *tenable* fictionalist account of a region of discourse that it display the theoretical and practical uses of merely accepted claims as fully reasonable when the attitudes that constitute acceptance are unpacked. So far as

I can see, the version of skepticism under discussion has no chance of satisfying this constraint.

7. Suppose you come to a new country and find a creature unlike any you've known before. It appears to be an animal of some sort, thought it is plantlike in other ways. It makes noises, but you can't tell whether it is trying to communicate. You wonder how it ought to be treated, and you notice that the locals treat it as a pet. They don't eat it or hunt it, but they do keep it on a leash or in a cage. You might wonder whether this is right. But until you've made up your mind, you might adopt a policy falling in with the locals. If someone stops you and asks you whether what you're doing is morally permissible, you might step back and say, 'You know, I really have no idea; but I've adopted this policy until I can make up my mind.' see Rosen (1984: 39) for discussion.

8. Compare Descartes (1960: 18ff):

[I]n order that I might not remain irresolute in my actions during the time my reason would oblige me to be so in my judgments, and so that I would not cease to live from that time forward as happily as I could, I formed a provisional moral code which consisted of only three or four maxims.

The first was to obey the laws and customs of my country... For, beginning already to discount my own opinion because I intended to submit them all to examination, I was assured that I could not do better than to follow those of the most prudent. And although there may be perhaps as sensible people among the Persians or the Chinese as among ourselves, it sees to me that the most useful would be to adapt my behavior to that of those with whom I have to live.

Apart from the appeal to prudence, this is compatible with the attitude I have attributed to the Pyrrhonist. Descartes' second maxim is:

to be as firm and resolute in my actions as I could, and to follow no less constantly the most doubtful opinions, once I had determined on them ... than I would be if they were very assured, imitating in this travelers who, finding themselves astray in some forest, must not wander, turning now this way now that, and even less stop in one place, but must walk always as straight as they can in a given direction and not change direction for weak reasons, even though it was perhaps only chance in the first place which made them choose it.

This may suggest that Descartes distinguishes sharply between acting in accordance with an opinion and believing that it is correct. However, Descartes continues:

And so it is that the actions of life, brooking no delay, it is a certain truth that when we are powerless to discern the truest opinions, we must follow the probable, and although we see no more probability in some than in others, we must nonetheless settle on some and consider them afterwards as no longer being doubtful, insofar as they relate to practice, but as very true and very certain, because the reason which has caused us to settle on them is itself such.

This involves two elements foreign to the stance we have attributed to the pyrrhonist. The first is the appeal to probability. Evidently, Descartes thinks that he can make some reasonable judgments about which opinions are more likely to be true; and insofar as he endorses these judgments and conforms his conduct to them, he has moral beliefs of the sort the pyrrhonist abjures. The second is the suggestion that for practical purposes it is necessary to convince oneself of the truth of the morality one accepts. It is unclear what it means to regard a proposition as 'no longer doubtful insofar as [it] relates to practice'. But on one natural construal this is a counsel of doublethink: when one is deliberating about what to do, one should wholeheartedly believe the morality one accepts. When one is reflecting one should withdraw this opinion and regard the principle only as a rule for action. Again, this has no analog in the pyrrhonist account. The pyrrhonist we have described acts on a rule—perhaps even resolutely—while suspending judgment on whether it points in the right direction. Descartes' analogy is apt. The traveler lost in the forest should adopt a policy of walking straight ahead in some direction or other. He *might* convince himself that the direction he has chosen is the right one. But this is obviously optional, and on the face of it quite unnecessary. He might proceed resolutely because he has resolved to do so, while fully and self-consciously acknowledging that he has no idea where he is going.

9. Some writers require models to conform to facts about the apparent sizes of the planets. Thus Simplicius:

Nevertheless, the theories of Eudoxus and his followers fail to save the phenomena . . . I refer to the fact that the planets appear at times to be near to us and at times to have receded. This is indeed obvious to our eyes in the case of some of them; for the star called after Aphrodite and also the star of Ares seem, in the middle of their retrogradations, to be many times as large, so much so that the star of Aphrodite actually makes bodies cast shadows on moonless nights.

(Translated in Heath, 1932: 68).

10. Plato lays down the principle that the heavenly bodies' motion is circular, uniform, and constantly regular. Thereupon he sets the mathematicians the following problem:

What circular motions, uniforms and perfectly regular, are to be admitted as hypotheses so that it might be possible to save the appearances presented by the planets?

(Simplicius, on *De Caelo*, translated in Duhem, 1969: 5).

11. When it comes to a choice between empirically equivalent hypotheses, Ptolemy appeals explicitly to simplicity. After a proof of the general equivalence between appeal to epicycles and the appeal to eccentrics (*Syntaxis* 3.4), Ptolemy writes:

> With these things explained, it is now necessary to take up the apparent irregularity or anomaly of the sun; because there is one only, and it is such that the time from the least movement to the mean is greater than the time from the mean to the greatest movement. For we find that this agrees with appearances. And this can be accomplished by either hypothesis:—(1) by that of the epicycle when the movement of the sun is in the direction of movement of the heavens on its arc at the apogee. But (2) it would be more reasonable to stick to the hypothesis of eccentricity which is simpler and completely effected by one and not two movements.
>
> (Hutchins, 1952: 93)

Duhem invariably treats such passages in which simplicity furnishes a ground for theory choice as evidence for a fictionalist attitude towards astronomical hypotheses. (See for example Duhem, 1969: 28.) Duhem never considers the possibility that for Ptolemy, the choice of the simpler hypothesis is grounded in the thought that what is simpler is more likely to be true.

12. A later work, the *Planetary Hypotheses*, contains a sustained account of the causes of the planetary movements that is clearly meant to cohere with the astronomical system of the *Syntaxis*.

13. For alternative translations of the passage based on more recent editions of the Greek text, see Sambursky (1962: 148ff) and Siovoranes (1996: 266).

14. Cf. the continuation of the passage from the *Hypotyposis* cited above:

> The account given of these mechanical hypotheses seems to be haphazard. Why, in each hypothesis, is the eccentric in this particular state—fixed or mobile—and the epicycle in that, and the planet moving either in a retrograde or a direct sense? What are the reasons for those planes and their separations—I mean the *real* reasons that, once understood, will relieve the mind of all its anguish?—this they never tell us.
>
> (Sambursky, 1962: 149)

15. Hypotyposis 9, in Sambursky (1962: 149).

16. For as Plato says in the Laws

> those sin against divinity who dare ascribe wandering to the celestial gods, in consequence of not knowing their order, their harmonious dance, and the equability of their motion. For inequability is alone [merely] apparent among them, through lation and circulation of their evolving circles, whether on

account of epicycles and eccentrics or from other causes. For all the hypotheses have not the same probability. But some of them, indeed, are remote from the simplicity of the divine natures . . .

(Proclus, 1820, 2: 221)

17. Elsewhere he suggests that that the appeal to epicycles and eccentrics is unnecessary, hinting that an astronomical system compatible with Plato's metaphysics was in fact available:

The spheres on which the planets move are now called by Plato 'circles', but not 'epicycles'. For he mentioned these nowhere, just as he did not mention the eccentrics among the circles. For it would be ridiculous to make some little circles move on every sphere in the direction opposite to its [motion], or make them part of the sphere, or of another substance, or eccentric spheres embracing the center without moving around it. For this undermines the common axiom of the physicists that every uniform motion is either around the center or away from it or towards it . . . Plato never moves the planets in any different way, *nor does he need such devices,* unworthy of divine things.

(Proclus, Commentary on Plato's *Timaeus*, 272 A–B, 284 C–D.)

18. After a thorough review of Duhem's evidence, the details of which are consonant with what we have seen above, Michael Gardner concludes that a number of ancient writers, including Proclus, held that the Ptolemaic theory was acceptable as a device for calculation but that it 'should not be accepted on a literal interpretation'. He goes on to add that 'persons who thought the theory was a convenient device but was untrue sometimes did, and sometimes did not, think it needed to be replaced by a convenient device that was also a true theory' (Gardner, 1983: 213). Unfortunately he does not cite an example of a theorist who expresses unalloyed satisfaction with the theory despite its acknowledged falsity.

19. Duhem does cite on compelling and altogether striking anticipation: in the *Guide of the Perplexed* Maimonides writes:

Know with regard to the astronomical matters mentioned that if an exclusively mathematical-minded man reads and understands them, he will think that they form a cogent argument that the form and number of the spheres is as stated. Now things are not like this, and this is not what is sought in the science of astronomy. Some of these matters are indeed founded on the demonstration that they are that way. Thus it has been demonstrated that the path of the sun is inclined against the equator. . . . But there has been no demonstration whether the sun has an eccentric sphere or an epicycle. *Now the master of astronomy does not mind this, for the object of that science is to suppose as a hypothesis an arrangement that renders it possible for the motion of the star to be uniform and*

> *circular with no acceleration ... and to have the inferences necessarily following from the assumption of that motion agree with what is observed.*
>
> (Maimonides, 1963: 273–4 quoted in Duhem, 1969: 34.)

So far as I have been able to determine, these remarks are an isolated anticipation and do not represent a larger trend.

20. For Osiander's career see Wrightman (1975).

21. The pioneering discussion of the group is Westman (1975b).

22. Translated in Jardine (1984: 39–40), my emphasis. Jardine's masterful book is an indispensable resource for further work on fictionalism in this period.

23. It is clear that Galileo was independently familiar with the view:

> The worst judgment that could fall upon Copernicus' book would be that some marginal notes would be added to the effect that this doctrine was introduced to save the appearances, in the same way that others have introduced eccentrics and epicycles without believing that they exist in nature.
>
> (Galileo to Dini, 23 March 1615.)

Galileo's goes on (210ff) to insist that those who understand these matters have not in fact rejected epicycles and eccentrics. Galileo's letter bespeaks an extraordinarily sophisticated and historically informed approach to the topic.

24. Bellarmine offers the view to Foscherini, but it seems clear that he (Bellarmine) did not endorse it. For Bellarmine's efforts in cosmology see Blackwell (1991: 40ff).

25. *De communibus omnium rerum naturalium principiis & affectionibus* (1562), quoted in Jardine (1984: 237).

26. See Gingerich (1973).

27. Scattered remarks on fictions are found throughout Bentham's work, but the main systematic treatments are to be found in the 'Fragment on Ontology' (1813–21) and the 'Essay on Logic' (1811–31), both published posthumously in Bentham (1843). The significance of Bentham's theory was first emphasized by C. K. Ogden (1932). The most significant recent treatment is the indispensable Harrison (1983).

28. It is possible for names like 'The Devil' which purport to refer to entities—in this case, animate creatures—of a genus which also contains real instances. For discussion, see Harrison (1983).

29. A body is said to be in motion. This, *taken in the literal sense, is as much as to say,* here is a body, called a motion; in this larger body, the other body, namely the really existing body is contained (Bentham, 1843: 195).

REFERENCES

Barker, Peter and Bernard Golstein (1998). 'Realism and Instrumentalism in Sixteenth Century Astronomy: A Reappraisal.' *Perspectives on Science*, 6.3: 232–57.

Barnes, Jonathan (1982). 'The Beliefs of a Pyrrhonist.' *Proceedings of the Cambridge Philological Society* N S, 28: 1–29. Reprinted in Burnyeat and Frede (1997).

Bentham, Jeremy (1843). *The Complete Works of Jeremy Bentham*, 8, John Bowring and William Tait, (eds.).

Blackwell, Richard J. (1991). *Galileo, Berllarmine, and the Bible: Including a Translation of Foscarini's Letter on the Motion of the Earth.* Notre Dame, Indiana: University of Notre Dame Press.

Brock, Stuart (2002). 'Fictionalism about Fictional Characters.' *Noûs*, 36.1: 1–21.

Burnyeat, Miles (1980). 'Can the Sceptic Live his Scepticism?' In Richard Rorty, Quintin Skinner, and Jerome Schneewind (eds.), *Philosophy in History: Essays in the Historiography of Philosophy.* Cambridge: Cambridge University Press, 1984. Reprinted in Burnyeat and Frede (1997).

Burnyeat, Miles, and Michael Frede (1997). *The Original Sceptics: A Controversy.* Hackett.

Copernicus, Nicholas (1995). *On the Revolutions of the Heavenly Spheres.* Charles Glenn Wallis (trans.). Prometheus Books.

Descartes, René (1960). *Discourse on the Method of Rightly Conducting the Reason and Seeking Truth in the Sciences,* III. In *Descartes, Philosophical Essays,* Lawrence J. Lafleur (trans). Indianapolis: Bobbs-Merril.

Duhem, Pierre (1969). *To Save the Phenomena: An Essay on the Idea of Physical Theory from Plato to Galileo.* E. Doland and C. Maschler (trans.). Chicago: University of Chicago Press.

Field, Hartry (1980). *Science Without Numbers.* Princeton: Princeton University Press.

—— (1989). *Realism, Mathematics and Modality.* Oxford: Basil Blackwell.

Fine, Arthur (1993). 'Fictionalism.' *Midwest Studies in Philosophy*, 18: 1–18.

Frank, Philipp (1950). 'Metaphysical Interpretations of Science, II.' *British Journal for the Philosophy of Science*, 1: 2.

Frede, Michael (1979). 'Des Skeptikers Meinungen.' *Neue Heft für Philosophie*, Heft 15.16: 102–29. Translated as 'The Sceptic's Beliefs' in Burnyeat and Frede (1997).

Gardner, Michael (1983). 'Realism and Instrumentalism in Pre-Newtonian Astronomy.' In J. Earman (ed.). *Testing Scientific Theories, Minnesota Studies in the Philosophy of Science,* 10. University of Minnesota Press.

Gingerich, Owen (1973). 'The Role of Erasmus Rheinhold and the Prutenic Tables in the Dissemination of Copernican Theory.' *Studia Copernicana*, 6: 43–62.

Harrison, Ross (1983). *Jeremy Bentham.* London: Routledged Kegan Paul.

Heath, Thomas (1932). *Greek Astronomy.* J. M. Dent and Sons.

Hutchins, Robert M. (ed.) (1952). *Ptolemy, Copernicus, Kepler, Great Books of the Western World,* 16. Encyclopedia Britannica, Inc.

Jardine, Nicholas (1984). *The Birth of History and Philosophy of Science.* Cambridge: Cambridge University Press.

Lloyd, G. E. R (1978). 'Saving the Appearances.' *Classical Quarterly,* 28: 202–22.

Maimonides, Moses (1963). *The Guide of the Perplexed.* Shlomo Pines (ed. and trans.). Chicago: University of Chicago Press.

Ogden, C. K. (1932). *Bentham's Theory of Fictions.* New York: Harcourt, Brace and Company.

Proclus (1820). *The Commentaries of Proclus on the Timaeus of Plato.* Thomas Taylor (trans.). London: privately printed.

Rosen, Edward (1984). *Copernicos and the Scientific Revolution.* Malabar, Florida: Kreiger.

Rosen, Gideon (1994). 'What is Constructive Empiricism?' *Philosophical Studies,* 74: 143–78.

Sambursky, Samuel (1962). *The Physical World of Late Antiquity.* Basic Books.

Sextus Empiricus (2000). *Outlines of Scepticism,* Julia Annas and Jonathan Barnes (eds.). Cambridge: Cambridge University Press.

Siovoranes, Lucas (1996). *Proclus: Neo-Platonic Philosophy and Science.* Edinburgh: Edinburgh University Press.

van Fraassen, Bas C. (1980). *The Scientific Image.* Oxford: Oxford University Press.

Westman, Robert S. (1975a). *The Copernican Achievement.* University of California Press.

—— (1975b). 'The Melanchthon Circle, Rheticus, and the Wittenberg Interpretation of the Copernican Theory.' *Isis,* 65: 165–93.

—— (1975c). 'Three Responses to the Copernican Theory: Johannes Praetorius, Tycho Brahe and Michael Maestlin.' In Westman (1975a).

Wrightman (1975). 'Andreas Osiander's Contribution to the Copernican Achievement.' In Westman (1975a).

2

Metaphor and Prop Oriented Make-Believe

KENDALL L. WALTON

I

Dolls and hobby horses are valuable for their contributions to make-believe. The same is true of paintings and novels. These and other props stimulate our imaginations and provide for exciting or pleasurable or interesting engagements with fictional worlds. A doll, in itself just a bundle of rags or a piece of moulded plastic, comes alive in a game of make-believe, providing the participant with a (fictional) baby. What in real life is a mere stick enables a child fictionally to ride around on a horse, the better to chase bandits or stray cattle. Paint on canvas and print on paper lead us into exciting worlds of mystery, romance, and adventure and guide our travels through them.

But props are not always tools in the service of make-believe. Sometimes make-believe is a means for understanding props. The props themselves may be the focus of our attention, and the point of regarding them as props in (actual or potential) games of make-believe may be to provide useful or illuminating ways of describing or thinking about them. Participating in the game may not be especially fun in itself and we may have little interest in the content of the make-believe world or the subject matter of our imaginings. A game may be cooked up simply to clarify or expose features of the props, simply so we can observe their role in it. This is make-believe in the service of the cognition of props. I call it *prop oriented* make-believe, and I contrast it to *content oriented* make-believe, whose interest lies in the content of the make-believe, in the fictional world. In *Mimesis as Make-Believe* I emphasized the latter, exploring the ways in which props of various kinds contribute to make-believe activities.[1] I will focus now on prop oriented make-believe.

II

Paper airplanes, like hobby horses and toy trucks, serve as props in games of make-believe. They make it fictional, i.e., true-in-the-world-of-make-believe, that they are airplanes flying through the air, climbing, diving, landing on a runway, crashing.[2] But the fun of making and playing with paper airplanes does not derive entirely, maybe not even primarily, from their role in make-believe. Children who know nothing of actual airplanes and who think of what we call paper airplanes merely as folded pieces of paper that behave interestingly when thrown, might enjoy throwing them, watching them glide, experimenting with the effects of different folds on their flight, and so on. One's interest may be in the paper constructions themselves, apart from any make-believe. Frisbees suggest a game in which fictionally they are flying saucers. But most frisbee enthusiasts seem to be interested in throwing, catching, and watching the plastic disks themselves, not in fantasies about space travel.

There is nevertheless a point in calling the paper constructions *airplanes* and the plastic disks *flying saucers*. These are convenient ways of indicating, for those who know about airplanes and flying saucers, what these toys are and how they work. The make-believe looks back toward the props themselves, rather than forward to the fictional truths the props generate; it is *prop oriented*.

Paper airplanes and frisbees thus differ from such props as hobby horses, non-flying airplane models (e.g., a model of the Wright brothers' airplane), and the kind of toy trucks that a child pushes around the floor. Merely manipulating or looking at *these* things is likely not to be much fun. One's interest is in the make-believe to which they contribute, in fictionally riding a horse or observing the Wright brothers' airplane or driving a truck.[3] In these cases make-believe looks forward to the content of the make-believe; it is *content oriented*.

Where in Italy is the town of Crotone?, I ask. You explain that it is on the arch of the Italian boot. 'See that thundercloud over there—the big angry face near the horizon', you say; 'it is headed this way'. Plumbers and electricians distinguish between 'male' and 'female' plumbing and electrical connections. We speak of the saddle of a mountain and the shoulder of a highway.

All of these cases are linked to make-believe. We think of Italy and the thundercloud as something like pictures. Italy (or a map of Italy) depicts a boot. The cloud is a prop which makes it fictional that there is an angry face.

Male and female plumbing or electrical connections are understood to be, fictionally, male and female sexual organs. The saddle of a mountain is, fictionally, a horse's saddle. But our interest, in these instances, is not in the make-believe itself, and it is not for the sake of games of make-believe that we regard these things as props. Our participation is minimal at best.[4] Imagining a boot, while seeing a map of Italy or seeing it in my mind's eye, may help me to understand your explanation of the location of Crotone. But I don't contemplate the Italian boot in the way one might contemplate Van Gogh's *Pair of Shoes* or even René Magritte's *The Red Model II*. Clouds *can* support extensive participation; one might, on a dreamy summer afternoon, fictionally examine the furrows of an angry face, wonder what it is angry about, and so on. One might be caught up emotionally in the fictional world the clouds present. But such involvement is unnecessary if the purpose is to identify which cloud you mean to point out. All this requires is to recognize which cloud can best be understood to be an angry-face-picture. To do that it may be helpful to have the experience of, fictionally, recognizing an angry face, but no further participation is called for; there is no need to be caught up emotionally in the fiction. The plumbing and electrical connections invite scarcely any participation in the game in which they are understood to be props, despite its sexy subject matter. The conscientious plumber does his job without, fictionally, leering at the fixtures. (This plumbing terminology can be vaguely titillating, however, and it might cause embarrassment, especially when one comes across it for the first time. These reactions suggest that a certain perhaps implicit participation in the game may be likely, perhaps even inevitable, whether or not such participation helps the plumber to keep track of which fixtures can be connected to which others.) We may speak of saddles of mountains and shoulders of highways without even thinking of make-believe, let alone participating in it, although no doubt such thoughts were present when these expressions were first introduced or learned.

Make-believe—recognition of the possibility of make-believe, at least—is useful in these cases, even if it is not exciting or pleasurable or edifying in ways games of dolls and games with paintings and novels are. It is useful for articulating, remembering, and communicating facts about the props— about the geography of Italy, or the identity of the storm cloud, or functional properties of plumbing and electrical fixtures, or mountain topography. It is by thinking of Italy or the thundercloud or plumbing connections as potential if not actual props that I understand where Crotone is, which cloud is the one being talked about, or whether one pipe can be connected to another. The purpose is cognitive, but what I learn is not about boots, angry faces (or anger), or sex. The subject matter of the (potential) make-believe is merely useful.

There is nothing profound about the cognitive role of make-believe in these examples. The facts it helps us to grasp and remember and communicate are mundane, and the make-believe is dispensable, a mere convenience. There are other ways of locating Crotone; we don't have to think of Italy as a boot. But make-believe, we shall see later, plays a more essential and extensive role in our understanding of props than is apparent from these examples.

Appreciation of visual and literary representations typically involves participation in content oriented games of make-believe, especially when the appreciation includes the experience of being 'caught up in the story' or 'emotionally involved' in the fictional world. But people sometimes find it convenient to devise *ad hoc* prop oriented games, often modifications of the standard content oriented ones, in describing the props themselves, the visual or literary representations, and their surroundings.[5] One might remark, for instance, that the author of a forthcoming novel murdered several of his characters with a pencil; this may be a way of pointing out that the author revised the novel so as to exclude those characters. The remark indicates a (possible) game of make-believe in which revising a novel in that manner makes it fictional that one kills characters with a pencil.

If the Metropolitan Museum borrows a portrait of Napoleon from the Louvre for a special exhibit and has it shipped to New York on the *Queen Mary*, one might observe that Napoleon is a 'passenger' on the *Queen Mary*, thus invoking a (possible) game in which the presence of a portrait on a ship makes it fictional that the subject of the portrait is a passenger. I don't know whether anyone else has thought of games like this, let alone participated in them. But there is nothing exotic about them, and it takes only the remark that Napoleon is a passenger on the *Queen Mary*, in a suitable context, to call the possibility of such games to mind. There is no need for anyone to explain them.

Here are some other comments that can be taken in similar ways:

'This statue isn't the original one. The Germans took the first Flaubert away in 1941, along with the railings and door-knockers. Perhaps he was processed into cap-badges.'[6]

'Christopher Robin had spent the morning indoors going to Africa and back [i.e., reading about Africa], and he had just got off the boat and was wondering what it was like outside, when who should come knocking at the door but Eyore.'[7]

'The chair behind the couch is not the stationary object it seems. I have travelled all over the world on it, and back and forth in time. Without moving from my easy seat I have met important personages and witnessed great events. But it remained for Kirk Allen to take me out of this world when he transformed the couch in my consulting room into a space ship that roved the galaxies.'[8]

These examples illustrate the pervasiveness of make-believe in thought and conversation, the prevalence of hints of, allusions to potential and often fragmentary games, in addition to sustained engagement with full fledged, established games when we appreciate works of art. They also illustrate how little it takes to introduce even rather novel games. The quotation from Lindner suffices to introduce an unusual game in which a patient's exotic tales of other worldly events make it fictional that the psychiatrist's chair is a space ship. We are constantly inventing new games of make-believe and communicating them to one another. This doesn't mean that we actively participate in these games. Many of them are prop rather than content oriented; our interest being not in the make-believe itself, but in the props. Thinking of the props as props in potential games of make-believe is a device for understanding them.

III

Many remarks that serve to suggest or imply or introduce or call to mind games of make-believe can themselves be 'moves' in the implied games, acts of verbal participation.[9] In saying 'Napoleon is a passenger on the *Queen Mary*' I might be pretending to assert that he is; it may be fictional, in the game my remark introduces, that in saying this I am claiming that Napoleon really is a passenger on the *Queen Mary*. One may thus call attention to a game of make-believe by engaging in it oneself. But the speaker need not actually participate in the game in order to call attention to it. There are different degrees and kinds of participation, and whether a speaker on a particular occasion does participate will depend on how we choose to understand this notion. (One relevant consideration will be whether, in saying 'Napoleon is a passenger on the *Queen Mary*' the speaker imagines herself to be asserting the literal truth of that sentence. But it may be none too easy to decide whether she does imagine this.) What matters is that to say 'Napoleon is a passenger on the *Queen Mary*' is to say something which obviously might be said in an act of verbal participation in a game of a certain salient kind, and that in doing this one implies, suggests, introduces, calls to mind, that kind of game.

The speaker is probably genuinely asserting something as well, whether or not she is pretending to assert something. Saying 'Napoleon is a passenger on the *Queen Mary*' is a colourful way of asserting that Napoleon's portrait is stowed aboard the ship. The colour consists in the utilization of make-believe as a device for asserting this to be the case; the speaker asserts it by using a sentence that might be used in pretending to assert that Napoleon is a passenger on the *Queen Mary*, whether or not she actually so pretends. She at least alludes to a (possible) act of pretended assertion, to an act of fictionally asserting, in the implied game of make-believe, that Napoleon is a passenger on the *Queen Mary*. She is saying, in effect, that fictionally to assert this would be, fictionally, to assert something true, that circumstances are such that it is fictional that Napoleon is a passenger on the *Queen Mary*. The circumstance that makes this fictional is the fact that Napoleon's portrait is aboard the ship.

So we have a way of describing the *Queen Mary* and Napoleon's portrait which depends on thinking of them as props in a game of make-believe of a certain sort. Likewise, to say 'That pipe is male' is a colourful way (a slightly off-colour way) of saying that the pipe is designed to fit inside another pipe, that it is threaded on the outside. The speaker implies a certain sort of game of make-believe in which being threaded on the outside makes it fictional that a pipe is male. She goes through the motions, at least, of fictionally asserting that the pipe in question is male, and in doing so she, in effect, claims it to be fictional that the pipe is male, i.e., she claims that it is threaded on the outside. The assertion amounts to the claim that certain circumstances obtain, namely, the circumstances that would make it fictional that she speaks truly if, fictionally, she asserts the literal truth of what she says.

Notice that the content of the assertions in these instances, as given by these glosses, includes no reference to make-believe. The speaker is simply describing features of the prop or props—features of things that are or would be props in games of the implied kind. But it is by invoking make-believe that the speaker says what she does about the props. Interest is focused on the props themselves; the envisioned make-believe provides a way of describing them.

If, or to the extent that, statements alluding to make-believe can be paraphrased in ways not involving make-believe, make-believe is not essential to what is said. But make-believe sometimes has a more essential role in describing and understanding props than it does in the examples I have given. Even so, the make-believe may be of no particular interest in itself; it may serve merely to clarify or illuminate the props. But it may be more or less indispensable for this purpose. It may do more than simply add colour or provide conveniently memorable or vivid ways of saying what could be said otherwise.

Men's restrooms are marked by stylized pictures of men on the doors; women's rooms by pictures of women. Icons of people in wheelchairs indicate facilities designed for the use of people with physical handicaps. These pictures are used in visual games of make-believe, but ones that invite only minimal participation.[10] On seeing them, one imagines recognizing a woman, or a man, or a person in a wheelchair; fictionally one does so. But that's about it. And this minimal participation is not fun or pleasurable or satisfying or exciting in the way that contemplation of pictures in art galleries is. The point, of course, is to learn something about the picture itself, the prop—that it is a man-picture or a woman-picture, for instance, and hence an indicator of the men's room or the women's room. (Our interest doesn't stop at the prop, in this case; our interest in it is instrumental. Nevertheless it is an interest in the prop apart from the make-believe world it contributes to, so the make-believe is prop oriented rather than content oriented.)

Iconic signs are usually very stylized and standardized. But I understand that the restrooms at the Orson Wells Cinema in Cambridge Massachusetts were marked by assorted stills of Katherine Hepburn and Cary Grant. Let's suppose that any recognizable woman-picture or man-picture, no matter what its depictive style and no matter what posture or attitude or environment the person is depicted in, can be used for the purpose. Every women's room door sports a different woman-picture. Some are in the style of Giotto; others mimic Rubens, or Vermeer, or Degas, or Picasso. (I will suppose that these are *bad* Giottos, Rubens, Picassos, etc., ones we would have little interest in contemplating. Our objective is still simply to identify women's rooms by identifying signs on their doors as woman-pictures.) Some women's room signs depict a seated woman nursing a child; others a woman playing tennis, or giving a lecture, or bathing, or climbing a mountain, or dancing, or descending a staircase. Some depict only a woman's face in close-up; others a silhouetted female figure in a vast landscape.

The variety of *visual designs* that serve to mark women's rooms is boggling. To identify them and distinguish them from those marking men's rooms by characteristics of line and shape would be hopeless. We succeed only if we use the designs as props at least to the extent of fictionally recognizing a woman, or a man, only if we 'see' a woman or a man 'in' them. *Then* we have no trouble. It is not usually hard to identify woman-pictures in the style of Giotto or Rubens or Degas as woman-pictures and to distinguish them from man-pictures, if we engage in the appropriate make-believe. Make-believe is not merely a convenience here, as it is in the case of male and female plumbing connections. A certain minimal participation in make-believe is essential; the mere thought of potential games of make-believe doesn't suffice.

Perhaps make-believe is *in principle* dispensable even here. Perhaps there is a complicated, disjunctive way of specifying members of the class of women's room indicators in terms of lines and shapes. (To keep things simple, I ignore the fact that as styles of depiction change new combinations of shapes may come to count as woman-pictures and women's room indicators.) But none of us can expect to come close to spelling it out. It is hard enough even to say very exactly what it is about a particular design that makes it a woman-picture; this requires more artistic ability or a better eye than most of us have, and an ability to articulate what one intuitively knows which few artists possess. Moreover, even if we had the relevant line and shape specification before us, the *unity* of the class of woman-pictures, the similarity among them, would not be apparent in it. It seems appropriate to classify these varied visual designs together only when we see them as woman-pictures.[11]

It is arguable that the property of being a woman-picture is not identical to that of possessing the complicated disjunctively specified design property. Perhaps the former depends on, or is supervenient on, the latter. Some may hold that being a woman-picture, like colours or moral properties or being funny, is a response dependent property,[12] the relevant response being that of seeing a woman in the design. The design property is not response dependent, or anyway it is not dependent on the same response.

By contrast, it would seem that 'saddle' (of a mountain), 'male connector' and 'on the arch of the Italian boot' are used to attribute properties having nothing essentially to do with make-believe.[13]

IV

It will have been evident that some of my examples are instances of metaphor. 'Saddle' applied to mountains and 'male' applied to plumbing fixtures are metaphors in anyones book, dead ones anyway. My other examples may be less comfortably thought of as metaphors: 'Napoleon is a passenger on the *Queen Mary*', 'Crotone is on the arch of the Italian boot', 'The ugly face in the sky is headed this way', and 'There is a man' said while pointing toward a men's room sign. The ground of the distinction is unclear, however. To speak of the saddle of a mountain is to think of the topography in question as though it is a representational sculpture, but one whose make-believe is oriented to the prop. 'It has been Grand Central Station around here all day' is a metaphor that involves thinking of the household in question as a kind of unwitting theatrical portrayal of Grand Central Station; one in which, again, the make-believe is prop oriented. The cases of the Italian boot, the angry face in the sky, and the rest room icons consist in regarding something as a representational picture whose make-believe is prop oriented. If 'saddle' and 'Grand Central Station' in these contexts are metaphors, why not also 'The ugly face in the sky is headed this way' and 'There is a man' said while pointing toward a men's room sign?

I am not going to propose a theory of metaphor. This is because I am very unsure what to count as metaphors, and because I am sceptical about whether anything like the class of what people call metaphors is a unified one, whether a single account will work for any reasonable refinement of that class. But I do want to explore the applicability of the notion of make-believe to some acknowledged metaphors, and to sketch some advantages of understanding these metaphors, at least, in terms of make-believe.

Other metaphors that plausibly involve prop oriented make-believe are easy to come by. 'Argument is war' and the family of metaphors subsidiary to it, including talk of claims being indefensible, criticisms being on target, winning and losing arguments, shooting down arguments, attacking and defending positions, and so on,[14] suggest a game in which what people say in the course of an argument generates fictional truths about acts of war. The arguers or observers of an argument participate in the game if they take argumentative behaviour to prescribe imagining acts of war, and imagine accordingly. But participation is not necessary for using and understanding the metaphors; it is enough to recognize or be aware of the game. The metaphors can work even if no one has ever participated in the game. The make-believe is prop oriented in that (or insofar as) it is the argument that one is interested in, and the make-believe war is thought of as a device for describing or understanding the argument.

In this case a single game or kind of game crops up intermittently but persistently in many different metaphorical utterances. Other metaphors of this sort include those deriving from the thought that 'time is money',[15] war metaphors applied to sports, and sports metaphors applied to war. More localized metaphors which also might be thought of as involving prop oriented make-believe include: 'Man is the cancer of the earth', 'Politician Jones started prairie fires on his campaign trip in the Midwest', 'an orgy of eating', and (at least before they died) 'bottle neck', 'traffic jam', 'waves of immigrants', 'chair leg', and 'mouth of a river'. (Metaphors that strike me as less plausibly amenable to this treatment include 'Time flies', 'Her spirits are rising', 'She always took the high road in business dealings', 'He knows which side his bread is buttered on', and 'Happiness is a warm puppy.' Perhaps not all of these are metaphors?)

The general idea is this: the metaphorical statement (in its context) implies or suggests or introduces or calls to mind a (possible) game of make-believe. The utterance may be an act of verbal participation in the implied game, or it may be merely the utterance of a sentence that *could* be used in participating in the game. In saying what she does, the speaker describes things that are or would be props in the implied game. It may be possible in favourable cases to paraphrase what she says about them with reasonable fidelity. Typically, the paraphrase will specify features of the props by virtue of which it would be fictional in the implied game that the speaker speaks truly, if her utterance is an act of verbal participation in it.

There are many variations on the theme, and many differences among metaphors. The example of rest room signs suggests that some metaphorical utterances are not paraphrasable, at least not in the way I mentioned, although they may still amount to descriptions of the (potential) props. Some metaphorical utterances may not be assertions at all, even if they are declarative in form. And metaphorical sentences are not always ones that might be used in acts of verbal participation in the implied games. Nevertheless, we are now in a position to clarify and explain much that has been said about metaphor. Then we can look at some of the variations.

V

Many have taken metaphor to involve the bringing together of two distinct *categories* or *realms* or *domains*. Nelson Goodman speaks of the (literal) use of predicates in one realm guiding their (metaphorical) application in another.[16] We can think of the two realms as (*a*) that of the props and the generating facts, and (*b*) that of the propositional content of the implied make-believe. The latter is the home realm of the predicates that are used metaphorically, the realm in which they have literal application (I. A. Richards' *vehicle*). The former is the new or target or foreign realm (Richards' *tenor*).

Goodman says little about how the predicates from one realm organize another. My suggestion is that (in the case of some metaphors anyway) the mechanism involves our thinking of objects of the new realm as props, as generating the fictionality of propositions concerning the home realm. The predicates 'male' and 'female' get applied to plumbing fixtures by means of our thinking of plumbing fixtures as props which generate fictional truths about sexual identities. 'Male' applies metaphorically to plumbing connections which make it fictional, in the implied game, that they are male.

This gives some content to talk of seeing or thinking of one kind of thing 'in terms of' another, under the influence of metaphors, or of metaphors 'yoking' different kinds of things together. Richard Moran speaks of metaphors getting us to adopt a perspective, to see one thing as *framed* by another.[17] This framing effect of metaphors is independent of and prior to the use metaphors sometimes have in making assertions. It will be present even when the metaphor is embedded in a context in which it is not asserted, when it is merely a question rather than an assertion, and when it is denied or negated.

All of this is accounted for if we think of the new perspective, the framing effect, as consisting in the metaphor's implication or introduction or reminder of a game of make-believe. 'The health of General Motors is improving' implies a game of make-believe; it gets us to think of corporations as props in a game (even if we don't participate in the game). It also serves to assert something about General Motors. But approximately the same game of make-believe is implied equally by the following: 'If General Motors' health is improving, unemployment will drop'; 'I wonder if General Motors' health is improving.' 'Is the health of General Motors improving?,' 'General Motors' health is not improving.' All of these statements have the same 'framing effect'; all of them introduce essentially the same game of make-believe. Probably 'Caterpiller is in robust good health' and 'Xerox has a slight cold' do so as well.

This account of the framing effect of metaphors, of their capacity to get us to see one kind of thing in terms of another, contrasts with two other tempting proposals. One is that it is a matter of seeing similarities. Regarding things (or states of affairs) of one realm as generating fictional truths, as prescribing imaginings, concerning another realm, is not essentially a matter of seeing similarities. Some principles of generation[18] are more or less conventional, and to the extent that they are, they are likely not to depend on similarities. (For example, halos on figures in Christian art make it fictional that they are saints.) One might have thought that 'metaphors' based on conventions cannot be metaphors. Granted, if there are simply conventions that 'slide' means one thing in photographic contexts and another in connection with children's playground equipment, the conventions merely define distinct literal meanings of the terms. But if there is a convention to the effect that a ridge connecting two higher elevations makes it fictional that there is a saddle, we still have a metaphor. Calling a topographic feature a saddle is not *simply* to say that it is a ridge connecting two higher elevations. Calling it this implies the game of make-believe in which the conventional principle of generation just mentioned holds. In this sense the speaker gets us to see or think of such ridges as saddles. (Not for the first time, of course; the convention is a familiar one. But the metaphor reminds us of the game.) The freshest, most lively metaphors may be ones that introduce games, principles of generation, that are new to us. But metaphors like *saddle* (of a mountain) are not dead in a sense that ought to make us deny that they are metaphors, so long as they invoke, remind us of, the game of make-believe, familiar though it is. So long as they do this, their use as applied to mountains is parasitic on their original literal senses, and it is their use in the home realm, their application to riding equipment, that guides their application to mountain topography.

It seems unlikely that metaphors like 'high' and 'low' pitches, and 'rising' and 'falling' melodies, are grounded in similarities between pitch relations and spatial relations, although they may be not merely conventional but in some way natural. I speculate that the association has a lot to do with the fact that more energy is usually needed to produce higher pitched sounds than lower pitched ones, just as upward movement requires more energy than downward movement. To sound a higher note on a wind or string instrument one blows harder or stretches the string tighter. But in order to understand metaphors like 'rising melodies' and 'low tones' we needn't know how they came about, how it happens that we associate pitches and spatial positions as we do. The utterance is not an assertion of a similarity or natural connection, or a pointing out of one. All that matters is that these metaphors do pick out for us a game of a certain sort. (Notice, incidentally, that, if age and familiarity are any indications, these metaphors are as dead as doornails. Yet they remain metaphors. Their make-believe is active—indeed it is content as well as prop oriented, as we shall see.)

Many metaphors are not reversible.[19] 'Life is hell' is very different from, 'Hell is life.' But similarity is presumably symmetrical. Life resembles hell in exactly the respects that hell resembles life. This should make us wary of construing metaphor in terms of similarity. My proposal explains this irreversibility nicely. *Generates fictional truths about* is not symmetrical. A ridge between two higher elevations makes it fictional that there is a saddle, but the reverse does not hold (not in the same game anyway).

A second tempting account of what it is to see one kind of thing in terms of another is that this is a matter of imagining things of the one kind to be of the other kind.[20] This is not my view. On my view it is a matter of taking things of one kind to prescribe imaginings about things of another kind, not (in general) imagining things of the first kind to be of the second. Understanding the dotted lines of a balloon in a cartoon to prescribe imagining that the words in the balloon are thought but not spoken, is not to imagine that the dotted lines have anything to do with unspoken thought; it is not to imagine anything of the dotted lines at all. The lines merely prompt and prescribe certain imaginings, imaginings about the character whose portrayal the balloon's stem points to.

Some props do prescribe and prompt imaginings about themselves, however. An actor playing Hamlet probably makes it fictional not only that a prince of Denmark hesitates, but that he himself (the actor) is a hesitating prince of Denmark. So we are to imagine something about the actor, the prop—that he is a prince of Denmark and hesitates. It may be that the props in the plumbing case and in the case of the mountain saddle are also objects. Probably participants in the game are not merely to imagine a saddle, this imagining being prescribed by features of the mountain, but are to imagine of the ridge that it is a saddle.

It is less clear in other cases that props in games implied by metaphorical utterances are also objects. Consider 'rising melody', 'broken chord', 'moving to a new key', 'wistful melody', a 'mountain of debt', a 'healthy' (or 'sick') corporation, and 'the sea is laughing'. If one were to participate in the game implied by 'moving to a new key', what would one imagine to be moving? The piece, the musical work? Perhaps one would just imagine something's moving, an instance of something moving, as one listens to the modulation. It is not easy to see how one might imagine a corporation to be (literally) healthy or sick. (Nevertheless, the corporation is the object of *interest*. It is a prop if not an object of prop oriented make-believe.)

I should mention, again, that understanding and appreciating a metaphor need not involve any actual imagining in any case. It is enough to recognize the implied game, to be aware of prescriptions to imagine in certain ways, without actually so imagining.

VI

The make-believe that metaphors involve is, I have suggested, prop oriented. Our interest is focused on the props, on the alien or target realm, the tenor. The make-believe is a device to clarify or illuminate the props. This may be so even if make-believe is essential for this purpose. But sometimes we have, even in cases of metaphor, something more like an intrinsic interest in the make-believe itself. The props may serve this make-believe, and metaphors may engage their service. One might want to make prop oriented make-believe a requirement for metaphor (or for the kind of metaphors that are based on make-believe). But make-believe can look forward to the content and back to the prop at the same time. Some metaphors that are said to be *essential* are Janus-like in this way.

Talk of 'broken chords' in music usually involves simple prop oriented make-believe. A passage consisting of broken chords is one that can be understood to make it fictional that chords (simultaneously sounding pitches of a single harmony) are broken apart. The property by virtue of which the passage makes this fictional is the sequential sounding of individual pitches of a single harmony. To say that there is a 'broken chord' in the bass is to say that the bass sounds individual pitches of a given harmony sequentially. The latter property is likely to be all we are interested in. The only point in using the metaphor, in invoking the make-believe, is to indicate this feature of the bass.

Contrast metaphors like 'high' and 'low' notes, and 'rising' and 'falling' (or 'descending') melodies. Roger Scruton calls these metaphors essential. We *hear* melodies rise and fall, he says, and this is a crucial aspect of musical appreciation. 'We don't just transfer the term; we transfer the movement.'[21]

I have no doubt that we do hear at least some rising melodies as rising. And if we didn't, or if we heard (what we call) rising melodies as falling, our musical experiences would be very different. By contrast, we rarely if ever hear 'broken chords' as broken. There is no hint of violence in the gently flowing arpeggios, the broken chord's of Bach's C-Major Prelude from the *Well Tempered Clavier*.

What does hearing a melody as rising (or hearing a melody rise) amount to? A reasonable first stab would be that it is hearing the melody in a way that involves imagining an instance of something's rising. One certainly does this when a rising melody illustrates a vocal text describing the rising of someone's soul into heaven, or when, in the case of pure instrumental music, the listener tacks onto the music a story about, let's say, the launching of a space ship. (One might close one's eyes and visualize the launching, accompanied by the music.) But one can hear a melody (as) rising without making up much of a story or visualizing something moving upward. I suggest that one's hearing of the melody may still involve imagining (an instance of) something's rising, although this imagining is probably very inexplicit (the thought that something is moving upward doesn't go through one's mind) and also indeterminate (there is no answer to the question what sort of thing one imagines to be moving upward or, probably, how far or fast it moves, or where it arrives). Could it be that one is just aware, vaguely, of how easy or natural it would be for the melody to elicit one's imagining of something's rising?

Imagining something's rising can be construed as participation in a game implied by the metaphor, 'the melody rises'. And the listener's interest is in part focused on this make-believe. So the orientation of the make-believe underlying this metaphor is to the content as well as to the prop.

Make-believe in this case is not essential in the way it is in the case of the rest room signs. In the rest room example, minimal imaginative participation was necessary to the prop oriented function of the make-believe; we cannot recognize men's and women's room indicators as such without seeing men and women in the designs. But the experience of hearing melodies rise, hearing them in a way that involves imagining upward movement, is surely not necessary for recognizing (what we call) rising melodies and distinguishing them from falling ones.[22] Let's say that pitches with higher frequencies are *timper* than those with lower frequencies, and that the latter are *tomper* than the former. Some melodies, 'rising' ones, proceed in a timpish 'direction', or better *timpishly*; others proceed *tompishly*.[23]

The point of the metaphors is not just to distinguish timper and tomper pitches and to identify timpish and tompish melodies; the make-believe looks forward to the content as well as back to the prop. The make-believe world in which ascendings and descendings occur is of interest in its own right. Although the metaphors are not essential to the prop oriented function their make-believe serves, they are important in pointing out and eliciting participation in the make-believe itself.

These metaphors do look back to the prop. We are interested in the props, the melodies, independently of their role in make-believe. Important structural features of music—balance, contrast, etc.—depend on timper and tomper relations of pitches and timpish and tompish qualities of melodies, apart from the make-believe our metaphorical ways of describing these properties introduce. There is the important difference between contrary and parallel motion in counterpoint. There is the significant change when a succession of timpish melodic fragments suddenly gives way to a strikingly tompish one.

It seems to me that metaphors indicating expressive qualities of music involve make-believe which, even more obviously than 'rising melody', are content as well as prop oriented. Consider 'wistful' melodies, and 'cheerful', or 'anguished', or 'angry', or 'calm' music. We *hear* music as wistful or cheerful or angry, i.e., in hearing it we imagine something's being wistful or cheerful or angry, and thereby participate in the implied game of make-believe. And this participation is itself an important focus of interest. Such expressive properties are also important to the formal structure of a piece;[24] the make-believe is oriented to the prop as well as to the content. But in these cases, like that of the rest room signs, one must participate in the make-believe in order to use the metaphors in classifying music or melodies. I cannot specify wistful melodies just by their formal or acoustic properties, any more than I can recognize man-pictures by their shape properties. So the make-believe implied by 'wistful melody' is essential in *both* of the ways I mentioned. It is essential in the way the make-believe of rest room signs is, and also in the way the make-believe implied by 'rising melody' is.

Ordinarily, I think, talk of the 'shape' of a sonata movement, where this refers to its formal structure, is prop oriented only. Talk of the 'shape' of a melody is content as well as prop oriented. And so is talk of 'moving' from one key to another. Although 'descending' melody, like 'rising' melody, looks both ways, 'falling' melody is often oriented to the prop but not the content. We may describe a melody as falling, although we hear it only as descending, not as falling.

VII

In what sense does a person, on hearing a metaphor or any utterance implying a prop oriented game of make-believe, become aware of the implied game? In what sense does the metaphor introduce one to or remind one of a game of make-believe? In the simplest cases one is made aware of and can articulate the game's principles of generation. Perhaps the game introduced by talk of mountain saddles consists entirely in the single principle that ridges connecting higher elevations make it fictional that they are saddles. Such talk may make us fully aware of this principle.

But we usually do not have such explicit knowledge even of the most standard and familiar content oriented games. I noted our inability to specify the principles of our make-believe games involving pictures, our inability to say what patterns of shape and colour constitute pictures of women or pictures of men. In this instance and in many others, we do not look to the principles for guidance in our engagement in the game. We do not formulate them for ourselves, and then use them to decide what fictional truths pictures generate, what participants are to imagine. The imagining comes first. On seeing a visual design, we simply find ourselves imagining a frog (for instance) and imagining seeing a frog, and because of this we take the design to make it fictional that there is a frog, and to be a frog-picture.[25] (The inference is defeasible, of course.) If one wants to spell out the principles of generation, one would have to read them off from our 'practice', noting what sorts of designs induce what imaginings (in normal or appropriately idealized observers under normal or appropriately idealized circumstances), and generalizing.[26]

Although we do not bear in mind specifications of the principles concerning what sorts of designs generate what fictional truths, we do have abilities and dispositions appropriate to pictorial games. We are disposed to imagine in prescribed ways on viewing designs of relevant sorts, and to recognize what fictional truths they generate. It is in this sense that we are cognisant of the games.

Picture games (many of them anyway) need no introduction. No one needs to imply or suggest them or remind me of them for me to be cognisant of them in the above sense. It does not take someone pointing to a design in a portrait museum or on a men's room door and saying, 'That is a man', to activate my disposition to imagine appropriately in response to pictures and to recognize what fictional truths they generate. On seeing a picture I (usually) respond automatically.[27]

We do need to be prodded to engage in or even to recognize many other games, however. This is what metaphorical utterances do. Even very familiar games may not automatically come to mind when I experience things that would be props in them. On observing a ridge between higher elevations, I do not always imagine a saddle, nor does it always occur to me that the ridge might be understood to make it fictional that there is a saddle—unless someone reminds me of the game by saying 'That is a saddle.' I might come across an instance of a 'weighty' argument, an 'under the table' payment, someone's coming 'out of the closet', a writing style with 'punch', or an 'unfolding' melody without the game of make-believe the metaphor implies occurring to me. I may need someone to remind me of the game by using the metaphor.

What metaphors do, in many cases, is to activate relevant dispositions or abilities, rather than to make us aware of the principles of generation. When someone describes a writing style as having punch or a melody as unfolding, I cannot say very well what characteristics of a writing style or a melody make these metaphorical attributions appropriate, which ones generate fictional truths about punches or about something's unfolding. But I may be prepared to recognize writing styles or melodies as having 'punch' or as 'unfolding'.

The dispositions that metaphors activate are often far more extensive than these, and may involve whole families of predicates, not just the one or ones originally used metaphorically. A comment that a computer remembers a phone number may prepare me to think of computers behaving so as to make it fictional that they forget things, that they calculate, make decisions, and even lose patience or complain about their handlers or give up on a task. Your describing your household as Grand Central Station might dispose me to describe mine as Coney Island, or as a cathedral on a Wednesday at midnight. Once someone establishes the precedent of describing people as animals by calling Jones a skunk, we may think of other people as, fictionally, being other animals (a tiger, beaver, pig, mouse, dinosaur). The remark that we are all in the same boat easily leads to a recommendation that we all row in the same direction. Metaphors often function something like the stipulative launching of a (content oriented) game of make-believe, which then grows naturally beyond the original stipulation. In suggesting 'Let's let stumps be bears', or pointing toward a stump and declaring, 'Watch out for the bear', a child may establish a game in which the presence of the stump makes it fictional that a bear is there. But the game is bound to be far richer than this. It may be understood, more or less automatically, that larger stumps count as larger bears and smaller ones as smaller bears, that an appropriately shaped stump makes it fictional that a bear is rearing on its hind legs; seeing a stump through the undergrowth will make it fictional that one sees a bear through the undergrowth, and children can behave in obvious ways so as to make it fictional that they run away from a bear in terror, or face it bravely, or offer it a blueberry ice-cream cone. Such extensions of the game the child introduced are more or less inevitable, but it took an introduction to get it started.

Metaphorical utterances, like stipulated launches of games of make-believe, enable us to *go on* in new ways, to apply the predicates used in the original metaphor to new cases, and to apply related predicates metaphorically. If possessing a concept consists in such abilities or dispositions to go on, as some have suggested, metaphorical utterances expand our repertoire of concepts. The new concepts are concepts of properties we might describe as those of being *metaphorically θ*—metaphorically unfolding, or metaphorically having punch, or being metaphorically under the table.

In uttering a metaphor one may assert that some such concept applies in a certain instance. But the introduction of the concept, the metaphor's role in enabling hearers to acquire it, is independent of the assertion. It is part of, or a result of, Moran's 'framing effect', which a given metaphor and its negation, as well as the same metaphor in nonassertive contexts, may possess equally. Insofar as we are unable to specify the features of props by virtue of which a predicate applies metaphorically to them, insofar as we just go on, we are likely to consider purported paraphrases of the assertions in terms of such features inadequate.[28]

VIII

Many metaphors, especially the more interesting ones, do not enable us to go on with assurance. They leave us uncertain or perplexed or in disagreement about applications of the original metaphorical predicate and others in its family. It is very unclear what games are introduced by 'Juliet is the sun', or by the description of a musical passage as a 'rainbow'.[29] Not only can we not specify the principles of generation, we are not prepared to identify with any assurance which people are metaphorically the sun and which are not (no matter how well we know them), or what musical passages are rainbows. Here is another example:

Art is dead. Its present moments are not at all indications of vitality; they are not even the convulsions of agony prior to death, they are the mechanical reflex actions of a corpse submitted to a galvanic force.[30]

What do moments of art have to be like to be (metaphorically) reflexes of a corpse, as opposed to convulsions of a person not yet dead? We can neither say with any confidence, nor can we very well recognize which description is appropriate for the present moment of art, or for other moments of art in this or another culture. To the extent that the concept a metaphor introduces is unclear, it will be unclear what (if anything) the speaker is asserting. But that may not be the point of the metaphor. Its point may be, in part, to provoke us to think about what sorts of games along suggested lines might be reasonable or natural or intriguing.

Even if the nature of the game implied by a metaphor is fairly definite and a fairly definite assertion is made, the metaphor's interest may lie neither in the assertion, nor in the introduction of new concepts. Consider 'There was anger in the rays of the sun.'[31] Perhaps the game this metaphor introduces is one in which all sunlight contains anger, in which sunlight always makes it fictional that there is anger (although one might choose not to participate in or think about the game in which this is so.) If this is right, the metaphor seems not to introduce any interestingly new concept, any new way of classifying things of the sort that might serve as props in the game. And the assertion (if there is one) is trivially true. What is of interest is the game of make-believe itself, but not simply the content of the make-believe, the fictional truth(s) generated by the sun's rays (roughly, the fact that fictionally there is anger). The make-believe may be content oriented, but it is prop oriented also. And the interest lies in the combination of the two views, in the sunlight's role as a prop in the envisioned game (not just a classification of sunlight that thinking of it as a prop might enable us to make). The metaphor shows us a way of regarding sunlight—as making it fictional that there is anger.

Many other metaphors would appear to be like this one. 'The sea is laughing' seems likely to be more significant as an expression of a way of regarding the sea or some manifestations of it—regarding it as a prop in the implied game—than as introducing a way of classifying states of the sea or as asserting something about the sea on the occasion of utterance.

Metaphors thus make such things as sunlight and the sea into something like representational works of art. A Japanese brush painting of a flower may be interesting not (or not merely) because of what it makes fictional, but because of how it makes it fictional, because of the manner in which the brush strokes work to generate the fictional truths. To see how they do is to regard them in a special way, and regarding them in this special way is an important part of one's aesthetic experience of the painting. It is the *function* of pictures such as the Japanese painting to serve as props in games of make-believe. This is not in general the function of sunlight and the sea. In particular social contexts metaphorical utterances accord them this function. Sunlight and the sea are 'found objects'. Metaphors do the finding.

NOTES

Originally published in *European Journal of Philosophy*, 1.1: 39–57. Thanks to Blackwell Publishing for permission to reprint. [Editor.]
This is the second of three Carl C. Hempel Lectures presented at Princeton University in May 1991. I gratefully acknowledge many helpful observations by the audience on that occasion, and by David Hills and Gideon Rosen.

1. Walton (1990).
2. To be *fictional* is to be (as we say) true-in-a-fictional-world, the world of a game of make-believe or a representational work of art, for instance. Features of props

are understood to make propositions fictional, to generate fictional truths. It is because a folded piece of paper falls to the ground that it is fictional that an airplane crashes. What is fictional in a game of make-believe is what participants in the game are to imagine to be true. Propositions that are fictional can be true as well. It is both true and fictional that something flies through the air, although it is only fictional, not true, that the flying object is an airplane. Participants in the game with the paper airplanes are to imagine that an airplane crashes, when the folded paper falls to the ground. See Walton (1990: Section 1).

3. One 'fictionally rides a horse' when one behaves so as to make it fictional, true-in-the-world-of-make-believe, that one rides a horse, e.g., when one prances around the house straddling a hobby horse, imagining oneself riding a (real) horse.

4. Compare *ornamental* representations, which involve thinking about a game of make-believe without participating in it. See Walton (1990: Section 7.6).

5. I have in mind what I called 'unofficial' games of make-believe, in Walton (1990: Section 10.4).

6. Barnes (1984: 1).

7. Milne (1928: 9).

8. Lindner (1954: 223).

9. See Walton (1990: Section 10.2).

10. See Walton (1990: 296).

11. Perhaps with enough practice we could learn to recognize woman pictures without either seeing women in them or explicitly identifying them by line and shape characteristics; perhaps we could learn to recognize a shape gestalt which they share.

12. See Johnston (1989).

13. The dictionary defines 'saddle' in the relevant sense as 'a ridge connecting two higher elevations', and 'male' as 'designed for fitting into a corresponding hollow part'. (*Webster's New Collegiate Dictionary*, 1979.)

14. Lakoff and Johnson (1980).

15. Ibid.

16. Goodman (1968: 74–80).

17. See Lakoff and Johnson (1980: 36); Davidson (1984); Moran (1989: 87–112).

18. 'Principles of generation' are principles specifying what features of props make what propositions fictional (i.e., true-in-the-fictional-world).

19. As Richard Moran (1989: 93) points out.

20. I. A. Richards (1936: 100–1, and elsewhere) speaks of imagining the tenor to be the vehicle. Richards seems to associate this view closely with the idea that metaphors involve resemblance.

21. Scruton (1983: 94–5).

22. It is curious that we have no convenient way of specifying the property of the melody, the prop, which this metaphor picks out, without using some variant of the metaphor. We even speak of *higher* and *lower* frequencies. But

nonmetaphorical predicates can easily be introduced. Nor is there an easy way of specifying legs of chairs without using that metaphor.

23. 'Timper' and 'tomper' do have a historical connection with spatial terms; I used spatial terms in the process of introducing them. But let's suppose that this historical connection is lost in the mists of history.

24. See Kivy (1990).

25. There is more to our response than this. We find ourselves not only imagining seeing a frog, but also imagining of our actual visual experience of the design that it is our perceiving of a frog. See Walton (1990: ch. 9).

26. Alternatively, we might understand the fictional truths to be generated by pictures' propensities to elicit certain imaginings in qualified viewers, rather than by their design properties. The principles of generation might be understood to specify what propensities make what propositions fictional. (Cf. my discussion of the *acceptance rule* for dreams, Walton, 1990: 44–9.)

27. This is not to deny that my propensity to imagine appropriately may depend on my having experienced various pictures in the past. And learning how to read new kinds of pictures—cubist ones, for instance—may require additional experience.

28. The metaphorical assertion that X is θ might, however, admit of a paraphrase of the following form: 'X is such as to make it fictional in game G that something (possibly X itself) is θ.' 'Jones is a squirrel' might be paraphrased as 'Jones has whatever it takes to make it fictional in game G that he is a squirrel.' This paraphrase is literal, I presume. But it is not the kind of paraphrase people look for. It does not get rid of the predicates that are metaphorical in the original.

29. Pablo Casals so described a passage of Beethoven's A-Major sonata for cello and piano, during a master class at Berkeley.

30. Marius de Zayas (1912). Quoted in Danto (1986: 81).

31. Mishima (1966).

REFERENCES

Barnes, Julian (1984). *Flaubert's Parrot*. New York: McGraw Hill.

Danto, Arthur C. (1986). *The Philosophical Disenfranchisement of Art*. New York: Columbia University Press.

de Zayas, M. (1912), 'The Sun Has Set.' *Camera Work*, 39: 17.

Davidson, Donald (1984). 'What Metaphors Mean.' In Davidson, *Inquiries into Truth and Interpretation*. Oxford: Clarendon Press.

Goodman, Nelson (1968). *Languages of Art*. Indianapolis, IN: Bobbs Merrill.

Johnston, Mark (1989). 'Dispositional Theories of Value.' *Proceedings of the Aristotelian Society*, Supplementary Volume, 63: 139–74.

Kivy, Peter (1990). *Music Alone: Philosophical Reflections on the Purely Musical Experience*. Ithaca: Cornell University Press.

Lakoff, George and Mark Johnson (1980). *Metaphors We Live By*. Chicago: University of Chicago Press.

Lindner, Robert M. (1954). 'The Jet-Propelled Couch.' In Lindner, *The Fifty Minute Hour: A Collection of True Psychoanalytic Tales*. New York: Holt, Rinehart, and Winston.

Milne, A. A. (1928). *The House at Pooh Corner*. New York: Dutton.

Mishima, Yukio (1966). *Death in Midsummer*. New York: New Directions.

Moran, Richard (1989). 'Seeing and Believing: Metaphor, Image and Force.' *Critical Inquiry*, 16: 87–112.

Richards, I. A. (1936). *The Philosophy of Rhetoric*. Oxford: Oxford University Press.

Scruton, Roger (1983). 'Understanding Music.' In Scruton, *The Aesthetic Understanding: Essays in the Philosophy of Art and Culture*. London: Methuen.

Walton, Kendall L. (1990). *Mimesis as Make-Believe: On the Foundations of the Representational Arts*. Cambridge, MA: Harvard University Press.

3

The Myth of the Seven

STEPHEN YABLO

Mathematics has been called the one area of inquiry that would retain its point even were the physical world to disappear entirely. This might be heard as an argument for platonism: the view that mathematics describes a special abstract department of reality lying far above the physical fray. The necessary truth of mathematics would be due to the fact that the mathematical department of reality had its properties unchangingly and essentially.

I said that it *might* be heard as an argument for platonism, that mathematics stays on point even if the physical objects disappear. However mathematics does not lose its point either if the *mathematical* realm disappears—or, indeed, if it turns out that that realm was empty all along. Consider a fable from John Burgess and Gideon Rosen's book *A Subject with No Object*:

> Finally, after years of waiting, it is your turn to put a question to the Oracle of Philosophy... you humbly approach and ask the question that has been consuming you for as long as you can remember: 'Tell me, O Oracle, what there is. What sorts of things exist?' To this the Oracle responds: 'What? You want the whole list?... I will tell you this: everything there is is concrete; nothing there is is abstract....'
>
> (Burgess and Rosen, 1997: 3)

Trembling at the implications, you return to civilization to spread the concrete gospel. Your first stop is [your university here], where researchers are confidently reckoning validity in terms of models and insisting on 1-1 functions as a condition of equinumerosity. Flipping over some worktables to get their attention, you demand that these practices be stopped at once. The entities do not exist, hence all theoretical reliance on them should cease. They, of course, tell you to bug off and am-scray. (Which, come to think of it, is exactly what you yourself would do, if the situation were reversed.)

Frege's Question

Frege in *Notes for L. Darmstaedter* asks, 'is arithmetic a game or a science?'[1] He himself thinks that it is a science, albeit one dealing with a special sort of logical object.[2] Arithmetic considered all by itself, just as a formal system, gives, in his view, little evidence of this: 'If we stay within [the] boundaries [of formal arithmetic], its rules appear as arbitrary as those of chess' (*Grundgesetze* II, section 89).[3] The falsity of this initial appearance is revealed only when we widen our gaze and consider the role arithmetic plays in our dealings with the natural world. According to Frege, 'it is applicability alone which elevates arithmetic from a game to the rank of a science' (*Grundgesetze* II, section 91).

One can see why applicability might be thought to have this result. What are the chances of an arbitrary, off the shelf, system of rules performing so brilliantly in so many theoretical contexts? Virtually nil, it seems; 'applicability cannot be an accident' (*Grundgesetze* II, section 89). What else could it be, though, if the rules did not track some sort of reality? Tracking reality is the business of science, so arithmetic is a science.[4]

The surprising thing is that the same phenomenon of applicability that Frege cites in *support* of a scientific interpretation has also been seen as the primary *obstacle* to such an interpretation. Arithmetic qua science is a deductively organized description of *sui generis* objects with no connection to the natural world. Why should objects like that be so useful in natural science = the theory of the natural world? This is an instance of what Eugene Wigner famously called 'the unreasonable effectiveness of mathematics'.[5]

Applicability thus plays a curious double role in debates about the status of arithmetic, and indeed mathematics more generally. Sometimes it appears as a *datum*, and then the question is, what *lessons* are to be drawn from it? Other times it appears as a *puzzle*, and the question is, what *explains* it, how does it work?

Hearing just that applicability plays these two roles, one might expect the puzzle role to be given priority. That is, we draw such and such lessons because they are the ones that emerge from our story about how applications in fact work.

But the pattern has generally been the reverse.[6] The first point people make is that since applicability would be a miracle if the mathematics involved were not true, it is evidence that mathematics *is* true. The second thing that gets said (what on some theories of evidence is a corollary of the first) is that applicability is explained in part by truth. It is admitted, of course, that truth is not the full explanation.[7] But the assumption appears to be that any further considerations will be specific to the mathematics involved and the application.[8] The most that can be said in *general* about why mathematics applies is that it is true.

One result of this ordering of the issues is that attention now naturally turns away from applied mathematics to pure. Why should we worry about the bearing of mathematical theories on physical reality when we have yet to work out their relation to mathematical reality? And so the literature comes to be dominated by a problem I will call *purity*: given that such and such a mathematical theory is true, what makes it true? Is arithmetic, for instance, true in virtue of (a) the behavior of particular objects (the numbers), or (b) the behavior of ω-sequences in general, or (c) the fact that it follows from Peano's axioms? If (a), are the numbers sets, and if so which ones? If (b), are we talking about actual or possible ω-sequences? If (c), are we talking about first-order axioms or second?

Some feel edified by the years of wrangling over these issues, others do not. Either way it seems that something is getting lost in the shuffle, viz., applications. Having served their purpose as a dialectical bludgeon, they are left to take care of themselves. One takes the occasional sidelong glance, to be sure. But this is mainly to reassure ourselves that as long as mathematics is true, there is no reason why empirical scientists should not take advantage of it. That certainly speaks to one possible worry about the use of mathematics in science, namely, is it defensible or something to feel guilty about? But our worry was different: Why should scientists *want* to take advantage of mathematics? What good does it do them? What sort of advantage is there to be taken? The reason this matters is that, depending on how we answer, the pure problem is greatly transformed. It could be, after all, that the kind of help mathematics gives is a kind it could give *even if it were false*. If that were so, then the pure problem—which in its usual form presupposes that mathematics is true—will need a different sort of treatment than it is usually given.

Retooling

Here are the main claims so far. Philosophers have tended to emphasize *purity* over *applicability*. The standard line on applicability has been that (i) it is evidence of truth, (ii) truth plays some small role in explaining it, and (iii) beyond that, there is not a whole lot to be said.[9]

A notable exception to all these generalizations is the work of Hartry Field. Not only does Field see applicability as centrally important, he dissents from both aspects of the 'standard line' on it. Where the standard line links the utility of mathematics to its truth, Field thinks that mathematics (although certainly useful) is very likely *false*. Where the standard line offers little *other* than truth to explain usefulness, Field lays great stress on the notion that mathematical theories are *conservative* over nominalistic ones, i.e., any nominalistic conclusions that can be proved with mathematics can also be proven (albeit often much less easily) without it.[10] The utility of mathematics lies in the *no-risk deductive assistance that it provides to the beleaguered theorist.*

This is on the right track, I think. But there is something strangely half-way about it. I do not doubt that Field has shown us a way in which mathematics *can* be useful without being true. It can be used to facilitate deduction in nominalistically reformulated theories of his own device: theories that are 'qualitative' in nature rather than quantitative. This leaves more or less untouched, however, the problem of how mathematics *does* manage to be useful without being true. It is not as though it benefits only practitioners of Field's qualitative science (it does not benefit Field-style scientists at all; there aren't any). The people whose activities we are trying to understand are practicing regular old platonic science.

How without being true does mathematics manage to be of so much help to *them*? Field never quite says.[11] He is quite explicit, in fact, that the relevance of his argument to *actual* applications of mathematics is limited and indirect:

[What I have said] is not of course intended to license the use of mathematical existence assertions in axiom systems for the particular sciences: *Such* a use of mathematics remains, for the nominalist, quite illegitimate. (Or, more accurately, a nominalist should treat such a use of mathematics as a temporary expedient that we indulge in when we don't know how to axiomatize the science properly.)

(1980: 14)

But then how exactly does he take himself to be addressing our actual situation? I see two main options.

Field might think that the role of mathematics in the *non*-nominalistic theories that scientists really use is *analogous* to its role in connection with his custom-built nominalistic theories—enough so that by explaining and justifying the one he has explained and justified the other. If that were Field's view, then one suspects he would have done more to develop the analogy.

Is the view, then, that he has *not* explained (or justified) actual applications of mathematics—but that is OK because, come the revolution, these actual applications will be supplanted by the new-style applications of which he *has* treated? This stands our usual approach to recalcitrant phenomena on its head. Usually we try to theorize the phenomena that we find, not popularize the phenomena we have a theory of.

Indispensability and Applicability

As you may have been beginning to suspect, these complaints have been based on a deliberate misunderstanding of Field's project.[12] It is true that he asks:

(d) What sort of account is possible of how mathematics is applied to the physical world?

(Field, 1980, vii)

But this can mean either of two things, depending on whether one is motivated by an interest in *applicability*, or an interest in *indispensability*.

Applicability is, in the first instance, a *problem*: the problem of explaining the effectiveness of mathematics. It is also, potentially, an *argument* for mathematical objects. For the best explanation may require that mathematics is true.

Indispensability is, in the first instance, an *argument* for the existence of mathematical objects. The argument is normally credited to Quine and Putnam. They say that since numbers are indispensable to science, and we are committed to science, we are committed to numbers. But, just as applicability was first a problem, second an argument, indispensability is first an argument, second a problem. The problem is: How do nominalists propose to deal with the fact that numbers have a *permanent* position in the range of our quantifiers?

Once this distinction is drawn, it seems clear that Field's concern is more with indispensability than applicability. His question is:

(d-ind) How can applications be conceived so that mathematical objects come out dispensable?

To *this*, Field's two-part package of (i) nominalistically reformulated scientific theories, and (ii) conservation claims, seems a perfectly appropriate answer. But we are still entitled to wonder what Field would say about:

(d-app) How are actual applications to be understood, be the objects indispensable or not?

If there is a complaint to be made, it is not that Field has given a bad answer to (d-app), but that he doesn't address (d-app) at all, and the resources he provides do not appear to be of much use with it.

Now, Field *might* reply that the indispensability argument is the important one. But that will be hard to argue. One reason, already mentioned, is that a serious mystery remains even if in-principle dispensability is established. How is the Fieldian nominalist to explain the usefulness-without-truth of mathematics in *ordinary*, quantitative, science? More important, though, suppose that an explanation can be given. Then *indispensability becomes a red herring*. Why should we be asked to *demathematicize* science, if ordinary science's mathematical aspects can be understood on some other basis than that they are true? Putting both of these pieces together: The point of nominalizing a theory is not achieved unless a further condition is met, given which condition there is no longer any need to nominalize the theory.

Non-Deductive Usefulness

That is my first reservation about Field's approach. The second is related. Consider the kind of usefulness-without-truth that Field lays so much weight on; mathematics thanks to its conservativeness gives no-risk deductive assistance. It is far from clear why *this particular form* of usefulness-without-truth deserves its special status. It might be thought that there is no other help objects can give without going to the trouble of existing. Field says the following:

if our interest is only with inferences among claims that don't say anything about numbers (but which may employ, say, numerical quantifiers), then we can employ numerical theory without harm, for we will get no conclusions with numerical theory that wouldn't be valid without it ... There are other purposes for which this justification for feigning acceptance of numerical theory does not apply, and we must decide whether or not to genuinely accept the theory. For instance, there may be observations that we want to formulate that we don't see how to formulate without reference to numbers, or there may be explanations that we want to state that we can't see how to state without reference to numbers ... *if such circumstances do arise, then we will have to genuinely accept numerical theory if we are not to reduce our ability to formulate our observations or our explanations*

(Field, 1989: 161–2, italics added).

But, *why* will we have to accept numerical theory in these circumstances? Having just maintained that the *deductive* usefulness of *X*s is not a reason to accept that *X*s exist, he seems now to be saying that *representational* usefulness is another matter. One might wonder whether there is much of a difference here. I am not denying that deductive usefulness is an important non-evidential reason for making as if to believe in numbers. But it is hard to see why representational usefulness isn't similarly situated.[13]

Numbers as Representational Aids

What is it that allows us to take our uses of numbers for deductive purposes so lightly? The deductive advantages that 'real' Xs do, or would, confer are (Field tells us) equally conferred by Xs that are just 'supposed' to exist. But the same would appear to apply to the representational advantages conferred by Xs; these advantages don't appear to depend on the Xs really existing either. The economist need not believe in the average family to derive representational advantage from it ('the average family has 2.7 bank accounts'). The psychiatrist need not believe in libido or ego strength to derive representational advantage from them. Why should the physicist have to believe in numbers to access new contents by couching her theory in numerical terms?

Suppose that our physicist is studying escape velocity. She discovers the factors that determine escape velocity and wants to record her results. She knows a great many facts of the following form:

(A) A projectile fired at so many meters per second from the surface of a planetary sphere so many kilograms in mass and so many meters in diameter will (will not) escape its gravitational field.

There are problems if she tries to record these facts without quantifying over mathematical objects, that is, using just numerical adjectives. One is that, since velocities range along a continuum, she will have to write uncountably many sentences, employing an uncountable number of distinct adjectives. Second, almost all reals are 'random' in the sense of encoding an irreducibly infinite amount of information.[14] So, unless we think there is room in English for uncountably many semantic primitives, almost all of the uncountably many sentences will have to be infinite in length. At this point someone is likely to ask why we don't drop the numerical-adjective idea and say simply that:

(B) For all positive real numbers M and R, the escape velocity from a sphere of mass M and diameter 2R is the square root of 2GM/R, where G is the gravitational constant.

Why not, indeed? To express the infinitely many facts in finite compass, we bring in numbers as representational aids. We do this despite the fact that what we are trying to get across has nothing to do with numbers, and could be expressed without them were it not for the requirements of a finitely based notation.

The question is whether functioning in this way as a representational aid is a privilege reserved to existing things. The answer appears to be that it isn't. That (B) succeeds in gathering together into a single content infinitely many facts of form (A) owes nothing whatever to the real existence of numbers. It is enough that *we understand what (B) asks of the non-numerical world*, the numerical world taken momentarily for granted.[15] How the real existence of numbers could help or hinder that understanding is difficult to imagine.

An oddity of the situation is that Field makes the same sort of point himself in his writings on truth. He thinks that 'true' is a device that exists 'to serve a certain logical need'—a need that would also be served by infinite conjunction and disjunction if we had them, but (given that we don't) would go unmet were it not for 'true'. No need then to take the truth-predicate ontologically seriously; its place in the language is secured by a role it can fill quite regardless of whether it picks out a property. It would seem natural for Field to consider whether the same applies to mathematical objects. Just as truth is an essential aid in the expression of facts not about truth (there is no such property), perhaps numbers are an essential aid in the expression of facts not about numbers (there are no such things).[16]

Our Opposite Fix

To say it one more time, the standard procedure in philosophy of mathematics is to start with the pure problem and leave applicability for later. It comes as no surprise, then, that most philosophical theories of mathematics have more to say about what makes mathematics true than about what makes it so useful in empirical science.

The approach suggested here looks to be in an opposite fix. Our theory of applications is rough but not non-existent. What are we going to say, though, about pure mathematics? If the line on applications is right, then one suspects that arithmetic, set theory, and so on are largely untrue. At the very least, then, the problem of purity is going to have to be reconceived. It cannot be: In virtue of what is arithmetic true? It will have to be: How is the line drawn between 'acceptable' arithmetical claims and 'unacceptable' ones? And it is very unclear what acceptability could amount to if it floats completely free of truth.

Just maybe there is a clue in the line on applications. Suppose that mathematical objects 'start life' as representational aids. Some systems of mathematicalia will work better in this capacity than others, e.g., standard arithmetic will work better than a modular arithmetic in which all operations are 'mod k', that is, when the result threatens to exceed k we cycle back down to o. As wisdom accumulates about the kind(s) of mathematical system needed, theorists develop an intuitive sense of what is the right way to go and what is the wrong way. Norms are developed that take on a life of their own, guiding the development of mathematical theories past the point where natural science greatly cares. The process then begins to feed on itself, as descriptive needs arise w.r.t., not the natural world, but *our system of representational aids as so far developed*. (After a certain point, the motivation for introducing larger numbers is the help they give us with the mathematical objects already on board.) These needs encourage the construction of still further theory, with further ontology, and so it goes.

You can see where this is headed. If the pressures our descriptive task exerts on us are sufficiently coherent and sharply enough felt, we begin to feel under the same sort of external constraint that is encountered in science itself. Our theory is certainly answerable to *something*, and what more natural candidate than the *objects* of which it purports to give a literally true account? Thus arises the feeling of the objectivity of mathematics qua description of mathematical objects.

Some Ways of Making As If [17]

I can make the above a bit more precise by bringing in some ideas of Kendall Walton's about 'making as if'. The thread that links as-if games together is that they call upon their participants to pretend or imagine that certain things are the case. These to-be-imagined items make up the game's *content*, and to elaborate and adapt oneself to this content is typically the game's very point.[18] At least one of the things we are about in a game of mud pies, for instance, is to work out who has what sorts of pies, how much longer they need to be baked, etc. At least one of the things we're about in a discussion of Sherlock Holmes is to work out, say, how exactly Holmes picked up Moriarty's trail near Reichenbach Falls, how we are to think of Watson as having acquired his war wound, and so on.

As I say, to elaborate and adapt oneself to the game's content is typically the game's very point. An alternative point suggests itself, though, when we reflect that all but the most boring games are played with *props*, whose game-independent properties help to determine what it is that players are supposed to imagine. That Sam's pie is too big for the oven does not follow from the rules of mud pies alone; you have to throw in the fact that Sam's clump of mud fails to fit into the hollow stump. If readers of 'The Final Problem' are to think of Holmes as living nearer to Windsor Castle than Edinburgh Castle, the facts of nineteenth-century geography deserve a large part of the credit.

A game whose content reflects the game-independent properties of worldly props can be seen in two different lights. What ordinarily happens is that we take an interest in the props because and to the extent that they influence the content; one tramps around London in search of 221B Baker street for the light it may shed on what is true according to the Holmes stories.

But in principle it could be the other way around: we could be interested in a game's content because and to the extent that it yielded information about the props. This would not stop us from playing the game, necessarily, but it would tend to confer a different significance on our moves. Pretending within the game to assert that BLAH would be a way of giving voice to a fact holding *outside* the game: the fact that the props are in such and such a condition, viz., the condition that makes BLAH a proper thing to pretend to assert. If we were playing the game in this alternative spirit, then we'd be engaged not in *content-oriented* but *prop-oriented* make-believe. Or, since the prop might as well be the entire world, *world-oriented* make-believe.

It makes a certain in principle sense, then, to use make-believe games for serious descriptive purposes. But is such a thing ever actually done? A case can be made that it is done all the time—not perhaps with explicit self-identified games like 'mud pies' but impromptu everyday games hardly rising to the level of consciousness. Some examples of Walton's suggest how this could be so:

Where in Italy is the town of Crotone? I ask. You explain that it is on the arch of the Italian boot. 'See that thundercloud over there—the big, angry face near the horizon', you say; 'it is headed this way'. . . . We speak of the saddle of a mountain and the shoulder of a highway. . . . All of these cases are linked to make-believe. We think of Italy and the thundercloud as something like pictures. Italy (or a map of Italy) depicts a boot. The cloud is a prop which makes it fictional that there is an angry face . . . The saddle of a mountain is, fictionally, a horse's saddle. But our interest, in these instances, is not in the make-believe itself, and it is not for the sake of games of make-believe that we regard these things as props . . . [The make-believe] is useful for articulating, remembering, and communicating facts about the props—about the geography of Italy, or the identity of the storm cloud . . . or mountain topography. It is by thinking of Italy or the thundercloud . . . as potential if not actual props that I understand where Crotone is, which cloud is the one being talked about.[19]

A certain kind of make-believe game, Walton says, can be 'useful for articulating, remembering, and communicating facts' about aspects of the game-independent world. He might have added that make-believe games can make it easier to reason about such facts, to systematize them, to visualize them, to spot connections with other facts, and to evaluate potential lines of research. That similar virtues have been claimed for metaphors is no accident, if metaphors are themselves moves in world-oriented pretend games. And this is what Walton maintains. A metaphor on his view is an utterance that represents its objects as being *like so*: the way that they *need* to be to make the utterance 'correct' in a game that it itself suggests. The game is played not for its own sake but to make clear which game-independent properties are being attributed. They are the ones that do or would confer legitimacy upon the utterance construed as a move in the game.

The Kinds of Making as If and the Kinds of Mathematics

Seen in the light of Walton's theory, our suggestion above can be put like this: numbers as they figure in applied mathematics are *creatures of existential metaphor*. They are part of a realm that we play along with because the pretense affords a desirable—sometimes irreplaceable—mode of access to certain real-world conditions, viz. the conditions that make a pretense like that appropriate in the relevant game. Much as we make as if, e.g., people have associated with them stores of something called 'luck', so as to be able to describe some of them metaphorically as individuals whose luck is 'running out', we make as if pluralities have associated with them things called 'numbers', so as to be able to express an (otherwise hard to express because) infinitely disjunctive fact about relative cardinalities like so: The number of *F*s is divisible by the number of *G*s.

Now, if applied mathematics is to be seen as world-oriented make-believe, then *one* attractive idea about pure mathematical statements is that:

(c) They are to be understood as *content*-oriented make-believe.

Why not? It seems a truism that pure mathematicians spend most of their time trying to work out what is true according to this or that mathematical theory.[20] All that needs to be added to the truism, to arrive at the conception of pure mathematics as content-oriented make-believe, is this: that the mathematician's interest in working out what is true-according-to-the-theory is by and large independent of whether the theory is thought to be *really true*—true in the sense of correctly describing a realm of independently constituted mathematical objects.[21]

That having been said, the statements of at least *some* parts of pure mathematics, like simple arithmetic, are legitimated (made pretense-worthy) by very general facts about the non-numerical world. So, on a natural under-standing of the arithmetic game, it is pretendable that $3 + 5 = 8$ because if there are three Fs and five Gs distinct from the Fs, then there are eight (F v G)s—whence construed as a piece of world-oriented make-believe, the statement that $3 + 5 = 8$ 'says' that if there are three Fs and five Gs, etc. For at least some pure mathematical statements, then, it is plausible to hold that:

(w) They are to be understood as *world*-oriented make-believe.

Construed as world-oriented make-believe, every statement of 'true arith-metic' expresses a first-order logical truth; that is, it has a logical truth for its metaphorical content.[22] (The picture that results might be called 'Kantian logicism'. It is *Kantian* because it grounds the necessity of arithmetic in the representational character of numbers. Numbers are always 'there' because they are written into the spectacles through which we see things. The picture is *logicist* because the facts represented—the facts we see through our numer-ical spectacles—are facts of first-order logic.)

There is a third interpretation possible for pure-mathematical statements. Arithmeticians imagine that there are numbers. But this a complicated thing to imagine. It would be natural for them to want a codification of what it is that they are taking on board. And it would be natural for them to want this codification in the form of an *autonomous* description of the pretended objects, one that doesn't look backward to applications. As in any descriptive project, a need may arise for representational aids. *Sometimes* these aids will be the very objects being described: 'For all n, the number of prime numbers is larger than n.' Sometimes though they will be *additional* objects dreamed up to help us get a handle on the original ones: 'The number of prime numbers is $\aleph_0$.'

What sort of information are these statements giving us? Not information about the concrete world (as on interpretation (w)); the prime numbers form no part of that world. And not, at least not on the face of it, information about the game (as on interpretation (c)); the number of primes would have been aleph-nought even if there had been no game. 'The number of primes is $\aleph_0$.' gives information about the prime numbers as they are supposed to be conceived by players of the game.

Numbers start life as representational aids. But then, on a second go-round, they come to be treated as a subject-matter in their own right (like Italy or the thundercloud). Just as representational aids are brought in to help us describe other subject-matters, they are brought in to help us describe the numbers. Numbers thus come to play a double role, functioning both as representational aids and things-represented. This gives us a third way of interpreting pure-mathematical statements:

(M) They are to be understood as prop-oriented make-believe with numbers etc. serving *both* as props and as representational aids helping us to describe the props.

One can see in particular cases how they switch from one role to the other. If I say that 'the number of primes is $\aleph_0$,' the primes are my subject-matter and $\aleph_0$ is the representational aid. (This is clear from the fact that I would accept the paraphrase 'there are denumerably many primes'.) If, as a friend of the continuum hypothesis, I say that 'the number of alephs no bigger than the continuum is prime', it is the other way around. The primes are now representational aids and $\aleph_0$ has become a prop. (I would accept the para-phrase 'there are primely many alephs no bigger than the continuum'.)

The bulk of pure mathematics is probably best served by interpretation (M). This is the interpretation that applies when we are trying to come up with autonomous descriptions of this or that imagined domain. Our *ultimate* interest may still be in describing the natural world; our *secondary* interest may still be in describing and consolidating the games we use for that purpose. But in most of pure mathematics, world and game have been left far behind, and we confront the numbers, sets, and so on, in full solitary glory.

Two Types of Metaphorical Correctness

So much for 'normal' pure mathematics, where we work within some existing theory. If the metaphoricalist has a problem about correctness, it does not arise there; for any piece of mathematics amenable to interpretations (C), (W), or (M) is going to have objective correctness conditions. Where a problem *does* seem to arise is in the context of theory-*development*. Why do some ways of constructing mathematical theories, and extending existing ones, strike us as better than others?

I have no really good answer to this, but let me indicate where an answer might be sought. A distinction is often drawn between *true* metaphors and metaphors that are *apt*. That these are two independent species of metaphorical goodness can be seen by looking at cases where they come apart.

An excellent source for the first quality (truth) without the second (aptness) is back issues of *Reader's Digest* magazine. There one finds jarring, if not necessarily inaccurate, titles along the lines of 'Tooth Decay: America's Silent Dental Killer', 'The Sino-Soviet Conflict: A Fight in the Family', and, my personal favorite, 'South America: Sleeping Giant on Our Doorstep'. Another good source is political metaphor. When Calvin Coolidge said that 'The future lies ahead', the problem was not that he was *wrong*—where else would it lie?—but that he didn't seem to be mobilizing the available metaphorical resources to maximal advantage. (Likewise when George H. Bush told us before the 1992 elections that 'It's no exaggeration to say that the undecideds could go one way or another.')

Of course, a likelier problem with political metaphor is the reverse, that is, aptness without truth. The following are either patently (metaphorically) untrue or can be imagined untrue at no cost to their aptness. Stalin: 'One death is a tragedy. A million deaths is a statistic.' Churchill: 'Man will occasionally stumble over truth, but most times he will pick himself up and carry on.' Will Rogers: 'Diplomacy is the art of saying "Nice doggie" until you can find a rock.' Richard Nixon: 'America is a pitiful helpless giant.'

Not the best examples, I fear. But let's move on to the question they were meant to raise. How does metaphorical *aptness* differ from metaphorical *truth*? David Hills (1997: 119–120) observes that where truth is a semantic feature, aptness can often be an aesthetic one: 'When I call Romeo's utterance apt, I mean that it possesses some degree of poetic power...Aptness is a specialized kind of beauty attaching to interpreted forms of words...For a form of words to be apt is for it ... to be the proper object of a certain kind of felt satisfaction on the part of the audience to which it is addressed.'

That can't be all there is to it, though; for 'apt' is used in connection not just with *particular* metaphorical claims but entire metaphorical frameworks. One says, for instance, that rising pressure is a good metaphor for intense emotion; that possible worlds provide a good metaphor for modality; or that war makes a good (or bad) metaphor for argument. What is meant by this sort of claim? Not that pressure (worlds, war) are metaphorically *true* of emotion (modality, argument). There is no question of truth because no metaphorical claims have been made. But it would be equally silly to speak here of poetic power or beauty. The suggestion seems rather to be that *an as-if game built around pressure (worlds, war) lends itself to the metaphorical expression of truths about emotion (possibility, argument).* The game 'lends itself' in the sense of affording access to lots of those truths, or to particularly important ones, and/or in the sense of presenting those truths in a cognitively or motivationally advantageous light.

Aptness is *at least* a feature of prop-oriented make-believe games; a game is apt relative to such and such a subject-matter to the extent that it lends itself to the expression of truths about that subject-matter. A particular metaphorical *utterance* is apt to the extent that (a) it is a move in an apt game, and (b) it makes impressive use of the resources that game provides. The reason it is so easy to have aptness without truth is that to make satisfying use of a game with lots of expressive potential is one thing, to make veridical use of a game with arbitrary expressive potential is another.[23]

Correctness in Non-Normal Mathematics

Back now to the main issue: what accounts for the feeling of a right and a wrong way of proceeding when it comes to mathematical theory-development? I want to say that a proposed new axiom *A* strikes us as correct roughly to the extent that a theory incorporating *A* seems to us to make for an *apter game*—a game that lends itself to the expression of more metaphorical truths—than a theory that omitted *A*, or incorporated its negation. To call *A* correct is to single it out as possessed of a great deal of 'cognitive promise'.[24]

Take for instance the controversy early in the last century over the axiom of choice. One of the many considerations arguing *against* acceptance of the axiom is that it requires us to suppose that geometrical spheres decompose into parts that can be reassembled into multiple copies of themselves. (The Banach–Tarski paradox.) Physical spheres are not *like* that, so we imagine, hence the axiom of choice makes geometrical space an imperfect metaphor for physical space.

One of the many considerations arguing in *favor* of the axiom is that it blocks the possibility of sets X and Y neither of which is injectable into the other. This is crucial if injectability and the lack of it are to serve as metaphors for relative size. It is crucial that the statement about functions that 'encodes' the fact that there are not as many Ys as Xs should be seen in the game to *entail* the statement 'encoding' the fact there are at least as many Xs as Ys. This entailment would not go through if sets were not assumed to satisfy the axiom of choice.[25] Add to this that choice *also* mitigates the paradoxicality of the Banach–Tarski result, by opening our eyes to the possibility of regions too inconceivably complicated to be assigned a 'size', and it is no surprise that choice is judged to make for an overall apter game. (This is hugely oversimplified, no doubt; but it illustrates the kind of consideration that I take to be relevant.)

Suppose we are working with a theory T and are trying to decide whether to extend it to $T^* = T + A$. An impression I do *not* want to leave is that T^*'s aptness is simply a matter of its expressive potential with regard to our original *naturalistic* subject matter: the world we really believe in, which, let's suppose, contains only concrete things. T^* may also be valued for the expressive assistance it provides in connection with the *mathematical* subject matter postulated by T—a subject-matter which we take to obtain in our role as players of the T-game. A new set-theoretic axiom may be valued for the light it sheds not on concreta but on mathematical objects already in play. So it is, for instance, with the axiom of projective determinacy and the sets of reals studied in descriptive set theory.

Our account of correctness has two parts. Sometimes a statement is correct because it is true according to an implicitly understood background story, such as Peano Arithmetic or ZFC. This is a relatively objective form of correctness. Sometimes though there is no well-enough understood background story and so we must think of correctness another way. The second kind of correctness goes with a statement's 'cognitive promise', that is, its being suited to figure in especially apt pretend games.

Our Goodmanian Ancestors

If mathematics is a myth, how did the myth arise? You got me. But it may be instructive to consider a meta-myth about how it might have arisen. My strategy here is borrowed from Wilfrid Sellars in *Empiricism and the Philosophy of Mind*. Sellars asks us to:

Imagine a stage in pre-history in which humans are limited to what I shall call a Rylean language, a language of which the fundamental descriptive vocabulary speaks of public properties of public objects located in Space and enduring through Time.

(Sellars, 1997: 91)

What resources would have to be added to the Rylean language of these talking animals in order that they might come to recognize each other and themselves as animals that *think*, *observe*, and have *feelings* and *sensations*? And, how could the addition of these resources be construed as reasonable?

(Sellars, 1997: 92)

Let us go back to a similar stage of pre-history, but since it is the language's concrete (rather than public) orientation that interests us, let us think of it not as a Rylean language but a *Goodmanian* one. The idea is to tell a just-so story that has mathematical objects invented for good and sufficient reasons by the speakers of this Goodmanian language: henceforth *our Goodmanian ancestors.* None of it really happened, but our situation today is as if it had happened, and the memory of these events was then lost.[26]

First Day, *Finite Numbers of Concreta.*

Our ancestors, aka the Goodmanians, start out speaking a first-order language quantifying over concreta. They have a barter economy based on the trading of precious stones. It is important that these trades be perceived as fair. To this end, numerical quantifiers are introduced:

$$\exists_0 xFx =_{df} \forall x(Fx \rightarrow x \neq x)$$
$$\exists_{n+1} xFx =_{df} \exists y(Fy \ \& \ \exists_n x(Fx \ \& \ x \neq y))$$

From $\exists_n x$ ruby(x) and $\exists_n x$ sapphire(x), they infer 'rubies-for-sapphires is a fair trade' (all gems are considered equally valuable). So far, though, they lack premises from which to infer 'rubies-for-sapphires is *not* a fair trade'. If they had infinite conjunction, the premise could be:

$$\sim(\exists_0 xRx \ \& \ \exists_0 xSx) \ \& \ \sim(\exists_1 xRx \ \& \ \exists_1 xSx) \ \& \ \text{etc.}$$

But their language is finite, so they take another tack. They decide to make as if there are non-concrete objects called 'numbers'. The point of numbers is to serve as measures of cardinality. Using $^*S^*$ for 'it is to be supposed that S', their first rule is:

(RI) If $\exists_n xFx$ then $^*n =$ the number of Fs^*, and if $\sim\exists_n xGx$ then $^*n \neq$ the number of Gs^{*}[27]

From $(\#x)Rx \neq (\#x)Sx$, they infer 'rubies-for-sapphires is not a fair trade'. ('The number of Fs' will sometimes be written '$(\#x)Fx$' or '$\#(F)$'.) Our ancestors do not believe in the new entities, but they pretend to for the access this gives them to a fact that would otherwise be inexpressible, viz., that there are (or are not) exactly as many rubies as sapphires.

Second Day, *Finite Numbers of Finite Numbers.*

Trading is not the only way to acquire gemstones; one can also inherit them, or dig them directly out of the ground. As a result some Goodmanians have more stones than others. A few hotheads clamor for an immediate redistri-bution of all stones so that everyone winds up with the same amount. Others prefer a more gradual approach in which, for example, there are five levels of ownership this year, three levels the next, and so on, until finally all are at the same level. The second group is at a disadvantage because their proposal is not yet expressible. Real objects can be counted using (R1), but not the pretend objects that (R1) posits as measures of cardinality. A second rule provides for the assignment of numbers to bunches of pretend objects:

(R2) *If $\exists_n xFx$ then $n = (\#x)Fx$*, and *If $\sim \exists_n xGx$ then $n \neq (\#x)Gx$*

The gradualists can now put their proposal like this: *every year should see a decline in the number of numbers k such that someone has k gemstones.* The new rule also has consequences of a more theoretical nature, such as *every number is less than some other number.* Suppose to the contrary that *the largest number is 6.* Then *the numbers are 0, 1, 2, . . . , and 6.* But *0, 1, 2, . . . , and 6 are seven in number.* So by (R2), *there is a number 7*.

Third Day, Operations on Finite Numbers.

Our ancestors seek a uniform distribution of gems, but find that this is not always so easy to arrange. Sometimes indeed the task is hopeless. Our ancestors know some sufficient conditions for 'it's hopeless', such as 'there are five gems and three people', but would like to be able to characterize hopelessness in general. They can get part way there by stipulating that numbers can be added together:

(R3) *If $\sim \exists x(Fx \& Gx)$, then $\#(F) + \#(G) = \#(F \lor G)$*.

Should there be two people, the situation is hopeless iff *$\sim \exists n$ #(gems) $= n + n$*. Should there be three people, the situation is hopeless iff *$\sim \exists n$ #(gems) $= ((n + n) + n)$*. A new rule:

(R4) *If $m = \#(G)$, then $\#(F) \times \#(G) = \#(F) + \ldots + \#(F)$* ($m$ times).

allows them to wrap these partial answers up into a single package. The situation is hopeless iff *$\sim \exists n$ #(gems) $= n \times$ #(people).*

Fourth Day, Finite Sets of Concreta.

Gems can be inherited from one's parents, and also from their parents, and theirs. However our ancestors find themselves unable to answer in general the question 'from whom can I inherit gems?' This is because they lack (the means to express) the concept of an ancestor. They decide to make as if there are finite sets of concreta:

(R5) For all $x_1, \ldots, x_n$, *there is a set y such that for all z, $z \in y$ iff $z = x_1 \vee z = x_2 \vee \ldots \vee z = x_n^*$.[28]

Ancestorhood can now be defined in the usual way. An ancestor of b is anyone who belongs to every set containing b and closed under the parenthood relation. Now our ancestors know (and can say) who to butter up at family gatherings: their ancestors.

Fifth Day, Infinite Sets of Concreta.

Gemstones are cut from veins of ruby and sapphire found underground. Due to the complex geometry of mineral deposits (and because miners are a quarrelsome lot), it often happens that two miners claim the same bit of stone. Our ancestors to decide to systematize the conditions of gem discovery. This much is clear: Miner Jill has discovered any (previously undiscovered) quantity of sapphire all of which was noticed first by her. But how should other bits of sapphire be related to the bits that Jill is known to have discovered for Jill to count as discovering those other bits too? One idea is that they should *touch* the bits of sapphire that Jill is known to have discovered. But the notion of touching is not well understood, and it is occasionally even argued that touching is impossible, since any two atoms are some distance apart. Our ancestors decide to take the bull by the horns and work directly with sets of atoms. They stipulate that:

(R6) If F is a predicate of concreta, then *there is a set y such that for all z, $z \in y$ iff Fz*,

and then, concerned that not all sets of interest are the extensions of Goodmanian predicates, boot this up to:

(R7) whatever x_1, x_2, ... might be, *there is a set containing all and only x_1, x_2 ...*[29]

Next they offer some definitions. Two sets S and T of atoms *converge* iff given any two atoms x and y, some s and t in S and T respectively are closer to one another than x is to y.[30] A set U of atoms is *integral* iff it intersects every set of atoms converging on any of its non-empty subsets. A set V of atoms all of the same type—sapphire, say—is *inclusive*, qua set of sapphire atoms, iff V has as a subset every integral set of sapphire atoms on which it converges. The sought after principle: Miner Jill can lay claim to the contents of the smallest inclusive set of sapphire atoms containing the bit she saw first.

Sixth Day, Infinite Numbers of Concreta.

Numbers have not yet been assigned to infinite totalities, although infinite numbers promise the same sort of expressive advantage as finite ones. Our ancestors decide to start with infinite totalities of concreta, like the infinitely many descendants they envisage. Their first rule is:

(R8) If $\forall x(Fx \rightarrow \exists!y\,(Gy\, \&\, Rxy))$ then $^*\#(F) \leq \#(G)^*$.

This is fine as far as it goes, but it does not go far enough, or cardinality relations will wind up depending on what relation symbols R the language happens to contain. Having run into a similar problem before, they know what to do.

(R9) For each x and y, *there is a unique ordered pair $< x, y >$*

(R10) *If $p_1, p_2, \ldots$ are ordered pairs of concreta, then there is a set containing all and only $p_1, p_2, \ldots$*

A set that never pairs two right elements with the same left element is a function; if in addition it never pairs two left elements with the same right element, it is a 1–1 function; if in addition its domain is X and its range is a subset of Y, it is a 1–1 function from X into Y.

(R11) *If there is a 1–1 function from $\{x\!: Fx\}$ into $\{x\!: Gx\}$, then $\#(F) \leq \#(G)^*$.

How many infinite numbers this nets them depends on the size of the concrete universe. To obtain a *lot* of infinite numbers, however, our ancestors will need to start counting abstracta.

Seventh Day, Infinite Sets (and Numbers) of Abstracta.

The next step is the one that courts paradox. (R7) allows for the unrestricted gathering together of concreta. (R10) allows for the unrestricted gathering together of a particular variety of abstracta. Now our ancestors take the plunge:

(R12) *If x_1, x_2, ... are sets, then there is a set containing all and only x_1, x_2, ...*

Assuming a set-theoretic treatment of ordered pairs, the sets introduced by (R12) already include the 1–1 functions used in the assignment of cardinality. Thus there is no need to reprise (R9); we can go straight to:

(R13) *If there is a 1–1 function from set S into set T, then #(S's members) ≤ #(T's members)*

(R12) will seem paradoxical to the extent that it seems to license the supposition of a universal set. It will seem to do that to that extent that 'all the sets' looks like it can go in for 'x_1, x_2, ...' in (R12)'s antecedent. 'All the sets' will look like an admissible substituend if the *de re* appearance of 'x_1, x_2, ...' is not taken seriously. But our ancestors take it *very* seriously. Entitlement to make as if there is a set whose members are x, y, z, ... depends on *prior* entitlements to make as if there are each of x, y, z, ... Hence the sets whose supposition is licensed by (R12) are the well-founded sets.

Much, Much Later, Forgetting.

These mathematical metaphors prove so useful that they are employed on a regular basis. As generation follows upon generation, the knowledge of how the mathematical enterprise had been launched begins to die out and is eventually lost altogether. People begin thinking of mathematical objects as genuinely there. Some, ironically enough, take the theoretical indispensability of these objects as a *proof* that they are there—ironically, since it was that same indispensability that led to their being concocted in the first place.

Worked Example

An oddity of Quine's approach to mathematical ontology has been noted by Penelope Maddy (1997). Quine sees math as continuous with 'total science' both in its subject matter and in its methods. Aping a methodology he sees at work in physics and elsewhere, Quine maintains that in mathematics too, we should keep our ontology as small as practically possible. Thus:

[I am prepared to] recognize indenumerable infinites only because they are forced on me by the simplest known systematizations of more welcome matters. Magnitudes in excess of such demands, e.g., beth-omega or inaccessible numbers, I look upon only as mathematical recreation and without ontological rights. Sets that are compatible with [Godel's axiom of constructibility v = l] afford a convenient cut-off...

(1986: 400).

Quine even proposes that we opt for the 'minimal natural model' of z f c, a model in which all sets are constructible *and* the tower of sets is chopped off at the earliest possible point. Such an approach is 'valued as inactivat[ing] the more gratuitous flights of higher set theory...'(Quine, 1992: 95).

Valued by whom? one might ask. Not actual set theorists. To them, cardinals the size of beth-omega are not even slightly controversial. They are guaranteed by an axiom introduced already in the 1920s (Replacement) and accepted by everyone. Inaccessibles are far too low in the hierarchy of large cardinals to attract any suspicion. As for Gödel's axiom of constructibility, it has been widely criticized—including by Gödel himself—as entirely too restrictive. Here is Moschovakis, in a passage quoted by Maddy:

The key argument against accepting v = l ... is that the axiom of constructibility appears to restrict unduly the notion of an *arbitrary* set of integers

(1980: 610).

Set-theorists have wanted to *avoid* axioms that would 'count sets out' just on grounds of arbitrariness. They have wanted, in fact, to run as far as possible in the other direction, seeking as fully packed a set-theoretic universe as the iterative conception of set permits. All this is reviewed in fascinating detail in Maddy (1997); see especially her discussion of the rise and fall of Definabilism, first in analysis and then in the theory of sets.

If Quine's picture of set theory as something like abstract physics cannot make sense of the field's plenitudinarian tendencies, can any other picture do better? Well, clearly one is not going to be worried about multiplying entities if the entities are not assumed to really exist. But we can say more. The likeliest approach if the set-theoretic universe is an intentional object more than a real one would be (A) to articulate the clearest intuitive conception possible, and then, (B) subject to that constraint, let all heck break loose.

Regarding (A), *some* sort of constraint is needed or the clarity of our intuitive vision will suffer. This is the justification usually offered for the axiom of foundation, which serves no real mathematical purpose—there is not a single theorem of mainstream mathematics that makes use of it—but just forces sets into the familiar and comprehensible tower structure. Without foundation there would be no possibility of 'taking in' the universe of sets in one intellectual glance.

Regarding (B), it helps to remember that sets 'originally' came in to improve our descriptions of non-sets. E.g., there are infinitely many Zs iff the set of Zs has a proper subset Y that maps onto it one-one, and uncountably many Zs iff it has an infinite proper subset Y that *cannot* be mapped onto it one-one. Since these notions of *infinitely* and *uncountably many* are topic neutral—the Zs do not have to meet a 'niceness' condition for it to make sense to ask how many of them there are—it would be counterproductive to have 'niceness' constraints on when the Zs are going to count as bundleable together into a set.[31] It would be still more counterproductive to impose 'niceness' constraints on the 1–1 functions; when it comes to infinitude, one way of pairing the Zs off 1–1 with just some of the Zs seems as good as another.

So: if we think of sets as having been brought in to help us count concrete things, a restriction to 'nice' sets would have been unmotivated and counterproductive. It would not be surprising if the anything-goes attitude at work in those original applications were to reverberate upward to contexts where the topic is sets themselves. Just as we do not want to tie our hands unnecessarily in applying set-theoretic methods to the matter of whether there are uncountably many space–time points, we don't want to tie our hands either in considering whether there are infinitely many natural numbers, or uncountably many sets of such numbers.

A case can be made, then, for (imagining there to be) a *plenitude* of sets of numbers; and a 'full' power set gathering all these sets together; and a plenitude of 1–1 functions from the power set to its proper subsets to ensure that if the power set isn't countable, there will be a function on hand to witness the fact. Plenitude is topic-neutrality writ ontologically. The preference for a 'full' universe is thus unsurprising on the as-if conception of sets.

NOTES

I am grateful to Jamie Tappenden, Thomas Hofweber, Carolina Sartorio, Hartry Field, Sandy Berkovski, Gideon Rosen, and Paolo Leonardi for comments and criticism. Most of this chapter was written in 1997 and there are places it shows. For one thing, a lot of relevant literature is simply ignored. Also various remarks about the state of the field were truer then than they are now (which is not to say they were particularly true then). My own views have changed too. Where the chapter speaks of '*making* as if you believe that *S*', I would now say '*being* as if you believe that S, but not really believing it except possibly per accidens' (see Yablo, 2002a). Related to this, mathematical objects may exist for all I know. I do not rule it out that '2 + 3 = 5' is literally true in addition to being metaphorically true, making it a twice-true metaphor along the lines of 'no man is an island'. I also do not rule it out that '2 + 3 = 5' is a maybe-metaphor, to be interpreted literally if so interpreted it is true, otherwise metaphorically. (Compare 'Nixon had a stunted superego', to use Jamie Tappenden's nice example.) I think that the existence issue can be finessed still further, but the margin is too small to contain my proof of this.

1. Beaney (1997: 366).
2. I am pretending for rhetorical purposes that Frege is still a logicist in 1919.
3. Geach and Black (1960: 184–7)
4. He speaks in *Notes for L. Darmstaedter* of 'The miracle of arithmetic'.
5. See Wigner (1967).
6. I am ignoring the Quine/Putnam approach here, first because Quine and Putnam do not purport to draw lessons from *applicability* (but rather indispensability), second because they do not purport to draw *lessons* from applicability. They do not say that we *should* accept mathematics given its applications; they think that we already *do* accept it by virtue of using it, and (this is where the indispensability comes in) we are not in a position to stop.
7. To suppose that truth alone should make for applicability would be like supposing that randomly chosen high quality products should improve the operation of randomly chosen machines. This seems to be what the Dormouse believed in *Alice in Wonderland*; asked what had possessed him to drip butter into the Mad Hatter's watch, he says, 'but it was the B E S T butter'. The best record of what I had for breakfast won't help science any more than the best butter will improve the operation of a watch.
8. Thus Mark Steiner (1998): 'Arithmetic is useful because bodies belong to reasonably stable families, such as are important in science and everyday life' (25–6). 'Addition is useful because of a *physical* regularity: gathering preserves the existence, the identity, and (what we call) the major properties, of assembled bodies' (27). 'That we can arrange a set [e.g., into rows] without losing members is an empirical precondition of the effectiveness of multiplication...' (29). 'Consider now *linearity*: why does it pervade physical laws? Because the sum of two solutions of a (homogeneous) linear equation is again a solution.' (30). 'The explanatory challenge... is to explain, not the law of gravity by itself, but the prevalence of the inverse square... What Pierce is looking for is some general physical property which lies behind the inverse square law, just as the principle of superposition and the principle of smoothness lie behind linearity' (35–6).
9. At least, not at this level of generality.

10. Some have questioned this claim, alleging a confusion of semantic conservativeness with deductive conservativeness. I propose to sidestep that issue entirely.

11. Field has pointed out to me that there are the materials for an explanation in the representation theorem he proves en route to nominalizing a theory. This is an excellent point and I do not have a worked out answer to it. Let me just make three brief remarks. First, we want an explanation that works even when the theory cannot be nominalized. Second, and more tendentiously, we want an explanation that doesn't trade on the potential for nominalization even when that potential is there. Third, the explanation that runs through a representation theorem is less a 'deductive utility' explanation than a 'representational aid' explanation of the type advocated later in this paper.

12. Deliberate now, anyway; it started out as an innocent misunderstanding. Thanks to Ana Carolina Sartorio for straightening me out on these matters.

13. Representational usefulness will be the focus in what follows. But I don't want to give the impression that the possibilities end there. Another way that numbers appear to 'help' is by redistributing theoretical content in a way that streamlines theory revision. Suppose that I am working in a first-order language speaking of material objects only. And suppose that my theory says that there are between two and three quarks in each Z-particle:

(a) $(\forall z)[(\exists q_1)(\exists q_2)(q_1 \neq q_2 \,\&\, q_i \varepsilon z \,\&\, (\forall r_1)(\forall r_2)((r_1 \neq r_2 \,\&\, r_j \,\varepsilon\, z) \rightarrow (r_1 = q_1 \text{etc.}))]$.

Then I discover that my theory is wrong: The number of quarks in a Z-particle is between two and *four*. Substantial revisions are now required in sentence (a). I will need to write in a new quantifier '$\forall r_3$'; two new non-identities '$r_1 \neq r_3$' and '$r_2 \neq r_3$'; and two new identities '$r_3 = q_1$' and '$r_3 = q_2$.' Compare this with the revisions that would have been required had quantification over numbers been allowed—had my initial statement been

(b) $(\forall z)(\forall n)(n = \#q \,(q \,\varepsilon\, z) \rightarrow 2 \leq n \leq 3)$.

Starting from (b), it would have been enough just to strike out the '3' and write in a '4.' So the numerical way of talking seems better able than the non-numerical way to efficiently absorb new information. Someone might say that the revisions would have been just as easy had we helped ourselves to numerical quantifiers $(\exists_{\geq n}x)$ defined in the usual recursive way. The original theory numbering the quarks at two or three could have been formulated as

(c) $(\forall z)[(\exists_{\geq 2}q)q \,\varepsilon\, z \,\&\, \neg(\exists_{\geq 4}q)q \,\varepsilon\, z)]$.

To obtain the new theory from (c), one need only change the second subscript. But this approach only postpones the inevitable. For our theory might be mistaken in another way: rather than the number of quarks in a Z-particle being two or three, it turns out that the number is two, three, five, seven, eleven, or... or ninety-seven—that is, the number is a *prime* less than one hundred. If we want to write this in the style of (c), our best option is a disjunction about thirty times longer than the original. Starting from (b), however, it is enough to replace '$2 \leq n \leq 3$' with 'n is prime $\& \, 2 \leq n \leq 100$.' True, we could do better if we had a primitive 'there exist primely many...' quantifier. But, as is familiar, the strategy of introducing a new primitive for each new expressive need outlives its usefulness fairly quickly. The only really progressive strategy in this area is to embrace quantification over numbers.

14. It is not just that for every recursive notation, there are reals that it does not reach; most reals are such that no recursive notation can reach them.

15. This point is also stressed by Balaguer. I first heard it from Gideon Rosen in 1990. He suggested defining the nominalistic content of a math-infused statement S as the set of worlds w such that w is indiscernible in concrete respects from some w^* where S is true.

16. Field does remark in various places that there may be no easy way of detaching the 'material content' of a statement partly about abstracta:

> the task of splitting up mixed statements into purely mathematical and purely non-mathematical components is a highly non-trivial one: it is done easily in [some] cases [e.g., '2 = the number of planets closer than the Earth to the Sun],' but it isn't at all clear how to do it in [other] cases [e.g., 'for some natural number n there is a function that maps the natural numbers less than n onto the set of all particles of matter,' 'surrounding each point of physical space-time there is an open region for which there is a 1–1 differentiable mapping of that region onto an open subset of R^4.']
>
> (Field, 1989: 235)

He goes on to say that:

> the task of splitting up all such assertions into two components is precisely the same as the task of showing that mathematics is dispensable in the physical sciences.
>
> (Field, 1989: 235)

This may be true if by 'mathematics is dispensable' one means (and Field does mean this) 'in any application of a mixed assertion. . . . a purely non-mathematical assertion could take its place' (235). But in *that* sense of dispensable—ideological dispensability, we might call it—truth is not dispensable either; there is no truth-less way of saying lots of the things we want to say. It appears then that ideological indispensability has *in the case of truth* no immediate ontological consequences. Why then is it considered to argue for the existence of numbers?

17. This section repeats some of Yablo (1998).

18. Better, such and such is part of the game's content if 'it is to be imagined. . . . *should the question arise*, it being understood that often the question *shouldn't* arise' (Walton, 1990: 40). Subject to the usual qualifications, the ideas about

make-believe and metaphor in the next few paragraphs are all due to Walton (1990, 1993).

19. Walton (1993: 40–1).

20. The theory might be a collection of axioms; it might be that plus some informal depiction of the kind of object the axioms attempt to characterize; or it might be an informal depiction pure and simple.

21. The intended contrast is with true-according-to-some-other-theory.

22. See Yablo (2002b).

23. Calling a figurative description 'wicked' or 'cruel' can be a way of expressing appreciation on the score of aptness but reservations on the score of truth. See in this connection Moran (1989).

24. Thanks to David Hills for this helpful phrase.

25. Thanks here to Hartry Field.

26. Earlier versions of this chapter had a fourteen-day melodrama involving functions on the reals, complex numbers, sets vs. classes, and more besides. It was ugly. Here I limit myself to cardinal numbers and sets.

27. F and G are predicates of concreta.

28. n here is schematic.

29. One might wonder how our ancestors acquired plural quantifiers, and whether they wouldn't have saved themselves a lot of trouble by acquiring them earlier.

30. Crucially for this definition, x and y can be material *or spatial* atoms. Our ancestors hold that all point-sized spatial positions are occupied by points of space; material atoms cohabit with some of these but not all.

31. Except to the extent that such constraints are needed to maintain consistency.

REFERENCES

Balaguer, Mark (1996). 'A Fictionalist Account of the Indispensable Applications of Mathematics.' *Philosophical Studies*, 83: 291–314.

—— (2000). *Platonism and Anti-Platonism in Mathematics.* Oxford: Oxford University Press.

—— (2001). 'A Theory of Mathematical Correctness and Mathematical Truth.' *Pacific Philosophical Quarterly,* 82: 87–114

Beaney, Michael (1997). *The Frege Reader.* Oxford: Basil Blackwell.

Burgess, John P. and Gideon Rosen (1997). *A Subject With No Object,* Oxford: Clarendon Press.

Field, Hartry (1980). *Science Without Numbers.* Princeton: Princeton University Press.

—— (1989). *Realism, Mathematics and Modality*. Oxford: Basil Blackwell.

Geach, Peter T. and Max Black. (1960). *Translations from the Philosophical Writings of Gottlob Frege*. Oxford: Basil Blackwell.

Hahn, L. and P. Schilpp (eds.) (1986). *The Philosophy of W. V. Quine*. La Salle, IL: Open Court.

Hills, David (1997). 'Aptness and Truth in Verbal Metaphor.' *Philosophical Topics*, 25: 117–153.

Horgan, Terrance (1984). 'Science Nominalized.' *Philosophy of Science*, 51: 529–49.

Maddy, Penelope (1997). *Naturalism in Mathematics*. Oxford: Clarendon Press.

Melia, Joseph (1995). 'On What There's Not.' *Analysis*, 55: 223–9.

Moran, Richard (1989). 'Seeing and Believing: Metaphor, Image, and Force.' *Critical Inquiry*, 16: 87–112.

Moschovakis, Y. (1980). *Descriptive Set Theory*. Amsterdam: North Holland.

Putnam, Hilary (1971). *Philosophy of Logic*. New York: Harper & Row.

Quine, Willard Van Orman (1951). 'Two Dogmas of Empiricism.' *Philosophical Review*, 60: 20–43. Reprinted in Quine (1961).

—— (1961). *From a Logical Point of View*, second edition. New York: Harper & Row.

—— (1986). 'Reply to Parsons,' in Hahn and Schilpp (1986).

—— (1992). *Pursuit of Truth*, revised edition. Cambridge: Harvard University Press.

Sellars, Wilfrid (1997). *Empiricism and the Philosophy of Mind*. Cambridge, MA: Harvard University Press.

Steiner, Mark (1998). *The Applicability of Mathematics as a Philosophical Problem*. Cambridge, MA: Harvard University Press.

Walton, Kendall L. (1990). *Mimesis and Make-Believe*. Cambridge, MA: Harvard University Press.

—— (1993). 'Metaphor and Prop Oriented Make-Believe.' *European Journal of Philosophy*, 1.1: 39–57.

Wigner, Eugene P. (1967). 'The Unreasonable Effectiveness of Mathematics in the Natural Sciences.' In *Symmetries and Reflections*. Bloomington, IN: Indiana University Press.

Yablo, Stephen (1998). 'Does Ontology Rest on a Mistake?' *Proceedings of the Aristotelian Society*, Supplementary Volume, 72: 229–61.

—— (2002a). 'Go Figure: A Path through Fictionalism.' *Midwest Studies in Philosophy*, 25: 72–102.

—— (2002b). 'Abstract Objects: A Case Study.' *Philosophical Issues*, 12: 220–40.

—— (forthcoming). 'Content Carving, Some Ways.' *Philosophical Quarterly*.

4

Modal Fictionalism and Analysis

SEAHWA KIM

Modal fictionalism was proposed as an attempt to keep the possible worlds framework but avoid the ontological commitment of this framework. While the modal realist analyzes modal claims by means of non-modal claims about possible worlds, the modal fictionalist takes this framework as a fiction, and analyzes modal claims in terms of the content of this fiction, calling it PW. Then, when P is an arbitrary modal claim, and P^* is the realist's translation of P, the modal fictionalist will assert every instance of the following schema:

(a) P iff according to PW, P^*.

Since modal fictionalism was proposed by Rosen, it seems that the most familiar complaint against it—that it is committed to the existence of possible worlds—has been answered by Noonan, Rosen, and Kim.[1]

There is one more obstacle to modal fictionalism. Anyone who is squeamish about abstract entities is likely to construe fictions and stories as concrete, contingent, and temporally restricted objects of some sort. But this raises a problem for modal fictionalism. If fictions are contingent and temporally restricted objects, how can the fictionalist account of modality be reconciled with the timelessness and necessity of modal truth without the assumption that the PW story itself is a timeless and necessarily existing abstract entity? In this chapter, I will develop an objection to modal fictionalism along these lines and examine several possible replies to it.

Objections: Modal and Temporal Objections

The objection begins from the premise: any sentence of the form 'According to F, P' cannot be eternally and necessarily true. There are a couple of things to clarify. First, the claims of the form 'According to F, P' or 'In F, P' should be understood as claims about the content of a story. For example, when Tom says 'I was thinking of including part of my diary in my autobiography, but I decided not to', the claim 'in Tom's autobiography, there might have been part of his diary' is not the sort of truth in a story claim we are concerned with. Second, when I say that a true claim of the form 'According to F, P' is not eternally and necessarily true, I mean that when this claim is evaluated at (or relative to) certain other times and at (or relative to) certain other worlds, it is not true. Consider the claim that there are horses. For this claim to be true at some time or at some world, the claim or the sentence 'there are horses' does not have to exist at that time or at that world. All that is required is that there be horses at that time or at that world. Platonistically speaking, what I mean when I say claims of the form 'According to PW, P' are not necessarily true is that the propositions which these claims express are not necessarily true.

With this in mind, consider the following statement:

> According to the Sherlock Holmes stories, there is a brilliant detective named 'Sherlock Holmes'.

Conan Doyle published his first Sherlock Holmes story in 1887. We ordinarily think that before that time, there were no Sherlock Holmes stories and therefore that claims about the content of the Sherlock Holmes stories were not true before 1887. The point is not that although this kind of claim had an objective and determinate truth-value, there was no way for us to find it out before the stories were written. The point is rather that at (or relative to) a time before the stories were written, claims of the form 'According to the Sherlock Holmes stories, P' were not true. As we ordinarily think, the above statement is true only after the Sherlock Holmes stories were written. And more generally, where F is an ordinary story with an ordinary history, that is, a story written or otherwise created by an author, claims of the form 'According to F, P' cannot be true at all times.

We also think that if there had been no Sherlock Holmes stories, any claim about the content of the Sherlock Holmes stories would not have been true. Again, the point is not that we could not have known what would have been true in these stories, but rather that claims about the content of these stories would not have been true. It is a contingent fact that Conan Doyle wrote the Sherlock Holmes stories. He might never have written them. Indeed, it might have been the case that no one wrote them. And if no one had written them they would not have existed. If this were the case, then any claims of the form 'According to the Sherlock Holmes stories, P' would not have been true. Since it is possible for any story to remain unwritten, no claims of the form 'According to F, P' can be necessarily true. Combining these two observations, we can say that as we ordinarily think, no claims of the form 'According to F, P', where F is a story with an ordinary history, can be true at all times and necessarily.

Why do we think in this way? Because we think that unless a story is written, unless the story exists, the content of that story is not yet determined, and hence that there is nothing true about the content of the story. That is, we ordinarily think phrases of the form 'According to a story F, P' imply that there is such a thing as the story F. At time t or at world w, it is true that according to a story F, P, only if F exists at that time and at that world. When F does not exist, 'According to F, P' is false.

Of course, I am not claiming that this is a logical implication. Sentences of the form 'According to a story F, P' don't have to be formally regimented as logically implying sentences of the form 'there is such a thing as the story F'.[2] It is more like an analytic implication in the sense that although 'Tom is a bachelor' does not logically imply 'Tom is not married', the former analytically implies the latter by virtue of their meanings. Our ordinary thought holds that the same applies to the relationship between claims of the form 'According to a story F, P' and claims of the form 'there is such a thing as the story F'. Just imagine someone who says, 'According to the Superman stories, Superman is vulnerable to Kryptonite', but then goes on to say 'but of course there are no Superman stories'. To the untutored ear, this sounds like a contradiction. The first premise of the objection, then, is that unless F exists at t (at w), claims of the form 'According to F, P' are not true at t (at w).

Now, consider the fictionalist analysis of modality. When P is a modal claim and P^* is its realist translation, the fictionalist asserts every instance of the schema:

(a) P iff according to PW, P^*.

Since the PW story is a story with an ordinary history,[3] our general principle would seem to apply. We may therefore argue as follows:

Argument (I)

(A) If F does not exists at t, then it is not true at t that according to F, P.

(B) For all times t before 1986,[4] the story PW does not exist at t.

(C) For all times t before 1986, it was not true at t that according to PW, P.

An exactly parallel argument can be given with respect to non-actual worlds in which there is no PW story:

Argument (II)

(A)* If F does not exists at w, then it is not true at w that according to F, P.

(B)* There is a world w at which PW does not exist.

(C)* At some world w, it is not true at w that according to PW, P.

Now, consider the following instance of (a):

Possibly there is a flying horse iff according to PW, there is a world at which there is a flying horse.

The fictionalist puts this biconditional forward as an analysis, and analyses are clearly supposed to hold at all times, so the fictionalist is committed to the eternal truth of the biconditional. Now we know that in (say) 1523, it was the case that there might have been a flying horse. The left-hand side was therefore true in 1523, long before the story PW was written. But since the PW story didn't exist before 1986, it was not the case in 1523 that according to PW, there is a world at which there is a flying horse. That is, the right-hand side was not true in 1523. Thus, fictionalism seems to imply that the modal claim 'possibly there is a flying horse' was not true before 1986. But this is absurd.

Again, since this biconditional is put forward as an analysis, and analyses are also supposed to hold necessarily, the fictionalist is committed to the necessary truth of the biconditional. It is quite plausible that the left-hand side is necessarily true. And yet the right-hand side is not necessarily true, because it is possible that the PW story does not exist. Thus, fictionalism seems to imply that this modal claim is at best contingently true. Now, the claim that the possible existence of a flying horse is a contingent matter is not absurd on its face. My point is that, even if the contingency of the modal claim is not absurd in every case, it is absurd to suppose that modal truth is in general contingent upon the existence of the fiction PW. We can easily think of a world at which there is a flying horse but there is no PW story, that is, a world at which the left-hand side is true but the right-hand side is false. Modal fictionalism seems to imply that even at this world the left-hand side is false because the right-hand side is false, even if there is a flying horse at this world. This is an unacceptable consequence.

The problems can be formulated as follows:

   (i) For all times *t* before 1986, it was not true at *t* that according to PW, *P* ((C) from the above).

  (ii) Modal fictionalism claims the truth of every instance of the schema (a) at every time *t*.

 (iii) Hence, modal fictionalism implies that no modal claim was true before 1986.

 (iv) But some modal claims were true before 1986.

  (v) Therefore, modal fictionalism is untenable.

  (i)* At some world *w*, it is not true at *w* that according to PW, *P* ((C)* from the above).

 (ii)* Modal fictionalism claims the truth of every instance of the schema (a) at every world *w*.

(iii)* Hence, modal fictionalism implies that no modal claim is true at worlds at which the story PW does not exist.

(iv)* Some modal claims are true at worlds at which the story PW does not exist.

  (v) Therefore, modal fictionalism is untenable.

The trouble, in a few words, is that modal fictionalism apparently has a consequence that before PW was written no modal claims were true, and that if PW had not existed no modal claims would have been true. But this is absurd.[5]

Rejecting (A) and (A)*: The Tenseless and Moodless Reading

How can the modal fictionalist reply to these objections? It seems that except for the first premises (i) and (i)*, all other steps of arguments from (i) to (v) and from (i)* to (v) are uncontroversial. The modal fictionalist must therefore reject these first steps by refuting the preliminary arguments (I) and (II).

The obvious candidates for rejection are steps (A) and (A)*:

  (A)   If *F* does not exists at *t*, then it is not true at *t* that according to *F*, *P*.

  (A)* If *F* does not exists at *w*, then it is not true at *w* that according to *F*, *P*.

These premises amount to the claim that 'According to F, P' should be read as equivalent to:

(1) There exists a certain story F, and according to F, P.

But the modal fictionalist may claim that this is not a natural reading. For example, consider a novelist who says to his friend, 'My next novel will be called "Triangle". I haven't written it yet, but I will tell you this: in "Triangle", a man has affairs with two women.' If he writes this novel at some later time, it would be natural to regard this earlier statement as true. Consider next a philosophy student who says 'Last night I wrote a paper in which I argued that there are no other minds, but I realized this was a crazy idea, so I erased it from my computer.' There is a sense in which this paper no longer exists, but we can still say truly that according to his paper, there are no other minds. In both cases, the 'story' F does not exist at t, and yet statements of the form 'According to F, P' seem to be true at t. Similar considerations apply in the modal case. Suppose someone was going to write a story about bears titled 'The Bear' and that he told people about his plans, but died before formulating the detailed plot of the story. When his friend says 'In "The Bear", there are bears', this seems true, even though the story did not, does not, and will not exist, but only might have existed.

These observations suggest that we should read 'According to F, P' not as equivalent to 'There exists a certain story F, and according to F, P', but rather as equivalent to 'There was or is or will be or might have been a certain story F, and according to F, P.' Then, the natural reading of any claim of the form 'According to PW, P' is:

(2) The PW story exists or has existed or will exist or might have existed, and according to PW, P.

Since (2) does not imply the existence of the story PW, the modal fictionalist can argue that (A) and (A)* are false, and he can also explain how statements of the form 'According to PW, F' can be true at all times and necessarily.

But this response is not satisfactory. First of all, the above 'counterexamples' to (A) and (A)* are not convincing. In the case of the philosophy paper, the natural thing to say after the paper has been destroyed is not 'According to his paper, there are no other minds', but 'It was the case that according to his paper, there are no other minds.' The modal case is especially unconvincing. The natural way for his friend to express his claim would be to say, not 'In "The Bear", there are bears', but 'There would have been bears in "The

Bear", if he had written it' or 'There were going to be bears in "The Bear"'. Thus, the tenseless and the moodless reading is not plausible.

More importantly, even if the tenseless and the moodless reading were plausible, this solution creates another problem for the modal fictionalist. Notice that (2) is equivalent to the following:

(2)# The PW story might have existed, and according to PW, *P.*

since 'exists or has existed or will exist' is redundant in (2). But (2)# is a modal claim, and modality is what the modal fictionalist was trying to analyze. On pain of circularity, the fictionalist cannot appeal to modality in solving problems which arise from his analysis of modality. Thus, the modal fictionalist cannot accept this solution.

Rejecting (A) and (A)*: Rigid Designation

There is another way to reject premises (A) and (A)*. It might be argued that 'PW' is a proper name, and proper names are rigid designators. There are two readings of this thesis. The weak reading is that a proper name refers to the same individual *x* at every world in which *x* exists. The strong reading is that a proper name refers to the same thing *x* at every world. The modal fictionalist may attempt to exploit the strong reading to solve the problem, insisting that 'PW' refers to PW even at worlds at which PW does not exist. Analogous accounts can be given about a proper name's referring to its referent at times at which its referent does not exist. Thus, it might be said that relative to 1980, 'PW' refers to PW even if PW does not exist at this time. Then there is no obstacle to a statement about the content of PW's being true at worlds and times at which PW does not exist. And if statements of the form 'According to PW, *P*' can be true even at times and at worlds at which the PW story does not exist, premises (A) and (A)* are false.

But this response is not satisfactory. Let's grant that 'PW' refers to PW at every time and at every world. This by itself does not show that statements of the form 'According to PW, *P*' can be true even at times and worlds at which PW does not exist. Suppose that all proper names are strongly rigid designators. Now, let's consider the name 'Socrates'. At times before Socrates was born, the statement that Socrates does not exist or that Socrates is not yet born were true. But there are statements about Socrates which were false at those times: 'Socrates exists', 'Socrates is famous', 'Socrates has married twice', etc.

At times after he died, the statement that Socrates was a teacher of Plato or that Socrates is admired by many people are true. But there are statements about Socrates which are not true at these times: 'Socrates exists', 'Socrates is not yet born', 'Socrates lives in Greece', etc. Likewise, at worlds where Socrates does not exist, the statement that Socrates does not exist or that Socrates might have existed are true, but the following are false at these worlds: 'Socrates exists', 'Socrates is a philosopher', 'Socrates will be born', etc.

In all of these example, 'Socrates' rigidly refers to Socrates, even at worlds and times at which he does not exist, but still some statements about him are true and some are false, and some of the false statements are false precisely because they imply the existence of Socrates at the relevant index. What the fictionalist has to show then is not just that 'PW' refers to PW at all times and at all worlds, but that statements of the form 'According to PW, P' can be true at worlds and times even if PW does not exist at these worlds and times. The claim that 'PW' is a strongly rigid designator itself does not show statements of the form 'According to PW, P' do not imply 'PW exists'.[6]

One might object in the following way. It is natural to think that even if there had never been any intelligent beings, and hence no theories, the laws of quantum mechanics would still have been true. That is, even if no theory or 'law' had ever been written down or thought of, quantum mechanics and its laws would still have been true. Then, can't we say the same thing about the PW story? Can't we say that PW and its content would still have been true even if there had never been a PW story? If so, then doesn't it show that claims about the content of a story F do not imply the existence of F?

I agree that the statement 'even if quantum mechanics considered as an artifact of human ingenuity had never existed, quantum mechanics would still have been true' is true. For a certain theory T to be true at some time or at some world, T itself does not have to exist at that time or at that world. Let's assume for the sake of argument that PW is true. One thing we can say about PW is that even if the PW story had never existed, the PW story would still have been true. But this statement is clearly different from the statement 'even if the PW story had never existed, it would have been the case that according to PW, there are many worlds'. And what the fictionalist needs to vindicate is this latter statement, not the former statement. What the statement 'even if quantum mechanics had never existed, it would still have been true' or the statement 'even if the PW story had never existed, the PW story would still have been true' says is this: quantum mechanics (the PW story) says that P, and even if quantum mechanics (the PW story) hadn't existed, P would still have been true. These statements do not show that claims of the form

'According to F, P' do not imply the existence of F. The statement which shows this is 'even if the PW story had not existed, it would have been the case that according to PW, there are many worlds'. But the above example does not support the truth of this statement, and hence does not support the claim that 'According to F, P' does not imply the existence of the story F.

Rejecting (B) and (B)*: Platonism about Stories

Another way to refute arguments (I) and (II) is to reject premises (B) and (B)*:

(B)   For all times t before 1986, the story PW does not exist at t.

(B)* There is a world w at which PW does not exist.

The modal fictionalist may claim that PW existed even before 1986, and that it exists necessarily. How can he claim this when we know that PW was written in 1986 and might not have been written at all? He can do this by claiming that stories are abstract entities. Since abstract entities are all standardly supposed to exist eternally and necessarily, as abstract entities, stories exist eternally and necessarily, too. Thus, whether or not someone actually writes them down, whether or not there is a concrete 'instance' of them, stories exist as abstract entities. On this view, although PW was first written down in 1986, it has existed always and it exists necessarily. So premises (B) and (B)* are false.

One might raise the following objection to this solution. If the modal fictionalist takes stories as abstract entities, he has to admit the existence of world-stories which the modal ersatzist identifies with possible worlds. But if there are world-stories, why should we be modal fictionalists instead of modal ersatzists?

I think the modal fictionalist has an answer to this. Even if there are world-stories which can represent possible worlds, we need to appeal to a modal notion in order to distinguish these world-stories from other stories. As we have seen, stories in general are not consistent or coherent. In order to say which stories are to count as possible worlds, we must distinguish the coherent or consistent world-stories from the rest. But this appeal to 'coherence' or 'consistency' is more than an appeal to logical possibility or logical consistency. It is an appeal to metaphysical possibility. Thus, unless it can be eliminated, the ersatzist analysis is circular. This was one of Lewis' objections to modal ersatzism. But if we let the PW story do all the work, there is no need to appeal to a modal concept like this. So there indeed is an advantage of being a fictionalist instead of an ersatzist. Adopting the platonist view of stories does not undercut the rationale for modal fictionalism.

Is this solution satisfactory for the modal fictionalist? Not entirely. First of all, even if we admit that stories are abstract entities, it is a mistake to assume that stories exist eternally and necessarily simply because they are abstract entities. It is quite plausible that some abstract entities do not exist eternally or necessarily. For example, some think that a set of concrete things does not exist all the time nor necessarily. Why not think of stories in the same way? Edward Zalta considers stories as abstract objects, but he does not consider them as existing necessarily and eternally. He says 'stories are abstract objects which . . . are authored by some existing thing. Hence, it is a contingent matter that there are any stories.'[7] What the fictionalist has to show is that stories are not contingent abstract entities, that they exist eternally and necessarily.

When he tries to show this, however, another problem arises. According to this view, every story exists necessarily and eternally and waits only for someone to 'select' it. But this does not square well with our ordinary views about stories or fictions. We think that authors are creators not selectors (or discoverers), that they make up the stories, and that stories come into being only when an author writes them down or thinks them up. We can find this uneasiness expressed in the following:

This [platonistic] conception of the ontological or metaphysical nature of musical and literary works is quite appealing—at least to those not already disposed to reject abstract objects on general grounds. . . . But it runs afoul of the view that novels and melodies are created by novelists and composers, and that creating a thing is—or at least entails—bringing that thing into existence.[8]

Although this passage is only concerned with literary fiction and music, I think the point applies to stories in general. Since we ordinarily think that authors create stories and that before they are created, stories do not exist, I think the platonistic view about stories is quite counter-intuitive. Given that the motivation for modal fictionalism is to respect our intuitions about what there are, this solution will make modal fictionalism less attractive.[9]

Rejecting (ii) and (ii)*: Timid Modal Fictionalism

It seems that any attempt to reject one of the steps in arguments (I) and (II) is not entirely satisfactory. But there is another way. The fictionalist can reject steps (ii) and (ii)* of the temporal and modal arguments:

(ii)   Modal fictionalism claims the truth of every instance of the schema (a) at any time *t*.

(ii)* Modal fictionalism claims the truth of every instance of the schema (a) at any world *w*.

That is, he can refute the objection by admitting that instances of the schema (a) are not true eternally and necessarily.

The modal fictionalist asserts every instance of schema (a). For example, he asserts the following biconditional:

> Possibly there is a flying horse iff according to P W, there is a world at which there is a flying horse.

But perhaps he does not have to assert that this biconditional is itself necessarily true or eternally true. What the fictionalist purports to do is to give a systematic fictionalist 'translation' for each and every modal claim, which yields the correct truth-value. But in doing this, the fictionalist does not have to give a biconditional which is necessarily and eternally true.

But we know the left-hand side, the modal claim, is necessarily true and that it was true before 1986, while the right-hand side, its fictionalist 'translation', is not necessarily true and that it was not true before 1986. How then can the fictionalist maintain that this modal claim is necessarily true and was true before 1986? He can do this by giving fictionalist translations to the following two claims:

(3) It is necessarily true that possibly there is a flying horse.

(4) It was true before 1986 that possibly there is a flying horse.

The fictionalist translations for these claims are:

(3)* According to P W, for all worlds, there is a world at which there is a flying horse.

(4)* According to P W, at all times *t* before 1986, there was a world at which there is a flying horse.

And since both (3)* and (4)* are true, the fictionalist can claim that (3) and (4) are true, and hence that the above modal claim 'Possibly there is a flying horse' is necessarily true and was true before 1986. The trick with modal claims with iterated modal operators or temporal indicators is to push all such operators within the scope of the story prefix. For example, in the case of modal claims with iterated modal operators like:

Necessarily, possibly *Q*.

the fictionalist gives the following translation:

According to PW, for all worlds there is a world at which Q.

In the case of modal claims with a temporal indicator like:

At t, P.

the fictionalist translation is:

According to PW, at t, P*.

with the tense in P* changed suitably.[10] By systematically applying this translation scheme, the modal fictionalist can give a proper translation for each and every modal claim.

Now, this response leads to a seemingly paradoxical consequence. The modal fictionalist can claim that a certain modal claim was true in 1145 even if there was no PW story at that time. He also can claim that a certain modal claim would have been true even if the story PW had never existed. That is, he can assert that the following claims are true:

(5) Even if there had been no PW story, it would have been true that there might have been a flying horse.

(6) Before PW existed, there could have been a flying horse.

He can assert these claims because the followings are clearly true:

(5)* According to PW, a world at which there is no PW story and there is a world at which there is a flying horse is closer to the actual world than any world at which there is no PW story and there is no world at which there is a flying horse.

(6)* According to PW, before PW existed (before 1986), there was a world at which there is a flying horse.

This seems a little paradoxical. The modal fictionalist seems to have asserted that modal truth consists in truth according to PW, but now he seems to be saying that the modal truth is modally independent of the existence of PW. And that sounds like a contradiction. But in fact the fictionalist should be able to assert both (5) and (6). Modal truths are timeless and necessary unlike truths about the existence of stories. He has to show that the timelessness and necessity of modal truth are compatible with the view that stories, including the PW story, are contingent and temporally restricted entities.

But an objection immediately arises. If the fictionalist's biconditional is neither eternally nor necessarily true, how can it be an analysis? Analyses are ordinarily supposed to be necessary. But the fictionalist analysis does not meet this condition. We have seen that biconditionals are not necessarily nor eternally true. Then, how can the fictionalist claim to provide an analysis of modality? Since the modal fictionalist cannot provide any general claim or biconditional which is necessarily true, he cannot claim that he provides an analysis of modality.

Because of this problem, I think this solution is available only for the timid fictionalist. The timid fictionalist takes modality as primitive. He does not aim to provide a theory or an analysis of modality. But he thinks the possible worlds framework is illuminating and useful, so he only wants license to move back and forth between modal claims and claims about possible worlds. For him, the biconditional 'P iff according to PW, P^{*}' guides such transitions. He only aims to provide 'a theory linking the modal facts with facts about the story PW'.[11] Since he does not purport to give an analysis, he does not need to provide a necessary biconditional. So, the timid fictionalist can adopt this solution. But the modal fictionalist who wants to give an analysis of modality cannot.

Rejecting (ii) and (ii)*: A New Analysis

There is another way to avoid the objections. The modal fictionalist can reject (ii) and (ii)*, and give a new analysis. That is, instead of the schema (a):

(a) P iff according to PW, P^{*}.

the modal fictionalist can provide a new analysis as follows:

(a)* P iff actually, presently, according to PW, P^{*}.

Here, the modal fictionalist introduces the actuality operator and 'presently' operator (or 'now' operator) into his analysis. According to the standard treatment of the actuality operator, a sentence of the form 'actually, P' is true iff P is true in the actual world, where 'the actual world' is rigid. Even at other worlds where P is not true, it is true at that world that actually, P, if P is true in the actual world. Thus, 'actually, P' is necessarily true if it is true at all. Also, with 'presently' operator, any sentence of the form 'presently, P' is true iff P is true presently (or now), where 'present' is rigid. Even at other times where P is not true, it is true at those times that presently, P, if P is true presently. Thus, 'presently, P' is true at all times if it is true at all.

Now, we know that for some P, 'According to PW, P' is true in the actual world and presently. Thus, the fictionalist can say that for these P, 'Actually, presently, according to PW, P' is true at all times and necessarily. For example, consider the following again:

> Possibly there is a flying horse iff according to PW, there is a world at which there is a flying horse.

The problem of this biconditional was that this holds only contingently and only at some times. It doesn't hold at worlds and times at which PW does not exist. But consider the following new analysis:

> Possibly there is a flying horse iff actually, presently, according to PW, there is a world at which there is a flying horse.

This biconditional holds at all times and necessarily. It holds even at worlds and times at which PW does not exist. For the right-hand side to be true at some world and time, 'According to PW, there is a world at which there is a flying horse' has to be true in the actual world and at present. And of course this is true in the actual world and at present. Thus, the right-hand side is necessarily and eternally true, and hence the left-hand side is also necessarily and eternally true. With the new analysis (a)*, the fictionalist can claim that he can show these biconditionals are necessarily and eternally true, and thus that he has provided a genuine analysis of modality.

If one thinks that this solution is not satisfactory, because it makes the fictionalist analysis modal by introducing the actuality operator as primitive,[12] I think, with a minor modification of (a)*, the fictionalist can improve the solution. Instead of (a)* which introduces the actuality operator, the fictionalist can give the following analysis:

> (a)** P iff at this universe, presently, according to PW, P^*.

The indexical 'this' has the same rigidifying effect as 'actually', but it is not a modal notion. With this new analysis (a)**, the fictionalist account of modality can be reconciled with the timelessness and necessity of modal truth without the assumption that the PW story itself is a timeless and necessarily existing abstract entity. Thus, I think this solution is the most satisfactory to modal and temporal objections.

Nolan anticipates this rigidifying solution, and gives an objection to it. According to him, the rigidifying solution still has the following unacceptable consequence:

> If there had actually been no Modal Fiction, no statement about contents of worlds would have been true according to it.[13]

We can modify this objection so that it applies to (a)** which covers the temporal case. Then, the objection is that (a)** still has the following unacceptable consequence:

> If there were no PW story at this universe, presently, no statement of the form 'at this universe, presently, according to PW, P^*' would have been true.

How can the modal fictionalist reply to this objection? I think the fictionalist can simply say that the above counterfactual has an impossible antecedent, because the PW story does exist at this world and presently, and thus it is vacuously true.

Conclusion

So far I have examined several possible solutions to the modal and temporal objections, and concluded that the rigidifying solution, that is, the solution which introduces a new analysis (a)**, is the most satisfactory.

But a worry remains. How can the fictionalist justify the claim that modal statements are true in virtue of the content of this contingent and temporally restricted story? I think the modal fictionalist should just admit that his view has this strange consequence. It is true that there is something bizarre in the thought that modal statements are true in virtue of the content of some fiction which might not have existed and didn't exist a long time ago. But although it is bizarre, it is still the case that modal statements are true in virtue of the content of some fiction.

Perhaps the biggest worry about (a)** is that, although it is necessary, it is *a posteriori* knowable, and since a biconditional can only count as an analysis if it is necessary and *a priori*, I fail to give an analysis of modality after all. I admit that this is a legitimate and serious worry, and that I cannot respond to it satisfactorily here. Perhaps the modal fictionalist can make a bold move and claim that an analysis does not have to be *a priori*. But I will sketch the following possible response to this worry and leave its answer for a future time. I can imagine the fictionalist might respond as follows: 'The biconditional the fictionalist proffers as an analysis of modality is necessarily and eternally true. We can teach people who don't know what possibility or necessity are by explaining them in terms of what is true according to the PW story. Moreover, the fictionalist account yields correct truth-values for modal statements. That is, just by considering what is true according to PW, the fictionalist can agree with ordinary people who only rely on their intuitions about modal truths. Also, if the principles which guide our thoughts about possibility or necessity are in some sense well captured by the postulates of the PW story, as Rosen suggests,[14] or if the postulates of the PW story somehow implicitly guide our thoughts about modality, then it seems plausible to think that this biconditional is not only necessary, but *a priori*. What more is required from an analysis?'

NOTES

I thank Gideon Rosen for helpful comments and discussions on earlier drafts of this chapter.

1. For the objection, see Gideon Rosen (1993) and Stuart Brock (1993). For the solutions, see Harold Noonan (1994), Gideon Rosen (1995), and Seahwa Kim (2002).

2. See Charles Chihara (1984: 73).

3. I think it is quite natural to think that the PW hypothesis is a story with an ordinary history. It was conceived or written by some people, and before that it didn't exist.

4. Or whenever the story first came into existence. It does not matter for our purposes when exactly this was: when Lewis first wrote it down, when he first thought it up, when Rosen first made the official postulates explicit, when some ancient author first conceived the doctrine of a plurality of concrete worlds, and so on. All that matters is that the story has not always existed. I chose the year 1986, and this is not a randomly chosen year, but the year David Lewis' monograph, *On the Plurality of Worlds*, was published.

5. Daniel Nolan (1997) raises the same kind of objection to modal fictionalism. I became aware of this only after writing the original version of this chapter, which was part of my doctoral dissertation.

6. Some might think that statements about Socrates' essential properties such as that Socrates is a human being are true at all times and at all worlds, and statements about the content of the story are like these because they are statements about essential properties of the story. But this is a controversial claim in two ways. First, many claim that what is true at all times and at all worlds is not that Socrates is a human being, but that if Socrates exists, he is a human being, which does not imply the existence of Socrates. Second, many claim that the content of a story is not its essential property. That is, many claim that a story can vary its content from world to world. I am not claiming that the modal

fictionalist should not argue along this line. But it seems to me that this solution makes modal fictionalism depend on too controversial a position.

7. See Edward Zalta (1983: 91).

8. See Harry Deutsch (1991: 209).

9. I would like to point out that I do not endorse the view that stories are contingent abstract entities. In my other paper, I attempt to make modal fictionalism fully nominalistic. See Seahwa Kim (2002).

10. If t is a past time, the past tense will be used, and if t is a future time, the future tense will be used. For example, 'At 1325, there might have been flying rabbits' is translated as 'According to PW, at 1325, there was a world at which there are flying rabbits', and 'At 2003, there might have been flying rabbits' is translated as 'According to PW, at 2003, there will be a world at which there are flying rabbits.'

11. See Gideon Rosen (1990: 354).

12. The actuality operator is a modal operator. With this operator as primitive, the fictionalist fails to give a thoroughly reductive analysis of modality. But the fictionalist can claim that this is not so bad. He can claim that although the fictionalist analysis will not be a reductive analysis, unlike the ersatzist analysis, it will not be circular in the sense that it appeals to metaphysical possibility in analyzing metaphysical possibility. Although the actuality operator is indeed a modal operator, it is not analyzable in terms of the usual box and diamond. Thus, the fictionalist can claim that he gives an analysis of modal notions. The same thing can be said about the fictionalist who takes the story prefix as a modal primitive. Also, since the story prefix applies to inconsistent sentences as well, there is a sense in which this primitive, the story prefix, is not clearly modal.

13. See Daniel Nolan (1997: 266).

14. See Gideon Rosen (1990: 353).

REFERENCES

Brock, Stuart (1993). 'Modal Fictionalism: A Response to Rosen.' *Mind*, 102: 147–50.

Chihara, Charles (1984). *Ontology and the Vicious-Circle Principle*. Ithaca, NY: Cornell University Press.

Deutsch, Harry (1991). 'The Creation Problem.' *Topoi*, 10: 209–25.

Kim, Seahwa (2002). 'Modal Fictionalism Generalized and Defended.' *Philosophical Studies*, 111: 121–46.

Lewis, David (1986). *On the Plurality of Worlds*. Oxford: Basil Blackwell.

Nolan, Daniel (1997a). 'Three Problems for "Strong" Modal Fictionalism.' *Philosophical Studies*, 87.3: 259–75.

Noonan, Harold (1994). 'In Defence of the Letter of Fictionalism.' *Analysis*, 54.3: 133–9.

Rosen, Gideon (1990). 'Modal Fictionalism.' *Mind*, 99.395: 327–54.

—— (1993). 'A Problem For Fictionalism About Possible Worlds.' *Analysis*, 53.2: 71–81.

—— (1995). 'Modal Fictionalism Fixed.' *Analysis*, 55.2: 67–73.

Zalta, Edward (1983). *Abstract Objects*. Dordrecht: D. Reidel Publishing Company.

5

Truth as a Pretense

James A. Woodbridge

Truth is a pretense. This bald statement might inspire "incredulous stares", but my aim here is to deflect this initial incredulity. To begin, then, my claim that truth is a pretense is really part of an analysis of truth-*talk*—the fragment of our talk (and thought) that employs the notion of truth.[1] Just this clarification probably deflects little skepticism, since it merely marks my view as some sort of fictionalism with respect to truth-talk. On a common understanding of fictionalist analyses, certain statements from a "way of talking"[2] understood fictionally may be "true in the fiction", but really all statements from this fragment of discourse are *false*.[3] Some of the abiding skepticism toward my initial claim likely comes from the recognition that this error-theoretic conception of fictionalism undermines itself when applied to truth-talk. The problem here is by now familiar: an account of truth-talk based on the thesis that all truth-talk is *false* (or, more broadly, *never true*) seems to presuppose a non-error-theoretic notion of truth-conditions, and so of truth.[4] And even if it did not, the claim that all instances of truth-talk are false is itself an instance of truth-talk, and so it would turn out to be false on this view. In fact, matters are even worse; this position would be *paradoxical* since it would say of *itself* that it was false.[5] Understood this way, a fictionalist interpretation of truth-talk is a non-starter.

Nevertheless, a fictionalist account of truth-talk is what I offer here. Of course, in doing so I will have to avoid the problematic, error-theoretic understanding of fictionalism, but that is precisely what the approach I take lets me do. My account explains truth-talk in terms of *semantic pretense*. The pretense approach applies coherently to truth-talk because on this variety of fictionalism some utterances understood this way still make genuinely true claims about the real world. The resulting pretense-based account of truth-talk amounts to a version of *deflationism* about truth. This provides some partial support for my view (along with others), as certain unusual features truth-talk exhibits—the duality of triviality and non-triviality truth-locutions display, and the talk's *prima facie* propensity for paradox—motivate pursuing some form of deflationism. Support for a pretense-based formulation in particular comes from this approach's agreement with the general deflationary strategies for dealing with truth-talk's unusual features. Even stronger motivation then comes from certain advantages a pretense-based view offers over other formulations of deflationism.

While my account explains truth-talk in terms of pretense, it still maintains that speakers typically use truth-talk to make serious assertions about the world. However, the serious assertions they make are not the ones that they seem to make. In the instances of truth-talk, uses of expressions like 'is true' and 'is false' appear to attribute properties—truth and falsity—to objects that the term expressions supposedly denote. These appearances are just part of a pretense on my view. There are no such properties as truth and falsity, and the expressions 'is true' and 'is false' do not even really play the linguistic roles they appear to play. We talk *as if* there are properties of truth and falsity in order to make certain serious assertions (not about truth) indirectly. The real value of the talk is that it lets speakers express a form of assertion that they otherwise could not express, in particular, it lets them formulate certain otherwise inexpressible generalizations. The account of truth-talk I develop here explains how the talk's invocation of pretense gives it this linguistic function. We should not, however, confuse the thesis that truth-talk involves pretense with the claim that saying something is true amounts to *pretending* it is true. Pretending something is true involves applying an additional level of pretense to something one would express indirectly via the pretense truth-talk already invokes. Truth-talk functions in virtue of pretense, but speakers use it to say (indirectly) how things are, not just how they pretend things are.

My goals for the rest of this paper are to motivate a pretense-based account of truth-talk and to show that in addition to being a coherent view, it also has certain theoretical advantages over other accounts of truth-talk. I start by explaining how truth-talk's unusual features provide initial motivation for deflationism in general. Then I lay out the basic details of the pretense approach (including how its application avoids generating an error theory). To show both that a pretense-based account is the best way to make good on deflationary aspirations and that it avoids a modified error-theoretic interpretation, I expand the standard account of semantic pretense by specifying a new distinction. I then explain the core pretense behind truth-talk, focusing on its satisfaction of the basic adequacy criteria that any account of truth-talk must satisfy, as well as its satisfaction of the central commitment of deflationism. Next, I discuss how to extend this account to cover the most interesting cases of truth-talk, the quantificational instances. Here (and in the discussion of the view's adequacy) I also highlight some of the advantages the pretense-based account offers in explaining certain aspects of truth-talk. Finally, I respond to some objections, including the most serious challenge to my view: the claim that we cannot explain truth in terms of pretense because we must appeal to truth to explain pretending.

Truth-talk, Deflationism, and Pretense

Truth-talk exhibits some unusual features that render it philosophically suspect. One such feature is a remarkable duality truth-locutions display.[6] In some cases the notion of truth seems vacuous or redundant. Claims like:

(1) It is true that crabapples are edible

appear to be trivial expansions of the sentences they embed; (1) is at least necessarily and *a priori* equivalent to (if not synonymous with):

(2) Crabapples are edible.

However, in other instances, the notion of truth does not seem trivial. For example, the claim:

(3) What Dex said is true

is not a trivial expansion of anything; it is not necessarily an *a priori* equivalent to any claim free of truth-locutions. The expression 'is true' is not redundant in an utterance like (3); removing it would turn a sentence into a singular term, resulting in a loss of content and a failure to express any thought.

Another suspicion-arousing feature truth-talk exhibits is a *prima facie* propensity for paradox. The central principles governing the notion of truth are the instances of the equivalence schema:

(ES) It is true that p iff p (= That p is true iff p).[7]

The problem is that some instances of truth-talk seem to generate contradictions in certain circumstances when we apply (ES) to them. This is especially clear for utterances that amount to formulations of the famous Liar paradox, for example, the sentence:

(4) The sentence labeled '(4)' does not express anything true[8]

The problem with sentences like (4) is well known. What (4) most plausibly expresses is that the sentence labeled '(4)' does not express anything true. So, what (4) expresses is true iff that the sentence labeled '(4)' does not express anything true is true. It follows from this and the relevant instance of (ES):

(ES$_4$) That the sentence labeled '(4)' does not express anything true is true iff the sentence labeled '(4)' does not express anything true

(and a little rephrasing) that (4) expresses something true iff (4) does not express anything true.[9]

Truth-talk's duality and propensity for paradox suggest that this way of talking is not completely straightforward. The general conclusion I draw is that we should approach the subject of truth from a *deflationary* perspective, rather than an inflationary one. The best way to understand deflationism "about truth" (henceforth, simply 'deflationism') is as a *meta*theory about truth-*talk*, rather than as a theory of *truth*. Viewing deflationism the latter way entangles the approach with independent philosophical issues concerning the nature and existence of properties. For example, if we took the central claim of deflationism to be that there is no property of truth (or even that there is no *substantive* property of truth), then any nominalist who rejects properties altogether would automatically be a deflationist.[10] But it is implausible to apply this classification to a nominalist who sees no difference between the functioning of truth-talk and that of, say, talk of what is and is not metal, or any other sort of "everyday" talk. As a view specifically about the topic of truth, the point of deflationism is to draw some sort of distinction here. Deflationism has consequences for the issue of whether there is a property of truth (and if so, what sort of property it could be), but the best way to understand the approach is as a view about truth-talk.[11]

We must be careful, however, about what sort of view about truth-talk we take deflationism to be. For reasons similar to those just rehearsed, we should also not take deflationism's primary concern to be which sorts of functions truth-talk performs, for instance, whether it plays an explanatory or normative role. This view of deflationism would also entangle the approach with independent philosophical issues, for example, those concerning the natures of explanation and normativity. The most plausible candidate for the central concern of deflationism is truth-talk's logico-linguistic functioning. The thesis that best captures deflationism's central commitment is the claim that truth-talk functions (logico-linguistically) in such a way that the instances of (ES) are *fundamental*.[12] What this means is that these equivalences neither require nor admit of any "deeper" analysis; their holding is not a matter of any underlying aspects of some property (truth) that truth-predicates attribute, or of any definitional connections holding between the concept of truth and more basic concepts. On deflationary views, the instances of (ES) are conceptually and explanatorily basic.[13]

Truth-talk's unusual features provide initial incentive for pursuing a deflationary account because views of this sort have an easier time dealing with them (in virtue of having less of an explanatory burden) than inflationary views do. There is no difficulty in accounting for the modal and epistemic status of the instances of (ES) if we take them to be fundamental in the sense just described. The necessity and *a prioricity* of these equivalences in turn accounts for the triviality of the truth-locutions in certain instances of truth-talk. Those that figure in the instances of (ES) are necessarily and *a priori* equivalent to certain sentences free of truth-locutions; those that do not figure in the instances of (ES) are not. There is thus a sense in which the truth-locutions make no significant contribution in cases of the first sort, but do in those of the second.

With regard to truth-talk's putative propensity for paradox, taking the instances of (ES) as fundamental allows deflationary views to accept the *prima facie* paradoxical sentences as genuinely paradoxical and to pursue a strategy of diagnosing and containing truth-talk's inconsistency, rather than one attempting to eliminate it.[14] This is not an option if we take the instances of (ES) to hold in virtue of the nature of a property the truth-predicate attributes on the left-hand side.[15] Given that many, if not most, actual instances of truth-talk "risk being paradoxical if the empirical circumstances are extremely (and unexpectedly) unfavorable",[16] solving the "diagnostic [and containment] problem" is probably an easier task than solving the "preventative problem".[17] Support for this thought comes from the seemingly relentless recurrence of paradox in the form of some strengthened version of the Liar in response to any proposed elimination.[18] Deflationary views might very well have a more difficult time in tackling the preventative problem, since various strategies (e.g., an appeal to truth-value gaps) might not be available to them, but one of the advantages deflationism offers over inflationism is that it makes solving this problem supererogatory and replaces it with what is arguably a less difficult task.[19]

A useful way to understand the position I advance here is as the claim that deflationism is the most promising approach to the topic of truth, and the best way to formulate a deflationary account of truth-talk is in terms of semantic pretense. I will specify the points on which I think a pretense-based formulation of deflationism scores better than current formulations presently, but an antecedent explanation of the approach I take will help make this clearer. The pretense approach is a recent fictionalist strategy that has produced illuminating analyses of some other philosophically suspect ways of talking. A central source of the approach is the account of the representational arts Kendall Walton presents in his book *Mimesis as Make-Believe*.[20] The best-known extension of Walton's views is the application of the pretense approach to our talk ostensibly of what does and does not exist (henceforth, 'existence-talk'). A central motivation for a pretense-based analysis of existence-talk stems from the problem of non-being, that is, the puzzle of negative existential claims like:

(5) Santa Claus does not exist.

According to the pretense approach, although claims like (5) can be genuinely true, they do not saddle speakers with paradoxical ontological commitments to nonexistent entities. This is because we should understand existence-talk in terms of a pretense. However, even though (5) functions in virtue of a pretense, a speaker could still use it to make a serious assertion about the world because of the special kind of pretense it involves.

The kind of pretense (5) involves is most familiar from children's games of make-believe. The interesting aspect of make-believe is that it is a kind of pretense in which some of what is *to be pretended* by participants in the game—some of what is *fictionally true* or *fictional*—depends on the state of the world outside of the game. Games of make-believe involve principles of generation, rules that determine the way actual circumstances (in particular, those pertaining to the features of the *props* the game employs) combine with the game's stipulated pretenses to determine what else is to be pretended (or, as I will say, what further pretenses are *prescribed*).[21] Within the context of a game of make-believe, then, we must distinguish between two kinds of prescribed pretenses: those that are the stipulative ground of the game—what is *expressly made-believe*—and those that are *generated from reality*.[22]

Because make-believe involves pretenses whose fictional truth depends systematically on real-world conditions, its use in the pretense approach results in a non-error-theoretic version of fictionalism. In using a pretense-employing utterance to make an assertion, one puts forward the pretenses the utterance displays as appropriate or prescribed. The principles of generation governing the game of make-believe the utterance is from determine that those pretenses are appropriate only under certain real-world conditions. Putting the utterance forward assertorically thus expresses a serious commitment to the obtaining of the required real-world conditions. A pretense-employing way of talking is therefore a way of making serious assertions *indirectly*, that is, of engaging in "indirectly serious discourse".[23] So, far from undermining any serious purposes that a way of talking serves, an appeal to make-believe can allow for and actually explain them if taking the talk at face value is problematic.

Consider existence-talk again. We can resolve puzzles about negative existentials by explaining existence-talk in terms of a game of make-believe that stipulates pretending that every putative referring expression has a bearer, and that uses of 'exists' attribute a discriminating property. We explain the serious purposes of existence-talk in terms of principles of generation making it fictionally true that a (pretend) referent has the (pretend) property of existence iff the referring expression as employed really refers to something, and fictionally true that a (pretend) referent does not have this (pretend) property iff the referring expression as employed does not refer to anything. Because of the dependency this establishes, an utterance like (5) makes a serious and genuinely true claim about how the world actually is, even though its doing so involves pretense. What (5) seriously asserts is that attempts to refer of the kind it displays will all be unsuccessful, something we know is correct.[24] Since pretense-employing utterances are not automatically false but in fact can be true, pretense-theoretic accounts are not automatically error theories. This placates the initial worry that a pretense-based account of truth-talk is incoherent.[25]

One of the reasons the pretense approach offers the best means of formulating a deflationary account of truth-talk is that it makes the most sense of deflationism's central commitment to the fundamentality of the instances of (ES). The pretense approach also fits particularly well with the general deflationary strategy for dealing with truth-talk's propensity for paradox. I elaborate on these points in the discussion below. Another point favoring a pretense-based formulation of deflationism is the fact that it accounts for some important aspects of truth-talk in a more satisfactory way than the current formulations offered by Paul Horwich, Hartry Field, and Robert Brandom. Of particular importance on this front is what some philosophers call "the generalization problem". This problem concerns the task of accounting for the role that truth-talk plays in generalizing on embedded sentence positions, as in the move from:

(6) If the Pope asserts that crabapples are edible, then crabapples are edible

to:

(7) Everything the Pope asserts is true.

I will explain the advantages a pretense-based account of truth-talk offers over the current formulations of deflationism with respect to the generalization problem (and a few other aspects of truth-talk) after presenting the make-believe behind truth-talk.

Extrinsic and Intrinsic Pretense

Before turning to the details of the game of make-believe behind truth-talk, it is important to explain the particular way that pretense figures in these utterances. The reason for this is twofold. First, it reveals an interesting affinity between deflationism and the pretense approach, supporting the idea that the latter offers the best way of formulating the former. Second, it makes clear why a modified charge of error-theoretic incoherence does not apply. The latter is an issue because even though the basic details of the pretense approach explain how uses of pretense-employing utterances can put forward genuinely true statements, there is still the worry that this approach has to assume that all such utterances are *literally* false. This would be problematic for a pretense-based account of truth-talk since it would require an antecedent notion of truth-conditions to apply to the instances of truth-talk taken literally (i.e., before the operation of any pretense). There is even the possibility that this would make the view paradoxical for reasons similar to those mentioned above.

We can accomplish these two tasks by drawing a distinction between two different ways that an utterance can invoke pretense. The basic difference has to do with whether pretense attaches to the utterance "from the outside", or whether pretense is integral to the utterance saying anything at all. In the first case, pretense is *extrinsic* to the utterance; in the second case, it is *intrinsic* to the utterance. Perhaps the most concise way of marking the difference is to say that a basic case of extrinsic pretense involves pretending of the proposition an utterance expresses, when we take it at face value, that it is true, while a case of intrinsic pretense also involves pretending of an utterance *that it expresses a proposition at all* when we take it at face value, in addition to pretending that this (pretended) proposition is true. However, I want to avoid explaining this distinction in terms of truth-talk (and proposition-talk) in order to skirt circularity worries. So I need a different account. A possible worry here is that any such account is just another statement of the proposition-based account, but my contention is that this is not the only way to interpret it. One could just as well reverse this order of explanation.

In the basic cases of extrinsic pretense (*first-order* extrinsic pretense),[26] we could take the utterance made literally. What I mean by this is that what a face-value or "straight" reading of the utterance gives is something that we could also, in some circumstances, take seriously—in the case of an assertoric utterance, as a genuine, direct statement about the actual world. Most metaphors of the form 'A is B' involve extrinsic pretense. Consider:

(8) Governor Arnold Schwarzenegger is the headliner of a bad lounge act.

One could take this sentence to make a serious statement about the world directly, that is, one could take it at face value. Taking or offering (8) metaphorically involves placing the face-value reading of the utterance in the context of a pretense. Specifically, (8) invokes a pretense consisting of a game of make-believe that prescribes pretending someone is the headliner of a bad lounge act whenever that person actually possesses certain features, features that really have nothing to do with headlining a lounge act.[27] The utterance's non-literal content, the serious claim it makes indirectly (namely, that Schwarzenegger has the pretense-prescribing features), depends on an antecedent literal content that (1) attaches to the whole utterance, and (2) depends compositionally on the literal contents of its parts in the usual way.

Intrinsic pretense is really what is important for my purposes here because that is what truth-talk involves. In cases of intrinsic pretense, the pretend statement an utterance makes is *not* something someone could offer as a serious statement in any actual circumstances. What a face-value reading of the utterance gives is something that could only be a pretend statement. We pretend that the utterance is meaningful when we take it at face value (i.e., without the operation of some pretense), but the only content there is to associate with it is the content the utterance puts forward indirectly in virtue of its role in the pretense. Typically the reason an utterance invokes pretense intrinsically is because there is no way to take some part of it seriously at face value. In other words, an utterance's lack of literal content as a whole usually results from the failure of at least one of its components to have any literal content.

Examples of intrinsically pretense-invoking utterances of this sort include cases employing fictional names or kind terms, as in:

(9) Quidditch is more about the Golden Snitch than the Quaffle or the Bludgers.[28]

The only content the terms 'Quidditch', 'Golden Snitch', 'Quaffle', and 'Bludgers' possess is that which the make-believe generated by J. K. Rowling's *Harry Potter* books gives to them.[29] Independent of that make-believe, these terms have no content to contribute to the content of (9) as a whole. Thus, pretense is integral to the utterance making any statement at all. Similar points hold for cases involving (restricted) quantification over domains of fictional objects, as one might interpret:

(10) All of Harry Potter's relatives are mean.[30]

We can find less literature-dependent cases in certain idiomatic expressions involving layers of pretense. For example, an utterance like:

(11) The puppy's gaze tugged at my heart strings

appears to invoke pretense intrinsically because not noly does it require pretending that gazes can tug on things (arguably an extrinsic pretense), but it is only in the context of a further pretense that there is anything for the puppy's gaze to tug. In fact, it is only in virtue of this pretense that the expression 'heart strings' has any sense. So there is no content we can assign to (11) without some appeal to pretense because at least one of its component expressions has no literal content to contribute to the whole.

We can find a type of component literal-content failure more relevant for present purposes in instances of *anthimeria*.[31] This figure of speech involves using a term that standardly functions as one part of speech as a different part of speech. For example, we might use a name as a verb, as in:

(12) Clinton nearly nixoned his presidency,

or we might use an adjective as a noun, as in:

(13) Gödel had a lot of smarts.[32]

The result is a neologism of sorts, but one that arises out of a kind of "word-play" derivative of the actual function and meaning of an existing term, rather than from explicit stipulation of a completely new word.

In cases of anthimeria, pretense enters at the level of functioning. 'Nixon' is a proper name and does not serve to specify an activity in any actual circumstances. Similarly, there are no actual circumstances in which 'smart' functions as a referential term.[33] In using these terms as in (12) and (13) we pretend that they function in these new ways. The pretense is most visible in the "coining" of a case of anthimeria, when one simply uses a term *as if* it already functions in the relevant novel way. Because prior to an invocation of this sort of pretense the expressions 'nixon' and 'smarts' do not really function as they appear to in (12) and (13), in these utterances these terms make no contribution to a literal content for the whole. Thus, we cannot take (12) and (13) seriously at face value, i.e., literally. However, this does not impede our ability to understand them. Interpreting (12) and (13) (and cases of anthimeria generally) does rely on the contents their components have in their standard uses, and these contents happen to be literal contents. But what is important here is the availability of contents provided by standard uses, not that they be literal contents.

According to a pretense-based account, truth-talk is like anthimeria in that it is just a pretense that the central expression it employs, 'is true', functions as it appears to function. Truth-talk is unlike anthimeria in that it is the *standard* use of 'is true' that involves pretense; pretense does not enter the picture only when an utterance forces this expression into some non-standard use. Truth-talk is thus a way of talking that invokes pretense intrinsically without depending on any literal content attaching to certain components of its instances. To understand this way of involving pretense better, it helps to consider a way of talking that exemplifies it more clearly: existence-talk.

The predicate-term 'exists' never has any pretense-independent content as any part of speech; the only content there is to associate with this expression is the content it gets from its role in a game of make-believe. Support for this thesis stems from the fact that the best understanding of 'exists' takes its standard use to invoke pretense in its very logico-linguistic functioning. Although claims like:

(5)   Santa Claus does not exist
(14) Christopher Robin exists

appear on the surface to perform the (internal) speech act of predication—to pick out objects with singular terms and to characterize or describe those objects (as lacking a property of existence in the first case and as having it in the second)—existence-talk does not really function in this way. We can see the not-fully-predicative nature of 'exists' from the absence of any informative analysis of its applicability conditions[34] of the form:

(E) $(\forall x)$ (x satisfies 'exists' iff x is F).

Given that for any object to be in the domain of a quantifier it must *be* (i.e., for those of us who reject Meinongian grades of being, it must exist), all one can and all one needs to give to account for the applicability of 'exists' is the formula:

(E′) $(\forall x)$ (x satisfies 'exists').[35]

This "analysis" reveals that the applicability conditions of 'exists' do not place conditions on the referents of the terms the instances of existence-talk employ. Although 'exists' functions *logically* as a predicate in existence-talk, the nature of its applicability conditions indicates that we should not take it to function as a genuine predicate in the full speech-act or logico-linguistic sense of serving to characterize or describe objects.[36] In order to characterize or describe objects, an expression must require something of objects that satisfy it.[37] Depending on the nature of the conditions it requires, the expression is either an analyzable predicate or a primitive predicate. There being no informative analysis of form (E) shows that 'exists' is not an analyzable predicate. So, if it is a predicate it is a primitive one. Primitive predicates still place conditions on the objects that satisfy them, so the basic form of their applicability conditions is:

(P) $(\forall x)$(x satisfies 'F' iff x is F).

The availability of an "analysis" of form (E′) where there is no analysans thus shows that 'exists' is not a primitive predicate. Of course, the substitution of 'exists' for both instances of 'F' in (P) yields a truth, but unlike any primitive predicate, for 'exists' this is not the final account of its applicability conditions since (E′) is available. Because 'exists' is neither an analyzable predicate nor a primitive predicate, it is not really a predicate (in the full, logico-linguistic sense of predication).

According to this line of thought, although we can use existence-talk to make true assertions about the real world, 'exists' does not function directly to offer genuine descriptions of any objects. But this is exactly what utterances employing this expression appear to do. So, existence-talk makes serious assertions indirectly by appearing to perform a logico-linguistic function it does not actually perform. Since there is no other role we could consider the standard function of 'exists,' we should see this way of talking as invoking pretense intrinsically, in a way that does not require associating any literal content with its central expression.

We can apply a similar line of reasoning to truth-talk. In the previous section, I claimed that certain aspects of truth-talk motivate a deflationary account. From there it is then a short step to a pretense-based account. The reasons just given for thinking that existence-talk involves intrinsic pretense parallel what deflationism says about truth-talk. Deflationary views consider the instances of the equivalence schema:

(ES)   It is true that p iff p (= That p is true iff p)

to be fundamental, that is, they claim that there is no deeper explanation for why these equivalences hold. This allows these views to deal with truth-talk's unusual features more effectively. But this attitude toward these equivalences also entails believing that, at least in the basic instances of truth-talk (those that figure in the instances of (ES)), the applicability conditions of the expression 'is true' place no conditions on any objects picked out by the terms these utterances employ, that is, by the 'that'-clauses. This suggests that 'is true' also does not really function predicatively in the full logico-linguistic sense.

The case of 'is true' differs from that of 'exists' in that (E′) involves no analysans while the instances of (ES) do.[38] However, the analyses are all the same in that none of them makes any reference on the right-hand side to any putative object the left-hand side offers as a satisfier of the supposed predicate. So in none of them do the applicability conditions involve placing conditions on the putative satisfiers. Deflationism thus involves viewing truth-talk as not fully predicative. Prosentential theorists like Brandom explicitly endorse a thesis even stronger than this, claiming that truth-talk is not even logically predicative.[39] But this seems too strong; 'is true' functions like a predicate in inference.[40] Moreover, the instances of truth-talk look exactly like cases of full-blown predication, and prosententialists offer no substantive account of why they take this form. We can resolve the apparent conflict between truth-talk's appearances and the denial that it is really predicative by recognizing the instances of truth-talk to invoke pretense at the level of logico-linguistic functioning. So an account of truth-talk in terms of intrinsic pretense fits especially well with the central commitment that gives deflationism its advantage in dealing with truth-talk's unusual features.

Identifying the pretense the instances of truth-talk involve specifically as intrinsic pretense also shows how a pretense-based account of truth-talk avoids the modified error-theoretic interpretation. There is a sense in which the instances of truth-talk are misleading on my account. Since the basic functioning of the expression 'is true' is not really predicative, it is not possible to make serious claims of the sort that:

(1′) That crabapples are edible is true

appears to make on the surface. So it is never correct to say that (1′) is true when we take it literally. But my account is not an error theory in any problematic sense because it is also never correct to say that (1′) is false when we take it literally, or even that (1′) is not true when we take it literally. The point is that we cannot really take (1′) literally, that is, we cannot assign it an interpretation on a face-value (which is not to say standard) reading. Truth-talk never puts forward genuine claims about the world *directly*, without the operation of any pretense. (1′) has *no* literal (i.e., pretense-independent) content at all because the standard use of 'is true' invokes pretense intrinsically. The only content regarding the real world we can associate with (1′) is the serious content it puts forward indirectly, in virtue of its role in a game of make-believe.

The Make-Believe behind Truth-Talk

The grounding, stipulated pretenses the game of make-believe behind truth-talk involves are as one might expect. The central component is a pretense that in a truth-attribution the expression 'is true' serves to describe referents of the term expressions it gets combined with by attributing to them a special property called "truth". So in the pretense, truth-talk is predicative in the full logico-linguistic sense. There is a definitional connection (in the pretense) between *being true* and *having the property of truth*.[41]

The game also stipulates pretending that the fundamental bearers of the property of truth (and that of falsity) are objects of a special sort called "propositions". This provides the best account of our linguistic and inferential practices. For example, we conclude that Dex believes something true when told that he believes what Corey said, that what she said is that crabapples are edible, and that it is true that crabapples are edible. The best way to understand talk of what people believe, assert, etc. is as talk ostensibly about propositions.[42] We use 'that'-clauses to specify what people believe, assert, etc., so we should take them to pick out propositions. 'That'-clauses are also the term expressions used in the basic instances of truth-talk, i.e., claims like:

(1) It is true that crabapples are edible.

Thus, we should understand the basic instances of truth-talk as ostensibly describing propositions. This means it should be part of the make-believe that propositions are the fundamental bearers of truth.

The basic instances of truth-talk appear to employ the expression 'is true' to attribute a property to propositions denoted in a special way by 'that'-clauses. We can consider this denoting special because 'that'-clauses *display* the propositions they pick out; they denote propositions *transparently*. Call the segment of truth-talk comprising (1) and its ilk "transparent propositional truth-talk". The particular form of claims like (1) involves an added compli- cation in that strictly speaking they combine 'is true' with the pronoun 'it'. This is unproblematic in these cases, however, since the pretense has it that the pronoun inherits its referent anaphorically from the relevant 'that' -clause.[43] We can eliminate this distracting complication by replacing (1) with its trivial syntactic variant:

(1′) That crabapples are edible is true.

On the surface, (1′) appears to involve the attribution of a property (truth) to a proposition denoted by a 'that'-clause. According to the present view, these appearances are part of a game of make-believe that involves parameters like those just described.

We can capture the key parameters of the make-believe behind truth-talk more precisely with the following schematic principles:

(PG1) (Πp)(The pretenses displayed in an utterance of 'The proposition that p has the property of truth' are prescribed (i.e., are part of what is to be pretended) iff p).

(PG2) (Πp)(The pretenses displayed in an utterance of 'The proposition that p has the property of falsity' are prescribed (i.e., are part of what is to be pretended) iff $\sim p$).

Because they use the universal substitutional quantifier 'Π' (understood as a device for encoding potentially infinite conjunctions), (PG1) and (PG2) encode collections of individual rules that result from filling in the schematic variable 'p' with declarative sentences from the substitution class associated with the quantifier. These individual rules are the game's principles of generation; they anchor the make-believe to reality by making some of what is to be pretended in the context of this game depend on how the world is. These principles extend the pretenses belonging to the game beyond the stipulated ones offered so far by making the appropriateness of certain additional pretenses follow from game-independent, real-world conditions.

For simplicity of expression, I will refer to (PG1) and (PG2) themselves as the principles of generation for the make-believe behind truth-talk. This will not affect any of the points I make here. The pretenses that these principles govern are those displayed in the instances of :

(15) The proposition that p has the property of truth.

(16) The proposition that p has the property of falsity.

(in which an English sentence goes in for 'p').[44] These utterances invoke pretense intrinsically by employing linguistic components (e.g., 'the property of truth') that are entirely creatures of the pretense. The basic principles of the make-believe give these linguistic components uses in the game and make utterances of the instances of (15) and (16) count as assertions in that context (i.e., make them at least *pretend* assertions). But these utterances have no life outside of the make-believe except that given to them *by* the make-believe. Principles (PG1) and (PG2) are what do this; they turn pretend assertion involving these utterances, which otherwise would have no serious application, into a way of making (indirectly) serious assertions that are not just about which pretenses the game prescribes.[45]

(PG1) and (PG2) thus determine precisely what serious assertions speakers make with the instances of (15) and (16). In making a pretend assertion with an utterance of either sort, e.g.:

(17) The proposition that crabapples are edible has the property of truth.

(18) The proposition that crabapples are edible has the property of falsity.

a speaker puts forward the intrinsic pretenses the utterance displays as appropriate or prescribed. Principles (PG1) and (PG2) stipulate that these pretenses actually have this status only under particular conditions. Part of what making a pretend assertion with (17) or (18) does, then, is express a serious commitment to the obtaining of the particular real-world conditions specified as necessary and sufficient by the relevant instance of (PG1) or (PG2). Given how these principles assign prescriptive conditions to the pretenses these utterances display, the serious assertion an utterance of (17) makes is that crabapples are edible, and the serious assertion an utterance of (18) makes is that crabapples are not edible.

A game of make-believe including (PG1) and (PG2) serves to institute a particular (indirect) semantic path for certain utterances. An instance of, say, (PG1) relates an assertion of the truth-attribution it mentions (and thus governs) to an assertion of the claim that appears on the right-hand side of the equivalence, by instituting something like the content-inheritance relation that prosententialists emphasize. With respect to serious content, the two claims are content equivalent. But the truth-attribution is not thereby content equivalent to the claim that the pretenses the truth-attribution displays are prescribed or appropriate, that is, to an assertion of what appears on the left-hand side of that instance of (PG1). The instances of (PG1) and (PG2) are material equivalences, not definitions. (PG1) makes appropriateness claims of the form schematized on its left-hand side materially equivalent in each case to an assertion of what goes in for 'p'. A truth-attribution is thus also materially equivalent to the relevant appropriateness claim, since the former is content-equivalent (with respect to serious content) to what goes in for 'p' in forming the relevant instance of (PG1). An appropriateness claim of the form that appears in an instance of (PG1) states very general correctness conditions for a (pretend-)assertion of the mentioned truth-attribution. Because the equivalence links the conditions said to obtain (that certain pretenses are appropriate or prescribed) to certain real-world conditions, these correctness conditions play a role in determining the (serious) content of the truth-attribution. However, that is the extent of the semantic relation between the truth-claim and the appropriateness claim.

One aspect of principles (PG1) and (PG2) that calls for some additional comment is a consequence of their use of the "non-standard" logical devices of substitutional quantification and sentence variables. Being basically conjunctions of schema instances, (PG1) and (PG2) do not offer general, unified conditions for the appropriateness of the pretenses the instances of (15) and (16) display. Instead, the individual instances of (PG1) and (PG2) each stipulate distinct conditions for the prescription of the pretenses in the relevant individual instances of (15) and (16). On the pretense-based account, the issue of what there is to say about the putative referents of the instances of '(the proposition) that p' being true becomes the issue of when the pretenses displayed in the instances of (15) are prescribed. According to (PG1), in each case there is nothing more to say about this than what an assertion of the sentence that goes in for 'p' says by itself.

Because a game of make-believe including (PG1) institutes an indirect semantic path for truth-attributions of form (15), giving each of them the same serious content as an assertion of the sentence that goes in for 'p' by itself, it thereby gives us all the instances of the schema:

(ES*) The proposition that p has the property of truth iff p.

Some of the other parameters of the make-believe discussed at the beginning of this section identify the pretenses that the corresponding instances of (15) display with those displayed by the instances of:

(19) The proposition that p is true.

So we can substitute (19) for (15) on the left-hand side of (es*). Dropping the expression 'the proposition' as superfluous, this yeilds all the instances of:

(es) That p is true iff p.

A pretense-based account of truth-talk including principle (PG1) as a principles of generation therefore satisfies the basic criterion of adequacy any account of truth-talk must satisfy, namely, that it generate all the instances of (es). The account also satisfies the central commitment of deflationism because the instances of (es) are fundamental on the pretense-based account of truth-talk, in the sense that they follow directly from the talk's logico-linguistic functioning. The explanation of this functioning essentially involves reference to a game of make-believe that includes a pretense that the instances of truth-talk attribute a property, but because this is just a pretense explaining how the talk works, it does not amount to a deeper explanation of these equivalences.

Another aspect of principles (PG1) and (PG2) that needs some discussion concerns the significance of the last appearance of the sentence variable 'p' in them. This variable functions on the right-hand side of each schema as a placeholder for sentences. These sentences specify real-world conditions prescribing the pretenses displayed in the sentences mentioned on the left-hand sides of the schema instances. It might seem, therefore, that only pretense-free sentences can go in for this variable, or that we must take any sentence going in for it seriously at face value. This is not the case. Equally viable substituends include sentences that themselves employ either extrinsic or intrinsic pretense, for instance, metaphors or (more importantly here) truth-attributions. One reason this is important is that an account of truth-talk must accommodate the indefinite iterability of truth-attribution. If it is true that snow is white, then it is true that it is true that snow is white. This consequent is itself true as well, and so on. Thus, the substitution class for the quantifier in (PG1) has to include truth-attributions, so the variable must admit pretense-employing utterances as well.

A second reason for allowing instances of truth-talk to fill in the variable on the right-hand side of (PG1) is that this is necessary if the pretense-based account is to provide a diagnosis of the Liar paradox. I explained above how substituting a Liar sentence like :

(L)   The proposition expressed by the sentence labeled '(L)' is not true.

in for 'p' in (ES) reveals an inconsistency in truth-talk. But on a pretense-based account this inconsistency is not worrisome; the account contains it appropriately. To begin with, truth-talk's inconsistency occurs entirely within the bounds of the pretense aspect of the talk. Because (L), like all truth-talk, invokes pretense intrinsically, the only way it might say something about the real world outside of the pretense is indirectly, by inheriting serious content from somewhere else (in part via the principles of generation of the make-believe). However, the utterance that (L) looks to for serious content happens to be one that invokes pretense intrinsically, namely (L) itself. Since this situation iterates indefinitely, there is never any serious content that attaches to (L). This lack of serious foundation can be thought of as a translation into the pretense framework of the informal notion of ungroundedness.[46] Call utterances without a serious foundation 'purely pretend' claims.[47] (L) and Liar sentences generally are all purely pretend claims. Because it is only in purely pretend claims that truth-talk exhibits its inconsistency, the bounds of the pretense completely contain it. No attribution of truth in itself generates an inconsistent claim about reality. While Liar sentences contain an ineliminable inconsistency, they do not say anything inconsistent about reality because the principles of generation governing truth-talk do not connect these claims with any content regarding states of affairs outside of the game. (L) makes no inconsistent claim about the real world; no serious inconsistency results.

We can illuminate the second stage of containment for truth-talk's inconsistency by comparing the situation with the Liar paradox to inconsistencies holding in works of fiction. There are two directions we can take this comparison. The first allows that in the context of the make-believe, Liar sentences generate contradictions. The situation is like that in a work of fiction that invites its audience to acknowledge a contradiction explicitly. A possible example of this sort of case is the lithograph, *Waterfall*, by M. C. Escher. We acknowledge in the make-believe the drawing invokes that the water is running up hill and not running up hill, and then we enjoy the sensation of paradox that ensues.[48] On this approach to the Liar, given (L) and (ES) we can derive a conjunction of the form 'p & $\sim p$', namely:

(20)   The proposition expressed by the sentence labeled '(L)' is true and the proposition expressed by the sentence labeled '(L)' is not true.

The conjuncts in (20) are both purely pretend claims, so it is only within the bounds of a game of make-believe that there is a contradiction. As in the case of the Escher drawing, we take the contradiction to be part of what the make-believe prescribes pretending, but we do not take it to entail that everything is to be pretended in the make-believe. The logic of the fiction is *paraconsistent*, that is, in it not all contradictions entail everything.[49] Similarly, we might take the logic of truth-talk to be paraconsistent, in which case (20) would not entail everything, not even just within the make-believe behind truth-talk. In fact, it might entail nothing further.

An alternative direction to take the comparison with inconsistencies in works of fiction is to disallow the explicit formation of the contradiction (20) in the first place. The inconsistency in truth-talk would remain in the form of a biconditional, but nothing further would follow from it. This is similar to how we treat accidental inconsistencies in works of fiction. For example, the Holmes stories as a whole are inconsistent about the location of Watson's sole war wound. The stories do not, however, invite readers to conclude that this wound is in his leg and not in his leg. If we treat the Liar paradox like an accidental inconsistency, (20) would not be a permissible consequence. Liar-like inconsistency would be something to note and avoid, but like the inconsistency about Watson's wound, it would be nothing to worry about since it would not undermine or trivialize the rest of the fiction by entailing everything in that context. Whether this amounts to another type specifically of paraconsistent logic, it is at least some sort of (non-adjunctive) non-classical logic. In any case, this approach results in the same sort of further containment of truth-talk's inconsistency as the previous one.

In both of these approaches to the Liar paradox, fully containing the inconsistency involves giving up classical logic. However, one of the advantages of formulating deflationism in terms of pretense is that this motivates an appealing localization of the deviation from classical logic. As far as "everyday" talk is concerned, it is as if logic is classical. Paraconsistency manifests itself only in truth-talk (and perhaps certain other related ways of talking) because the ineliminable inconsistencies arise only within this fragment of discourse and furthermore only within the bounds of the make-believe behind the talk. Dealing with the Liar paradox by claiming that logic is paraconsistent is just an instance of a general approach we already take to inconsistencies in fiction, so the same sort of localization occurs. Thus, the strategy of diagnosing and containing truth-talk's inconsistency in terms of paraconsistent logic fits particularly well with a pretense-based formulation of deflationism. Other formulations of deflationism can make this move in trying to deal with the Liar, but they offer less motivation for this strategy and any localization.

Still, since other formulations of deflationism can adopt a paraconsistent logic, this strategy does not clearly favor a pretense-based formulation. However, something that does is the way that a pretense-based account of truth-talk deals with the generalization problem. Explaining this involves extending the make-believe introduced above so that it also covers quantificational instances of truth-talk, for example, claims like:

(7)　Everything the Pope asserts is true

(21)　Something Dex asserted is true.

It is in claims of these sorts, especially those like (7), that truth-talk plays its most important role. Universal claims like (7) allow us to express generalizations not about truth that we could not otherwise express—they allow us to generalize on the embedded sentences in a claim like:

(6)　If the Pope asserts that crabapples are edible, then crabapples are edible.

From the deflationary perspective, fulfilling this function is truth-talk's central purpose.

In order for the pretense-based account to cover claims of these forms, we must add additional principles of generation to the game of make-believe considered so far. The generalization (7) is (a contraction of) an instance of the general form:

(22)　$(\forall x)(Fx \rightarrow x$ is true$)$

in which 'F' symbolizes 'is asserted by the Pope'. Claims of form (22) involve pretenses governed by the principle for universally quantified truth-talk:

(UQ)　The pretenses displayed in an utterance of the form '$(\forall x)(Fx \rightarrow x$ is true$)$' are prescribed iff (Πp)(the pretenses displayed in an utterance of the form '$(\exists x)(Fx \ \& \ x =$ the proposition that $p)$' are prescribed $\rightarrow p$).[50]

Existentially quantified truth-attributions like (21) have the general form:

(23)　$(\exists x)(Fx \ \& \ x$ is true$)$.

(21) is an instance of (23) in which 'F' symbolizes 'is asserted by Dex'. Claims of form (23) involve pretenses governed by the principle for existentially quantified truth-talk:

(EQ) The pretenses displayed in an utterance of the form '$(\exists x)(Fx \ \& \ x$ is true)' are prescribed iff (Σp)(the pretenses displayed in an utterance of the form '$(\exists x)(Fx \ \& \ x =$ the proposition that $p)$' are prescribed & p).[51]

Extending the make-believe behind truth-talk with these principles requires also taking utterances of the general form:

(24) $(\exists x)(Fx \ \& \ x =$ the proposition that $p)$

as pretense-involving. The full story about quantificational truth-talk thus also includes a pretense-based account of *proposition-talk*. The need for such an account in the present context is hardly surprising, given of the tight connection between the notions of truth and proposition. However, a pretense-based account of proposition-talk is not an *ad hoc* demand that the present account of truth-talk requires just for consistency. There are independent reasons for thinking that the best explanation of our talk putatively about propositions (e.g., in attitude ascriptions) is in terms of semantic pretense.[52] My preference is for a fairly radical version of this sort of account, one that specifies the possession of certain use-theoretic features like inferential or conceptual role as the real-world conditions prescribing a pretense that something (e.g., an utterance) is related (in some way) to some proposition (pretend-)denoted by a 'that'-clause.[53] Essentially what this amounts to is giving a non-truth-theoretic account of content (or better, of *attributions* of content, i.e., "meaning-talk") in which an appeal to pretense explains both how we manage to talk about the use-features in question with utterances that seem unsuited to the task and the utility of doing so. Given that any deflationary account of truth-talk must rely on and eventually produce a non-truth-theoretic account of meaning, this is not a burden peculiar to my formulation of deflationism.

The main advantage the pretense-based account of truth-talk offers over other formulations of deflationism is its ability to account for truth-talk's special generalizing role without attributing to it any non-standard logical functioning involving devices like substitutional quantification and sentence variables. Of course, in stating the principles of generation that govern truth-talk, including those governing quantificational instances, even I have had to *use* substitutional quantification and sentence variables to express the real-world conditions prescribing the pretenses truth-attributions invoke. But on my view this is simply due to the fact that the only way to express these conditions in a natural language is *indirectly*, with pretense-employing utterances of the very sort that these principles explain. Truth-talk functions as a surrogate for these non-standard logical devices, by deploying standard logical devices, such as predication and objectual quantification, in the context of a particular pretense. The non-standard devices in question are not actually at work in the talk's logical functioning. The pretense-based account thus avoids a serious problem that confronts some of the current formulations of deflationism.

The problem threatening these other views stems from the fact that they take the complicated sorts of logical devices mentioned above to be part of truth-talk's actual logical functioning. This does give these formulations of deflationism at least something approximating an account of how the talk performs its definitive generalizing function, but in the end it undermines their attempts to explain truth-talk's role here. A fairly extreme version of this approach involves interpreting the main quantifiers in utterances like (7) substitutionally. This is the strategy Brandom's prosentential account of truth-talk employs. Understanding (7) as a contraction of:

(25) Everything (one can assert) is such that if the Pope asserts it, then it is true.

Brandom's view takes 'it is true' as it functions in (25) to be something like an "open" prosentence, each instance of which depends anaphorically on what the quantifier supplies to fill in the variable 'it' in forming that instance.[54] Since anaphora is a relation between linguistic items, the quantifier does not supply things that any part of (25) *talks about*; both occurrences of 'it' serve as substitution variables rather than object variables. An account of the quantifier as functioning to pick out a class of things (linguistic items serving as the anaphoric antecedents of a variable prosentence) to which the tokens of the variable connect "referentially" (by the relation of *anaphoric reference*)[55] gives utterances like (7) a structure that is at least superficially similar to that of ordinary generalizations. *Prima facie*, then, Brandom's view provides truth-talk with a role that seems to account for the way the talk enables us to generalize on the embedded sentences in statements like:

(6) If the Pope asserts that crabapples are edible, then crabapples are edible.

This sort of appeal to substitutional quantification is also available to a "Fieldian" disquotational account of truth-talk as a strategy for explaining the talk's special generalizing function. The thought here is that in generalizing on (6), an instance of truth-talk like (7) provides all the instances of the schema:

(26) If the Pope asserts that p, then p.

We can formulate a kind of "generalized" version of this schema by prefixing (26) with a universal substitutional quantifier as in:

(27) (Πp)(the Pope asserts that $p \to p$).

The problem is that even if (27) counts as a generalization of (6), there is no way to express a claim of this form informally in a natural language (at least directly) because there are no (atomic) expressions playing the role of schematic sentence variables. This is where truth-talk comes in, as a means of expressing something equivalent to (27) in natural language.

According to Field's account, we can axiomatize the functioning of truth-talk with a generalized version of the equivalence schema like:

(GES) (Πp)(that p is true iff p).[56]

The availability of this formula allows us to derive from (27) an equivalent claim that one might hold is expressible in a natural language, namely:

(28) (Πp)(the Pope asserts that $p \to$ that p is true).

The reason we might claim that (28) is expressible informally is that here the variable 'p' occurs only in the nominalizing context of a that-clause. This means that (28) uses the variable only as part of a variable *term*-expression, 'that p.' Because 'that p' is a variable nominal term, we can translate it (and so cover every use of 'p' in (28)) into natural language as a pronoun, as in the "open" sentence:

(29) If the Pope asserts it, then it is true.[57]

Because in the context of Field's view the things the instances of 'that p' pick out in the instances of (28) are exactly what make up the substitution class of its substitutional quantifier (computationally typed tokens of the sentences of the speaker's idiolect), there is a sense in which the quantifier "supplies" all the different things that "fill in" the occurrences of 'it' in (29) when we "bind" the open sentence with the quantifier.[58] This is the motivation for claiming that we can express (28) informally with a universally quantified claim like:

(7) Everything the Pope asserts is true.

Truth-talk's generalizing role lets us use claims like (7) to express fertile generalizations that impact on matters not involving truth but that we cannot formulate except by employing truth-talk.[59] By interpreting the initial quantifiers in claims like (7) substitutionally, Brandom's prosentential view and a "Fieldian" disquotationalism would provide truth-talk with a role that seems *prima facie* to account for the desired generalizing from claims like (6).[60] However, beyond just the implausibility of attributing this more complicated logical functioning to the quantificational expressions of ordinary language, the problem with this appeal to substitutional quantification, as Anil Gupta has pointed out, is that there is a logical gap between what a substitutionally quantified schema provides (a conjunction of the instances of the schema) and a genuine generalization.[61] This casts serious doubt on the adequacy of taking the substitutional quantifier approach to explain truth-talk's generalizing role. Because the pretense-based account explains truth-talk's generalizing role without interpreting the quantifiers in general truth-attributions substitutionally, it avoids Gupta's objection. This gives the account a clear advantage over Brandom's view since he has to give quantifiers truth-talk employs a substitutional interpretation.[62] The advantage the pretense-based account has over Field's view requires further consideration, however, since there is an alternative way the latter can read universally quantified claims like (7), one that provides Field with a different, less overtly problematic approach to the generalization problem.[63]

This alternative understanding of Field's view also avoids treating the quantifiers in instances of quantificational truth-talk substitutionally. However, even on this different approach, Field's view does not take the logical form of a claim like (7) to be (22). Instead, Field understands it as something like:

(30) $(\forall x)[Fx \rightarrow (x = \text{that } p \rightarrow \text{that } p \text{ is true})]$.[64]

We can factor in the operation of 'is true' more completely by taking into account Field's understanding of (the instances of) the equivalence schema:

(ES) That p is true iff p.

Field takes (ES) to axiomatize a cognitive equivalence amounting to the substitutability in most contexts (except inside quotation marks and intentional attitude constructions) of what appears on either side of an instance of (ES) for what appears on the other.[65] Thus, on his view, a claim of form (30) is cognitively equivalent to one of the form:

(31) $(\forall x)[Fx \rightarrow (x = \text{that } p \rightarrow p)]$.

So, an instance of truth-talk like (7) is a way of making a claim of form (31)—the sort of fertile generalization on a claim like (6) that we are after.

This approach to quantificational truth-talk differs from the previous "Fieldian" approach in two ways. First, the main quantifier in (31) is objectual, so this approach avoids the problematic logical gap Gupta has identified. Second, this approach drops substitutional quantification altogether (both here and in treating (ES) itself as "general" instead of appealing to (GES)) in favor of the weaker approach that employs just schemata involving sentence variables like 'p' (that can appear inside and outside quotation mark devices, including 'that'-clauses), subject to certain rules of inference.[66] Nevertheless, in spite of these improvements, I maintain that the pretense-based account still offers certain advantages over Field's view. On his view, truth-talk itself still involves non-standard logical devices (schematic sentence variables) in its actual logical functioning. One merit of the pretense-based account is that it avoids postulating logical devices of this sort at work in natural language, even to this lesser degree.

There is a sense in which the pretense-based view and Field's view agree on the logical form of what a general truth-attribution says. After all, given how (UG) identifies the real-world conditions prescribing the pretenses that claims like (7) display, the logical form of the serious assertions made indirectly by such claims is fairly similar to what Field attributes directly to truth-talk itself. So the two approaches coincide at the level of what (7) seriously asserts.[67] The main difference between the two views emerges in their accounts of how speakers make an assertion with this logical form. On Field's view they do it directly because (31) is the logical form of (7) itself; on the pretense-based view speakers make an assertion with the schematic logical form indirectly, through the operation of make-believe in their utterances. One advantage of the pretense-based view, then, is that it offers more explanation of *how* truth-talk makes the claims we take it to make. Field's view can certainly explain *why* we should think that speakers assert something with the postulated logical form. Recall that deflationists hold truth-talk's most important role to be that of allowing speakers to generalize on the sentences a claim like (6) embeds, by uttering something like (7). Asserting (7) commits a speaker to everything the Pope asserts, but without requiring that she affirm each of those things explicitly and individually. If fulfilling this task really is the whole purpose of a general truth-attribution like (7), its making an assertion with logical form (31) would accomplish this directly. So, for a deflationist, the thesis that this particular job is truth-talk's central function explains why we should think general truth-attributions put forward claims with this form. What Field's view leaves without substantive explanation, however, is *how* truth-talk accomplishes this by using an expression that looks unsuited to the task, one whose grammatical role makes it look like it is in fact doing something else.

Of course, substantive how-explanations of this sort are not always necessary. Ordinary language quantificational expressions function grammatically as nominal terms, but they do not function logically like ordinary referential expressions, and the explanation of how they pull off the very different logical task they perform is quite simple: *they just do; that is their job*. But this non-substantive sort of answer is not always appropriate. One might be able to offer arguments explaining why, say, we should read existence-talk as making metalinguistic claims about referential success and failure, or explaining why we should take intentional-attitude ascriptions to involve some hidden indexicality to modes of presentation, but in cases like these there would still be a need for accounts of *how* these ways of talking manage to put forward claims with these unobvious logical forms. The reply 'they just do' is unsatisfying in these cases because the putative divergences of logical from grammatical form lack the transparency the quantificational-expression case exhibits. The divergence shows up in the inferential behavior of quantificational expressions; understanding how the logical form differs is part of knowing how to use them properly. This is not the case for more opaque divergences, including, I claim, that occurring in truth-talk.

We cannot plausibly maintain that the logical/grammatical divergence Field postulates for truth-talk has the sort of transparency the quantificational-expressions case exhibits. Thinking it does would involve attributing an implausible level of logical sophistication—including an understanding of schematic sentence variables—to anyone who knows how to use truth-talk. Moreover, there is no apparent explanation for transparency here, since the divergence does not show up in the inferential behavior of 'is true'; on the contrary, this expression's behavior mirrors that of an ordinary, property-attributing predicate. These points might not concern Field much, however, since he is perfectly willing to characterize his view as offering a more precise, technical notion meant to replace the ordinary notion of truth.[68] If we consider his notion of truth a replacement concept designed for a particular job, then we can say that it has a transparent (because stipulated) divergence of logical form. But since we cannot make this claim about ordinary truth-talk, a non-revisionary deflationist who attributes a divergent logical form to the (serious) assertion made with a general truth-attribution needs a substantive explanation of *how* such an utterance manages to make such an assertion. The pretense-based view thus has an explanatory advantage over Field's view, at least as an account of ordinary truth-talk, since in addition to endorsing the same why-explanation as the latter, the pretense-based view also offers a how-explanation of the desired sort.[69]

According to a pretense-based account of truth-talk including rule (UQ), the serious assertion an utterance of (7) makes *indirectly* has a logical form that generalizes schematically on the sentences (6) embeds. Although the quantifier (7) employs operates in the ordinary, objectual way, and the expression 'is true' functions like an ordinary property-attributing predicate, here these familiar logical devices operate in the context of a make-believe that assigns to the pretenses (7) displays prescriptive real-world conditions we cannot specify directly without introducing complex, non-standard logical devices like substitutional quantification and schematic sentence variables. Thus, because of the way the pretense approach determines the serious assertions pretense-employing utterances make indirectly, the appeal to pretense here explains *how* an utterance that looks unsuited to the task manages to make an assertion with such a different logical form. At the same time, since the pretense-based view does not interpret the main quantifier in claims like (7) substitutionally, it does not open the logical gap that undermines certain other formulations of deflationism. It also avoids postulating any non-standard logical devices at work in truth-talk's actual functioning. To reiterate a point made earlier, on my view truth-attributions themselves do not involve such devices in any way (not even in their 'underlying logic'). Rather, it implements these new logical roles indirectly by employing simpler logical devices already available in a natural language, the important factor being that here it does so in the context of a particular pretense. Because the pretense-based account deals with the generalization problem in this logico-syntactically conservative way, it fits especially well with one of the motivating thoughts behind the deflationary impulse: Truth-talk allows us to effect schematic generalizations *without* having to incorporate new, complicated logical devices into our language.[70] Brandom and Field have to abandon this thought in one way or another as they attempt to deal with the generalization problem; the pretense-based account does not.

Objections and Replies

I have already replied to the challenge that my view is incoherent because, as a version of fictionalism, it amounts to an error theory of truth-talk. The particular way pretense figures in truth-talk prevents the account from being an error theory (in any problematic sense anyway). However, even though my view avoids this worry, my application of the pretense approach to truth-talk extends the reach of semantic pretense beyond any previous application, and to a domain of discourse that might appear off limits— even to those who employ the approach elsewhere. One might think the application to truth-talk is illegitimate because of the apparently explanatory role that truth-talk typically plays in applications of the pretense approach.[71] However, the use of truth-talk in explanations of other applications of the pretense approach does not preclude applying the approach to truth-talk itself. There is nothing inconsistent about using one semantic pretense to explain another. In fact, although it might be a surprising result, there would be no inconsistency if applying the pretense approach to truth-talk entailed that the only way to explain some semantic pretenses was indirectly, through the use of some (other) semantic pretense.

A slightly stronger objection someone might raise is that this kind of account ignores the obvious fact that speakers making truth-attributions do not think of themselves as pretending anything, and pretending is not something one can do unintentionally.[72] In response to this objection, let me first reiterate that my view does not claim that employing truth-talk amounts to *pretending* that things are true. Pretending that something is true involves intentionally applying a higher-order extrinsic pretense to something truth-talk already expresses indirectly via its intrinsic invocation of pretense. Speakers cannot unintentionally pretend something is true, but they can invoke the pretenses that utterances involve without thinking of themselves as pretending anything because semantic pretense requires only *shallow* pretenses.

The point of calling the pretense an utterance employs "shallow" is to indicate that a speaker's use of it does not require that she *actively* engage in any pretending. Speakers do not actually have to play the game of make-believe that explains a way of talking in order to employ the talk. The pretense approach is a way of explaining how fragments of language function; it is not an account of what speakers do. A speaker may be aware that an utterance involves pretense somehow, but she might only allude to the pretense that explains the utterance rather than engage in it.[73] In fact, a speaker can make a pretense-employing utterance without even being aware that it involves any pretense.[74] She might just know that an utterance of this form is a way of making some point without having much of an idea of how it accomplishes this feat, or even without being completely clear on precisely what point the utterance makes.[75] This last possibility is simply another facet of the social dimension of content externalism—just as, by relying on his linguistic community (in particular, certain experts), one can refer, e.g., to elm trees without knowing any of their essential features, so too can one assert something he does not (and possibly even cannot) understand by using truth-talk to *co*-assert with someone who does.[76] In any case, what ordinary speakers take themselves to be doing is not particularly relevant here. Viewed from the outside we can say that it is *as if* someone employing truth-talk actively plays the game of make-believe sketched above. But a shallow pretense is more like a figure of speech one employs than a game one is playing; it is a figure of speech we can best explain in terms of an implicated game of make-believe.

The final objection I will address here is the one that poses the most serious challenge to a pretense-based account of truth-talk. The charge is that we cannot explain truth-talk in terms of pretense because the explanations of pretense and the activity of pretending rely on the notion of truth. If this notion played an ineliminable role in explaining pretense, a role the pretense-based account of truth-talk could not cover, then the attempt to provide a complete account of this talk in terms of semantic pretense would be self-undermining.[77] This is a genuine worry because the best way to understand pretending is as a special kind of imagining, and the most concise account of imagining, e.g., that a is F, is in terms of regarding the proposition that a is F as being true, regardless of whether it is true.[78] However, objecting to a pretense-based account of truth-talk on the basis of this observation pushes the point beyond its legitimate purchase. While we *can* explain pretense in a way that employs truth-talk, it is also possible to account for pretending without appeal to the notion of truth.

The account of pretending I have in mind stems from the deflationary thesis that truth-talk is just a device for canceling semantic ascent, or, more generally, for denominalizing sentence nominalizations (e.g., expressions of the form 'that a is F'). The thought is that we can attain a truth-talk-free account of pretending by "semantically descending" from the proposition- and truth-involving account mentioned above. As a first pass at this, explain pretending that a is F in terms of regarding the subject of the embedded sentence as being how the sentence says it is on a face-value reading, whether it is that way or not. So we explain pretending that a is F is in terms of adopting the attitude prescribed in:

(32) Regard a as being F, regardless of whether it is F.

Obviously this does not cover all scenarios. One will attempt to regard a in some way only if he believes that a really exists. Similarly, one will take something to be F only if he thinks being F is really a way something can be. So the attitude (32) prescribes underlies pretending that a is F only when this involves the application of extrinsic pretense to a literal (face-value) reading of 'a is F'. For example, we explain pretending what (8) taken literally says, that is, pretending that Arnold Schwarzenegger is (literally) the headliner of a bad lounge act, in terms of the attitude prescribed in:

(33) Regard Governor Arnold Schwarzenegger as being the headliner of a bad lounge act, regardless of whether he is the headliner of a bad lounge act.

However, complications arise once we move beyond this straightforward sort of case. If one does not believe both that a exists and that things can (literally) be F, then one will not take a literal reading of the sentence 'a is F' to provide anything one might pretend. All the sentence might provide for someone to pretend would be something an utterance of it would say indirectly through the operation of some prior pretense. In other words, *pretending* that a is F under these conditions involves the application of extrinsic pretense to something that an utterance of 'a is F' would assert indirectly, via the intrinsic pretense it invoked. For example, consider the scenario in which one pretends that Santa Claus gets skinny every summer, in full awareness that there is no Santa Claus.[79] The embedded sentence in this case invokes pretense intrinsically because the name 'Santa Claus' is a fictional name drawn from what we can call the 'Santa Claus'-story.[80] Following Walton's analysis of what he calls "ordinary statements" concerning works of fiction, the use of a fictional name like 'Santa Claus' in, for example:

(34) Santa Claus gets skinny every summer

makes a serious assertion about the story that supplies the name.[81] So *pretending* that Santa Claus gets skinny every summer (when one knows there is no Santa Claus) involves an additional layer of pretense beyond that already at work in (34). We explain this additional pretense in terms of adopting the attitude prescribed in:

(35) Regard the 'Santa Claus'-story as portraying a jolly, fat man called "Santa Claus" who lives at the North Pole, brings presents to good children on Christmas Eve, who rides a sleigh pulled by flying reindeer, . . . , *and who gets skinny every summer*, whether the story portrays this or not.[82]

In both of the scenarios considered so far there is a match between how the person pretending takes the name and how the name functions: the pretender takes it to refer when it does and takes it not to refer when it does not. There are also, however, two possible scenarios involving mismatches of these two aspects: (i) the potential pretender takes the name not to refer when it actually does; (ii) the potential pretender takes the name to refer when it actually does not. We can analyze the first mismatch scenario in the same way as the matching scenario just discussed. Whether the name actually refers is insignificant; what matters for the pretenses that the use of the name specifies is that the potential pretender takes the name not to refer.[83] In such a situation the pretending involves adopting an attitude like the one (35) prescribes.

The second mismatch scenario is not so simple and requires more comment. Consider a case in which a child who believes that Santa Claus exists attempts to *pretend* that Santa Claus gets skinny every summer. She will not adopt an attitude toward the 'Santa Claus'-story; rather, she will attempt to regard Santa Claus in some way. But since there is no Santa Claus, this attempt will fail, and she will not succeed in pretending anything. This is not as counterintuitive as it might sound. The child is not, after all, *pretending* that Santa Claus exists and then adding the further pretense that he gets skinny—nor is she *believing* that Santa Claus both exists and gets skinny every summer. It is quite possible for her to do either of these things (although the explanations of what she does might be somewhat complicated). Part of the point of distinguishing the various scenarios is to contrast *de dicto* and *de re* cases. The current scenario is akin to a *de re* attitude ascription. Resistance to the idea that the child's attempt to pretend will fail most likely arises from thinking of this case in *de dicto* (or at least ambiguous) terms, that is, as a case of pretending that Santa Claus gets skinny every summer. There is no problem with the child doing this when we read it *de dicto*, but then it is closer to the second matching scenario. Because the distinguishing factor in the current scenario is that the child *believes* that Santa Claus exists, we should read this case *de re*, that is, as one in which she attempts to pretend of that (supposedly existing) object that it gets skinny every summer. Her attempt fails because there is no such object. It is only when a potential pretender takes the name as a fictional (or merely empty) name that we can use a sentences like (34) to specify the content of a pretense.

The possibility of these different scenarios indicates a need for a more inclusive account of the attitude pretending that *a* is *F* involves than the one (32) illustrates. Because there are possible cases of pretending that *a* is *F* in which the claim '*a* is *F*' itself involves pretense, we need to modify the idea that we regard the subject of the embedded claim as being the way a face-value reading of the sentence describes it. What pretending that *a* is *F* involves is regarding the *serious* subject of '*a* is *F*' as being how the utterance *seriously* describes it, whether it is that way or not. This account of pretending applies generally, both to situations that involve applying extrinsic pretense to a claim that we take literally (as in pretending that Arnold Schwarzenegger headlines a bad lounge act), and to situations in which pretending that *a* is *F* involves applying extrinsic pretense to something that a claim that itself invokes pretense intrinsically expresses indirectly (as in pretending that Santa Claus gets skinny every summer). In fact, the first pass account (32) offers still works as an account of the first sort of scenario because (32) is a special case of the general account for instances of first-order extrinsic pretense. I maintain that a truth-talk-free account of pretending constructed along these lines will address the circularity challenge and allow for the application of the pretense approach to truth-talk without threat of incoherence. And even if an account based on the points just made cannot completely avoid circularity, this does not automatically mean that a pretense-based account of truth-talk is incoherent. It would simply mean that we can explain pretending itself only indirectly, through the use of some semantic pretense.[84]

Concluding Comments

I have presented a pretense-based deflationary account of the fragment of truth-talk that putatively describes propositions transparently denoted with 'that'-clauses. This is an important start, but further work must extend the account offered here in at least two ways. First, it must extended it to truth-talk ostensibly describing propositions denoted opaquely (e.g., by expressions like 'what Corey believes'), and to truth-talk purporting to describe things other than propositions (e.g., sentences). These extensions will require a pretense-based account of proposition-talk, in particular, talk of expressing a proposition. This is no small task, but as mentioned above, it is just a version of the demand for a non-truth-theoretic account of meaning(-talk) that all deflationists face.

Second, further work must extend the account to cover the other traditional semantic notions: reference and predicate-satisfaction.[85] The pretense-based accounts of these ways of talking will parallel my account of truth-talk in that they too will explain how certain apparently predicative ways of talking allow us to make indirectly serious assertions we could not otherwise make, by means of appearing to say something else. And as the principles of generation from the make-believe behind truth-talk underwrite (ES), the pretense-based accounts of the other semantic notions will underwrite the similar schemata governing them:

(R) $(\forall x)$ ('n' refers to x iff $n = x$)

(S) $(\forall x)$ (x satisfies 'F' iff Fx).

These extensions are the issues that the larger project this chapter introduces should address next. Further work then includes the task of determining how a pretense-based account of truth-talk impacts related subjects (e.g., proposition-talk, propositional-attitude-talk, property-talk, existence-talk, and identity-talk). The account offered here addresses some of the basic concerns truth-talk raises and provides the foundation for a suggestive line of inquiry into the important family of issues related to the functioning of truth-talk.

Notes

Comments and criticisms from many people helped shape this chapter. I would like to thank Mark Crimmins, Hartry Field, David Hills, Jim Joyce, Michael Lynch, Doug Patterson, Stephen Schiffer, Jason Stanley, David Velleman, Ken Walton, and Steve Yablo. Thanks also to Ray Buchanan and Joshua Schechter. Special thanks goes to Brad Armour-Garb for the many conversations we have had about deflationism and related topics over the past few years.

1. By 'truth-talk' I primarily mean that fragment of our talk (and thought) that involves the terms (or concepts) 'true', 'false', 'truth', 'falsity', and such cognates as 'being right', 'being so', etc. Taken broadly, truth-talk also includes talk involving such technical notions as reference and satisfaction. The scope of my concern at this stage is truth-talk in the former, narrower sense.

2. A way of talking is a loosely bounded fragment of discourse (and thought) centered around some expression (concept) or family of expressions (concepts)—e.g., modality, numbers, truth—or around some mode or figure of speech—e.g., metaphor, irony, hyperbole.

3. Field (1989: 2) describes this error-theoretic sense of fictionalism but also points out that this is not the only way to understand the general approach. See also Price (2003: 188) for a statement of this worry about fictionalism regarding semantic notions.

4. See Boghossian (1990: 167, 174–5) for a fuller account of this kind of objection to such a view.

5. I say more about the paradoxical aspect of truth-talk below.

6. See Frege (1918: 6) and Soames (1999: 21–2).

7. Claiming as I do here that utterances of the forms 'It is true that p' and 'That p is true' are trivial syntactic variants involves a commitment to treating 'that'-clauses as referential expressions. Schiffer (1996) presents arguments for doing so. Here I take them as referential expressions, but only in the context of a pretense. I will say a bit more about this below.

8. This is a *strengthened* version of the Liar formulated to foil attempted solutions in terms of truth-value gaps or the claim that Liar sentences do not express anything. Even the latter strategy is self-defeating if we apply it to (4).

9. Note also that in the case of (4), its paradoxical nature is due to the contingent fact that I have labeled it '(4)' rather than anything intrinsic to the sentence itself. The sentence would not be paradoxical if I had labeled it '(A)'—unless, of course, I also applied the label '(4)' to 'The sentence labeled "(A)" expresses something true,' in which case (4) and (A) would form a paradoxical loop. See Kripke (1975: 691–2).

10. Kirkham (1992: 311).

11. It turns out to be a necessary condition for a view of truth-talk to count as deflationary that it takes the talk not to attribute any substantive property, but this is not a sufficient condition for counting as deflationary, and thus is not deflationism's definitive commitment.

12. See Horwich (1998: 121, 126–8, 138). This general understanding of deflationism covers a variety of more specific "realizing" formulations of the approach. The three most developed formulations in the current literature (the "current formulations") are: Paul Horwich's Minimal Theory (MT), presented in Horwich (1998); Robert Brandom's operator version of Prosententialism (OP), presented in Chapter 5 of Brandom (1994); and Hartry Field's Pure Disquotationalism (PD), presented in Field (1994). Field (2001c) presents an account of 'that'-clauses that would allow him to explain his *disquotational* view in terms of (ES).

13. On Horwich's MT these equivalences are brute axioms, in the sense of being logico-linguistically basic. Field's PD and Brandom's OP take the instances of (ES) as explanatorily and conceptually basic, but not as brute. Rather, on the latter two views these equivalences are immediate consequences of truth-talk's basic logico-linguistic functioning.

14. Although not explicitly deflationary, Graham Priest's dialetheism is the best-developed example of this approach to the paradoxes. See Priest (1979) and (1998).

15. I am assuming, of course, that there cannot be "inconsistent" properties—properties that certain things have if, and only if, those things do not have those properties. If one finds this assumption questionable (perhaps by taking

reality to be inconsistent?), then he should take my point here to be just that deflationary views are more flexible in pursuing the "diagnose and contain" strategy with respect to the Liar paradox, since one does not have to assume that reality is "inconsistent" (whatever that might mean) to do so.

16. Kripke (1975: 692).

17. See Chihara (1979) on the diagnostic problem/preventative problem distinction.

18. See Priest (1998: 421). As evidence for this point, consider the following cases. Sentence (L_1): 'The sentence labeled "(L_1)" is not stably true' challenges rule-of-revision solutions. Sentence (L_2): 'The sentence labeled "(L_2)" is not definitely true' confronts indeterminacy solutions. Sentence (L_3): 'The sentence labeled "(L_3)" is not true in any context (or at any level of the hierarchy)' confronts contextual/indexical solutions.

19. I should note that this does not hold for all deflationary views. As it currently stands, Horwich's MT needs to solve the preventative problem as much as any inflationary view does. So the Liar may pose even more of a problem for MT than it does for inflationary views. This would change if Horwich gave up the claim that MT is a theory of *truth itself* and offered it just as a theory of the *concept* of truth. He seems to be leaning slightly in this direction in the postscript to Horwich (1998: 141–2), although his explicit position is still that MT is a theory of truth itself and that we must eliminate the paradoxicality from the Liar paradox (ibid.: 36–7, 136).

20. Walton (1990).

21. Walton (1990: 37–8). To avoid circularity, I replace Walton's use of 'fictional' and Crimmins's related and more perspicuous use of 'fictionally true' (1998: 4–6) with explanations in terms of what is *to be pretended* or what pretenses are *prescribed*. I use 'prescribed' here simply as a means of saying that something is both permissible (or appropriate) and obligatory (in so far as the question of its normative status arises). A pretense being prescribed thus means that given certain assumptions (e.g., that one is playing a particular game of make-believe), circumstances will antecedently settle that one should include this pretense in what he pretends, should the issue of what to pretend on that front arise.

22. Crimmins (1998: 5).

23. Ibid.: 32.

24. See Walton (1990: ch. 11) for the details of this way of applying the pretense approach to existence-talk. Evans (1982: ch. 10) and Kroon (1996) develop slightly different pretense-theoretic accounts.

25. The pretense approach thus offers a direct response to the worries about self-application failure that Huw Price considers regarding fictionalism about truth and other semantic notions. See Price (2003: 188).

26. Higher-order levels of extrinsic pretense are possible, for example, second-order extrinsic pretense involves merely pretending that it is to be pretended that a is F, etc. Second-order extrinsic pretense involves a change in how we regard the

subject in the pretense (from being F to having the features required to be fictionally F in a first-order pretense). Third- and higher-orders of pretense involve a change in subject (from a to games of make-believe themselves) as well.

27. See Walton (1993) for the details of the role of make-believe in (much) metaphor. What I add here is a specification of the type of pretense many cases involve as extrinsic, in particular, *first-order* extrinsic.

28. See Rowling (1998: 166–70). For the uninitiated, Quidditch is a sport played by wizards on flying brooms. It involves three types of balls: a Quaffle, two Bludgers, and a Golden Snitch.

29. See Walton (1990: ch. 10) for the relevant account of "ordinary statements" concerning works of fiction.

30. The pretense approach and the notion of intrinsic pretense might explain not only uses of fictional names and "fictional quantification", but also uses of merely *empty* names and "empty quantification". See note 82.

31. Preminger and Brogan (1993: 74). Thanks to David Hills for the suggestion.

32. See Yablo (2000: 214, 223).

33. In the case of 'smarts' this might be too strong, but if so this is only because this expression is now a case of *dead* anthimeria (on analogy with dead metaphors, as in 'The bottle has a long neck'). Even if this term is now a referential English expression, it still has no referent, and it seems highly plausible that it entered the language via the kind of pretense about its functioning that I describe. After all, its meaning is parasitic on the meaning of the adjective that an utterance like (13) uses as a noun. (*Mutatis mutandis* for the pretend verb 'to nixon'.)

34. I do not mean anything too heavy-duty by 'analysis' here—just an account specifying when the mentioned expression is applicable to some object. The most precise form of this involves the specification of (when available) discriminating conditions that are necessary and sufficient for the expression's correct application.

35. Evans (1982: 348) makes a similar point, although without drawing the conclusion I draw from it.

36. Functioning *logically* as a predicate is a matter of how a term behaves in inference. We can see that 'exists' functions as a predicate logically from its behavior in inferences like that from 'Santa Claus and the tooth fairy do not exist' to 'There are things that do not exist.' Functioning as a predicate *logico-linguistically* includes this inferential behavior, but it includes more as well (in particular, characterizing or describing the referent of the term expression to which the putative predicate attaches).

37. This claim pertains to the most general applicability conditions for the expression. The truth of a claim like 'Dex is happy iff Corey is nearby' is not a counter-example even though it implies 'Dex satisfies "is happy" iff Corey is nearby.' A statement of the *general* applicability conditions for 'is happy' has the form '$(\forall x)(x$ satisfies "is happy" iff x is F).' The same point applies to other putative counter-examples like

'Space is Euclidean iff for any straight line L and any point not on that line, exactly one line co-planer with L passes through that point without intersecting L.' The form of the general applicability conditions for 'is Euclidean' is something like '$(\forall x)(x$ satisfies "is Euclidean" iff x is a spatial structure such that . . .).' Thus, the right-hand side of any instance of these applicability conditions does place conditions on the subject from its left-hand side.

38. There is also the difference that (ES) is an analysis *schema* rather than an actual general analysis, so each instance of (ES) is itself an analysis of a particular application of 'is true'. This does not affect the present point. An additional difference is that in the instances of (ES), the putative predicate is used rather than mentioned, but this is also unimportant here, since each is trivially equivalent to an instance of: '(ES') That p satisfies "is true" iff p.'

39. The classic presentation of prosententialism is Grover, Camp, and Belnap (1975). Brandom's version of the approach appears in Brandom (1994: ch. 5). On this view, the expression 'is true' is an operator that attaches to terms denoting sentences (or "sentence-*tokenings*" as Brandom would say) to form *prosentences*, the sentential analog of pronouns. Like pronouns, prosentences inherit their content anaphorically, in this case from another sentence.

40. See Horwich (1998: 125).

41. *Mutatis mutandis* for 'is false' and the pretend property of falsity.

42. See Alston (1996: 14). I say "*ostensibly* about propositions" because proposition-talk also gets a pretense-theoretic account on my overall view. I will not discuss this in detail here (I do in Woodbridge (MS)), but briefly, I accept the arguments in Schiffer (1996) for propositions being "language-created" entities, but not those for their being "language-independent" entities. We *talk* as if they are, but this is just a semantic pretense serving other expressive purposes, e.g., that of talking about computationally typed mentalese sentences in my head for the purpose of describing (via analogy or comparison) mentalese sentences in other heads. (See Field (2001c), on 'that'-clauses and content attributions.)

43. Although we can break claims like (1) down syntactically into the expression 'it is true that . . . ' and a sentence, this decomposition does not represent the underlying logical form of these claims. Even in (1), the truth-locution functions ostensibly as a predicate, combining with a referring term; it does not function as an operator modifying a sentence.

44. I do not mean to imply that making utterances in English is an essential part of the pretenses identified in this way. One might engage in the relevant pretenses by making utterances in some other language or by having certain thoughts.

45. We can make serious assertions with utterances expressing stipulated pretenses belonging to the game, e.g., 'Propositions are the basic truth-bearers' or 'Truth is a property of propositions', but the serious assertions made will be that the pretenses displayed in the utterances are part of the content of the make-believe.

46. See Kripke (1975) and Grover (1977).

47. The contrast is with *partially* pretend claims, e.g., non-pathological instances of truth-talk, such as 'It is true that crabapples are edible.' Partially pretend claims generally are claims that employ pretense to make serious claims about the world indirectly.

48. Thanks to Ken Walton for the example.

49. See Priest (1998: 410–12).

50. There will also be an analogous principle for the segment of truth-talk involving quantificational attributions of falsity. We can obtain this rule by replacing 'is true' in the mentioned formula on the left-hand side with 'is false' and 'p' in the consequent on the right-hand side with '$\sim p$'.

51. As in the case of (UQ), there is a principle analogous to (EQ) for existentially quantified attributions of falsity. 'Σ' is the existential substitutional quantifier, which is a device for encoding a (potentially infinite) disjunction.

52. See Crimmins (1998).

53. I develop an account of this sort in Woodbridge (MS).

54. See Brandom (1994: 302).

55. Brandom (1994: 304).

56. Field (1994: 259, 267, 268). Field also discusses an approach that drops substitutional quantifiers and just takes schemata employing sentence variables as themselves generalized. I consider this alternative below. In discussing both approaches I am paraphrasing what Field says about the *disquotational* schema: '(DS) "p" is true iff p', in light of the account of 'that'-clauses Field now finds attractive (what he calls "LV" in Field (2001c)). According to LV, 'that'-clauses are just a means of picking out computationally (rather than orthographically) typed sentences of the speaker's own idiolect. Thus, on Field's view, the equivalence schema: '(ES) It is true that p (= That p is true)' is really the basis of a disquotational (rather than propositional) account of truth-talk.

57. This step involves the assumption that 'that'-clauses pick out the things speakers assert. Combining Field's PD with LV somewhat complicates this thesis. According to LV, 'that'-clauses pick out sentences belonging to the idiolect of the person using them (interpreted as that person interprets them). But while I can assert (29) indiscriminately, much of what comes out of the Pope's mouth are not sentences belonging to my idiolect. So really we need to loosen (28) to something along the lines of: '(28') (Πp)(Pope assertorically utters something *that means* that $p \rightarrow$ that p is true)' where we understand meaning-talk as LV explains it.

58. Although, unlike an objectual quantifier, it does not supply them referentially as things the claim talks about.

59. Field (1999: 533).

60. Because it is a propositional view, Horwich's MT cannot make use of substitutional quantification in this way. As a result, however, MT has even less to say about truth-talk's generalizing role, and because of its structure it is basically sunk by the generalization problem.

61. See Gupta (1993).

62. As part of his normative-inferentialist approach to meaning, Brandom actually endorses a substitutional interpretation of quantification generally. (See Brandom (1994: 434–5).)

63. This is the reason for my use of scare-quotes above around 'Fieldian', to distance the application of the above strategy to a disquotational account from Field's actual view. In fact, Field has urged something like the following alternative reading on me as his intended one (recognizing the above strategy for the sort of Trojan Horse it is).

64. It is important to keep in mind the explanation of Field's take on 'that'-clauses from above and note 56. Since on his view, 'that'-clauses amount to a kind of quotation with which a speaker can refer to computationally typed sentences of her own idiolect, (30) involves identifying objects the quantifier supplies with sentences, not with propositions, and applying the truth-predicate to sentences, not to propositions. Thus, like (ES), (30) is still part of a *disquotational* account of truth-talk.

65. Field (1994: 251, 251 n.2, 268). See also Field (2001a: 142 n. 1). Cognitive equivalence is thus a non-intensional notion for Field. Again, I am translating what Field says about (DS).

66. Field (1994: 259) and (2001b: 141–2). The details of these rules are not important for present purposes, but I should note that I find the particular rules Field offers problematic. In fact, my worries apply to any rules that would be strong enough for Field's purposes. I pursue this objection in Woodbridge (2003).

67. However, as indicated in the comments about proposition-talk above, I think that Field needs to modify his understanding of 'that'-clauses to include an element of pretense. We can take the analysis LV offers to capture the serious content proposition-talk puts forward indirectly via the semantic pretense it involves. This fits better with our linguistic and inferential practices involving 'that'-clauses and avoids the problems that follow from taking terms like 'what Corey asserted/ believes' as literally denoting sentences (or sentence-tokenings). For instance, one does not have to think (implausibly) that our ordinary notions of belief, assertion, etc. are relations to sentences; instead one can retain the intuitive thought that each is (or at least purports to be) a relation to a proposition—that is, something that we assert, believe, etc. *by means of* uttering sentences or having mental states (that perhaps involve mental sentence-analogs).

68. Field (1994: 277–8). This revisionary attitude is also apparent in Field's talk of "incorporat[ing] schematic letters for sentences into the language" (ibid.: 259) and Field (2001b: 141) and of "reasoning with" and "accepting" schemata (Field (2001b: 147–8)).

69. With respect to treating Field's view as a replacement proposal, understanding ordinary truth-talk in terms of semantic pretense offers both a theoretical and

practical advantage over accepting this revision because on the pretense approach truth-talk involves fewer and simpler syntactic resources.

70. Horwich (1998: 4 n.1, 37).

71. Consider, for example, the use of 'fictionally true' in the brief sketch of the pretense-based account of existence-talk given above. Truth-talk plays a similar role in Mark Crimmins' discussion of the pretense approach and his applications of it to attitude ascriptions and identity-talk in Crimmins (1998). See also Stephen Yablo's application of the pretense approach to possible-worlds-talk in Yablo (1996).

72. At least the first conjunct seems to be one of the fundamental objections Richard (2000) raises against semantic pretense.

73. See Walton (1990: 406–11) on statements belonging to "unofficial" games of make-believe.

74. Crimmins (1998: 10, 14–15). One must be aware of the shallow pretense, however, if one is to have a full understanding of both what is said and how it gets said (ibid.: 3).

75. In the case of truth-talk, the explanation of this might be the fact that 'is true' has no literal content. Yablo (2000: 223–4) points out that we often mistake standard usage for literal usage. Thus, we might fail to notice that standard usage involves pretense, especially if there is no literal content with which to contrast the non-literal (standard) content.

76. See Putnam (1975) on the role of the linguistic community (and in particular, of experts), in referring.

77. This would be akin to the sort of general objection to deflationism developed in Boghossian (1990).

78. Velleman (2000: 251). On Velleman's view, both imagining and believing involve accepting a proposition, that is, both are ways of regarding a proposition to be true. He claims that the difference is that, unlike imagining, believing a proposition involves regarding it as true with the aim of doing so only if it is true.

79. For simplicity, I will contrast cases that differ only with respect to one's position on the existence of *a*. The same points apply *mutatis mutandis* for cases that involve giving up the possibility that things can literally be *F*, and for cases in which one rejects both.

80. The 'Santa Claus'-story is the familiar, standard, culturally salient story in which the term 'Santa Claus' centrally figures. This rules out deviant stories employing the name, and stories portraying someone with the same features as those the 'Santa Claus'-story portrays someone named 'Santa Claus' as having, but which are "about someone else" (i.e., which use a different fictional name with the intention of portraying a different (fictional) person). This does not rule out stories in other languages or from other cultures (e.g., the French 'Papa Noël'-story) from being the "same story" or from portraying the "same" (fictional) person.

81. I take this to follow from the explanation given in Walton (1990: 403).

82. We can give an analogous account of pretenses involving names one takes as merely empty names not drawn from established works of fiction (as opposed to specifically fictional names that are). Just as the serious assertion one makes with an utterance employing the name 'Santa Claus' as a fictional name is about the 'Santa Claus'-story, the serious assertion one makes with an utterance employing what he takes as a merely empty name (e.g., 'Vulcan') is about the (mini-)theory or "lore" surrounding the use of that name (e.g., the 'Vulcan'-lore). Therefore, pretenses described using merely empty names involve regarding the associated "lore" as including various claims, regardless of whether it does.

83. In my use of 'the name' here I am simplifying things by proceeding as if we individuate names orthographically rather than (at least partially) semantically. In fact, the latter seems more plausible to me, but then the name we take not to refer would be a different (though homophonic) name from the one that does refer. If so, and if one's linguistic community employed the latter name, that would not automatically falsify one's belief that this particular orthographic item does not refer, even if one intended to use it as his linguistic community does. Rather, it would be indeterminate which name one was using, and we could resolve this indeterminacy in either direction depending on whether the speaker gave up the intention or the belief upon discovering this conflict. Thus, we must qualify the claim that what matters is how one takes the name, factoring in the social aspects of content externalism referenced in the paragraph connected with note 76. But this qualification does not undermine the claim, as the flexibility in resolving the indeterminacy just mentioned indicates.

84. See Yablo (1998: 249 n.50). This would not be a problem, since it would just be a fact about the extent of our linguistic and explanatory capacities and would *not* constitute a vicious regress in which one must already be pretending in order to *begin* pretending.

85. We might think that pretense-based accounts of these notions receive initial motivation from the Berry Paradox involving expressions like 'the least number not describable in less than eighteen syllables' and the Heterological Paradox involving predicates like '. . . is not true of itself.'

References

Alston, William P. (1996). *A Realist Conception of Truth*. Ithaca, NY: Cornell University Press.

Boghossian, Paul (1990). 'The Status of Content.' *Philosophical Review*, 99: 157–84.

Brandom, Robert (1994). *Making It Explicit*. Cambridge, MA: Harvard University Press.

Chihara, Charles (1979). 'The Semantic Paradoxes: A Diagnostic Investigation.' *Philosophical Review*, 88: 590–618.

Crimmins, Mark (1998). 'Hesperus and Phosphorus: Sense, Pretense, and Reference.' *Philosophical Review*, 107.1: 1–47.

Evans, Gareth (1982). *The Varieties of Reference*, John McDowell (ed.). Oxford: Clarendon Press.

Field, Hartry (1986). 'The Deflationary Conception of Truth.' In Graham McDonald and Crispin Wright (eds.), *Fact, Science and Morality*: 55–117. Oxford: Basil Blackwell.

—— (1989). *Realism, Mathematics and Modality*. Oxford: Basil Blackwell.

—— (1994). 'Deflationist Views of Meaning and Content.' *Mind*, 103: 249–85. Reprinted in Field (2001a: 104–40).

—— (1999). 'Deflating the Conservativeness Argument.' *Journal of Philosophy*, 96: 533–40.

—— (2001a). *Truth and the Absence of Fact*. Oxford: Clarendon Press.

—— (2001b). 'Postscript to "Deflationist Views of Meaning and Content".' In Field (2001a: 141–56).

—— (2001c). 'Attributions of Meaning and Content.' In Field (2001a: 157–74).

Frege, Gottlob (1918/77). 'Thoughts.' In Peter T. Geach (ed.), *Logical Investigations*: 1–30. New Haven: Yale University Press.

Grover, Dorothy L. (1977). 'Inheritors and Paradox.' *Journal of Philosophy*, 74: 590–604.

Grover, Dorothy L., Camp, L. Joseph, Jr., and Nuel D. Belnap, Jr. (1975). 'A Prosentential Theory of Truth.' *Philosophical Studies*, 27: 73–125.

Gupta, Anil (1993). 'A Critique of Deflationism.' *Philosophical Topics*, 21: 57–81.

Hills, David (1997). 'Aptness and Truth in Verbal Metaphor.' *Philosophical Topics*, 25: 117–53.

Horwich, Paul (1998). *Truth,* second edition. Oxford: Clarendon Press.

Kirkham, Richard (1992). *Theories of Truth*. Cambridge, MA: The MIT Press.

Kripke, Saul A. (1975). 'Outline of a Theory of Truth.' *Journal of Philosophy*, 72: 690–716.

Kroon, Frederick (1996). 'Characterizing Non-Existents.' *Grazer Philosophische Studien*, 51: 163–93.

Lewis, David (1978). 'Truth in Fiction.' *American Philosophical Quarterly*, 15.1: 37–46. Reprinted in Lewis (1981a: 261–75).

—— (1981a). *Philosophical Papers*, 1. Oxford: Oxford University Press.

—— (1981b). 'Postscripts to "Truth in Fiction".' In Lewis (1981a: 276–80).

Preminger, Alex, T. V. F. Brogan, *et al.* (1993). *The New Princeton Encyclopedia of Poetry and Poetics*. Princeton: Princeton University Press.

Price, Huw (2003). 'Truth as a Convenient Fiction.' *Journal of Philosophy*, 100: 167–90.

Priest, Graham (1979). 'The Logic of Paradox.' *Journal of Philosophical Logic*, 8: 219–41.

—— (1998). 'What is so bad about Contradictions?' *Journal of Philosophy*, 95: 410–26.

Putnam, Hilary (1975b). 'The Meaning of "Meaning".' Reprinted in *Mind, Language, and Reality: Philosophical Papers*, 2: 215–71. Cambridge: Cambridge University Press.

Richard, Mark (2000). 'Semantic Pretense.' In Anthony Everett and Thomas Hofweber (eds.), *Empty Names, Fiction, and the Puzzles of Non-Existence*: 205–32. Stanford: CSLI Publications.

Rowling, J. K. (1998). *Harry Potter and the Sorcerer's Stone*. New York: Scholastic Press.

Schiffer, Stephen (1996). 'Language-Created, Language-Independent Entities.' *Philosophical Topics*, 24: 149–67.

Searle, John R. (1969). *Speech Acts: An Essay in the Philosophy of Language*. Cambridge: Cambridge University Press.

Soames, Scott (1999). *Understanding Truth*. Oxford: Oxford University Press.

Tarski, Alfred (1944). 'The Semantic Conception of Truth.' *Philosophy and Phenomenological Research*, 4: 341–75.

Velleman, J. David (2000). 'On the Aim of Belief.' Reprinted in *The Possibility of Practical Reason*: 244–81. Oxford: Clarendon Press.

Walton, Kendall L. (1990). *Mimesis as Make-Believe*. Cambridge, MA: Harvard University Press.

—— (1993). 'Metaphor and Prop-Oriented Make-Believe.' *European Journal of Philosophy*, 1.1: 39–57.

Woodbridge, James A. (MS). 'Propositions as Semantic Pretense.'

—— (2003). 'Deflationism and the Generalization Problem.' *Logica Yearbook 2003*: 285–97. Prague: Filosofia, Institute of Philosophy, Academy of Sciences of the Czech Republic.

Yablo, Stephen (1996). 'How in the World?' *Philosophical Topics*, 24.1: 255–86.

—— (1998). 'Does Ontology Rest on a Mistake?' *Proceedings of the Aristotelian Society*, Supplementary Volume, 72: 229–61.

—— (2000). 'Aprioricity and Existence.' In Paul Boghossian and Christopher Peacocke (eds.), *New Essays on the A Priori*: 197–228. Oxford: Oxford University Press.

6

Belief about Nothing in Particular

FREDERICK KROON

It is easy nowadays—so Nathan Salmon declares approvingly in *Frege's Puzzle*—to get caught up in 'direct-reference mania', the widespread philosophical conviction that the semantic content of a proper name, demonstrative, or other simple indexical is not descriptive but directly involves the particular that the term refers to.[1] This *Direct Reference* program (DR) faces enormous problems, of course—problems that persuaded Russell long ago to reject the program for all but the most immediate of referring devices (his logically proper names) and to prefer a description-theoretic treatment for ordinary proper names. With the demise of description theories, however, the question of how to deal with these problems has once again begun to occupy center stage.[2]

Among the most famous of these problems is the crop of problems stemming from the phenomenon of empty names—in particular, what sense to make of true negative existentials and belief reports containing empty names, given that DR interprets such sentences as having parts that lack semantic content.[3] Problems of this kind have given rise to a batch of solutions that aim to preserve the spirit of DR, the best-known of them broadly neo-Fregean in nature. The present chapter, which focuses on empty names in belief reports, argues that no such solution can work, and that something altogether different is necessary to solve the most difficult version of this problem: the problem of why speakers would *knowingly* use empty names to report beliefs. I shall defend a kind of pretence solution to this latter problem, but one that differs from existing pretence accounts in its explanation of why pretence is bound to play an important role once we assume DR.

The Problem of Empty Names in Belief Reports

DR, it has often been argued, yields the wrong results when applied to belief reports containing empty names in the 'that'-clause. Take the following examples, one containing a fictional name, the other the name for a failed posit of natural science:[4]

(1) Smith believes that Poirot has a moustache,

and:

(2) Pièrre [a nineteenth-century French amateur astronomer] believed that Vulcan was larger than Mercury.

The problem that confronts us can be summarized as follows. First, (1) and (2) have no propositional object of belief if DR is right—there is nothing to be believed. Even if we suppose, as many of DR's proponents do, that belief reports standardly import reference to modes of presentation under which objects are thought, it is hard to see how this could help: The presence of modes doesn't make the absence of objects any more palatable.[5] But since what goes for the 'that'-clause must go for the entire sentence, it now follows that (1) and (2) also don't express propositions, and so *a fortiori* don't express *true* propositions. Yet there is surely a clear sense in which (1) and (2) may well be true. This is so even if we can be persuaded that the unembedded sentences 'Poirot has a moustache' and 'Vulcan is larger than Mercury' themselves lack propositional content. The situation isn't much improved if, following a suggestion of Kaplan (1989), we hold that sentences containing empty names express gappy or unfilled propositions. (1) and (2) strike us as clear candidates for truth, yet it is difficult to see why structures that *would* be propositions if certain names referred deserve to be called 'propositions' when they don't refer, and how gappy 'propositions' of this kind can be true or false.[6]

Call this problem about belief reports that embed empty names the 'no [complete] proposition' problem. There is also another problem. Let the 'deliberate use [of empty names]' problem be the problem posed by competent speakers who are fully aware (or at least believe) that the embedded names in their belief reports lack a reference, but despite this still persist in using the names in the reports (presumably because they believe the reports to be true). This is precisely how we usually understand the context of utterance of (1) and (2), of course; we take the speaker to know that the Poirot stories are fiction and that Vulcan-theory is a failed theory of astronomy. Note that when speakers are unaware that the names are empty, our intuitions about cases like (1) and (2) are rather less clear. They strike us as true in one sense, although we also think they betray a mistake—an especially serious one in the case of (1). Lacking a clear intuition about such cases, let us set them aside. I say a bit more about such cases later.

Descriptive Solutions and Why they Fail

The problem of empty names in belief reports thus divides into at least two problems, the 'no proposition' and 'the deliberate use' problems. It is tempting to solve both by allowing some exceptions to DR. In particular, we might think that where N is an empty name, the semantic function of N is not to stand for some particular individual but to express an individual concept or sense, perhaps a speaker-dependent sense: something like *the world-famous little Belgian detective called 'Poirot'* in the case of 'Poirot' and *the unique planet whose behavior caused such-and-such perturbations in the orbit of Mercury* in the case of 'Vulcan'. Call this the *strong descriptive solution* to the problem of empty names in belief reports. It claims that statements like (1) and (2) are equivalent in meaning to (partly) descriptive statements like 'Smith believes that the world-famous little Belgian detective called "Poirot" has a moustache' and 'Pièrre believed that the unique planet whose behavior caused such-and-such perturbations in the orbit of Mercury was larger than Mercury.' This dispatches the 'no proposition' problem (such statements don't contain empty directly referential terms and express perfectly ordinary propositions) as well as the 'deliberate use' problem (empty names mean the same as empty descriptions on this proposal, and presumably there is no difficulty understanding why we sometimes use empty descriptions).[7]

But the strong solution faces some obvious difficulties. To explain the possibility of true belief reports, it must suppose that reporters of such beliefs always know the relevant descriptive concepts that the believers associate with such empty names, not just the ones that the reporters themselves associate with the names. And this, as we'll see below, is quite implausible, even if we weaken the strong descriptive solution so that it requires only a determinate disjunction ('X believes either that the F_1 is G, that the F_2 is G, or. . . .'). In addition, there appears to be no ordinary name that is in principle immune from being thought empty (something that for Russell established the descriptive nature of all ordinary 'proper names'). That is why it makes sense to say something like 'We can't be absolutely certain that Aristotle existed; but if he did, he was the greatest philosopher of all time.' Such a statement is deliberately formulated to be true whether or not the name 'Aristotle' is empty, and it suggests that speakers who use empty names, whether deliberately or not, do not draw a principled semantic distinction between such names and ordinary non-empty names—it suggests that there is no special category of descriptive empty names to contrast with the class of directly referential non-empty names.

But even if descriptions don't give the meaning of names, perhaps they specify some of what is pragmatically implicated rather than semantically expressed by an utterance of a belief report containing a name. The *weak descriptive solution* to the problem of empty names in belief reports directs us to find a descriptive proposition naturally associated with such a belief report that doesn't depend on there being an object of reference for the name and is pragmatically implicated rather than semantically expressed.[8] In the case of (1), this solution might yield something like our earlier 'Smith believes that the world-famous little Belgian detective called "Poirot" has a moustache', but construed this time as a statement that is pragmatically implicated rather than equivalent in meaning to (1). In the case of (2), it might yield something like 'Pièrre believed that the unique planet whose behaviour caused such-and-such perturbations in the orbit of Mercury was larger than Mercury.' The solution then says that our sense that claims like (1) and (2) may well be true is misplaced: its real source is our sense that such pragmatically implicated claims may well be true.

While the weak descriptive solution seems initially more promising than the strong, I doubt that it is in the end any more successful. To begin with, consider our earlier insistence that any viable solution to the problem of empty names in belief reports should provide an answer to the 'deliberate use' problem, the problem of why speakers would knowingly use empty names. The weak descriptive solution provides no such answer. Indeed, on the standard Gricean understanding of pragmatic constraints on conversation we might well wonder how the knowing use of empty proper names could possibly be reconciled with, in particular, the Gricean maxims of Quality and Quantity. How could knowingly using an empty name possibly show that the speaker is trying to make a contribution that is true rather than false, and one that is as informative as necessary for the purpose of the conversation? Why not use the implicated statement itself?

Unlike this first objection, the second objection to be described—which I'll call the 'unknown mode' objection—also affects the strong descriptive solutions. It can be taken in the first instance as an objection to various familiar ways in which supporters of DR have tried to cope with the problem that we apparently can't always substitute co-referring names for each other in belief reports, *salva veritate*. Supporters of DR have usually tried to solve this problem by arguing that belief reports typically invoke modes of presentation of some kind, whether through pragmatic implication (Salmon, 1986; Soames, 2002), or semantically (Richard, 1990; Crimmins, 1992). But in many cases there doesn't even seem to be a determinate *type* of mode of presentation available to the speaker. Take a telling example given by Schiffer.[9] Suppose we are having a casual conversation about the French Riviera, when Stella, a non-philosopher who likes to drop names, informs us that:

> (3) Jean Luc Godard believes that Brigitte Bardot is selling her villa in St Tropez and moving to Liverpool.

As Schiffer points out, it seems clear that nothing specific is communicated hereby about the kind of way Godard thinks of Bardot, let alone the other properties and objects that feature in the report.[10] We can't, for example, rely on the fact that Stella uses the name 'Brigitte Bardot,' since Stella's own name-dropping tendencies suffice to explain her choice. Despite this, the belief report seems no less intelligible than reports where a great deal more is known about modes available to the believer.

The difficulty for the weak and strong descriptive solutions to the problem of empty names is that there are cases like (3) that are equally silent about the relevant modes of presentation for embedded names but where the names are empty. Recall that for views that espouse such solutions, the burden of what makes the reports true or false falls on the believers' attitude to certain propositions that contain descriptive modes of presentation in place of the missing referents. But if the speaker can't even specify a determinate *type* of mode, then she doesn't have a belief of the right kind to report—one that has all the specificity of a belief about a particular individual, apart from the fact that there is no particular for it to be about.[11]

Here are two cases of this kind. Some mistakes about what there is in the world might be quite pervasive, and not—as in the case of 'Vulcan'—simply attributable to the failure of a specific scientific theory. Consider Schiffer's 'Brigitte Bardot' case, and now imagine that Bardot doesn't in fact exist, with apparent references to this person rooted in an extremely elaborate, pervasive hoax (even apparent sightings are based on deception). Consider someone who has been made aware of this, and who, on the basis of hearing Stella utter (3), exclaims:

(4) Jean Luc Godard actually believes that Brigitte Bardot is selling her villa in St Tropez and moving to Liverpool!

The situation is just about as bad as before. There is virtually no hint about which mode of presentation is relied on by Godard. On the weak as well strong solution, therefore, there is no specific belief, or even specific *type* of belief, to be reported on. I take this to be completely counterintuitive. In some sense or other, when the speaker utters (4) he reports on a specific belief, and the report may well be true.

The following is an example that makes the same point but involves a belief report containing a fictional name ('Poirot'). Suppose we know that Smith has heard of Hercule Poirot, having either read (parts of) some of the Agatha Christie stories, or watched (parts of) movies like *Death on the Nile*, or heard others talk about these fictional works, or heard about Poirot in classes on the nature of fiction, or... (and so on). Suppose we are now told: 'Smith believes that Poirot has a moustache.' Is there really implicit reference here to some relatively specific mode of presentation that is part of what is expressed or implicated by 'Smith believes that Poirot has a moustache?' Scarcely. We have no right to assume anything very much about how Smith represents Poirot. While the options are no doubt more limited than with ordinary names, they remain vast. In addition to the more usual scenarios, imagine that the speaker heard Smith exclaim: 'He has a moustache!' on the basis of watching part of *Death on the Nile* (falling asleep before he saw much more and never appreciating that the person was called 'Poirot', that he was a famous Belgian detective, and so on). Even this kind of situation might confirm the report 'Smith believes that Poirot has a moustache.'[12]

Defective Belief Reports and the Role of 'Engagement'

As we saw earlier, the weak descriptive solution to the problem of empty names in belief reports has difficulty with the 'deliberate use' problem facing DR. The solution finds it hard to motivate the choice of (1) and (2) as an appropriate way of phrasing belief in associated descriptive propositions if the speaker thinks that the names are empty. The 'missing mode' objection now suggests that the weak and strong descriptive solutions will (often) not be able to come up with associated descriptive propositions. The 'no [complete] proposition' problem therefore remains unsolved. What else remains for the proponent of DR?

In what follows I shall describe a rather different approach, one that shows no such reliance on specific modes of presentation and at the same time offers a natural solution to the 'deliberate use' problem. To motivate the approach, I want to return to our starting point: the thought that the phenomenon of empty names in belief reports presents DR with a potentially devastating challenge. The thought was that belief reports containing empty names give all the appearance of expressing true/false propositions. Both critics and proponents of DR then take it to be a constraint on a viable semantic theory that it should account for this appearance.

It is simply not true, however, that there is always such an appearance. Some belief reports are deeply defective because of the way in which embedded empty names fail to refer—so deeply defective that at first sight they lack any appearance of expressing a proposition. Cases of this kind, I shall argue, should lead us to modify our appreciation of the problems that face DR, and argue for a different style of solution to such problems.

Thus consider the claim:

(5) Jones believes that man is about to attack him.

where Jones has sincerely uttered the sentence 'That man is about to attack me!', and where both speaker and audience are in a position to grasp Jones' demonstrative reference, should there be any people in the area demonstrated. But suppose that Jones is delusional; there are no people where Jones is pointing, something that is utterly clear to the speaker and audience alike. Of course, this is a case involving a demonstrative description, not a name, but the difference is unimportant; just let Jones introduce a name for 'that man', for ease of reference ('That man—I'll call him "Psycho"—is about to attack me!'). Question: has the speaker spoken truly? Hardly. If Jones was delusional, we and the audience would hardly accept the speaker's claim as true (or, indeed, false). Indeed, it seems that the speaker would have to be equally delusional to report Jones' belief in this way. While there are lots of true belief reports in the neighbourhood of (5) (such as 'Jones believes that *there is a man nearby* about to attack him', etc.), (5) appears not to be one of them. This is an intuition that appears to confirm DR's suspicion of sentences containing empty names and demonstratives.

At least, that is our intuition when we consider the audience's response to (5) as one that is totally disengaged, delivered *sub specie aeternitatis*, as it were. But now suppose instead that the audience is appropriately engaged with the situation that prompted the utterance of (5). Suppose they have an interest in Jones' behaviour and condition. Imagine, for example, that they comprise psychiatrists who are sympathetically talking him through his condition, and that one of them hits upon the truth: 'Now I see why you are so worried. You are afraid of that man in the corner.' (5) might be the report that sums up this discovery. If so, the speaker's utterance of (5) is likely to strike this audience as a clear truth, while saying 'Jones does not believe that that man is about to attack him' will strike them as clearly false. Not reporting Jones' belief this way in Jones' presence might even strike people as unconscionably insensitive, something that ought to be forbidden by a psychiatrists' Code of Ethics. A later report, no longer made in the presence of whatever prompted the delusion, might simply say that 'Jones believed that Psycho—the guy he saw in the corner—was about to attack him.' (Just about any kind of term might be used to report Jones' belief. The psychiatrist's choice of therapy for Jones might even dictate that she use the second-person pronoun 'you' when describing Jones' belief, as in: 'Jones believes you are about to attack him. We know what you are up to, so go away!')

My suggestion is that our assessment of (5) as true is only appropriate from the point of view of such an engaged perspective. Similarly, if a speaker is aware of Jones' delusion, her attempt to describe Jones' belief in (5) and related reports is only intelligible if we see her as speaking from such an engaged perspective. If we try to offer a disengaged assessment of (5), we are bound to see (5) as deeply defective—precisely, as it seems, because what is being said depends crucially on the availability of a referent for 'that man'.

This suggestion leaves us with a number of challenges: first, how to understand the relevant notion of an 'engaged perspective', and, secondly, how to apply this account to ordinary belief reports like (2) that do not seem to rest on an engaged perspective.

Belief and Pretence

These challenges are best answered, I believe, by appealing to the notion of pretence or make-believe in the form developed by Kendall Walton (1990). In Walton's influential development of the idea of make-believe, children as well as adults play games of make-believe on the basis of props that mandate that they imagine certain things.[13] Thus a children's game may require its participants to imagine that certain oddly shaped stumps are bears, that ropes are lassoes, and that an action done to a stump is an action against the corresponding bear (putting a rope around a stump, for instance, means a bear is being lassoed). Similarly, adults are participants in a game of make-believe when they read a novel that mandates their imagining that certain events really happened (that there really was a famous self-important little detective called 'Poirot' who had a moustache, for example). Something is fictionally true, true in the pretence or make-believe, when it is thus mandated to be imagined.

If DR is right about names in standard contexts, then we can even assume that names are typically used as devices of direct reference in the scope of the pretence adopted by consumers of works of fiction. For when we make-believe that the world is a certain way, and from this imaginative perspective use language to describe the world, part of our pretence involves imagining that the way language applies to the world accords with a certain semantics— presumably, the semantics that language actually has, unless we are deliberately imagining language to have some kind of non-standard semantics.[14] Assuming DR, this means that it is true in the pretence that the names we use are devices of direct reference, making a direct contribution to the expression of object-dependent propositions and designating their referents in this (imagined) world on the basis of the usual sorts of relationships of acquaintance. If so, fictional names need not present the DR-theorist with much of a worry. For the DR-theorist they are then likely to be directly referential in the only sense that counts: when they are used, they are used in the scope of a pretence in which they function as devices of direct reference. The same is true of demonstratives used in the course of watching a play (for example, 'That man is about to attack his wife!', said while watching *Othello*).

Now consider Jones and his psychiatrist. When Jones says: 'That man is about to attack me!' his utterance suffers from a serious defect. There is an intuitive sense, made official by DR, in which he has failed to say anything. But when his psychiatrist murmurs in response: 'Let's see how we deal with that man', the psychiatrist cannot be accused of a similar confusion, since there is no serious intent to single out a demonstratively salient individual. The psychiatrist simply goes along with Jones' delusion, doing *as if* Jones really can perceive someone and so is in a position to use the demonstrative correctly. The psychiatrist pretends that the world conforms, in this way at least, to Jones' beliefs, and then deliberately speaks from the perspective of that pretence. What we earlier called her engaged perspective is a pretend-perspective. Note that what is true in this pretence will partly depend on certain decisions the psychiatrist makes, perhaps determined by what form of therapy she deems appropriate. Thus she might continue: 'You are *wrong* to think he is about to attack you; let's go up to him' or 'You are *right* to think he is about to attack; let's move away.' The delusional Jones is not playing games, so can't set the rules; the psychiatrist is, and can.

Of course, it might be an exaggeration to call what the psychiatrist is doing 'indulging in make-believe'. Her pretence is not richly imaginative, but deliberately shallow and opportunistic. After all, part of the reason for adopting it is that it forms part of a therapeutic plan to help eradicate the very circumstances—Jones' delusionary visions—that prompted its adoption in the first place. Nonetheless, it seems proper to say that the psychiatrist is involved in pretence, if only in the relatively weak sense that she is doing *as if* the world is a certain way in order to achieve a certain purpose (not, this time, the intrinsic pleasure of indulging in make-believe, but to help a patient).

We can let the case of non-fictional empty names and demonstratives go the same way. Suppose we are in discussion with Vulcan-believers. One way for unbelievers to conduct the conversation is to go along with Vulcan-believers: 'So tell me, where will Vulcan be a year from now?' This might enable them to learn more about Vulcan-theory from the inside; it might even allow them to demonstrate to Vulcan-believers that Vulcan doesn't exist, by showing up inconsistencies. Speakers who do this are involved in a bit of pretence, pretending to accept an alien ontology in order to communicate effectively with those embracing it. Of course there is little by way of *phenomenological* evidence to suggest that such speakers are involved in pretence, but I think that appearances are deceptive in this case. Unlike the imaginative involvement required of the psychiatrist, which is centered on the psychiatrist herself (her senses, her perceptual environment), speakers who indulge in Vulcan-talk imagine only that the world conforms to a certain theory. The phenomenology of their imagining is therefore bound to be different—there is a sense in which far less is required of them.

Of course, there is no reason why speakers should be close in time to Vulcan-believers for this kind of talk to have a point. We might wish to continue Vulcan-talk, going along with Vulcan-theory in order to articulate its content in a way that mimics how Vulcan-believers would have done it, or perhaps to challenge the way they applied the theory. (For another example, consider the way a historian of science might say: 'It was wrong to say, as some phlogiston theorists did, that phlogiston had negative weight. Other claims central to their chemistry ensured that phlogiston must have had a small, if negligible, weight.') Here too, therefore, there is scope for an appeal to a form of make-believe. Likewise with talk involving myths and legends, falling as they do between mere fiction and theories.

What about statements reporting, rather than giving expression to, such alien beliefs: Jones' beliefs or those of Vulcan-believers, say? They are bound to go the same way. The reporting of propositional attitudes is in fact a familiar activity in games of make-believe. Thus in our earlier example of the 'stumps-are-bears' game, participants in the game may truthfully remark: 'Johnny thinks he has lassoed a bear, but he hasn't' (perhaps Johnny fails to see that his rope has slipped off the stump). Ken Walton showed long ago how to extend this model to the case of belief concerning fiction. Taking the movie *Death on the Nile* to be the appropriate prop, for example, it seems entirely appropriate to report Smith's reaction to that movie from the perspective of the make-believe that the movie is a reliable record of actual events involving a world-famous Belgian detective called 'Poirot'. That way we get (1).

Now consider our psychiatrist as she conveys Jones' fears to her colleagues. In the presence of Jones, there may be little choice about how to report what Jones believes. If she is to report Jones' belief in a non-patronizing way that fairly captures how Jones views its content, the psychiatrist had better play along with Jones' delusions. Against that pretend-background, certain reports about what Jones believes are clearly true, others false. In particular, her utterance of (5) is true. And not only (5), but even a more blatantly *de re* report like:

(5′)   Jones believes, about that man in the corner, that the latter is about to attack him.

or (worse, in some ways) a quantified belief report like:

(5″)   There is a man in that corner who, so Jones believes, is about to attack him.

All these reports strike us as true once we grant the sympathetic sense in which (5) counts as true.

In exactly the same way, it seems entirely appropriate to report Pièrre's Vulcan-beliefs from the perspective of the pretence that our benighted forebears were right to posit a planet they called 'Vulcan' that caused certain perturbations in Mercury's orbit. Against that pretend-background, the speaker's utterance of (2) is true. And not only (2), but also associated sentences like:

(2′)   Vulcan is one of a number of planets that Pièrre believed to be larger than Mercury,

and:

(2″)   There is a planet posited by nineteenth-century astronomers, and dubbed 'Vulcan', that Pièrre believed to be larger than Mercury.

As in the case of our delusional Jones, speakers quite properly utter such sentences in full knowledge (or even just belief) that there is no Vulcan.[15] If there is a need to show that they know how things really stand, all they need to do is utter a concessive disclaimer ('Of course, we know it doesn't really exist, that it was wrongly posited'), an option also open to our psychiatrist should someone question her utterance of (5)–(5″).

Let's briefly review where we stand. Earlier, we were left with a two-fold challenge: how to understand the notion of an 'engaged perspective' that played such a crucial role in securing a charitable understanding of (5), and how to apply this account to ordinary belief reports like (2) which do not seem to rest on an engaged perspective. The answer, I suggested, came from the idea of pretence or make-believe, resulting in a certain *pretence* account of belief reports containing empty names. (Strictly speaking, of course, a pretence account of this kind merely requires speakers to *believe*, not know, that certain names are empty. If speakers want to describe what agents believe from the point of view of the commitments held by these agents, the belief— or even just the suspicion—that these commitments are false is enough to prompt adoption of the pretence.)

What about cases where speakers are not *pretending* that certain empty names they use are non-empty, but where they simply assume, falsely, that the names are non-empty? Earlier I set such cases aside on the grounds that our intuitions about them were oddly mixed. By appealing to pretence, however, we are able to cast light on such cases as well. Suppose we accept the view that speakers implicitly take names and demonstratives to be devices of direct reference. If those names are empty, they and their embedding sentences lack content. In understanding this about (1) and (2) as used by those who are unaware that 'Poirot' and 'Vulcan' are empty, we therefore also understand the seriousness of the mistake they make—an egregious mistake in the case of (1) since the name 'Poirot' is not even intended to be used as a name for an actual person. So understood, therefore, (1) and (2) strike us as defective, deeply so in the case of (1). But in understanding the mistake, we also know how to make up for it. On hearing (1) and (2), we—as critical but charitable listeners—implicitly represent the names they embed as fully functional, and hence as non-empty. We do this by implicitly *pretending* that they are fully functional, that the world we inhabit is such as to imbue such sentences and the component sentences they embed with propositional content (e.g., by imagining, as before, that *Death on the Nile* is a reliable record of actual fact, or that Vulcan-theory is genuinely true). That explains why hearers are able to hear (1) and (2) as, in a sense, true. Because it is hard to separate the unmassaged use of (1) and (2) from the use of the same sentences as heard through the ears of charitable, conniving hearers, such claims can sound both confused and true.[16]

Externally Oriented Pretence

Let us return to the case that mainly interests us, that of belief reports containing empty names known or believed by the reporters to be empty. Clearly the story told so far can't be the whole story. On the pretence account, belief reports involving names that are known to be empty can scarcely be said to be true in the strict sense. Asked to say what Jones really believes, out of earshot of Jones, the psychiatrist must surely answer: 'Jones believes that there is a man in that corner who is about to attack him' rather than (5): 'Jones believes that *that man* is about to attack him.' To the extent that in uttering (5) she acts as if the world has features that she really believes it lacks, there is surely a sense in which she dissimulates. She no doubt does this for an excellent reason (perhaps it is part of her therapy for Jones), but it is one that is hard to square with the strict truth of her report. For the same reason, the pretence account must admit that saying 'Smith believes that Poirot has a moustache' or 'Pièrre believed that Vulcan was larger than Mercury' is, in a sense, to dissimulate. These reports are at best fictionally true, true from the perspective of the pretence. But don't we have the strong impression—an impression we somehow need to capture—that the reports are *genuinely* true?

One answer to this objection is simply to decree that a sentence that is fictionally true in this way is, in the relevant sense, simply true; that this is what truth amounts to for such sentences. Such is the view explicitly adopted by Gareth Evans in Evans (1982). (At least, he adopts it for the case of sentences like (1), which are rooted in an extended game of make-believe based on a prop—a book or a movie, say—whose purpose is to facilitate such make-believe.) And such a view seems right for those cases. The sense in which a sentence like (1) counts as true cannot be separated from the way it counts as true in the pretence based on treating certain props (movies, novels) as reliable records of fact. One way to see this is as follows. Exactly the same circumstances that make it true to say: 'Smith believes that Poirot is a world-famous little Belgian detective who has a moustache' would make it true to say: 'Smith believes that some world-famous little Belgian detective has a moustache.' Any conversation that counts the first as true in the relevant sense would also count the second as (*a fortiori*) true. (The speaker might utter the second if he has forgotten Poirot's name, say.) Pretence aside, however, the speaker may be fully aware that Smith has no such existential belief. She may know that Smith refuses to believe that there are any famous Belgian detectives anywhere.

Contrary to appearances, therefore, (1) doesn't really present DR with a problem, for once we take account of the pretence-background to the speaker's utterance of (1) we see that the name 'Poirot' functions as a standard non-empty name.[17] But none of this helps us with (2). While the speaker who utters (1) may know full well that Smith doesn't really believe that there ever was such a person as Poirot, it is undeniable that Pièrre really did believe that there was a planet of the kind described in Vulcan-theory. So even if the pretence theory fully explains the sense in which (1) is true, it doesn't fully explain the sense in which (2) is true.

To understand that sense, we need to draw a distinction. Children playing games and readers of novels are typically caught up in what we might call 'internally oriented' pretence. As participants, they are interested in the world of the fiction and its goings on. But in externally oriented pretence, we pretend that the world is a certain way, not in order to pursue the imaginative thought that the world is that way but to say something about the real world that provides the props for our pretence.[18] Consider our earlier example of Johnny and the 'stumps-are-bears' game. The real-world circumstance that Johnny has put a rope around the stump makes it fictional that a bear has been lassoed. The latter fictional truth is what interests him as he triumphantly prods the stump with a stick. So here we have internally oriented pretence. But it is not what interests his mother, for example, as she tells him that 'this hunter gets no dinner if he doesn't leave the bear alone for a spell'. Mother is involved in externally oriented pretence, affirming the real world circumstance that makes her claim true in the make-believe—the fact that Johnny will get no dinner if he doesn't stop prodding the stump. (More generally, she asserts a proposition that is true at a world w iff w contains a (real) circumstance that makes her utterance fictionally true relative to w. This incorporates the fact that real possibilities, such as Johnny's possibly putting a rope around two stumps at the same time, make for fictional possibilities—Johnny possibly lassoing two bears at the same time.)[19]

Like other talk involving fictional names, belief reporting involving fictional names is, I suggest, typically a matter of internally oriented pretence.[20] So, I think, it is with (1). But (2), and its fellow reports (2') and (2''), are different. The pretence underlying an utterance of (2) is externally oriented pretence: The speaker, engaging in the pretence that the world contains a unique [actual] planet responsible for the perturbations in the orbit of Mercury in the manner described by Vulcan-theory (a planet thus far unobserved, but one that people can nonetheless talk and speculate about in much the same way as they can about other objects in the world), affirms a certain real world circumstance, namely the one that makes her belief report true in this pretence. (That is what she asserts about the actual world. More generally, she asserts a proposition true in a world w if w contains a circumstance that makes her utterance fictionally true relative to w.) Interpreting (2) this way will not only make it clear why it strikes us as a report attributing a genuine, seriously entertained belief (unlike (1)), but will also explain the virtues of using empty names this way, fully aware that they are empty (the 'deliberate use of empty names' phenomenon for the case of non-fictional names).

So what genuine, non-pretended belief attribution would make (2)–(2″) true in the scope of the pretence? Well, given the unavailability of a referent for 'Vulcan' outside of the pretence, the easiest way of understanding what is being attributed is in terms of some kind of descriptive 'mode of presentation' of a representational kind: Pièrre held a certain belief involving a descriptive mode of presentation that—in terms of best fit—represents nothing if construed from outside of the pretence, and represents the planet Vulcan if construed from the point of view of the pretence that there really is a planet called 'Vulcan' responsible for such-and-such perturbations in the orbit of Mercury. Which belief? The answer seems clear in this case. Since we know that Pièrre was an amateur astronomer, he is likely to have known the authoritative reference-fixing description for 'Vulcan', and so the belief being ascribed to him is presumably something like the belief that the [actual] planet responsible for such-and-such perturbations in the orbit of Mercury— the actual Vulcanish planet, for short—is larger than Mercury. (The inclusion of the rigidifier 'actual' ensures that the descriptive representation is treated as rigid, which is surely what is intended. It reflects an important world-centred aspect of the believer's representation, just as the inclusion of 'I' in descriptive representations of the form *the [actual] person I am acquainted with in such-and-such ways* reflects an important egocentric aspect. And it is needed if we are to have a sensible account of the modal content of what is asserted with a statement like (2)—an account of what makes such an assertion true at worlds other than the actual world.)[21]

This kind of answer is, of course, close to the answer proposed by descriptive solutions to the 'no proposition' problem, so it is important to stress the differences between those solutions and the present account. One difference is that on the present account such a descriptive representation doesn't capture anything like the meaning of 'Vulcan' or the contribution it makes to propositions expressed with the use of sentences containing the name. For DR the contribution made by 'Vulcan' can only be an object: that is, the planet Vulcan if 'Vulcan' is understood from inside the pretence that there is such a planet, no object otherwise. The role of Pièrre's representational mode is quite different. It is what, from the perspective of the pretence, makes the belief a belief about Vulcan. (Despite the rhetoric, none of this is meant to assume any particular representationalist philosophy. In particular, I hope that an account of this kind is right even if there are no special mental entities that do the representing. My reference to representations gets its cash-value from the idea that believers represent the world as being a certain way, and that what makes it fictionally true to say that Pièrre has a belief about Vulcan is that he represents the world as containing a unique actual planet fitting the conditions of Vulcan-theory.)[22]

A second difference is that the present account does not insist that we know in any detail what belief is being attributed through the speaker's reliance on external pretence. The specificity of a belief report like (2) results in large part from its engagement in the (external) pretence that there is such an object as Vulcan, and that Pièrre therefore has a belief about a specific object. That kind of specificity may go hand-in-hand with fairly detailed knowledge of the mode of presentation available to the agent of the belief report, but it is also compatible with substantial lack of knowledge. In truth, we can't even be sure in the case of Pièrre. Imagine that the speaker in the case of (2) is talking about what Pièrre believed at a time when Pièrre had forgotten much of what he previously knew about Vulcan; perhaps at that time Pièrre deferentially represented Vulcan as the [actual] planet called 'Vulcan' by expert astronomers, in which case it is the way expert astronomers relied on Vulcan-theory's theoretical description of Vulcan that makes it the case that Pièrre's belief counts—from within the pretence—as a belief about Vulcan. So long as context makes it clear that this is Pièrre's situation, we have a determinate grasp on his descriptive belief. If not, we only have a grasp on something a bit more disjunctive.

In other cases, we may have far less of a grasp on the descriptive belief being reported. The reason is that there may be vastly more ways in which the believer could have represented the world, leading directly to the problem of the 'unknown mode'. In particular, there could be representations based on various forms of perceptual acquaintance, something explicitly ruled out in the 'Vulcan' pretence. Consider again a belief report like (4), uttered in a situation in which the speaker knows that 'Bardot'-references, sightings, etc., rest on an extremely pervasive hoax, and where she wants to describe whatever genuine belief Godard has in a way that doesn't presuppose any knowledge of relevant modes. In this case, she can do no better than pretend that reference with the empty name 'Bardot,' associated demonstratives and other devices of reference is successful after all; that there is no hoax but just an immensely varied set of ways in which she and others can be acquainted with a particular person called 'Bardot.' The speaker is thereby able to assert that Godard has a certain genuine (descriptive) belief, namely one which can be described, once it is assessed from the perspective of her pretence, as the belief that Bardot is selling her villa in St Tropez and moving to Liverpool—perhaps this is the descriptive belief that the person called 'Bardot' with whom he is acquainted in such-and-such ways is selling her villa in St Tropez . . ., or the descriptive belief that the person he knows as his neighbour is selling her villa in St Tropez . . ., or . . . Since the speaker lacks knowledge of the mode, she can't be much more specific, and so she only manages to assert what is in effect an indeterminate, disjunctive proposition concerning Godard's real beliefs.

Despite this indeterminacy, (4) retains the surface specificity of an ordinary belief report such as (3). The usefulness of the sort of pretending that induces such specificity despite the indeterminacy should not be underestimated. As we saw earlier, it typically occurs as part of an empathetic, imaginative engagement with certain alien views—views the speaker regards as errone- ous—that has rewards of its own. We now see that, not infrequently, such empathetic, imaginative engagement yields an efficient and reliable way in which to understand what sorts of representations might feature in a believer's real beliefs, even when it is well-nigh impossible to give a determinate description of these beliefs.[23]

Let me finish this discussion by addressing, all too briefly, an apparent difficulty for a theory of this kind. As the theory has been presented, there seems to be no reason for its account of the representations that (2) and (4) attribute to believers to stop with descriptive Vulcan- or Bardot-representa- tions. In talking about what genuine beliefs are reported by (2) or (4), we should surely treat the representations that make something a belief about Mercury or Liverpool as no less descriptive, if only because there seems to be no relevant principled difference between empty and non-empty names. (As we saw earlier there is a good sense in which *any* name might be empty.) But now we have a problem, for such a descriptivist view conflicts with a widely accepted doctrine about the externalist nature of *de re* belief.

My own view is that the supporter of DR should hold two doctrines that are sometimes thought to be incompatible: First, the semantic contribution of a name is as DR says it is, namely its referent; secondly, what makes it true to say that a person has a belief about X is that she has a partly descriptive representational mode of presentation of X, typically one that represents X in terms of some type of relationship of acquaintance between the believer and X. In the case of a name like 'Mercury', this might be *the celestial body I have heard of under the name 'Mercury' by others, the celestial body I am now looking at through this telescope*, and so on. A view of this kind has prominent supporters,[24] but, of course, a great many detractors as well, in particular those who accept some kind of externalist account of what makes something X the subject of a belief. I'll make two brief points in defence of such a position before making an irenic suggestion. The first point is that a more elaborate account of the position would make it clear that not just any acquaintance-based descriptive representations would suffice. We should look to acquaintance-based descriptive representations that are appropriately resilient, ones that capture how believers would be disposed, on reflection, to describe the objects of their belief, not ones that they would offer on demand. (There is nothing ad hoc about this. Something like a condition of resilience is surely needed if our belief reports are supposed to explain behaviour reliably; and note that even ordinary descriptive representations are subject to correction in this way—what makes Pièrre's belief a belief 'about Vulcan', as it were, is that some appropriate resilient descriptive representation in his possession represents Vulcan from the perspective of the pretence, not that just any description that Pièrre takes to describe Vulcan does so.) Secondly, there are situations in which we ascribe beliefs about some object X, but where no externalist account can work, for example beliefs about Neptune, at a time when Neptune was known only as the planet responsible for certain perturbations in the orbit of Uranus. (We can even do this in the case of Mercury: in some contexts, merely having the belief that 'the closest planet to the sun is certain to have a surface temperature in excess of 1,000 degrees Celsius' can count as believing that 'Mercury has a surface temperature in excess of 1,000 degrees Celsius.') Descriptivism about representational modes is therefore a position that is attractively general in scope.

The irenic suggestion is just this. Without buying into a fight about what really warrants describing a person's belief by means of a belief report whose 'that'-clause contains a name, we can simply say that such a belief report is used to assert the claim that the person has a belief involving an appropriate way of representing the object named, whether the representing is done descriptively or in a way that is *de re* and dependent on the causal and even social antecedents of the speaker's conception of a thing (philosophers can speculate about how the trick is done).[25] This story will encompass the names 'Mercury', 'Bardot', and 'Liverpool' as used in (2) and (3), no less than the names 'Vulcan' or 'Bardot' as used in (2) and (4), and will not depend on any particular account of representation. From such a perspective, the only relevant feature that differentiates 'Mercury', 'Bardot', and 'Liverpool' in (2) and (3) from 'Vulcan' or 'Bardot' in (2) and (4) are certain background referential assumptions. In the former case, the speaker *believes* that there are represented objects, since he believes that the names in question genuinely refer; in the latter case, the speaker *make-believes* that there are represented objects.

This picture retains the desired symmetry between names that are (believed to be) empty and names that are (believed to be) non-empty, enabling us to explain why it is so easy for someone to agree with (2), for example, yet express a kind of disagreement by adding: 'And, by the way, I happen to think that Mercury doesn't really exist either—the idea that there is such a planet is based on a massive hoax.' The speaker is here challenging the first speaker's background referential belief where 'Mercury' is concerned, and, in a smooth transition, replacing it with an attitude of doing *as if* there is such a planet in order to describe the beliefs of those taken in by the hoax. To all appearances, the shift occurs without a clear shift in our understanding of the belief that is being attributed to Pièrre. In general, a picture of this kind holds that belief reports embedding names don't so much serve to *specify* what is believed (namely, certain singular propositions, so that the attributed beliefs are wide) as *characterize* what is believed, relying on context and pretence to help the characterization along. I take such a picture to be strongly supported in the case of empty names (given DR), and I have now argued that, in the absence of any principled difference between empty and non-empty names, we should accept it for all belief reports containing names.[26]

This completes my explanation of why belief-reporters knowingly use empty names (more generally, names they believe to be empty), an explanation that invokes the pleasure and usefulness of imaginative play, even when the orientation of such play is external.

One final comment. When talking about non-fictional empty names, I concentrated on what we might call the unapologetic use of such names: the deliberate use of a name like 'Vulcan' without the concession that the name's referent doesn't exist. Often, however, speakers who are aware the names they use are empty will indicate through the use of negative existentials that the names are empty. In particular, a speaker might prefer to state (2) in the apologetic form:

> (2*) Vulcan doesn't exist, but Pièrre believed that it did and that it was larger than Mercury.

Locutions like (2*) suggest that there is an intimate connection between the problem of negative existentials and belief reports containing empty non-fictional names.[27] From the perspective of the pretence account this is something to be expected, since pretence theorists tend to prefer a pretence account of negative existentials. Take Walton's view that a speaker who utters the negative existential 'Vulcan doesn't exist' does so from the perspective of the pretence that Vulcan-theory is successful, and by doing so asserts that certain non-pretended referring-attempts—the kind that, in the scope of the pretence, successfully secure reference to Vulcan—fail to secure reference to anything.[28] Using the gloss provided above, we can take such attempts to be those relying on appropriate descriptive specifications like 'the planet responsible in such-and-so a way for such-and-such perturbations in the orbit of Mercury', 'the planet called "Vulcan" by other astronomers', and so on. The claim that Pièrre believed that Vulcan exists can then be given exactly the same treatment as (2) itself. Pièrre genuinely believed that there was a planetary body responsible in the appropriate way for specified perturbations in the orbit of Mercury, and thus had a genuine belief that the speaker is then able to describe, from inside the scope of the pretence, as the belief that Vulcan exists. Apologetic versions of belief reports containing empty non-fictional names thus have a pretence treatment that is entirely continuous with the pretence treatment afforded to non-apologetic versions.

NOTES

This chapter began as a commentary on a paper by Bill Lycan on his paratactic approach to belief reports, both presented at Victoria University of Wellington. Thanks to Lycan and M. J. Cresswell for useful comments. I am also grateful to an anonymous reader for Oxford University Press, and especially to Jonathan McKeown-Green.

1. Salmon (1986). Strictly speaking, Salmon takes the 'theory of direct reference' to be the theory that such terms are non-descriptive, although he also holds the

neo-Russellian view that their semantic (information) value is what they refer to. I shall follow the common trend of using 'theory of direct reference' for the stronger neo-Russellian view. See also Kaplan (1989) and Soames (1987, 2002). Recanati (1993) allows for a species of semantic value or content that includes modes of presentation as well as individuals.

2. See Russell (1956). Most influential in producing the demise has been Kripke (1980), initially published in 1972 as an article.

3. Apart from their importance to DR, statements of this kind are of critical relevance to fictionalist programs. If we want to be fictionalists about the role that a particular kind of term plays in a certain type of discourse involving the term, we better have an appropriate way of making sense of the truth of the statement that *t* doesn't exist, that it is only *fictional* that *t* exists, that ordinary folk believe that *t* has such-and-such properties despite *t* not existing, and so on (where '*t*' is replaced by a term of the relevant kind). In particular, we better not find ourselves positing special 'non-existent' entities to make sense of the truth of such statements, for that would cast doubt on our fictionalist credentials.

4. Poirot is Agatha Christie's fictional detective, Hercule Poirot—hero of works like *Taken at the Flood, The Murder of Roger Ackroyd*, and *Dead Man's Folly*. Vulcan is the planet that was (unsuccessfully) posited by Urbain Le Verrier in 1859 to explain the advancing perihelion of Mercury's orbit around the sun, perturbations later explained by Einstein's theory of relativity as a mere byproduct of the Sun's gravitational field. (Le Verrier's hypothesis followed his earlier successful positing of a new planet, Neptune, to explain certain perturbations in the orbit of Uranus.) Throughout this chapter, I am taking it for granted that the names 'Poirot' and 'Vulcan' are genuinely empty, a view accepted by most Millians although it is disputed by Nathan Salmon, who argues that such names denote abstract artifacts of some kind (Salmon, 1998; see also Soames, 2002: 89–95). Salmon agrees, however, that there are (rare) cases of genuinely empty, 'thoroughly non-referring' names, so the problem of how to understand belief reports involving empty names will not disappear even if Salmon is right about 'Poirot' and 'Vulcan.' For criticism of Salmon's view, see Reimer (2001) and Kroon (2003).

5. Accounts that invoke modes of presentation include Stephen Schiffer's 'hidden indexical theory', the 'unarticulated constituents' account of John Perry and Mark Crimmins, Mark Richard's 'Russellian Annotated Matrix' theory, and Recanati's 'quasi-singular proposition' account.

6. For more on 'gappy' or 'unfilled' propositions, see Braun (1993), Adams and Stecker (1993), and Reimer (2001). Unlike the other authors, Braun argues that sentences containing empty names express unfilled propositions that nonetheless have a truth-value; in particular, the atomic sentence 'Vulcan is larger than Mercury' expresses a *false* unfilled proposition because there is no referent for 'Vulcan' to make it true, while the compound sentence (2) expresses a *true*

unfilled proposition because Pièrre was in the appropriate belief-state. (In fact, assuming there was no founder of Rome named 'Romulus', Braun's view implies that a sentence like 'Romulus is larger than Mercury' expresses the same false unfilled proposition as 'Vulcan is larger than Mercury', resulting in the odd consequence that 'Pièrre believes that Romulus was larger than Mercury' expresses the same true unfilled proposition as (2).) Despite the ingenuity of Braun's proposal, I share the reservations that some Millians have about the idea of truth-valued unfilled propositions (Reimer 2001; but cf. Braun 2005).

7. Here I assume a Russellian understanding of definite descriptions. On a Straw-sonian understanding, the use of the definite description would involve a presupposition on the speaker's part that there is an object of the described kind. But that would leave the Strawsonian in the same kind of boat as DR: the belief report, even when phrased descriptively, would not be used to make a truth-valued statement.

8. See, for example, Adams, Stecker, and Fuller (1992), and Adams and Stecker (1993).

9. Schiffer (1995). Schiffer here addresses only hidden-indexical theories, but it seems clear that examples of the kind presented are also a problem for pragmatic theories.

10. Still, not just anything counts. As Schiffer points out, Goddard's simply over-hearing an unrecognized person say that she was moving wouldn't make the report true, even if this person was in fact Bardot.

11. Crimmins (1992) claims that in cases like (3) speakers still have a grasp, albeit a thin one, on the notions involved. We can take Stella to be talking about Godard's notion for Bardot, identified, if nothing else works, as *the one she is talking about* (173ff). But this identification provides far too little content for the purposes of the weak descriptive solution, which wants notions to do duty for missing referents, and hence to leave us with genuinely informative belief claims despite the absence of referents.

12. The belief report might arise as follows. Someone holds up a digitally adjusted shot (from the movie *Death on the Nile*) of Poirot without the moustache, says that he is a fictional detective called 'Poirot' who solved a famous case in *Death on the Nile*, and asks whether anyone has an opinion as to how the picture misrepresents Poirot. The response that 'Smith believes that Poirot has a mous-tache' would be perfectly true in this situation.

13. See Walton (1990). For purposes of the present chapter, I take the ideas of pretending, imagining, or making believe to be well enough understood and more or less equivalent.

14. Kripke (1973) uses a principle of this kind (which he calls the 'Pretence Principle') to argue that the case of fiction is unable to provide us with a crucial test for choosing among theories of naming.

15. Speakers can, of course, indulge in such pretence without having the correct views about the world. It is enough that they believe, or even suspect, that Vulcan-theory is false, or that there really is no person in the corner about to attack Jones. This is all to the good, for it allows an appeal to pretence to solve the following more general difficulty facing DR. Suppose you believe that certain names or demonstratives are empty, whether or not they are in fact empty, and then use them to report beliefs. Assuming you also accept DR, it then follows that you implicitly accept that your reports don't have true/false propositional content, which seems bizarre. The pretence view as it has been developed so far suggests that such reports do have propositional content, but (if you are right about the names being empty) only from the point of view of the pretence.

16. Responding to Crimmins' treatment of the occurrence of empty names in belief contexts in Crimmins (1992), Kent Bach comments: '[S]uppose that on Christmas Eve one child says to another, "Billy believes that Santa Claus will be coming tonight." Crimmins denies that the "that"-clause expresses a proposition for Billy to believe. But the speaker thinks it does, and his belief report may well be true' (Bach, 1993: 440). Bach clearly thinks ordinary language-users would count such a report as literally true if Billy was sincere in his prediction. But I think most of us would be torn. We would count such a report as no more, or less, true, than a fully *de re* report like 'There is someone who Billy thinks will come tonight, namely Santa,' which normal speakers would regard as a trivial variant on the earlier report.

17. The speaker may need to highlight the pretence background of (1), but generally only when the contrast between reality and make-believe becomes an issue. Thus, in response to Jones's impatient retort: 'Smith knows as well as anyone that there is no such person as Poirot', the speaker is likely to point out that she is simply playing along with the Poirot stories and movies—and to take Jones to task for being pedantic.

18. The terms 'internally/externally oriented make-believe [or pretence]' roughly map onto Walton's terms 'content oriented make-believe' and 'prop oriented make-believe' (Walton, 1993).

19. See Crimmins (1998) and Richard (2000).

20. This is not always so, of course. It is not so with 'Smith believes that it is true in the Poirot stories that Poirot has a moustache' or 'Smith believes that Poirot is far cleverer that any living detective', for example.

21. In brief: given the speaker's pretence and what is in this case implicated about the relevant [rigidified] representations available to the believer, we should say that his utterance of (2) is fictionally true relative to a world w iff (i) in w Pièrre believes that the Vulcanish planet of w is larger than Mercury, and (ii) it is also true in the pretence that the Vulcanish planet of w is the actual Vulcanish planet. But when is (ii) the case? The only reasonable answer, I think, is that the identity

should hold outside of the pretence. Since outside of the pretence 'the actual Vulcanish planet' rigidly picks out no object at all, it follows that what is asserted with (2) is true at w so long as Pièrre has such a descriptive belief at w, and there is no Vulcanish planet at w. A view of this kind seems especially plausible when we consider a pretence in which a speaker's term secures reference to an actual object once this term is evaluated apart from the pretence. Thus consider the psychiatrist's utterance of (5). If, unbeknownst to the psychiatrist, Jones really did see a man, it seems clear that what the psychiatrist asserts is true at a world w only if Jones' demonstrative representation of 'that man' in w picks out the very person he actually saw. (Cf. also Crimmins' remarks on modal content in Crimmins, 1998: 26ff. For elaboration and criticism of Crimmins' position, see Richard, 2000.)

22. In particular, I hope that the account is consistent with a 'map' theory of belief. See Lewis (1994) and Jackson (1996).

23. Cf. Recanati (2000: 225–6). Recanati argues that the fictive, or pretended, ascription of a singular belief about, say, Santa Claus can amount to a factive, or non-pretended, ascription of a pseudo-singular belief, where the latter has all the features of a singular belief apart from the lack of an object for the name 'Santa Claus'. (Because this is virtually all that Recanati has to say about pseudo-singular beliefs, it is unclear how close his views are to the kind of views I have defended in this chapter.)

24. See, for example, Lewis (1994: 424–5).

25. For more on *de re* modes, see Bach (1987) and Recanati (1993). Cf. also Devitt's account of belief ascription in Devitt (1995). Although Devitt is well known for a certain version of externalism, this account is similarly liberal in the kind of representational meanings he allows.

26. Much more can, and should, be said about this general perspective. Recent defences include Shier (1996) and (in a version less tied to a descriptivist account of the representations underlying the use of names) Bach (1997). Neither philosopher has anything to say about the case of empty names, although if I am right that provides one of the best pieces of evidence for a view of this kind. (Still, the omission is not surprising, since the case of empty names spells trouble for the way Shier and Bach understand the connection between a belief report embedding a name and the belief ascribed by way of the report.)

27. Note that unless Smith was confused about the status of the name 'Poirot' in (1), we don't similarly say: 'Smith believes that Poirot existed and had a moustache.' That again argues for a substantial difference between belief reports containing fictional names and those containing non-fictional names.

28. Notoriously, Walton's view seems to misdescribe the modal content of negative existentials. For related pretence views, see Crimmins (1998) and Kroon (2000).

REFERENCES

Adams, Fred, Robert Stecker, and G. Fuller (1992). 'The Semantics of Thoughts.' *Pacific Philosophical Quarterly*, 73: 375–89.

Adams, Fred, and Robert Stecker (1993). 'Vacuous Singular Terms.' *Mind and Language*, 9: 387–401.

Bach, Kent (1987). *Thought and Reference*. Oxford: Oxford University Press.

—— (1993). 'Sometimes a Great Notion: A Critical Notice of Crimmins' *Talk about Beliefs.' Mind and Language*, 8: 431–41.

—— (1997). 'Do Belief Reports Report Beliefs?' *Pacific Philosophical Quarterly*, 78: 215–41.

Braun, David (1993). 'Empty Names.' *Noûs*, 27: 449–69.

—— (2005. 'Empty Names, Fictional Names, Mythical Names.' *Noûs*, 39.

Crimmins, Mark (1992). *Talk About Beliefs*. Cambridge, MA: MIT Press.

—— (1998). 'Hesperus and Phosphorus: Sense, Pretense, and Reference.' *Philosophical Review*, 107.1: 1–47.

Devitt, Michael (1995). *Coming to our Senses*. New York: Cambridge University Press.

Evans, Gareth (1982). *The Varieties of Reference*. John McDowell (ed.). Oxford: Clarendon Press.

Jackson, Frank (1996). 'Mental Causation.' *Mind*, 105: 377–413.

Kaplan, David (1989). 'Demonstratives.' In Joseph Almog, John Perry, and Howard Wettstein (eds.), *Themes from Kaplan*. Oxford: Oxford University Press.

Kripke, Saul A. (1973): 'Reference and Existence.' John Locke Lectures (unpublished).

—— (1980). *Naming and Necessity*. Cambridge, MA: Harvard University Press.

Kroon, Frederick (2000). '"Disavowal through Commitment" Theories of Negative Existentials.' In Anthony Everett and Thomas Hofweber (eds.), *Empty Names, Fiction and the Puzzles of Existence*. Stanford: CSLI Publications.

—— (2003). 'Quantified Negative Existentials.' *Dialectica*, 57: 149–64.

Lewis David (1994). 'Reduction of Mind.' In Samuel Guttenplan (ed.), *A Companion to the Philosophy of Mind*. Oxford: Basil Blackwell.

Recanati, François (1993). *Direct Reference: From Language to Thought*. Oxford: Basil Blackwell.

—— (2000). *Oratia Obliqua, Oratia Recta*. Cambridge, MA: MIT Press.

Reimer, Marga (2001). 'The Problem of Empty Names.' *Australasian Journal of Philosophy*, 79: 491–506.

Richard, Mark (1990). *Propositional Attitudes*. Cambridge: Cambridge University Press.

—— (2000). 'Semantic Pretence.' In Anthony Everett and Thomas Hofweber (eds.), *Empty Names, Fiction and the Puzzles of Existence*: 205–32. Stanford: CSLI Publications.

Russell, Bertrand (1956). 'The Philosophy of Logical Atomism.' In R. C. Marsh (ed.), *Logic and Knowledge*. London: George Allen and Unwin.

Salmon, Nathan (1986). *Frege's Puzzle*. Cambridge, MA: MIT Press.

—— (1998). 'Nonexistence.' *Noûs*, 32.3: 277–319.

Schiffer, Stephen (1995). 'Descriptions, Indexicals, and Belief Reports: Some Dilemmas (But Not the Ones You Expect).' *Mind*, 104: 107–31.

Shier, David (1996). 'Direct Reference for the Narrow Minded.' *Pacific Philosophical Quarterly*, 77: 225–48.

Soames, Scott (1987). 'Direct Reference, Propositional Attitudes, and Semantic Content.' *Philosophical Topics*, 15: 47–87.

—— (2002). *Beyond Rigidity: The Unfinished Semantic Agenda of Naming and Necessity*. New York: Oxford University Press.

Walton, Kendall L. (1990). *Mimesis as Make-Believe*. Cambridge, MA: Harvard University Press.

—— (1993). 'Metaphor and Prop Oriented Make-Believe.' *European Journal of Philosophy*, 1.1: 39–57.

7

Fictionalist Attitudes about Fictional Matters

Daniel Nolan

A pressing problem for many non-realist[1] theories concerning various specific subject matters is the challenge of making sense of our ordinary propositional attitude claims related to the subject in question. Famously in the case of ethics, to take one example, we have in ordinary language *prima facie* ascriptions of beliefs and desires involving moral properties and relationships. In the case, for instance, of 'Jason believes that Kylie is virtuous', we appear to have a belief which takes Kylie to be a certain way. If Jason desires that Kylie acts as she ought, he appears to have a desire which has as its content that Kylie perform actions of a certain sort (that is, the actions that she ought to perform). However, for non-cognitivists in ethics who reject the idea that sentences such as 'Kylie is virtuous' or 'Kylie acts as she ought' are in the business of making truth-apt claims, or representing that certain moral features are possessed by objects or events, or even, in extreme cases, that such claims express propositions at all, the semantic analysis of the example propositional attitude claims made about Jason will have to be non-standard. (This is merely an application of the well-known 'Frege–Geach problem' (see Geach, 1965) to the case of embedding moral vocabulary in propositional-attitude ascriptions.)

The problem is by no means restricted to ethics, of course: to mention quickly some other examples, those who do not think that conditional statements (or indicative conditional statements) express propositions (Adams, 1975) will have difficulty making sense of beliefs that certain conditionals hold, or desires that certain conditionals hold. Similarly for expressivists about probability judgements, or aesthetic claims, or modal claims; or traditional instrumentalists about scientific claims (in which such claims are not truth-apt, but perform a function analogous to a calculating device) when it comes to dealing with apparently innocuous claims about scientists' beliefs and desires. Again, those who take terms in a target discourse to be literally meaningless have trouble describing the psychological attitudes of their opponents (consider for example the traditional verificationist attitude to theology, faced with the task of characterizing the beliefs of the theologians, or the desires of the theologians for salvation, or an afterlife, or for avenging angels to strike the godless verificationists down, as it might be . . .); and the list of non-realist views which face such problems goes on. It is not that non-realist theories must face such problems (some do not), but rather that such problems are common.

Non-realists need not respond to the challenge of providing the semantics for belief and other propositional attitude contexts by providing truth-conditions for statements involving propositional attitudes about the relevant subject matters (ethics, conditionals, physics, theology, or what-have-you): though they may do so. However, what is more important in accounting for our linguistic practices is that these theories should explain the acceptability, or assertibility, or appropriateness of some propositional attitude claims over others—why, for example, it is right on a given occasion for a non-realist about conditionals to say that Bob believes that if it rains, it will pour, but not to say that Bob believes that if it rains, aliens will land. The story of acceptability or appropriateness of propositional attitude ascriptions may of course be given primarily in terms of truth-conditions: it may just be that we sort claims about the relevant propositional attitudes into the good and bad ones primarily by sorting them into the true and the false ones. However, sorting the acceptable from the unacceptable may be done in other ways—it may be a matter of assertibility rather than truth, or some non-cognitive account of the distinction we observe in our ordinary usage of the relevant propositional attitude ascriptions might be given. Without some such account, the non-realist about a certain subject matter cannot provide an account of many of our commonplace uses of the relevant vocabulary in attitude ascriptions which have much intuitive plausibility. This will not displease all non-realists, especially those who are of a revisionist bent—they may be inclined to let the chips fall where they may on this issue. If good sense cannot be made of something like our standard practices of ascribing the relevant propositional attitudes, however, this is a result which would deny us forms of speech which are both pervasive and important. Conversely, a non-realist theory unable to salvage such pervasive and important ways of talking which are apparently in good order incurs an unpleasant theoretical cost relative to its rivals.

Troubles for Non-Realism

One standard way to address this challenge for non-realists of different sorts is to adopt one of a family of so-called 'quasi-realist' approaches to the discourse in question (see most famously Blackburn, 1984, 1993, and Gibbard, 1990). These are designed to make sense of such propositional attitude ascriptions, and often to allow that apparently innocuous instances of such ascriptions are indeed assertible, and perhaps also true (or quasi-true) as well. The question of how acceptable this style of answer is to the question of the truth-conditions for propositional attitude ascriptions involving the problematic discourse (ethical, conditional, mathematical or whatever) and more generally providing a criterion for distinguishing 'acceptable' from 'unacceptable' propositional attitude ascriptions in a given area of discourse is beyond the scope of my present task. However, the projectivist and quasi-realist strategies for dealing with the relevant propositional attitude ascriptions (involving putative propositions concerning a subject matter to be treated in a projectivist or quasi-realist way) by and large share three serious drawbacks. First is that such treatments are typically programmatic, and do not spell out in detail even what the proposed solution is meant to be.[2] This is of course not an objection in principle, since future work could produce proposals with the needed detail. Second is that such treatments produce semantic non-uniformity, with the assertion conditions and truth-conditions of some statements (the projectivist or quasi-realist ones) being treated differently from the claims to be given a straightforward realist treatment.[3] At least this is so at the level of the most perspicuous assertion- and truth-conditions, since the quasi-realist may construct more realist-like semantic conditions for the quasi-realist statements at later stages of the procedure of mimicking realist semantics (Blackburn makes a start at this in Blackburn, 1988, and elsewhere). Third is that these treatments are relatively complex compared to realist treatments, or so I judge (claims about relative simplicity or complexity of semantic theories being very hard to establish). Fourth, and finally, a standard concern is that these treatments are of dubious consistency, especially when theories motivated by non-cognitivist theoretical commitments go too far in providing a cognitivist treatment of the discourse in question in the course of 'recovering' putatively realist characterizations of that discourse. This paragraph is not intended as a refutation of projectivism or quasi-realism, of course, but rather to mention some standard concerns about such strategies.[4]

Error-theories, which hold that the realist is right about the semantics and truth-conditions of the claims of a target discourse, are a class of alternatives to realism which do not face the same sorts of Frege–Geach challenges as non-cognitivist, quasi-realist and (some) minimalist theories do. This is because the error-theorists agree with realists that the expressions in the vocabulary associated with the subject matter in question receive the orthodox semantic treatment: It is simply that the relevant (positive) claims are all false. The difficulty with the most straightforward versions of error theories is that they avoid semantic trouble with the relevant vocabulary, but at the cost of dispensing with the use of the vocabulary altogether. Since the vocabulary of many areas is very useful, even when some have suspicions about realist understandings of the claims in question (e.g., platonist treatment of mathematical claims, scientific realist treatments of claims about unobservables, moral realist treatments of claims in ethics, or whatever), there is a reluctance to abandon the discourse altogether. This is of course one of the motivations for some non-cognitivist and quasi-realist approaches, especially those which are conceived of as proposals for linguistic reform rather than uncovering the way the particular pieces of language had been used all along.

Fictionalism: A Happy Medium

Fictionalism can be seen as a happy medium between an 'eliminativist' approach which takes the relevant discourse to be largely incorrect and therefore also unacceptable and to be dispensed with, on the one hand; and approaches which do not interpret statements in the relevant discourses as having a standard realist semantics, on the other (with the consequent need to explain from scratch the statements' roles in indirect contexts of all sorts, including propositional attitude contexts). One standard fictionalist approach is to take the positive statements of a certain region of discourse (whether it be about mathematics, or possible worlds, or storybook characters) to be literally speaking false, but nonetheless worth using and recording for some theoretical purpose or other. So, for example, Hartry Field (1989), a fictionalist about mathematics, held that statements committed to the existence of mathematical entities are all false, but many are nevertheless very useful, both in science and for everyday purposes.[5]

Taken this way, fictionalism is indeed a version of an error theory, taking all the positive statements of a given theory to be literally false. (A restriction to 'positive' statements is needed, since in most vocabularies it will be possible to formulate both a sentence and its negation, and the fictionalist need not suggest that both of these are false! An error theorist about phlogiston denies that there is any phlogiston, that phlogiston plays an important role in the burning of metals, and so on, but need not deny, for example, that phlogiston is *absent* in an evacuated jar, or that phlogiston is *not* emitted in a wide range of reactions.) As a matter of terminological stipulation, let me distinguish fictionalism from a more standard variety of an error theory, according to which the discourse in question should be abandoned also—call this latter variety of an error theory 'eliminativism', after Churchland's position on the posits of folk psychological theories (beliefs, desires, emotions, etc.) in the philosophy of mind (see, e.g., Churchland, 1981).

It may be useful to extend the use of the term 'fictionalism' to cover other positions which are extremely functionally similar. One would be a position which does not commit itself to the positive claims of the target discourse being *false*, but merely refrains from committing itself to the truth of the claims. A well-known example is Bas van Fraassen's (1980) line on theories in the natural sciences which are committed to unobservable entities (viruses, benzene rings, isotopes, electrons, quarks, or whatever). Van Fraassen argues, not that scientific theories committed to such entities are false, but rather that we have no reason to think they are true, and recommends a studied agnosticism. His so-called 'epistemic instrumentalism' is extremely similar to fictionalism: like paradigmatic fictionalism, he agrees with the realist about the semantics of the language, and what it is doing (it is purporting to describe a realm of objects too small to be sensed, rather than some non-representational function), and like standard fictionalism he justifies the continued employment of the theories in question on grounds other than their truth (or probable truth).

Another cluster of positions similar to the standard fictionalism of, for example, Field, is an approach which takes sentences of a target discourse to fail to be true, but not to be false either: either because they take some other truth-value or values, or because they fail to have truth-values altogether, despite their surface appearances. Nonetheless the cluster in question take the claims of the theory to be worthy of continued use nonetheless, for some purpose or purposes other than stating the truth in the relevant area. (One might hold this position if one had a view that held that the appearance of non-referring names in a theory rendered sections of it truth-valueless, or if one held that predicates not associated with instantiated properties likewise resulted in truth-value gaps,[6] or for a variety of other reasons.)

In both the case of van Fraassen and the cluster of options which take a theory to be useful despite being not-true-but-not-false-either, the structure of the views are the same in most relevant respects as the structure of the standard, error-theoretical fictionalism. I shall therefore include these cases under the rubric 'fictionalism', though I am happy to regard this usage as a matter of stipulation, at least for purposes of this chapter.

It is part of fictionalism, so defined, that statements of a certain sort are not to be taken as true (for one reason or another), despite being such that we should continue to make use of them. But what use are we to make of them? I take it that there are at least two important components of this question: the question of how one is to use these statements, and the question of why we should do so: what point might such an exercise have, that could not be better served in another way?

The question of why we should persist in, in some sense, employing a theory even when we do not take it to be true may have different answers from case to case. The first sort of advantage often claimed may include convenience for reasoning about matters of fact, as in Field's mathematical fiction in Field (1989), or as in 'timid' modal fictionalism, which takes a fiction of possible worlds to be useful in part for convenience in reasoning about the literal truth or falsehood of claims cast in terms of modal operators.[7] Another convenience claimed for some fictionalist strategies is the ability to generate predictions or generalizations about matters of fact which are not otherwise in practice available, as in for instance fictionalism about unobservables in the style of van Fraassen (1980). It is very plausible that we could not in practice have made the successful predictions about observable objects we now make without deploying theories about unobservables (even if we did not have to believe in those theories). Just think of what chemistry would look like if we had never been entitled to speculation about the molecular constitution of various observable stuffs, or to imagine how one might invent a functioning television set without any theory about the behaviour of small electric charges. Fictionalists will no doubt argue that there are other advantages available as well (for a slightly more detailed list, see Nolan, Restall, and West), and no doubt fictionalist proposals in particular areas will often claim advantages specific to that particular domain.

The question of how exactly the discourse should continue to be used in spite of its admitted falsity (or at least in spite of a lack of a commitment to its truth) is one which different theorists will answer differently. Some account of how it is legitimate to continue to utter the sentences in question (whether the sentences are ones involving commitment to mathematical objects, physical unobservables, moral states of affairs, or whatever the fictionalism involves) will be a central part of this answer. The question of what sort of legitimacy this talk will have is potentially a very controversial one, and this controversy may mirror the controversy about the status of sentences in and about paradigm fictions: Some will see the relevant claims as only pretend assertions, not genuinely asserted at all by those who utter them in fictional contexts (as in Searle's treatment—see Searle, 1979); or true when uttered in the appropriate contexts because they are implicitly prefixed with something like 'according to the fiction' (Lewis, 1978); false, but true under a presupposition (the supposition of the relevant theory) (Hinckfuss, 1993) and so assertible in the context in which that presupposition is in place; or false, but assertible for some other reason. It does not matter for the substance of this chapter what kind of account of sentences uttered in fictional contexts is appropriate: whether they are literally truth-valueless but nevertheless licensed for some reason or other; or literally false but nonetheless assertible (or otherwise licensed as utterances); or even true, and thus assertible, but with misleading surface form; or some combination of these depending on facts about the context of utterance. Let me use 'fictional assertion' as a general term for what is done in fictional contexts with those sentences which taken literally and at face value are false, but which may be uttered as if they were being asserted in the context of the fiction: But note that this choice of terminology is not intended to take any stand on the exact nature of this activity (even whether or not it is assertion, properly speaking).

This characterization of 'fictional assertion' is meant to cover even the case of a family of currently popular fictional approaches that take the use of a sentence in a fictional context to change its semantic value, often in a radical way: a change greater than implicitly affixing it was a 'in the fiction' operator, for example. In the fictionalism of Crimmins (1998) or the 'figuralism' of, e.g., Yablo (2002a), or in the work of other fictionalists influenced by Walton (1990: ch. 10), the semantic value of an utterance in a fictional context will often be a literally true proposition about the non-fictional world: whatever it is that would make the sentence uttered fictionally appropriate to utter given the game of fiction in force, for example. The assertibility of a sentence in a fictional context then is determined from its semantic value in the way that the assertibility of ordinary sentences is. However, for these fictionalists, the semantic value a sentence in fact has when uttered in a fictional context will still normally be different from the semantic value of that sentence when uttered in literal contexts (if it has one), or the semantic value one would take it to have if one took it at 'face value': it is the proposition expressed by a 'literal' use that these fictionalists take to be false (or they take the sentence if used literally to be truth-valueless). This form of fictionalism suffers from drawbacks of semantic non-uniformity and semantic complexity which might be thought costly in the same way that these features were drawbacks of the quasi-realist approach, and since the fictional context infects the meaning of the sentences they may not have the advantage of being able to 'piggy-back' on the realist's treatments of indirect contexts, so they may not seem the most attractive versions of fictionalism when it comes to the advantages claimed for fictionalism at the start of this chapter. Still, it is clear that they fall under the 'fictionalist' umbrella, in that claims that are not *literally* true can still be usefully used for a variety of purposes.

The fictionalist must also provide an account of how we mix our talk which is to be taken fictionally with that part of our theories and assertions which we do wish to take literally. No doubt the story will vary from fictionalist proposal to fictionalist proposal. But some features will typically be in common. There will be a realm of discourse which the fictionalist takes literally (a 'base discourse'), and a fiction which will have its contents depend in a systematic way on what is literally true in the language of the base discourse.[8] For a fictionalist about unobservables, the 'base discourse' might be statements about observables, for a fictionalist about mathematics the base discourse might be, in a given application, the language of (de-mathematicized) physics, and for a moral fictionalist the base discourse might include such things as statements about how people in fact behave and will behave, and what it is desirable to do or rational to do, all things considered. We may, following Field, use the term 'bridge laws' for the statements which connect what is literally true in the base discourse with what is true in the fiction, and vice versa. It is these bridge laws that allow us to infer from something's being fictionally true (e.g., that the patient's cells contain a given virus) something about what is literally true (the patient will be delirious and vomiting), and will enable us to go from what is literally true to what is true according to a given fiction (e.g., from the claim that infants are dying of starvation to the claim that according to the moral fiction, something very morally bad is happening). Note that once the bridge laws are stipulated, it may turn out that there are things true according to the fiction which are not known to be true according to the fiction by the fiction's users. For a particularly vivid example, consider the modal fictionalism discussed in Rosen (1990), where the bridge laws ensure *all* of the truths about the actual world are also represented by his fiction to be true of the actual world.

Note that one thing that bridge laws will almost always do is to 'import' into the theoretical fiction many claims that are also literally true. So, for example, a fictionalist about unobservables will not only fictionally believe in their pieces of laboratory equipment, such as electron microscopes,[9] but will not literally believe in electrons: nevertheless, it will be true according to their fiction both that electrons exist, and that electron microscopes exist. After all, their theory will do things like describe the interactions between laboratory equipment and sub-atomic particles, and so it should be true according to that theory that there are such things as the electron microscopes it says interacts with electrons. Or in the case of moral fictionalism, it should be true according to the moral fiction that there are such events as killings, for example, since the moral fiction should say that some killings are wrong: and if some killings are wrong, then that implies that there are some killings. Theoretical fictions will often represent many things which are in fact true as well as propositions which are only fictionally true: in this respect they resemble novels where not only are there entirely fictional characters, but where the fictions also make representations about real personages like Napoleon or Hamlet (and real objects like the Sun and the Moon, real cities like London, etc.), and say true things about those real people and objects.

The fictionalist will then hopefully provide some reason to suppose that using the bridge laws to make inferences about what is literally true will not lead us astray, in the way that employing false theories for prediction and explanation so often does. Take a case where, for example, we use the bridge laws to go from something we take literally to something true according to the fiction, reasoning to something else true according to the fiction, and then inferring something new about what is literally true using the bridge laws again. A fictionalist might try to persuade us that this detour is harmless by giving a proof that for a given fiction and bridge laws it *cannot* lead from literal truth to literal falsehood (see, e.g., Field's, 1989, Conservativity result). Or the fictionalist might argue that there are less than conclusive, but still strong, reasons to suppose that using the theory is reliable (for example a fictionalist about unobservables could argue that it is the scientific method which puts us in the position to rely on a theory arrived at in the right way to give us accurate predictions given some data). Let us assume for the purposes of this chapter that a fictionalist in a given area has specified their principles for generating a fiction, the bridge laws which allow us to pass between what is fictional and what is literal, and some reason to suppose that moving back and forth between the domain of fiction and the domain taken literally will not, when done properly, lead us into literal errors.

Fictionalism and Propositional Attitudes

Since the preferred varieties of fictionalism agree with the realist about the semantic behaviour of the statements in the target discourse (albeit a semantics which takes the positive predicates to never in fact be literally satisfied, and the distinctive ontology which is putatively referred to by the positive statements to not ever be successfully referred to), fictionalists can provide a straightforward and attractive account of the meaning of the target vocabulary, and the meaning of that vocabulary in negations, disjunctions, conditionals, and normal propositional attitude ascriptions. In the case of propositional attitude ascriptions, 'Jason believes Kylie is virtuous' is not very different semantically from 'Jason believes Kylie is tall' or 'Jason believes Kylie is phlogisticated'. While in the first and third cases Jason has a belief which is bound to be actually incorrect, the belief ascription and the belief itself *qua* belief are none the worse for that. Similarly in the case of desire: if Jason desires that Kylie act as she ought, he desires that Kylie's actions should have a certain feature (albeit, for the fictionalist, one they will not, and perhaps cannot, have). There is no need to spin a new semantic structure out of whole cloth for moral language for the moral fictionalist, and *mutatis mutandis* for the fictionalist about unobservable physical entities, or mathematical objects, or possible worlds, or what-have-you.

All is not quite plain sailing for the fictionalist in this respect: for while fictionalists can avail themselves of the semantic machinery available to the realist, this will help against the specter of the Frege–Geach difficulties only if the realists have semantic machinery that can make sense of areas of discourse which are infected with a failure to 'correspond to the world' in the right way. If the realist is saddled with a view according to which names that do not refer to objects are meaningless, or predicates that do not express instantiated properties are meaningless, the fictionalist may not be able to rest content on the realist's laurels. Still, there are attractive accounts of content which do allow that people can have literal beliefs and desires which are appropriately described using non-referring terms and predicates which lack a (non-null) extension, and many people will find one of these accounts congenial in any case.[10]

While a fictionalist does not therefore face standard Frege–Geach-like challenges concerning the relevant propositional attitudes in the most straightforward class of cases (or at least they need not), they do face an analogous challenge in a slightly different class of situations. On the assumption that the normal users of moral language have realist attitudes (at least implicitly), the above story is straightforward. The story is not so straightforward when fictionalists come to describe their own attitudes, or the attitudes of other fictionalists. This is of concern especially to a fictionalist who hopes to convince those around her of the truth of fictionalism in a given area. Speaking literally, of course, fictionalists can say what one would expect, given that they are error theorists: Moral fictionalists do not believe slavery is morally wrong, for example, indeed they believe it is not morally wrong (and perhaps even morally permitted, depending on how one draws the positive/negative distinction within moral vocabulary). Furthermore, modal fictionalists of the sort discussed by Rosen (1990) literally believe there is only one possible world; mathematical fictionalists of Field's stripe literally believe there are no prime numbers; and so on.

Despite this, fictionalists may well sometimes find it convenient to talk as if they and their fellow fictionalists have positive moral attitudes of various sorts. For example, a moral fictionalist who is prepared to utter the sentence 'abortion is wrong', when asked what his opinion of abortion is, might naturally reply 'I believe that abortion is wrong.' More usefully, we need devices for reporting the positions of others. A fellow moral fictionalist Bill regularly utters the sentence 'abortion is wrong', seeks to prevent abortions from occurring, donates money to right-to-life organizations, etc. When asked about Bill's attitude to abortion, it would be convenient to be able to say that Bill believes that abortion is wrong (. . . impermissible, . . . ought not occur, etc.). Similarly, it may be convenient to ascribe Bill moral desires. Bill, like Jason, above, might also desire that Kylie be virtuous, or at least it would be convenient to talk this way, even while admitting ascriptions of 'positive' beliefs and desires to self-conscious fictionalists will not be literally true.

While it may be convenient to fictionally impute these psychological states to oneself or to other fictionalists, the various fictions employed by fictionalists, whether they be fictionalists about mathematics, or microphysics, or possible worlds, or morality, or whatever it might be, will need to be extended if the fictionalist wishes to indulge in this extended pretence. For the question of what beliefs and desires one has is a matter of descriptive psychology, rather than of mathematics, or microphysics, or possible worlds, or morality, or whatever: even an eliminativist about, e.g., morality will admit that people have beliefs about the moral statuses of things (outcomes, events, people, properties, or whatever), and desires concerning the moral status of things: though many such beliefs will be held to be untrue by an eliminativist, and many of the desires misguided. Likewise, even an eliminativist about the microscopic realm (should there be such a person) should admit that many people have beliefs about objects too small to see, and desires concerning them (e.g., about the presence of disease-causing bacteria and viruses, or chances of radioactive decay of atoms in a particular sample), even though, again, the eliminativist about the microscopic realm would take such beliefs and desires to be mistaken or misguided. What psychological states people have will typically be taken to be something that is a matter of fact, rather than a matter of fiction.[11]

The fictionalist seems to be faced with a dilemma: either extend the fiction to cover fictional ascriptions of certain beliefs, desires and other attitudes, for example, in the case of a moral fictionalist, beliefs that certain outcomes are morally good or bad, certain actions morally obligatory or forbidden; or give up talking as if fictionalists have positive beliefs, desires, and so on, of the relevant sort. The challenge facing the fictionalist is like that facing other anti-realists: not so much to justify the truth of certain claims about propositional attitudes, but if possible to provide for the *acceptability* of the kinds of propositional-attitude-ascription sentences fictionalists would be tempted to produce once fictionalism spread through a population. Either they must revise their practices, and give up talking as if each other has (for example) positive moral beliefs; or they must provide for the acceptability of talk as if their fellow fictionalists have the relevant beliefs and desires, even though those propositional attitudes are not literally held, and even though a fictionalist may not be in general an anti-realist about propositional attitudes.

If the fictionalist passes up the opportunity to extend the fiction to cover what they are to say about their own attitudes and the attitudes of other fictionalists, they give up on several benefits which fictionalists should be concerned to retain—several of which were mentioned earlier. There is the immediately obvious one of keeping a familiar and psychologically convenient way of everyday talking—in this case our everyday practices of ascribing attitudes about various subject matters to ourselves and others. There is also the advantage of communication about first-order issues, and people's attitudes towards them, in ordinary circumstances without having to mention people's commitment to literal error theories ('Well, Bill doesn't really believe that abortion is wrong, it's just that . . .'). When, for instance, a fictionalist about unobservables is asked about what his or her opinion is about radiation levels outside a leaking reactor, if they have a way of talking as if they have a positive opinion, they can get to the main point, rather than detouring through mention of their more philosophical concerns. A nuclear scientist asked by a reporter about his beliefs concerning the effect of fallout would risk unhelpfulness and producing confusion if the best she could honestly say was 'Well, I don't believe that there is any radiation at all, let alone harmful effects of radiation, but. . . . '

If it is indeed true, as I suggested above, that fictionalists can gain an advantage in expressing claims over more austerely nominalist rivals, then a fictionalist who lacks the ability to extend their fiction to talk as if other fictionalists and they themselves have apparently committed attitudes will also be deprived of the ability to capture the content of a fellow fictionalist's attitudes in the convenient way that, for example, moral language sometimes allows: if I would like to say that Jack (a fellow fictionalist) believes we should put more effort into defending the right of free speech than the right of security of property, or even if I want to say that Jill (also a fictionalist) tries to be charitable (on the assumption that the concept of charity is a thick moral concept and not merely a descriptive one), I shall be hard pressed to say what I mean if I am not allowed to help myself to the pretence that Jack has beliefs about the value of rights, and Jill has beliefs and desires about how one might be charitable. For paraphrasing the claim about Jack or the claim about Jill into sentences which are literally true of their psychological states is by no means a straightforward matter. Similarly, if I wish to talk as if a van Fraassenite director of health believes that the rapid spread of a certain virus is caused by vitamin deficiencies (while not literally saying any such thing, knowing that the director lacks belief both in viruses and vitamins), trying to say literally what the health director *does* literally believe about the population in question, its diet, and its health, without mention of vitamins or antibodies, is not straightforward.

It is in the spirit of fictionalism to try to retain these sorts of advantages, so it is worthwhile investigating what a fictionalist can do in the way of providing a way of fictionally ascribing moral attitudes to themselves and other fictionalists, despite the problem that they will also need to be able to make literal claims about the psychological states of fictionalists at the same time. Before we begin to outline how this might be done, we must stress an important condition for a solution to the problem of extending, for example, the moral fictionalist pretence to (at least some) claims about moral attitudes. This is the problem of higher-order attitudes: attitudes about attitudes. For suppose we wish to pretend that Anne believes that capital punishment is wrong. We may also wish to talk as if Belle, who knows Anne well, believes (or even knows) that Anne has that attitude. And that Cath has discovered from talking to Belle that this is what Belle takes Anne's attitude to be, and that Dale believes that Cath's belief about Belle's belief is mistaken . . . and so on. When all of them are self-conscious fictionalists, and know the others to be, however, the story will start to get very complicated. For Anne does not literally think capital punishment is wrong, and Belle, knowing of Anne's fictionalism, will not literally believe that Anne literally believes that capital punishment is wrong, and Cath, knowing of Anne's fictionalism and Belle's awareness of it, will not literally believe that Belle believes that Anne is opposed to capital punishment . . . so new pretences will need to be introduced at each step, and presumably in a systematic way.

Nor should it be thought that the need to handle higher-order attitudes is only a product of a philosopher's desire to produce a theory adequate even for obscure cases. For our attitudes to other people, and in particular their attitudes, are among the most commonplace and central features of our mental lives. Far more time is spent finding out about other people and their beliefs and desires (as well as their fears, hopes, expectations, suspicions, etc.) than virtually any other subject. Furthermore, much of our epistemic access to the world is a result of our access to the attitudes of others. To be able to make proper use of testimony, we need to know how to tell from what people say what they believe, what their intentions were in saying so, and so on. So much of what we know about others' attitudes is itself discovered through our access to people's beliefs concerning those others and their attitudes. It may be unusual, but by no means a philosopher's fantasy, that we, e.g., read a report in a newspaper or magazine which is a second- or third-hand retelling of an incident which is evidence that a knowledgeable insider takes an important figure to have a particular attitude. This would produce at least fifth-order attitudes in us: and it is easy to add some more levels if I discover my friend A has been informed by my friend B about the report, which B read in the paper. We rarely notice how many levels of nested attitudes occur in our everyday life. It may be, of course, that after a certain point the need to provide for nested attitudes becomes more fanciful—five-hundredth-level attitudes seem unlikely to be very common, if there are any at all. Still, the ability to talk and behave as if there are such higher-order attitudes be able to serve some of the same purposes of communication about each other, and indirectly about the world, as ascribing first-order propositional attitudes.

Higher-order attitudes ultimately to do with people's moral attitudes are a special case of higher-order attitudes, but the usefulness of talk about them can be explained in the same sorts of terms as the justification of the need for higher-order attitude ascriptions in general. To talk as if others have moral beliefs, for example, and that yet others might be useful sources of testimony about those beliefs, enables us to gain important evidence about important values that people cherish. Knowledge of how someone is liable to act is often gained through discovering what the realist would describe as the extent to which they are motivated in a moral way (they have desires about moral attributes of some sort or another): being able to talk as if some people are villains, others dutiful, yet others indifferent, and to be able to evaluate reports to this effect that are made to us, clearly seems to be useful in our dealings with our fellow human beings. Likewise, being able to talk as if a group of fictionalist mathematicians have certain hunches about what statements are theorems and which are not, or talk as if a particular mathematician wants to investigate a certain mathematical structure, is useful for understanding and predicting what that mathematician will say or do (and may shed light on what the mathematician is trying to communicate, insofar as knowing where someone is 'coming from' is often an important part of ensuring successful communication). So making room for a fictionalist to assert higher-order attitude ascriptions is not just an interesting philosophical challenge—it is likely to be very important in practice, should fictionalism become widespread.

Of course, making room for these fictional attitude reports, both of the basic sort and of the higher-level sort, is even more important if fictionalism is in fact already widespread in any area. Plausibly it is: talk in physics of rigid rods or ideal gases is often treated as fictionalist, a case can be made that teleological talk in contemporary evolutionary biology is best seen as a useful fiction, and some fictionalists want to argue that our everyday talk of abstract objects, alternative outcomes, and other puzzling entities is *already* fictionalist (e.g., the figuralist position in Yablo, 2002). Such fictionalists should think that we already (implicitly at least) deploy an extended fiction that people have the attitudes we normally say they do about such matters, or be prepared to explain why there is so much widespread error when we say that people have the beliefs and desires we ascribe to them.[12] The former seems preferable.

A Solution

With this complication in mind, let us discuss one obvious way in which a fictionalist might develop the ability to talk as if they and others have attitudes about a subject matter, without thereby having literally to possess those attitudes. Let us begin with the case of belief ascriptions, since this is an important case in its own right, as well as having significance as the propositional attitude which must be treated with particular caution if the fiction is to avoid incoherence: for it must be possible both literally to take someone to be a fictionalist about mathematics (and thus literally believe there are no positive truths about sets, functions, numbers, or whatever) and fictionally be a believer of standard mathematical claims (and thus fictionally believe that there are positive truths concerning sets, functions, numbers, etc.)—and to be able to say both in successive breaths without either fictionally or literally contradicting oneself, and without imputing contradiction (either literally or fictionally) to the believer in question.

Let me discuss the specific case of moral fictionalism, even though the remarks I will make about moral fictionalism will generalize in an obvious way. Suppose we are moral fictionalists and that we would like to say, speaking loosely, that a fellow fictionalist Bill believes that abortion is wrong—even though, speaking literally, he believes nothing of the sort, being a moral fictionalist. Under what literal circumstances would we want our extended moral fiction to have as part of its content that Bill believes that abortion is wrong? One thing that many philosophers have wanted to do is tie belief to appropriate assertion—the thought being that prima facie one has done something wrong by one's own lights if one asserts something one does not believe. Now, moral fictionalism has already provided for conditions for Bill to appear to assert 'abortion is wrong': He is to utter that sentence only when he takes it that the moral fiction claims that abortion is wrong. (Of course he is not required to utter the sentence whenever he takes it to be true according to the moral fiction that abortion is wrong, otherwise he would be constantly parroting the sentence.) So given that we have conditions for Bill to find 'abortion is wrong' fictionally assertible (whether fictional assertion is to pretend to assert, to assert under presuppositions, to assert something about the content of fiction, or whatever), we have a building block to build a condition for fictional belief.

In a literal case, there is a sense in which I am right to assert p just in case it is true that p, but I believe that I am right to assert p just in case I believe that p. So, if it is right for Bill to 'fictionally assert' 'abortion is wrong' just in case it is true according to the moral fiction that abortion is wrong, then we might try constructing the extended fiction (EF for short) so that it says that Bill believes abortion is wrong just in case Bill takes himself to be in a position to assert that abortion is wrong, that is, just in case he takes it to be the case that according to the moral fiction, abortion is wrong.

A similar line of thought provides us with one natural suggestion for handling the fictional ascription of higher-order attitudes which 'ground out' in moral attitudes. Let us say that Carl is a fictionalist about morality who knows Bill and what Bill thinks, including that Bill is also a moral fictionalist. We are inclined to say in such a case that, loosely speaking, it is appropriate to say that Carl believes that Bill believes that abortion is wrong. Of course, Carl does not literally believe this, since he knows full well that Bill does not believe anything is morally wrong, strictly speaking. Still, Carl does believe that Bill takes himself to be in a position to fictionally assert that abortion is wrong, and does believe that, according to EF, Bill believes that abortion is wrong. So just as it was true according to the EF that Bill believed abortion is wrong just in case Bill believed that according to the moral fiction, abortion is wrong, we shall say that according to EF, Carl believes that Bill believes that abortion is wrong, just in case Carl believes that, according to EF, Bill believes that abortion is wrong. And it is true according to EF that Dennis believes that Carl believes . . . just in case Dennis believes that according to the EF fiction, Carl believes . . . and so on. To sum up the general rule as a slogan (using the language of as-if): It is as if X believes that p just in case X believes it is as if p. Or in the language of 'according to the fiction', where p is a moral claim, or a claim about a belief about a moral claim, or a higher-order claim of the relevant sort, (a claim about a belief about a belief about a moral matter, or a claim about a belief about a belief about a belief about a moral matter, or . . .)

(According to EF, X believes that p) iff (X believes that according to EF, p).

As well as this rule for importing content into the EF (from right to left), and going from claims about what is true according to the fiction to something which is literally the case (left to right), we should also include the ground-level fiction as a part of the extended fiction. That way the biconditional will hold in a case of the non-iterated fictional belief ascriptions. (According to the fiction Bill believes that abortion is wrong iff Bill believes that according to the fiction, abortion is wrong.) Otherwise the EF would not represent that abortion is wrong, so Bill, our competent fellow fictionalist, would not be expected to believe that it did. One could set the scheme up to handle the ground-level case separately, if one so desired, and keep the ground-level fiction out of the extended fiction, but in the standard case that would be needlessly complicated.

It is surprisingly straightforward to extend this EF fictional biconditional to attitudes other than belief, and mixtures of different attitudes. Take the case of desire: to be specific, a case where we would like to be able to say, loosely speaking, that Bill desires that Kylie be virtuous. Again, strictly speaking, Bill may desire no such thing, being a fictionalist and not believing that anyone is, nor is likely to be, literally virtuous, for Bill holds that there is strictly speaking no such thing as virtue. We can say that according to EF, Bill desires that Kylie be virtuous: and by analogy with the case of belief we shall say that this is the case just when Bill desires that according to the fiction Kylie be virtuous.

This needs to be understood the right way, of course. When we say (speaking loosely) Bill desires that Kylie be virtuous, we would normally mean that he wants Kylie's character to conform to the standards in fact prescribed (according to the fiction) in order to be virtuous. We do not normally mean that he desires that the standards of virtue be changed (or the fiction about such standards be changed) so that Kylie's actual disposition, however it may be, counts as virtuous by the lights of the standard. Nor do we mean that Bill would be happy with either option (Kylie's character conforming to the actual standard, or the standard's prescriptions being in line with Kylie's actual character), even though both would do for making it the case that according to the fiction about virtue, Kylie is virtuous.

However, this understanding is not a resource that needs to be particularly appealed to by a moral fictionalist. Anyone ascribing moral desires ought to recognize the distinction. If our realist Jason desires that Kylie be virtuous, he will normally desire that Kylie's character conforms to the actual standards (whatever they are), rather than desiring that the standards endorse Kylie's character (however it happens to be). This is so even though both directions of conformity are ways Kylie's character and the standards can be brought into harmony. (Perhaps the latter is impossible if the standards for virtue hold of necessity—but one can still desire impossible things, especially if one does not know they are impossible.) Just as in principle character and principles can be brought into harmony by changing one or the other, in principle character and fictional principle can be brought into harmony by controlling character or controlling the fiction. We are normally to understand someone who (loosely speaking) desires a person to be virtuous (or act rightly, or produce good outcomes) desires that the fiction says that they do, but that the fiction says that they do because their features are such that the actual fiction gives the result that their character is virtuous (or acts are right, or consequences are good), rather than the desire being that the fiction turn out to endorse whatever the actual character, acts, or consequences happen to be, or desiring one or the other indifferently. When understood this way, the fictional ascriptions of desire look natural: when we say (fictionally) that Bill desires that Kylie be virtuous, what makes our saying so appropriate is ultimately largely facts about Bill's desires concerning Kylie's character. Similarly, our fictional ascription of his desire that she acts rightly is legitimate largely because of desires he literally has about her actions, his fictional desire that the outcomes of her actions are good is the product of his non-fictional desires concerning those outcomes, etc.

With this caveat, which will also be needed when ascribing moral hopes, moral disgust, and various other attitudes, an account generalized from the one for belief can be simply given for propositional attitudes:

(According to EF, $X \Phi$s that p) iff ($X \Phi$s that according to EF, p).

This can be used for mixed cases above the first-order cases as well: if it is appropriate to fictionally assert 'Bob believes that Bill desires that Kylie be virtuous', this will be because Bob believes that it is true according to the EF fiction that Bill desires that Kylie be virtuous.

This will tell us when to fictionally assert that some person X has a propositional attitude Φ that p. We should also add another condition, to specify when we can fictionally assert that X does *not* have a propositional attitude Φ that p.[13] A separate clause is needed, since the mere fact that it is not the case that one proposition A is true in a fiction does not establish that not-A is true in that fiction: fictions are famously incomplete, and may not say anything either way about certain subject matters (it would be odd to assume that every fiction must represent one way or another about the price of cabbages in Istanbul, for example). An additional clause is not difficult to supply, however: we can ensure that the EF is complete in respect of the relevant psychological attitudes (that is, that for each attitude with each relevant content, the EF either says X has it or it does not), for instance by stipulating another bridge law:

(According to EF, it is not the case that $X \Phi$s that p) iff (it is not the case that $X \Phi$s that according to EF, p).

This bridging principle should probably be restricted to fictionalists in our fictionalist community: In cases where there are mixed communities of genuine believers and fictionalists, we may not wish our extended fiction to say that some genuine believers do not believe that p, simply on the basis that they have no opinion about the fictionalists' extended fiction!

Other methods are no doubt available for specifying how to fill out the rules governing the EF to specify when a statement of the form (According to the EF, it is not the case that $X \Phi$s that p) holds, but this one seems adequate. (Another would be some sort of principle ensuring that the fiction was complete in some respects—so that, e.g., if there was not something which forced the fiction to represent that $X \Phi$s that p, it defaulted to representing that not-$(X \Phi$s that $p)$.) The reason why we want our fiction to make claims about when people do not hold certain attitudes is that we want to also specify when it is appropriate, in the extended fiction, to deny that, for example, Bill believes abortions are obligatory. And of course talk about beliefs and desires about what other people do *not* believe and desire can mix with higher-order belief and desire ascriptions, so we would like a treatment that can iterate smoothly.[14]

What if the Ground-Level Fiction Contains Propositional Attitude Attributions?[15]

The story just given works in the simplest case, when the ground-level fiction does not itself contain any claims about what propositional attitudes people hold. Some ground-level discourses a fictionalist may be interested in will be like this: Field's fiction of containing only a portion of mathematical physics, for example. But others will not: the base fiction for a moral fictionalist will include claims about what people believe and desire, and moral evaluations of those (for instance, it may say that Jill's desire to kill Jack is wrong, or that Jack's desire to give to charity is virtuous). A basic fiction might endorse these claims for a variety of reasons. In the case of moral fictionalism, many of the propositional attitude ascriptions will be there because of import principles from what is literally the case, as in the previous two examples. Or it may only be fictionally true in the basic fiction that certain beliefs and desires are possessed at all. Take for example an anthropological fiction, where for convenience anthropologists on occasion talk to each other as if there really are the demons and helpful spirits that some tribe they are studying say that there are. (This pretence might be for convenience in talking about the tribe's religious activities, or to achieve a better understanding of the tribe's world-view, or whatever.) Then when the anthropologist says the demons want boys to fail their manhood tests, or that the good spirits believe that they will eventually defeat the demons, or whatever, these belief and desire ascriptions are not part of what the anthropologist takes to be literally the case, but are not part of an extended fiction either: they are part and parcel of the ontology of the basic fiction, which is an ontology of spirits, their behaviour and their attitudes.

It would be silly if we applied the biconditional developed in the previous section to extended fictions based on ground-level fictions that already contain propositional attitude ascriptions. Once we import the ground-level anthropological fiction, the extended fiction will have true according to it that the good spirits believe they will win. We should not conclude from this that it is literally the case that the good spirits believe that, according to the extended fiction, they will win. Presumably neither in fiction nor in reality do the spirits have opinions about the anthropologists' fiction. This is even more obvious when the ground-level moral fiction says, for example, that Jack believes that putting a cheque in the mail is an effective way to give to charity (the ground-level moral fiction will have true according to it much that is also literally true when those propositions are relevant to what the story should say is good or bad, right or wrong). We should not think automatically that Jack believes that, according to an extended moral fiction, putting a cheque in the mail is an effective way to give to charity. Jack may not even be a moral fictionalist, and may never have heard of a moral fiction. (He may not even have moral concepts—I presume it is possible to know how to give to charity even if one is amoral enough not to see much point, and the outcomes of an amoral person's actions can still be assessed for degree of moral value.)

Fortunately, the wrinkle we need to add when the ground-level fiction contains propositional attitude ascriptions is not very complex. The import rule for the extended fiction need not be altered: when someone Φs that, according to the extended fiction, p, we can allow that the extended fiction represents that person as Φing that p. When the extended fiction represents that someone Φs that p, though, that may not be because that person literally Φs that according to the extended fiction, p. The other way it could have happened via the content of the ground-level fiction. So the 'export rule'—what we can tell about what is going on outside EF from the contents of EF—will be disjunctive. When it is true that according to EF, X Φs that p, then *either* X Φs that, according to EF, p *or* according to the ground-level fiction, X Φs that p. (There may even be unusual cases when both disjuncts are satisfied.) Depending on the rules for the ground-level fiction, we may then be able to infer something about what is literally the case about X—but that is a story to leave to the specification of the ground-level fictions. The disjunctive rule is less convenient, but in many cases it will be reasonably clear which disjunct we should think is applicable—we can tell that what the EF says about one spirit's belief about another spirit's belief is in the EF because it was in the anthropologists' ground-level fiction, but the belief of our colleague about a spirit's belief is due in all likelihood to the import bridge law used to set up EF.[16]

An equivalent tweak should be made for our biconditional about when EF represents that X does *not* Φ that p. The import half of the biconditional can remain unchanged (again, perhaps with the restriction of the values of X to members of our fictionalist community), and the export conditional may have to be disjunctive: when according to EF, X does not Φ that p, then either X does not Φ that, according to EF, p, *or* according to the ground-level fiction, X does not Φ that p. This, incidentally, may point the way to how we can have an extended fiction which handles both realists and fictionalists: if a base fiction says that a realist Φs that p when that realist does indeed Φ that p, (and that the realist does not Φ that p just in case the realist literally does not Φ that p), but stays silent about the relevant ascriptions to fictionalists, then the extended fiction will represent both realists and fictionalists having attitudes of the relevant sort, thus giving us the ability to compare and contrast the attitudes that the fictionalist (fictionally) has and the realist (fictionally and literally) has.

Limitations and an Alternative

Cases of non-propositional attitudes do not seem to be as straightforward to deal with. This sort of case includes the situation in which it is as if a fictionalist about unobservable physical entities is surprised by the behaviour of some subatomic particle, or when it is as if a moral fictionalist hates a criminal's wickedness, or in general when fictionalists have the fictional counterparts of likes or dislikes for fictional entities, or the counterparts of reliance or distrust, or whenever we are tempted to say that it is true according to the fiction that the fictionalist has some non-propositional but intentional attitude: an attitude to a thing, or event, or state, or property or relation, rather than an attitude which, on the surface at least, is an attitude involving a proposition (such as the attitudes of belief that.... , desire that..., hope that..., etc.). Partly I suspect this is a reflection of the broader problem of explicating apparently non-propositional attitudes to non-existent objects. It may also be that such attitudes are less well understood. I have sympathy for views which attempt to account for what I have been calling non-propositional attitudes in terms of complexes of propositional attitudes of one sort or another, or possibly complexes of propositional attitudes and emotional states (where the relevant emotional states are not in turn understood as states directed towards non-propositional objects). If such an approach could be established, then the problem of 'non-propositional attitudes' would be solved, for the attitudes in question could be analyzed in terms of propositional attitudes, and the account provided for them applied.[17] However, for those who resist this reduction, clearly the account of how these attitudes could be incorporated into a suitable extended fiction would have to take a different form.

Note that this extended fiction (the EF fiction I have been discussing) may be useful in some contexts for many people who are not themselves necessarily fictionalists about any of the typical subjects. For it is not only fictionalists that will want to talk about the attitudes of fictionalists, and it would be just as unnatural and inconvenient for a non-fictionalist attempting to describe the attitudes within a group of fictionalists (especially higher-order attitudes) without employing the EF fiction as it would be for fictionalists. Talking as if fictionalists have attitudes involving the relevant subject matter, and that they have attitudes to each other's attitudes in such areas will be useful for fictionalists and non-fictionalists alike, particularly if fictionalism becomes common in a given group. What a moral fictionalist's attitudes are will be of interest to non-fictionalists about morality as well as moral fictionalists, and given the convenience of talking as if even moral fictionalists have moral beliefs and desires about morally characterized states of affairs, even a non-fictionalist about morality who needs to deal with such fictionalists will find the extended fiction expedient.

One headache that will arise from this extended fictionalizing is distinguishing literal propositional attitude reports from their fictional counterparts. For people may have literal attitudes about another's moral beliefs as well as have them fictionally. For example, Hiero might literally believe that Bill believes that abortion is wrong: through seeing Bill in action and not yet realizing that Bill is a fictionalist. And Igor might (fictionally) believe that Hiero believes that Bill believes that abortion is wrong—perhaps through hearing a report from Hiero, but Igor's not realizing that Hiero wasn't speaking fictionally, but was instead speaking literally. And Julia might (literally) desire that Igor believe that Hiero believe that Bill believes that abortion is wrong—she may wish to correct Igor's misapprehension about Hiero. At each stage of iteration, attitudes can be held literally or only according to EF, opening up a range of possible misunderstandings that could fill an epic comedy of errors. (Whether they could contribute to an interesting or entertaining comedy of errors is another matter.) Distinguishing pretence from seriousness is always a challenge to a greater or lesser extent when fictionalists are about: but the skills we have developed through growing up in a media age should prove adequate to the task.

It is an unfortunate feature of this iterative EF pretence, with its apparently complex methods for determining what is fictional in higher-order cases and need to draw fine distinctions between literal beliefs and fictional beliefs and the higher-order beliefs of both sorts, and the possibility of mix-ups between them and the higher-order ramifications of those mix-ups results in a system that does seem a little more complex than the realist's ascription of propositional attitudes about morality to fellow realists. It is perhaps at this point that the quasi-realist will retort to our earlier charges about their difficulty in dealing with propositional attitude ascriptions that the necessarily complex story they had to tell about higher-order attitudes is not one that the fictionalist can afford to scoff at, and perhaps (*perhaps!*) this is a fair *ad hominem*. Though I will wait for a worked-out story from the quasi-realist camp about higher-order attitude ascriptions before I might agree that their problem in this area is on a par with the fictionalist strategy put forward above.

In any case, there is an alternative strategy the moral fictionalist might attempt: a strategy for retaining much of the expressive and simplifying power of moral language (though perhaps not all of the other advantages), without having to extend the pretence to our psychological ascriptions of moral beliefs and moral desires, and the higher-order beliefs and desires associated with them. This would be to talk about what our fellow fictionalists believe or desire, not about moral matters, but about what is true *according to the moral fiction*. Instead of (falsely but appropriately) asserting that Bill believes abortion is wrong, we could instead assert that Bill believes that according to the moral fiction abortion is wrong. (Or perhaps that he believes that according to his particular moral fiction abortion is wrong, if there is more than one acceptable moral fiction.) Similarly, instead of saying that Bill desires that Kylie be virtuous, we might say that Bill desires that according to the moral fiction, Kylie would be virtuous. If this route is taken, higher-order ascriptions can just be treated literally: if Ella is aware of Bill's views on abortion (and moral fictionalism), we might say that Ella believes that Bill believes that according to the moral fiction (or Bill's moral fiction) abortion is wrong, if Ella wants to pass the news about Bill to Francine, we can say that Ella desires that Francine believes that Bill believes that abortion is wrong according to the moral fiction: but if Ella wants to deceive Francine into thinking Bill a realist, she will desire that Francine believes that Bill believes that abortion is wrong *simpliciter*. Likewise with the innumerable other iterations of higher-order attitudes.

The great advantage of this second proposal is that the higher-order attitudes require no extra mention of fiction or use of pretence at all—they are treated in the standard manner in which higher-order attitudes are treated when any other subject is involved.[18] As a result, this strategy avoids the risk of confusing literal attitude ascriptions with fictional ones, since all ascriptions are literal, and cases are distinguished by whether or not the first-order attitudes are about moral states of affairs or only about what is true in the moral fiction. The disadvantage of this latter strategy is that it departs further from non-fictionalist usage than the first strategy, and so is less convenient in that respect. In addition, because it requires explicit mention of the moral fiction in its attitude ascriptions when we are dealing with fictionalists, meta-ethical matters may intrude into discussions where they are not wanted: for instance many practical discussions aimed at coordinating actions taking into account people's attitudes to the relevant proposals.

Of course, the two alternatives are not entirely exclusive: as long as people are clear about what is being done, the two strategies could both be employed at different times. The extended fiction is best suited to occasions where talking like a realist is most convenient, and using the literal method of ascription is most useful where avoiding confusion between literal attitude ascriptions and only pretended ascriptions is particularly important. I leave it to future fictionalist communities (and commentators thereon) to decide on their conventions in this matter.

Conclusion

Dealing with propositional attitude ascriptions which directly or indirectly involve attitudes about fictional states of affairs is a point of some complexity in the rounding out of a fictionalist position, as well as a headache for those who need to talk about fictionalists' attitudes. But once accomplished, we may note that the strategy can be applied, not only in the standard cases of fictionalism or its cousins usually mentioned in the philosophical literature, but also in the comparatively commonplace case of talking of literary fiction. If we hear it said that Zelda believes that Yank believes that Batman and Robin were lovers, we are unlikely to assume that Zelda believes that Yank literally accepts the existence of Batman and Robin and their activities. If Zelda tells her friend Wendy about Yank, while we might say that Zelda desires that Wendy believe that Yank believes that Batman and Robin were lovers, we again may not think that Zelda desires that Wendy come to literally believe such a thing about Yank—it is unlike what her desire would be in a case, say, where Zelda is trying to convince Wendy that Yank is so delusional he cannot distinguish real life from comic book worlds any more. A similar practice of employing extended fictions to discuss higher-order attitudes is tempting here.

This chapter smoothes a wrinkle in fictionalist projects which has for too long remained unnoticed: perhaps because fictionalists are often more concerned to set out and defend a fictionalist position as one which an individual can maintain in good philosophical conscience, rather than as one which is primarily conceived of as an attitude which is held in a practical manner by a community of inquiry. (Not that the former is unimportant—I am tempted to think it a precondition for the latter.) The housekeeping it does is important for another purpose also, mentioned at the beginning: to the extent that a fictionalist claims that their position is to be preferred to theories offering various non-realist semantic analyses due to the Frege–Geach problems which plague such rivals, the fictionalist had better be able to handle any analogous problems they face, such as the one concerning fictional propositional attitudes discussed in this chapter. The usefulness of propositional attitude talk is manifest—in showing that the fictionalist can use it in questionable areas with a clear conscience, this paper makes a useful addition to nearly any fictionalist's toolkit. In addition, it should prove helpful for those interested in talking *about* fictionalists and their attitudes (loosely speaking): and it may prove useful even for those who may not embrace fictionalism in any widespread way, and who do not have much occasion to discuss the opinions of fictionalists, but who nonetheless wish to embrace fictionalism or an analogue about certain very limited subjects such as ideal gasses or the characters of literary fiction.

NOTES

Thanks to audiences at the Australasian Association of Philosophy meeting, Indiana University Bloomington, Keele University, the University of Leeds, the University of Massachusetts at Amherst, and the University of Rochester for useful comments and feedback; with thanks in particular to Phil Bricker, Chris Daly, André Gallois, Jay Garfield, David Lewis, Graham Oppy and Tamar Szabó Gendler. Especial thanks to

Greg Restall and Caroline West for collaboration in work from which this chapter developed. Remaining shortcomings of the chapter, of course, are not the fault of all those who have helped!

1. 'Realist' is a slippery term, and so 'non-realist' will be no less slippery. I mean 'realism' about a particular subject matter here primarily as a doctrine that claims putatively concerning such a subject matter are truth apt, some of them are indeed true, and that such claims are to be assessed more-or-less at face value when providing the semantics for such claims. (The last is vague, but perhaps unavoidably so, given the variety of actual and possible semantic treatments available.) The distinction between realist and non-realist claims can be made more precise in specific areas where needs be. Note that for present purposes I am not concerned to distinguish 'realism' from, e.g., theories of subject matters which take the truth of the relevant claims to be mind-, language-, concept- or evidence-dependent. So many constructivists and idealists will fall into the 'realist' camp for present purposes.

2. Blackburn (1988), for example, admits as much, at least as far as his 'slow track' is concerned: and his 'fast track' proposal seems equally programmatic (though perhaps it is meant to allow that no more than programmatic remarks need to be made).

3. Exempted from this charge may be global projectivists or quasi-realists, if such there be.

4. For more discussion on the drawbacks of quasi-realism in this regard, see Nolan, Restall and West, 'Moral Fictionalism and the Rest', forthcoming.

5. A classic example of a fictionalist about a very wide range of things (and on some readings everything!) is the classic work of Hans Vaihinger (1924). Vaihinger takes whole classes of statements we are inclined to believe as in fact false, but useful to assert and employ in theories.

6. Walton (1990) endorses both of these reasons for taking some of the sentences of some fictions to literally lack truth-value (and indeed not to express propositions literally).

7. A characterization of 'timid' modal fictionalism and the difference between it and some other varieties can be found in Nolan (1997).

8. Or perhaps unsystematically, for those fictionalists who think there is no systematic way that fictional truths in a given area are generated from a fiction and what is literally true. Walton (1990: ch. 4) claims that the mechanisms for generating fictional truths in the case of paradigm fictions are 'complex and unsystematic'.

9. They may not think those pieces of equipment literally deserve the name 'electron microscopes', if they do not literally believe those pieces of equipment interact with electrons: but whether a standard name for a certain sort of artifact is an apt one is a different question from the question of whether there are such artifacts. Even if they would not want to literally use such an expression to refer to that equipment, they still believe in the pieces of equipment I am talking about.

10. Ironically, some have seen in fictionalism a way to defend a thesis that non-referring names are meaningless when used literally: see Crimmins (1998).

11. The case of fictionalism about propositional attitudes themselves would be an exception, and would not face the problem raised by this chapter, at least in the form in which it is presented here. Fictionalism about propositional attitudes faces particular and apparently severe difficulties of its own, however: difficulties which I shall not pursue in this paper.

12. I imagine Yablo at least would be happy to say that our report, e.g., that most high school students believe that $7 + 5 = 12$ is to be treated in a similar 'figuralist' way to the way he thinks that we treat '$7 + 5 = 12$', should it turn out that we are not ordinarily realists about numbers. This chapter can be seen as a story about how the 'figuralist' mechanism generates the fictional truths about our propositional attitudes concerning, e.g., numbers: though the mechanism to be discussed should be equally applicable to fictionalist strategies which lack the particular commitments that Yablo has.

13. I am indebted to a questioner at Indiana for stressing the importance of this point.

14. A fictionalist may wish to have other rules for generating the content of the extended fiction, besides importing the content of the relevant ground-level fiction and the content which is imported because of the right-to-left side of the bridge-law biconditional discussed. For instance, we may wish the extended fiction to sometimes make it fictionally the case that an action of an agent is caused by a combination of beliefs and desires which someone has according to that extended fiction, even if the action is literally only caused by attitudes literally possessed by that person. Or we may wish to have some principle about truth so that we can use a truth predicate in the extended fiction so we can say e.g. everything that Bob believes about electrons is false (or whatever).

15. I am indebted to Jay Garfield for stressing the need to be clear about this more complicated case.

16. The reader is invited to speculate about how useful this fiction would be if we were dealing with a tribe who believed in spirits that both did anthropology and had opinions about fictionalism. It is usually possible to think of possible situations where convenient fictions would not have been convenient.

17. This is not quite the end of the story if some so-called non-propositional attitudes involve emotional states, and it is thought that when one reacts to fiction, one reacts not with genuine emotion but with fictional-emotion of some sort. Then this would need to be added to the account of what it was to have such a 'non-propositional attitude' according to a fiction. I have no wish to take a position on this question of emotional involvement in fiction here.

18. There still may be multiple introductions of mentions of the fiction in those complicated cases where we might normally be tempted to say that there are moral evaluations of states of affairs involving higher-order attitudes which have

at the base level an attitude involving the (a) moral fiction: For example, if Ella would violate a confidence were she to tell Francine about Bill's attitude to abortion, Gerry might disapprove of Ella's desire to tell: indeed it may be that Gerry believes that according to the moral fiction it is wrong that Ella desire that she (Ella) bring it about that Francine believes that Bill believes that according to the moral fiction abortion is wrong. These extended cases, even if they occasionally induce headaches, do not cause any additional problem in principle for this strategy, and it may be noted will be somewhat complex even in straightforward cases where all participants are moral realists.

REFERENCES

Adams, Ernest W. (1975). *The Logic of Conditionals*. Dordrecht: D. Riedel.

Blackburn, Simon (1984). *Spreading the Word*. Oxford: Oxford University Press.

—— (1988). 'Attitudes and Contents.' *Ethics* 98: 501–17. Reprinted in Blackburn (1993a).

—— (1993a). *Essays in Quasi-Realism*. New York: Oxford University Press.

Churchland, Paul (1981). 'Eliminative Materialism and the Propositional Attitudes.' *Journal of Philosophy*, 78.2: 67–90.

Crimmins, Mark (1998). 'Hesperus and Phosphorus: Sense, Pretence and Reference.' *Philosophical Review*, 107.1: 1–47.

Field, Hartry (1989). *Realism, Mathematics and Modality*. New York: Basil Blackwell.

Geach, Peter T. (1965). 'Assertion.' *Philosophical Review*, 74: 449–65.

Gibbard, Allan (1990). *Wise Choices, Apt Feelings: A Theory of Normative Judgment*. Cambridge, MA: Harvard University Press.

Hinckfuss, I. (1993). 'Suppositions, Presuppositions and Ontology.' *Canadian Journal of Philosophy*, 23.4: 595–617.

—— (1996). 'Instrumental Theories: Possibilities and Space and Time.' In P. J. Riggs, (ed.), *Natural Kinds, Laws of Nature and Scientific Methodology*. Dordrecht: Kluwer Academic Publishers.

Lewis, David (1978). 'Truth in Fiction.' *American Philosophical Quarterly*, 15.1: 37–46.

Nolan, Daniel (1997a). 'Three Problems for "Strong" Modal Fictionalism.' *Philosophical Studies*, 87.3: 259–75.

Nolan Daniel, Gregory Restall, and Caroline West (forthcoming). 'Moral Fictionalism versus The Rest.' *Australasian Journal of Philosophy*.

Rosen, Gideon (1990). 'Modal Fictionalism.' *Mind*, 99.395: 327–54.

Searle, John R. (1979). *Expression and Meaning*. Cambridge: Cambridge University Press.

Vaihinger, Hans (1924). *The Philosophy of 'As If'*. C. K. Ogden (trans.). London: Kegan Paul.

van Fraassen, Bas C. (1980). *The Scientific Image*. Oxford: Oxford University Press.

Walton, Kendall L. (1990). *Mimesis as Make-Believe*. Cambridge, MA: Harvard University Press.

Yablo, Stephen (2002a). 'Go Figure: A Path Through Fictionalism.' *Midwest Studies in Philosophy*, 25: 72–102.

8

What we Disagree about when we Disagree about Ontology

Cian Dorr

1. Some Tribes

There was once a land inhabited by many tribes. For a long time, each of the tribes was isolated from all the rest. When they finally made contact, all were amazed to discover how similar they were to one another. All of them spoke languages with exactly the same syntax—that of English. Nevertheless, it soon became clear that there were systematic behavioural differences among the tribes. These differences were reflected in the tribes peoples' reactions to:

> *The Special Composition Question*: Under what circumstances do several things compose something?

or its more explicit variant:

> Under what circumstances is there an object having each of several things as parts, every part of which shares a part with one of them?

It turned out that, while each tribe had taken it for granted that the answer to this question was completely obvious and unproblematic, different answers to this question were current among the different tribes. The tribe of *Universalists*, for example, would unhesitatingly answer 'Always: For any things whatsoever, no matter how scattered and miscellaneous they might be, there is something they compose.' The *Nihilists* favoured the answer

'Never: There are no composite objects, only simple ones.' The *Organicists* answered 'Just in case their activity constitutes a life.'[1] The *Stuck-Togetherists* answered 'Just in case they are all sufficiently tightly stuck together.' And so on for each of many other tribes. The rest of the tribes' verbal behaviour was as one would expect, given these differences. So, for example, in the circumstances where a Universalist would say 'take a chair', Nihilists and Organicists would invariably say 'take some things arranged chairwise'.

Once the tribes had learned of one another's existence, two views about the nature of the differences between the tribes became popular. Some claimed that the tribes were all speaking the same language: what distinguished them was the difference in their *beliefs* about the question expressed by the words 'Under what circumstances do several things compose something?' in their common language. Others favoured a conciliatory view, according to which each tribe had its own language. When the Organicists said things like 'There are no nonliving composite objects', they were, despite appearances, not really contradicting what the Universalists expressed by the words 'There are many nonliving composite objects.' In fact, the sentence expressing each tribe's characteristic answer to the Special Composition Question was a true sentence of that tribe's language.[2]

In the first part of this chapter (sections 2–5), I will consider the question how proponents of the conciliatory view should conceive of the differences between the languages of the tribes. Although the idea that there are many different possible languages which differ systematically in the truth-values they assign to general ontological claims has had many distinguished adherents—among them Carnap (1950), Putnam (1987), and Hirsch (2002)—none of them, to my knowledge, has given a fully general semantic account of these differences: one which shows the speakers of any given language how to state semantic theories for all the other languages. Opponents of the view have suspected that the challenge cannot be met (see, e.g., Sider MS). I will show how, by borrowing some ideas from contemporary work on fictionalism, a conciliator can give a uniform compositional semantics for all the different tribes' languages, which will work just as well no matter which language the conciliator might happen to be speaking.

The remainder of the chapter will consider what those who favour the conciliatory view about these imaginary tribes ought to say about the ongoing debate about the Special Composition Question among ontologists at the actual world. There are appealing lines of thought which might lead a conciliator to adopt one of the following claims about that debate:

(i) The Special Composition Question is easier to resolve than many ontologists think: All we need to do is look closely at the way ordinary people talk about composite objects.

(ii) The Special Composition Question is highly indeterminate: Many logically inconsistent answers to it are such that there is no fact of the matter as regards whether they are true.

(iii) The ontologists debating the Special Composition Question are in the same situation as our imaginary tribes: Each ontologist speaks an idiolect in which his or her favoured answer to the Question is true.

(I will use 'scepticism' as a blanket term to cover all three of these views, together with various intermediate positions.) My main aim will be to argue that these lines of thought are mistaken. In fact, if conciliators pay close attention to what ontologists actually think they are doing, they will see that they should really say that the Special Composition Question, as debated by ontologists, has a univocal, determinate answer, namely the Nihilists' one.

2. Variation in the Meanings of Quantifiers

For the sake of exposition, then, let's suppose that the conciliators are right. Sentences like 'Whenever there are some things, they compose something' and 'There are chairs' mean different things in the languages of different tribes, since they have different truth-values in the languages of different tribes. If so, then presumably some of the words in these sentences also vary in meaning between the different languages.[3]

Which are the variable words? Given the nature of the divergence between the languages, one might naturally expect that *mereological* vocabulary—predicates like 'part', 'compose', and 'simple'—will be variable. But this can't be the only difference between the languages, since 'there are chairs' varies in meaning but doesn't contain any mereological vocabulary. One way to explain this variation would be to add a great many ordinary predicates like 'chair' to the list of variable words. Indeed, in view of the variation in the meaning of sentences like 'There are exactly ten things'—surely if this sentence were true in Nihilish, it would be false in Universalese—if we adopt this approach we shall have to include even very general predicates like 'thing' ('object', 'entity', etc.) on the list of variable words.[4] Perhaps this approach can be made to work. But I think there is a much better, more economical explanation for the variation in the meaning of sentences:

namely, the hypothesis that the *quantifiers*—by which I mean words like 'some', 'all', 'most', 'few', 'something', 'everything', 'whenever', 'always', as well as words like 'ten' when they occur as determiners—are variable in meaning.[5] Once this variation in the meaning of quantifiers has been recognized, there is no evident need to posit variation in the meanings of predicates like 'part', 'chair', and 'thing'.[6]

The quantifiers can't be the only variable words, since some variable sentences don't contain any quantifiers. For example, 'Mars is red' is true in Universalese but untrue in Organicese. To explain the variability of sentences like this, we will also need to recognize some sort of variation in the meaning of names, demonstratives and indexicals.[7] But it's the variability of the quantifiers that is most relevant to the general ontological claims we're concerned with, so let's investigate that first.

3. Conciliatory Semantics for the Quantifiers

What, then, is the nature of this variation in the meanings of the quantifiers? If we happen to be Universalists, we will find this question easy to answer: we can characterize the meaning of a given quantifier in any other tribe's language as a *restriction* of the meaning it has in our language, Universalese. Suppose, for the sake of definiteness, that we adopt the view that the semantic value of 'something' is a property of properties: 'something *F*s' is true just in case the semantic value of '*F*s' instantiates the semantic value of 'something.' Then we can say that just as 'something' in Universalese expresses the property *being instantiated*, so 'something' in Organicese expresses the property *being instantiated by some simple or living thing*.

But what are we to say if we are Organicists trying to characterize the meaning of 'something' in Universalese? We can't say, of course, that there are things that are in the ranges of their quantifiers but not of ours: claims like this are self-defeating. But there must be *something* for us to say. Given that the truth-values of sentences in Universalese depend somehow on which things there are, and what they are like, surely there must be some systematic story to be told about how this dependence works.

(We certainly can imagine radically impoverished languages, blind to whole realms of facts. For example, some people might find the discoveries of modern astronomy so disturbing that they decide to make them inexpressible: they agree among themselves to speak a new language in which 'something' means what 'something within a light year of the centre of gravity of the solar system' means in English, and similarly for other quantifiers. In Astronomically Impoverished English, the sentence 'The truth-values of sentences in ordinary English depend on which things there are, and on what they are like' is false.[8] If we somehow found ourselves speaking such a language, we would have a good reason to institute a linguistic reform. But it seems to me that we would need very special reasons to interpret any community as speaking a language that was impoverished in this way. Besides, it is hardly in the spirit of the conciliatory view to say that while the Universalists can give an adequate semantics for Organicese, the Organicists cannot return the favour.)

How, then, are we to specify the semantic value of 'something' in Universalese, if we are Organicists? One thing we can see immediately is that it cannot be an *extensional* property of properties: it is sometimes instantiated by only one of two coextensive properties.[9] For if we assume that the words 'large', 'inanimate', and 'non-self-identical' mean the same in Organicese and in Universalese, we can truly make the following speech:

> Although the predicates 'large and inanimate' and 'non-self-identical' are coextensive in Organicese, and hence in Universalese, the sentence 'something is large and inanimate' is true in Universalese, whereas the sentence 'something is non-self-identical' is not.[10]

This speech would of course be false in the mouths of the Universalists. No matter what language we are speaking, we can truly say, 'The word "something" is extensional in our language, since an instantiated property cannot be coextensive with an uninstantiated one.' This shows that the word 'extensional' expresses different properties in Organicese and Universalese.[11] There's nothing surprising about this: the definition of 'extensional' contains several quantifiers, so of course it will inherit the variability in the meaning of the quantifiers.[12]

Given that we're looking for a non-extensional property of properties, an obvious strategy is to specify the meaning of 'something' in Universalese using some sort of modal or conditional operator. One approach that promises great generality involves employing counterfactual conditionals. The idea is that the Organicists should say something like:

(1) The word 'something' in Universalese expresses the property of being a property which would be instantiated if composition were universal.

Or better (to avoid the thought, which an Organicist might find natural, that if composition were universal, it would have to be because of the truth of the bizarre pan-vitalist hypothesis that the activity of any things whatsoever constitutes a life):

(2) The word 'something' in Universalese expresses the property of being a property which would be instantiated if things remained arranged exactly as they actually are, except that there were just enough new things to make it true that composition is universal.

This semantics can be generalized straightforwardly to other quantifiers; the natural way of doing this will have the desired consequence that the sentence 'whenever there are some things, there is something they compose' is true in Universalese. It can also be generalized straightforwardly to the languages of other tribes: we need only substitute a statement of the central dogma of the tribe whose language we are trying to interpret for the sentence 'Composition is universal' in the antecedent of the counterfactual. Finally, nothing depends on the fact that we have been considering these theories as stated in Organicese. If they work in Organicese, they will work just as well in any of the other tribes' languages.[13]

4. Objections to the Counterfactual Semantics

4.1. Counterfactuals with Impossible Antecedents

Many philosophers have held that counterfactuals with impossible antecedents are all vacuously true. If this view were correct, it would spell trouble for the counterfactual semantics. For presumably, if the conciliatory view is correct, 'Everything is simple or living' is a necessarily true sentence in Organicese; if so, 'It is impossible for composition to be universal, if all actual things are arranged just as they actually are' is true in Organicese, so the counterfactual that features in (2) has an impossible antecedent. If all such counterfactuals were true, it would follow that the semantic value of 'something' is a property instantiated by all properties whatsoever! However, there is every reason to disbelieve the claim that all counterfactuals with metaphysically impossible antecedents are vacuously true. Here are some plausible counterexamples:

(3a) If I were a bird, I would have feathers.
(3b) If it were necessary that there are no donkeys, it would be necessary that there are no talking donkeys.

(3c) If there were unicorns, there would be horse-like creatures with horns on their foreheads.

(3d) If all and only married men were bachelors, most politicians would be bachelors.

These examples do indeed pose a challenge for the project of giving a formal semantics for the counterfactual conditional. But: (i) There are even worse challenges facing those who would give a formal semantics for other kindred notions, such as the indicative conditional. (ii) Some good work has been done on responding to these challenges (see, e.g., Nolan, 1997b). And (iii) if you are still determined not to understand counterfactuals with impossible antecedents, you should feel free to substitute 'According to the fiction that...' wherever I have written something of the form 'If it were the case that...': For we surely can understand claims about what is the case according to impossible fictions in such a way that such claims are not all vacuously true (see Rosen, 1990).

4.2. 'Actually'

If we use counterfactuals—or modal operators of any sort—in our account of the variation in the meanings of the quantifiers, we will, rather surprisingly, find that we have to add the words 'actual' and 'actually' to our list of variable expressions. For consider the true Universalese sentence:

(4) Something actually is a chair.

If we treated 'actually is a chair' as invariant, our Organicists' semantic theory for 'something' would entail that (4) is true iff the property *actually being a chair* would be instantiated if composition were universal. But in that case (4) would have to be false. Since nothing is a chair at the actual world, nothing would have been *actually* a chair no matter how things had been different.

It's not hard to come up with an appropriate account of the variability of 'actually': We need only take the semantic value of 'actually' in Universalese to be the same as that of the compound operator 'actually, if composition were universal' in Organicese.[14] Since 'actually' plays the very same logical or conceptual role in all the tribes' languages, it is surprising to learn that it varies in meaning in this way. Then again, one doesn't have to be a radical holist to think that the semantic properties of an expression are not determined by that expression's conceptual role taken in isolation, but rather by its conceptual role taken in conjunction with those of certain other expressions in its language.

4.3. Semantic Claims

Consider the following sentence of Universalese:

(5) All the central dogmas of the Organicists are true.

Given that we are assuming the conciliatory view, we must count (5) as true. But how are the Organicists to account for its truth? Assuming that the quantifier is the only relevant variable expression in (5), the counterfactual semantics entails that (5) is true iff:

(5*) If composition were universal, then all the central dogmas of the Organicists would be true.

But (5*) seems, at first sight, to be false (in Organicese). For the central dogmas of the Organicists are sentences like 'there are no nonliving composite objects'. If composition had been universal, there would have been nonliving composite objects, and so this sentence would have been false.

One might be tempted to respond to this objection by claiming that the predicate 'true' (understood as applying to utterances, or sentences of arbitrary languages) expresses different properties in Organicese and Universalese. But even if an approach along these lines could be made to work, we should be loath to take this step. It is one thing to propose that when the members of different tribes appear to disagree about *ontology*, they are really talking past one another. It is quite another thing, and much stranger, to propose that even when they explicitly endorse the conciliatory view, and start saying things like 'In your language, the sentence "There are no nonliving composite objects" is true', they are still somehow talking past one another.

I think that it would be better to respond to this objection by claiming that (5*) is in fact *true* in Organicese. The idea is that the Organicists should reason to themselves along the following lines:

If composition were universal, we Organicists would still be going around uttering sentences like 'There are no nonliving composite objects'; but we would be speaking a different language from the one we actually speak. The proposition expressed in *that* language by 'There are no nonliving composite objects' is one that would be true, even if composition were universal.

This idea—that a change in the facts about what it takes for composition to occur, without any change in the Organicists' behaviour, could suffice for such a radical change in the meaning of the Organicists' sentences—may initially seem bizarre. But it strikes me that anyone who finds the conciliatory view plausible should, on reflection, find this idea plausible as well. What underlies the conciliatory view is a limited principle of charity: a correct interpretation of some language-users will never impute to them systematic error as regards the ontology of composite objects, at least if their discourse about composite objects is internally consistent. If this is right, the speakers of any language can truly say to themselves that if the ontological facts had been systematically different, the principle of charity would have made a different interpretation of their speech correct.[15]

4.4. Translation and Fine-Grained Contexts

Given a semantic theory for one language stated in another language, there will be a natural way to read off a *translation manual* from the first language into the second language. The Organicists' counterfactual semantic theory for Universalese suggests that we could translate an arbitrary Universalese sentence into Organicese by inserting the expression 'If composition were universal, it would be the case that . . .' in front of every quantifier. (In fact something more complicated than this will be required to deal with quantifiers that are not in subject-position, as in 'Everyone loves someone.') The translations we arrive at by using this algorithm will often be quite complex. For example:

(6) Some star is such that many planets orbit it

will become:

(6*) If composition were universal, some star would be such that if composition were universal, many planets would orbit it.

But typically this complexity is eliminable. (6*), for example, is logically equivalent to:

(6**) If composition were universal, some star would be such that many planets orbit it.[16]

If we blindly apply this algorithm to all Universalese sentences, problems will ensue. Consider the (presumably true) Universalese sentence:

(7) Most dogs believe that there are rocks

The algorithm would lead us to translate this into Organicese as:

(7*) If composition were universal, most dogs would believe that if composition were universal, there would be rocks.

But (7*) seems dubious. We might well think that most dogs are not sophisticated enough to have this counterfactual belief; and the truth of the antecedent of the counterfactual wouldn't make them any more sophisticated.

Again, consider the Universalese sentence:

(8) If there were no nonliving composite objects, composition would be universal.

Intuitively, this is false, despite the impossibility of the antecedent. But the algorithm would lead us to translate (8) as follows:

(8*) If it were the case that (if composition were universal, there would be no nonliving composite objects), then it would be the case that (if composition were universal, composition would be universal).

This is hard to make sense of, but there is a strong case for regarding it as true—perhaps vacuously true—in virtue of its logically true consequent.[17]

Is this a problem for the counterfactual semantics? If it is, it is a general problem for the sort of semantics that assigns entities like *properties* as semantic values. For example, although the word 'water' expresses the property *being H_2O*, it would be a mistake to translate the true sentence:

(9) All dogs believe that there is water

into the intuitively false sentence:

(9*) All dogs believe that there is H_2O.

Likewise, it would be a mistake to translate the intuitively false sentence:

(10) If water were an element rather than a compound, all water would be H_2O

into the much more bizarre, but apparently true:

(10*) If H_2O were an element rather than a compound, all H_2O would be H_2O.

It may be that the style of semantic theory in which properties are assigned as semantic values is simply not up to the task of giving an adequate compositional account of sentences like these. If so, we will presumably need to find some more 'fine-grained' style of semantic value to make the necessary distinctions between expressions which correspond to the same property.[18] But I know of no reason to expect any *special* difficulties in the task of adding the right sort of fineness of grain to the counterfactual semantics.

I am tempted to say no more than that: But perhaps it would help if I sketched one style of approach to adding the necessary fineness of grain which, while it doesn't solve all the puzzles of substitutivity, does at least give us a neat explanation of what is wrong with the translations of (7)–(10) as (7*)–(10*). The idea is that whereas syntactically simple expressions pick out the properties and relations they express 'directly', syntactically complex expressions pick them out 'by description', as the properties and relations constructed in such-and-such ways out of such-and-such other properties and relations. So, to take a simple example, the syntactically complex term 'frozen water' picks out the property it expresses—the property of being ice—as the conjunction of the properties *being frozen* and *being water*. This explains why 'ice' and 'frozen water' are not intersubstitutable in propositional attitude ascriptions: To believe that there is frozen water in the glass, one must not only believe that there is ice in the glass, but believe that proposition in a certain articulated way. It also explains why 'ice' and 'frozen water' are not intersubstitutable in certain counterfactuals with impossible antecedents. For it to be true that, if it had been the case that *P,* there would have been frozen water in the glass, what must be true is that, if it had been the case that *P,* the glass would have contained an instance of whatever property would in that case have been the conjunction of *being frozen* and *being water*—which might be something other than being ice, if *P* describes an impossible situation in which *being ice* fails to be the conjunction of *being frozen* and *being water.*[19]

Applied to the counterfactual semantics, the idea would be that 'something' in Universalese expresses a certain property of properties *directly,* a property which the complex Organicese expression 'is a property which would have been instantiated if composition had been universal' expresses only under a description which characterizes its structure. Dogs do believe propositions involving this property of properties—for example, the proposition that results when it is predicated of the property of being a rock—but they do not pick it out in the articulated manner which would be required for (7*) to be true. And counterfactuals like (8), which concern impossible situations in which the property has a different structure from the one it actually has, can differ in truth value from sentences like (8*), in which the property is picked out as the occupant of a certain structural role.

5. Conciliatory Semantics for Names

How can these conciliatory semantic theories be extended so as to account for
the variation in the meanings of proper names between the different tribes'
languages? One thing that we can see straight away is that in general, we can't
expect semantic theories on which names are assigned their *referents* as semantic
values, so that a simple subject–predicate sentence is true if the semantic value
of the subject instantiates the semantic value of the predicate. For the Organicists must recognize that 'Mars is a red planet' is true in Universalese despite the
fact that nothing instantiates the property of being a red planet.[20] Instead, the
semantic value of a name should be taken to be something like a *property of
properties*—an entity of the same general sort as the semantic values of quantifiers. On this approach, 'Mars is a red planet' will be true in Universalese iff
the semantic value of 'is a red planet' in Universalese (i.e., the property *being a
red planet*) instantiates the semantic value of 'Mars' in Universalese.

How should the Organicists characterize the semantic value of 'Mars' in
Universalese? If they have the name 'Mars' in their language—for them, of
course, it will be an empty name—they can mimic the counterfactual
semantics for the quantifiers:

(11) The word 'Mars' in Universalese expresses the property of being a
property that would be instantiated by Mars, if composition were
universal.

This will only work, of course, if we can truly say (in Organicese) that Mars
would exist if composition were universal. This sounds reasonable enough to
me; but there are some views about empty names according to which
sentences involving empty names in this way are always untrue.[21] In any
case, it can hardly be maintained that it is only thanks to the fortuitous
presence in their language of appropriate empty names that the Organicists
can give an adequate semantic theory of names in Universalese. In the absence
of appropriate empty names, the semantics must proceed piecemeal. It might
be suggested that each name of Universalese should be associated with a
certain set of simple things, giving us a semantics along the following lines:

(12) The word 'Mars' in Universalese expresses the property of being a
property that would be instantiated by the unique planet composed
by the members of S, if composition were universal.

But this seems to be too simple: it will fail to account for the truth in
Universalese of the sentence 'It could have been the case that Mars had

different parts.'[22] To get around this sort of problem, we will need to substitute for 'the unique planet composed by the members of S' some description of which we can truly say, in Universalese, that it expresses an *individual essence* of Mars—a property possession of which is necessary and sufficient for being Mars. Something along the lines of 'the unique planet composed by the members of the unique F set', where F expresses some complicated property of sets of simples, might do the trick.[23]

This sort of semantics for names has the same sort of problems with propositional-attitude contexts that I discussed for the case of the quantifiers in section 4.4. Prima facie, it looks as if we will have trouble accounting for the truth, in Universalese, of sentences like:

(13) Many people believe that Mars is red but do not believe that the unique planet composed by the members of the unique F set of simples is red,

and the falsity of sentences like:

(14) If Mars had not been composed by the members of any F set of simples, the unique planet composed by the members of the unique F set of simples would not have been composed by the members of any F set of simples.

Perhaps there is no way to give an adequate semantic account of sentences like this one without introducing some new, more fine-grained element into our semantic theory. One sort of approach to providing the needed fineness of grain is closed to the conciliator: the Organicists cannot say that the semantic value of 'Mars' is, or involves, a certain object, namely Mars, in a way that the semantic value of the description 'the unique planet composed by the members of the unique F set of simples' does not. But this is not the only possible approach. Indeed, for any account we might give of the difference between the semantic values of 'water' and 'H_2O' (for example, the one sketched at the end of section 4.4), it should be possible for the Organicists to give an analogous account of the differences between the semantic values in Universalese of 'Mars' and the description that gives its individual essence.

6. Folk Mereology

Let's step back from all these semantic details and take stock. How is the thought experiment of the tribes supposed to bear on our actual situation?

Unlike the tribespeople, ordinary English speakers don't have an answer to the Special Composition Question on the tips of their tongues. Nevertheless, there are many general principles about the circumstances under which composition occurs which we *treat* as if we were perfectly confident of their truth, even though we generally don't feel called upon to assert them. For example, if I were to tell you that my child put one block on top of another block, and put a third block on top of that, and put a fourth block on top of that, and that no other blocks were nearby, and you believed me, you would be apt to report me as having said that my child made a stack of four blocks. In moving back and forth like this between a claim about the blocks and a claim about the stack, you are implicitly treating the sentence 'If some blocks are stacked up one on top of another, then there is a stack that they compose' as if you were very confident of its truth. Call the theory that comprises all the general claims about composition which we typically take for granted in this way *folk mereology*.

Here is an argument for the truth of folk mereology. Folk mereology plays the same general sort of role for the community of ordinary English-speakers that each tribe's central dogmas play for that tribe. But the thought experiment of the tribes shows us that any sentences which play that sort of role in a community will express truths in that community's language. Hence, the sentences that comprise folk mereology express truths in ordinary English. Let's call this the *argument from charity*, since its second premise is a highly circumscribed version of the principle of charity.[24]

A complication: it may have been an oversimplification to assume that there is a *single* set of principles about composition which guide our talk about composite objects in all ordinary contexts. Perhaps we have several different, incompatible practices for talking about composite objects, of which we choose whichever best serves our communicative purposes. In that case, it would be natural to conclude that the quantifiers in ordinary English are context-sensitive, so that different general claims about composite objects are true in different contexts. We might be motivated to posit this sort of context-sensitivity by considering certain paradoxes: jointly inconsistent sets of intuitively compelling sentences. For example, there is the celebrated paradox of the statue and the lump. On the one hand we want to say that the atoms arranged statuewise compose only one object; on the other hand, we want to say that they compose at least two, on the grounds that the statue has been around much longer than, would be easier to destroy than, is worth more than . . . the lump of clay. Perhaps the thing to say is that each of these claims is true in the context in which it would be most likely to be asserted, although there is no context in which both are true.

The argument from charity is silent about the truth-values of those general claims about composition that are consistent with but not entailed by folk mereology (or by the theory that plays the role of folk mereology in a given context). But there is a natural line of thought that might lead one from the conciliatory view to the conclusion that all such questions are indeterminate in truth value. Consider a tribe whose characteristic mereological doctrine is relatively unspecific: for instance, the Stuck-Togetherists, who propound a doctrine they express using the words 'Several things compose something just in case they are sufficiently tightly stuck together', but never say anything very specific about the degree of tightness required. It seems unacceptably arbitrary to claim that anything much more specific than this doctrine is determinately true in their language. The only way to avoid this arbitrariness is to claim that their current language is indeterminate, having each of the languages which they might end up speaking if they adopted a more specific version of the doctrine as an admissible precisification. It is arguable that speakers of ordinary English are in an analogous situation. If so, any suitably general question about composition which is not resolved by folk mereology will be indeterminate.[25]

7. Ontological Disagreement

If the argument from charity is sound, the right methodology for investigating questions about the ontology of composition, expressed in ordinary English, is the methodology of ordinary language philosophy.[26] That doesn't entail that these questions are trivial or uninteresting: It may not always be obvious what, if anything, folk mereology has to say about a given question. Nevertheless, this picture plainly conflicts with many ontologists' conception of what they are talking about. This class clearly includes ontologists like van Inwagen (1990), whose theories are blatantly inconsistent with folk mereology. But even ontologists whose theories are not in such obvious conflict with folk mereology may make it clear, by the nature of the arguments that they give for their own views, and by the seriousness with which they take the views of their opponents, that they don't think that what they are doing is answerable to the methods of ordinary language philosophy. They mean to be doing something much less parochial. Is there any way, if we accept the conclusion of the argument from charity, to avoid the conclusion that all these ontologists are just wrong?

Of course there is: we can claim that the ontologists in question—call them 'foundational ontologists'—are not speaking ordinary English. Their language may instead be a sort of professional jargon in which certain expressions—in particular the quantifiers—have special senses, distinct from their senses in ordinary English. The most cursory look at these ontologists' linguistic behaviour suffices to make this interpretative hypothesis look compelling. Although many foundational ontologists are disposed to utter sentences which conflict with folk mereology, like 'there are no chairs', when they are engaged in ontological debates, the rest of the time they behave just like everyone else, uttering sentences like 'there are too many chairs in my office'. And even those foundational ontologists whose linguistic behaviour is less variable than this seem to take their colleagues' strange dispositions in their stride; they do not display the blank incomprehension which would be the natural response to people one took to be alternating between contradictory assertions.[27]

Further confirmation for the hypothesis that the language of ontology is distinct from ordinary English can be found by looking at what ontologists themselves think is going on. Opinions vary, of course; but many ontologists make remarks that suggest that they hold something like this view. Here, for example, is what van Inwagen says about the relation between his claims and ordinary opinion:

[W]hen people say things in the ordinary business of life by uttering sentences that start 'There are chairs...' or 'There are stars...' they very often say things that are literally true.... [A]ny of the propositions that an English speaker might express by uttering 'There are two very valuable chairs in the next room' on a particular occasion...is, I would argue, consistent with the propositions that I, as metaphysician, express by writing the words 'There are no chairs.'

(van Inwagen, 1990: 101)

Indeed, the idea that certain bits of language have distinctive meanings in the mouths of philosophers must be as old as philosophy itself. When Thales said 'All is water', did he really mean to be contradicting the propositions that ordinary people would express using sentences like 'There is very little water in the Arabian Desert'?

Once we have recognized the possibility that the language of ontology is distinct from ordinary English, we can no longer rely on the argument from charity to establish the truth of folk mereology in the language of ontology. The most salient thing about the ontologists' usage is the fact that they don't take any sentences about composition for granted in the way each tribe takes its characteristic dogma for granted. So there is no very direct route from the conciliatory view of the tribes to any particular view of ontological debate.

However, if we embrace the 'two languages' picture, it does seem reasonable to ask the ontologists to explain what they are talking about in ordinary English—to teach the uninitiated how to speak their special jargon. I don't see why the ontologists should refuse to take up this invitation. I imagine the proffered explanation will look something like this:

> What we debate in the ontology room is the question what there is *strictly speaking*—what there *really, ultimately* is—what there is *in the most fundamental sense*. Of all the many meanings a quantifier like 'something' might have, one is *special*. This is the one in terms of which all the rest are to be analyzed; it is the one such that to find out what there is in *this* sense would be to fulfill the traditional metaphysical goal of comprehending reality *as it is in itself*. When we do ontology, our quantifiers bear these special meanings.

There is no reason why someone who endorsed the argument from charity would have to find this explanation unsatisfactory. Nevertheless, many philosophers certainly will find it unsatisfactory. They will deny that there is any relevantly 'special' interpretation of the quantifiers. They need not go so far as to reject the very idea that some languages could be better-suited than others for capturing the structure of reality 'as it is in itself';[28] they need only claim that this goal can be achieved equally well in many different languages, in which different meanings for the quantifiers lead to different answers to the Special Composition Question.

What should these sceptically minded philosophers say about the language of ontology? As I already mentioned in section 1, there seem to be three main possible views:

(i) Ontologists' attempts to break free from the shackles of ordinary language are unsuccessful. Even in the context of the ontology room, folk mereology is true 'by default'.

(ii) The special practices of ontologists succeed in freeing language from the constraints imposed by ordinary usage, but they do not succeed in imposing any new constraints to take their place. As a result, the language of ontology is highly indeterminate, so that none of the disputed answers to the Special Composition Question has a determinate truth-value.

(iii) The special practices of ontologists succeed in freeing language from the constraints imposed by ordinary usage; but the result of this is linguistic fragmentation. In the idiosyncratic language spoken by a given ontologist, that ontologist's general claims about composition are all true.

The differences between these interpretative views don't matter much for my purposes. They all entail, in one way or another, that foundational ontologists are deeply mistaken about the nature of their own practice.

8. Strategy

So far, then, we have stalemate. The foundational ontologist maintains that there is a special, 'metaphysically basic' set of meanings for the quantifiers. The sceptic denies this, or claims not even to understand the expressions used by the ontologist in explaining the relevant notion of specialness. How can we move the debate forward?

The task faced by the ontologist is to initiate the sceptic into the practice of foundational ontology, by articulating, in terms even the sceptic will understand, a criterion by which the language of ontology can be distinguished from all the many other candidate languages which one might be tempted to interpret ontologists as speaking. To win at this game, we will need to convince the sceptic that the criterion we articulate fulfils certain desiderata:

(i) It should be *satisfied* by some language—and not just by toy languages, but by some language that is a candidate to be the language of ontology.[29]

(ii) It should be *discriminating*. Ideally, it should be satisfied by exactly one of the candidate languages; but if it is satisfied by more than one, they should at least agree as regards the answers to general ontological questions like the Special Composition Question. This will be enough to ensure that such questions have determinately and univocally correct answers in the language of ontology.

(iii) It should be *faithful* to the practice of foundational ontology. It would be ideal if foundational ontologists were all disposed, irrespective of their ontological views, to agree that the language in which they conduct their debates is one that satisfies the criterion. Failing that, we should be able to make it plausible that foundational ontologists are implicitly committed to accepting our criterion: it should articulate some basic presupposition that unifies and makes sense of some facts about foundational ontological debate which would otherwise seem puzzling and arbitrary.

Suppose we can convince the sceptic that our criterion meets all three of these desiderata. Then, I think, the sceptic would have to agree that actual foundational ontologists are properly interpreted as speaking a language

satisfying the criterion in question.[30] Such an interpretation is clearly preferable, from the point of view of charity, to an interpretation according to
which ontologists are speaking a language in which folk mereology is guaranteed to be true, or speaking a radically indeterminate language, or speaking
many divergent idiolects.[31] Foundational ontologists think that they are
debating genuine questions, with determinate answers, which do not merely
reflect the idiosyncrasies of 'our conceptual scheme'. If we can, we should
interpret them in such a way that this self-conception is correct.

I should emphasize that it is not a requirement for success that the sceptic
should be left, after we have finished our initiation, regarding the questions
debated by ontologists as open questions. It may well be that the sceptic will
end up saying, 'Oh, if *that's* what you've been talking about all this time, I see
that I have agreed all along with those ontologists who maintain that *P*, and that
I have disagreed with those ontologists who maintain that not-*P*.' (In fact, this
will be the state of play at the end of the chapter: if my argument works, it will
convince would-be-sceptics that they have really been Nihilists all along.)
It would be worrisome if the sceptic could present us with an *obviously sound*
argument for the claim that '*P*' is true in the language(s) that satisfy our
criterion, for then we would have to worry that we were being unduly uncharitable in interpreting ontologists who deny '*P*' as speaking such a language. But
if the (former) sceptic's argument for the claim that '*P*' is true in the language of
ontology is based on controversial premises which many non-sceptical opponents of the claim that *P* will deny, we need not be concerned.

The question how foundational ontologists should be interpreted is in-
timately bound up with a question about the proper interpretation of
modifiers like 'strictly speaking', 'really', 'ultimately' and 'fundamentally'. If
we can agree that foundational ontologists should be interpreted as speaking
some single, reasonably determinate language, distinct from ordinary English, we should also agree that at least one legitimate function of these
modifiers in ordinary English is to force whatever is within their scope to
be interpreted as it would be in that language. The point of prefixing a
sentence with one of these modifiers is to encourage one's hearers to look for
some unusual interpretation of one's words that is somehow salient and
interesting, but that would normally be rejected on the grounds that it fits
too poorly with our ordinary communicative purposes. Consider, for example, how we manage to work out what someone would intend to convey
by using the words 'nothing is *really* solid'. Among the properties that are
similar enough to the property we normally attribute using the word 'solid',
one stands out as especially salient—the property of containing no empty

space at all. Many words aren't like this. For example, there isn't any obvious sense to be made of the claim that the things ordinarily called chairs aren't *really* chairs at all (although they really do exist). If the sceptic is right, the quantifiers are more like 'chair' than 'solid'. The space of possible interpretations of the quantifiers is homogeneous: there is nothing to make any given unusual interpretation stand out as especially interesting and salient. But if we can convince the sceptic that some feature possessed by one of these interpretations makes it (reasonably) determinately correct as an interpretation of the quantifiers in the language of ontology, surely the sceptic will have to agree that this feature also makes this interpretation salient and interesting in the way that matters to the interpretation of modifiers like 'really'. It's not as if foundational ontologists are a community of eccentrics who assign some arbitrary nonstandard meanings to the quantifiers just for the sake of being different. Any interpretation that can manage to be uniquely correct for such an extraordinarily varied group of speakers must be quite remarkable in some way. Moreover, the ease with which generations of students have been inducted into the practice of foundational ontology is evidence that the basic presuppositions of that practice cannot be wholly alien to our ordinary thought, even if their role there is not central enough to overcome the force of the argument from charity.

Although the communicative function of the word 'literally' in most contexts is very similar to those of the other modifiers I have been concerned with, we would be inviting confusion if we used this modifier in the same way as the others, characterizing foundational ontology as concerned with the question what *literally* exists. For the use of 'literally' is complicated enormously by its having come to play a central role in theorizing about language by linguists and philosophers. The question whether ordinary sentences like 'this table is solid oak' are sometimes literally true, as opposed to being merely pragmatically appropriate, is regarded as a weighty theoretical matter, with empirical implications about the structure of our linguistic capacities. I'm sure that important empirical questions are at stake in these debates about where to draw the line between semantics and pragmatics, although I'm inclined to doubt that there's only one such question.[32] But if we think that the only way to put a distance between our ontological claims and what we assert the rest of the time is to claim that only the former sentences are literally true, we will make these empirical questions look more important than they really are. It would certainly be interesting if, as Stephen Yablo (1998, 2000) has claimed, ordinary talk about numbers and other abstracta is similar in some relevant respect to paradigmatically non-literal uses of language in metaphor and make-believe.[33] It would be even more interesting if such an analogy could be made out in the case of ordinary talk about chairs. But we would be conceding altogether too much to the sceptic if we adopted a conception of the subject-matter of ontological debate on which nominalists who don't think that ordinary folk are mistaken as regards the existence of numbers, and Nihilists or Organicists who don't think that ordinary folk are mistaken as regards the existence of chairs, must be committed to psychological claims like these.

The remainder of this chapter will be devoted to considering various criteria by which one might attempt to distinguish the language of ontology from other languages. I will begin, in sections 9 and 10, by considering two criteria which, though they have been thought by some to provide the key to the interpretation of ontological debate, are in my view wholly unsatisfactory. Then, in section 11, I will consider a third criterion, which seems more promising, although it too is flawed. In succeeding sections I will show how this criterion can be improved upon. Finally, in section 17, I will argue that the final version of the criterion does meet all three of our desiderata, and hence that the sceptic should accept it as providing a correct and determinate understanding of the subject-matter of ontological debate. If this argument works, it will also show that the sceptic should take ontologists to be speaking a language in which Nihilism is the correct answer to the Special Composition Question.

9. Ontological Disagreement as Pragmatic Disagreement

Carnap (1950) thought that the only way to make charitable sense of debates about general ontological principles was to interpret them as pragmatic debates about whether it would suit our purposes to adopt 'frameworks' (i.e., languages) in which the principles in question were true. This interpretative proposal can be understood as a criterion for distinguishing the language of ontology from other languages:

> *Criterion 1*: The language of ontology is the language that it would best suit our purposes to speak, among the candidate languages.

Could this be the key to understanding the debates of foundational ontologists?

There certainly *could* be a practice that worked like this. We could use the sentence 'composition is universal' to convey that our purposes would be optimally well-served by speaking a language in which 'composition is universal' expressed a truth. Perhaps there are even some actual philosophers who are properly interpreted as engaging in such a practice. But it seems quite obvious that this characterization is very far from being faithful to the self-conception of most foundational ontologists. Ontologists whose theories conflict dramatically with folk mereology are generally perfectly happy to admit that it would be awkward and impractical were we to make a practice of asserting only those sentences that are consistent with their theories; and their more 'commonsensical' opponents don't find this position in any way *incoherent*. It is just too obvious that most of our purposes would be worse served if we had to go around saying things like 'the things arranged chairwise are under the things arranged tablewise' instead of 'the chair is under the table'. (Of course, ontologists whose theories conflict with folk mereology will grant that there would be *something* desirable in our adopting the cumbrous mode of speech: if we talked in this way, we would be less apt to be led by linguistic appearances into holding erroneous views about what really, fundamentally, ultimately exists. But we can't legitimately appeal to *this* kind of 'purpose' if we are attempting to teach the language of ontology to a sceptic who refuses to understand this sort of talk.)

This is not to say that Carnap must be wrong to think that ontological debate is best interpreted in accordance with Criterion 1. But an interpretation as unfaithful as this, on which the views of so many ontologists turn out to be so easily refuted, could be acceptable only as a last resort. Before we give in, we should try hard to find a criterion that comes closer to satisfying our desiderata.

10. Absolutely Unrestricted Quantification

Of the various meanings a quantifier might have, some are *restrictions* of others. For example, the meaning of 'something' in Organicese is a restriction of its meaning in Universalese. If we think of these meanings as properties of properties, we will explain this by appealing to the fact that the former property entails the latter.[34] One of the things ontologists are apt to say when asked to clarify the meanings of their quantifiers is that they intend to be quantifying *without restriction*, over everything there is. Is there any way to interpret these remarks as expressing some criterion by which the language of ontology might plausibly be distinguished from other languages?

These remarks admit of a 'deflationary' interpretation, on which they could equally well be made by the members of any of the tribes. If the Universalists are anything like us, they will sometimes say things like 'every bottle is empty' to convey the information that they could have conveyed by saying 'every bottle in the house is empty'; similarly, the Organicists will sometimes say things like 'all atoms arranged bottle wise are arranged empty-wise'. This phenomenon is naturally explained by positing a context-dependence in the quantifiers.[35] On the deflationary interpretation, quantifying unrestrictedly just means occupying a context such that the semantic value of a quantifier in one's language in any other context is a restriction of its semantic value in one's language in that context.[36] This interpretation is clearly useless for our purposes, since it does nothing at all to distinguish the language of ontology from any other language.

If the notion of unrestricted quantification is to do any work for us, we will need to find a more ambitious way to interpret it. Say that a quantifier is *absolutely unrestricted* just in case it has a meaning which is not a restriction of any other possible quantifier-meaning. We could try taking this to be the distinguishing mark of the language of ontology:

> *Criterion 2*: The language of ontology is one in which all quantifiers are absolutely unrestricted.

This criterion is unsatisfactory, for two reasons. First, it is doubtful whether it is really *faithful* to the practice of foundational ontology. True, ontologists do go on about how they mean to be 'quantifying unrestrictedly'. But can we really charitably interpret these claims as claims to be using absolutely unrestricted quantifiers? It seems altogether too obvious that Universalism would be the true answer to the Special Composition Question in any language with absolutely unrestricted quantifiers. For Universalism is true in Universalese, and hence it is true in any language with quantifiers of which the quantifiers in Universalese are restrictions. On this interpretation, foundational ontologists who reject Universalism are in an unstable position: to refute them, we only have to convince them that Universalese is a *possible* language, which we might do by showing how to give a counterfactual semantics for the quantifiers of Universalese. If we can find one, we should prefer a more charitable interpretation, on which the Special Composition Question cannot be so straightforwardly resolved.

Secondly, there is a good argument that Criterion 2 is unsatisfiable. Starting with any language L, one can find a new language L' such that the meanings of the quantifiers in L are restrictions of their meanings in L'. For no matter how numerous the things at the actual world may be, we can always construct a counterfactual whose antecedent sends us to a world where there are some new things that don't exist at the actual world, by making judicious use of the 'actually' operator. This counterfactual can then be used to specify, in L, the meanings of the quantifiers of L'. For example, we could define the new meanings of the quantifiers as follows:

'Something' in L' expresses the property of being a property that would have been instantiated if there had been an angel more powerful than any actual angel, and everything else had been just as it actually is.

Or, if we wanted something more abstract, we could take advantage of Russell's paradox:

'Something' in L' expresses the property of being a property that would have been instantiated if there had been a set having as members all and only those things which actually are not members of themselves, and everything else had been just as it actually is.

The original meaning of 'something' will be a restriction of these new meanings: in the first case, to things other than the most powerful angel; in the second case, to things other than the set which has as members all and only those things other than itself that are not members of themselves. Thus, once we recognize that counterfactuals can be used in this way to extend the space of possible quantifier-meanings, we will see that there can be no such thing as an absolutely unrestricted quantifier.[37]

11. Constraints on Analyticity

The counterfactual semantic theories described in section 3 are designed with a view to entailing that each tribe's characteristic dogma is a *true* sentence of that tribe's language. However, they naturally suggest the stronger claim that each tribe's characteristic dogma is an *analytic* sentence of that tribe's language. For surely—one might think—translation must preserve analyticity and syntheticity: analyticity is truth in virtue of meaning, and translation is preservation of meaning. But if we translate between the languages of the tribes in the way naturally suggested by the counterfactual semantic theories, we will find that the translation of any tribe's dogma into any other tribe's language is an analytic truth. For example, the Universalist dogma 'Any objects are such that something is composed by them' will be translated into Organicese as the analytic truth 'If composition were universal, then any objects would be such that if composition were universal, some object would be composed by them.'

This comes as no surprise: at least since Carnap (1950), scepticism about the genuineness of ontological disagreement has been closely allied with the view that ontological claims are typically analytic when true. Conversely, those who take ontological disagreement seriously have tended to find it obvious that controversial ontological claims like the answers to the Special Composition Question are synthetic, if they accept the analytic/synthetic distinction at all.[38] These sociological facts suggest a strategy for distinguishing the language of ontology from other candidate languages. If we could find some principled basis for ontologists' judgements of syntheticity—some general, non-arbitrary condition satisfied by uncontroversially analytic truths, but not satisfied by the disputed ontological claims—we could characterize the language of ontology as one in which the only analytic truths are those that satisfy the condition.

What could the condition be? There is an long and influential tradition in philosophy according to which *existential* sentences—sentences which assert the existence of an entity of some sort—can never be analytic. This is a common theme in responses to putative a priori proofs of the existence of God, by Hume:

Whatever we conceive as existent, we can also conceive as non-existent. There is no being, therefore, whose non-existence implies a contradiction. Consequently there is no being whose existence is demonstrable.

(Hume, 1779/1997, part 9)

and Kant:

I can not form the least concept of a thing which, should it be rejected with all its predicates, leaves behind a contradiction.

(Kant, 1781/1965, B 623–4).

If we picked out the language of ontology as one in which existential sentences are never analytic, we would succeed in ruling out the analyticity of a great many ontological claims: the claim that there are numbers, for example. Unfortunately, the disputed answers to the Special Composition Question are not existential: they are all consistent with—indeed, entailed by—the hypothesis that there is nothing at all. If we want our characterization of the language of ontology to entail that none—or at most one—of these sentences is analytic, we will need something stronger than the ban on existential analytic truths.

What we are looking for, I think, is something like this:

Criterion 3: The language of ontology is one in which all analytic truths can be transformed into logical truths by replacing nonlogical expressions with their conceptual analyses.[39]

Since it is quite clear that the Special Composition Question can't be settled by conceptual analysis (of nonlogical vocabulary), Criterion 3 has the intended result of entailing that none of the disputed answers to the Special Composition Question are analytic truths in the language of ontology. If this doesn't strike you as obvious, all I can do is challenge you to come up with a remotely plausible conceptual analysis of 'part', or of any other predicates, which allows any of the answers to be transformed into a logical truth. I predict you will fail.

Many philosophers in the tradition which agrees with Hume's and Kant's claim about the impossibility of existential analytic truths have implicitly or explicitly endorsed something like Criterion 3. Moreover, those who do endorse Criterion 3 tend to find it very obvious—obvious enough to make one wonder whether those who deny it are not speaking a different language altogether. So this criterion is faithful to at least one important strand in the actual practice of foundational ontology. Can we argue that all foundational ontologists are in some sense implicitly committed to Criterion 3? I think there is a case to be made that they are: that any language whose quantifiers were 'ultimate' and 'fundamental', as the quantifiers of the language of ontology are supposed to be, would have to conform to Criterion 3. The meanings of the quantifiers in the languages of the tribes are rich and distinctive: Particular answers to the Special Composition Question are, as it were, written into the meanings of the quantifiers, which is how they get to be analytic truths. 'Ultimate' and 'fundamental' meanings for the quantifiers, by contrast, are austere. Their capacity for generating analytic truths is minimal: it is exhausted by their capacity for generating *logical* truths, in accordance with the fundamental rules of inference common to all the tribes' quantifiers. Since this is also true of other logical vocabulary, like the truth-functional connectives and the identity sign, the analyticity of any sentence in the language of ontology that is *not* a logical truth must be due entirely to the distinctive meanings of its constituent nonlogical expressions. But the capacity of a nonlogical expression, such as a predicate, for generating analytic truths is revealed by conceptual analysis.[40] Thus, the only analytic sentences in the language of ontology are those whose analyticity can be revealed by logic and the conceptual analysis of nonlogical expressions.

12. Problems with Analyticity

The obvious thing for the sceptic to say about Criterion 3 is that it isn't *satisfied*. There may be toy languages in which all analytic truths can be transformed into logical truths by substitution of conceptual analysis, but no candidate to be the language of ontology is like this. You can't just *stipulate* that such-and-such sentences are to be synthetic—there may not be any appropriate synthetic subject matter for them to have. (Consider how you would react to someone who attempted to stipulate that the claim that everything is self-identical should be synthetic.)

I see no easy way to argue that Criterion 3 is satisfied. But let's postpone further discussion of this desideratum for a while (I will take it up again in section 15). For now, it will be more useful to consider certain grounds a sceptic might have for denying that Criterion 3 is *discriminating*. There is, in fact, a good case to be made that *any* criterion that takes the form of a constraint on analyticity will fail to be discriminating: if it is satisfied by any of the candidate languages, it will be satisfied by many of them, in which a wide range of answers to the Special Composition Question are true.

Why were we supposed to think that each tribe's central dogmas were analytic in that tribe's language? The only reason I gave for this claim was the fact that these sentences are mapped onto analytic truths in other languages by the translation manuals naturally associated with the counterfactual semantics. But this isn't a good reason. It may be that a perfect translation will always preserve analyticity and syntheticity; but if so, the translation manual associated with a true semantic theory need not always be perfect. For example, we can truly say that the French word 'eau' expresses the property of being H_2O, as does the French word 'H_2O'; but the translation of 'Toute l'eau est H_2O' as 'All H_2O is H_2O' fails to preserve syntheticity.

Of course, in this case a better translation, namely 'All water is H_2O', is ready to hand. But this need not always be the case. Consider the inhabitants of Titan, where the oceans are made of liquid methane. The Titanians have never encountered water outside of chemistry labs, so their only word for water is a chemical name that plays the same sort of role in their language that the expression 'H_2O' plays in ours. The best the Titanians can do, if they want to translate our sentence 'All water is H_2O', is to use the same sentence they would use to translate our sentence 'All H_2O is H_2O'.[41] But this need not prevent them from stating a true semantic theory about our word 'water': they can truly say that 'water' in English expresses the property of being H_2O.[42]

Note, furthermore, that Titanian doesn't seem intuitively to be an impoverished language, like Astronomically Impoverished English. It would be absurd for the Titanians to advocate linguistic reform on the grounds that, without an expression corresponding more closely to the English word 'water', they would be unable to express the important chemical fact expressed by the English sentence 'Water is H_2O.' So there is no general reason to expect non-impoverished languages to contain perfect translations of the sentences of other languages.[43] Hence, if we want to deny that the Universalese sentence 'Composition is universal' has a perfect translation into Organicese—as we presumably will if we regard this sentence as synthetic—we will not thereby be committed to regarding Organicese as an impoverished language. I can see no good reason to hold that there is a closer relation between Organicese and Universalese than between Titanian and English.

Thus, it is open to the sceptic to maintain that the tribal dogmas are all synthetic truths. And even if there is some other reason to think that the tribal dogmas are analytic, I see nothing to stop us from imagining other candidate languages, just like the tribes' languages in the assignment of truth values (at least to sentences not containing the operator 'it is analytic that'), but differing from them as regards which of the truths are analytic. Hence, any criterion that takes the form of a constraint on which sentences are allowed to be analytic will, if it is satisfied by any of the candidate languages, be satisfied by many of them, and the languages that satisfy it will disagree as regards the answer to the Special Composition Question.

13. Constraints on Necessity

Analyticity, it seems, is too fine-grained a notion for our purposes. What could we put in its place? Perhaps we should focus instead on *metaphysical necessity*. Clearly the counterfactual semantic theories do at least entail that each tribe's characteristic dogma is a metaphysically necessary sentence of that tribe's language. So if we could find some natural, nonarbitrary condition satisfied by none (or at most one) of the answers to the Special Composition Question, we could characterize the language of ontology as one in which the only metaphysically necessary sentences are those that fulfill this condition, and this characterization would succeed in distinguishing the language of ontology from all (or all but one) of the languages of the tribes.

What could such a condition be? Obviously it wouldn't work to require necessary truths to be transformable into logical truths via *conceptual* analysis, since that would entail that 'all water is H_2O' is not a necessary truth of the language of ontology. But there is another notion of analysis to which we can appeal: *metaphysical* analysis. This is the sort of analysis we report by saying things like 'to be a square is to be a quadrilateral with equal sides and angles', 'to be water is to be H_2O', or 'for x to be hotter than y is for the mean kinetic energy of the molecules of x to be higher than that of the molecules of y'. Claims of this sort provide us with a canonical form of explanation of necessary truth, just as conceptual analyses provide us with canonical explanations of analytic truth. The proposal worth considering, then, is that the language of ontology is one in which all necessity admits of this sort of canonical explanation:

> *Criterion 4*: The language of ontology is one in which all *metaphysically necessary* truths can be transformed into logical truths by replacing nonlogical expressions with their *metaphysical* analyses.[44]

It seems to me only slightly less obvious that the Special Composition Question cannot be settled by metaphysical analysis (of nonlogical vocabulary) than that it cannot be settled by conceptual analysis. Analyses of 'part' and other predicates which would allow any answer to the Special Composition Question to be transformed into a logical truth or falsehood seem just as implausible whether they are considered as metaphysical or conceptual analyses. Thus, Criterion 4 has the intended consequence that all these sentences are metaphysically contingent. So, unlike Criterion 3, Criterion 4 is discriminating enough to rule out the identification of the language of ontology with any of the languages of the tribes.

To my mind, the idea that all necessary truths can ultimately be explained by metaphysical analysis has considerable intuitive force. When I'm in the mood in which Hume's and Kant's strictures against the *analyticity* of existential claims seem compelling, the idea that existential claims could be *necessary* seems equally mysterious; moreover, it seems mysterious how there could be any necessary truths whose necessity did not flow from metaphysical analyses of nonlogical expressions. Unfortunately, my intuitions in this regard seem to be out of step with those of other foundational ontologists. Most foundational ontologists take it for granted that the true answer to the Special Composition Question, whatever it might be, is metaphysically necessary: they apparently see nothing especially mysterious about how any claim of that sort could be necessary. Thus, it is, to say the least, doubtful whether Criterion 4 is really *faithful* to the practice of foundational ontology. One might legitimately be concerned that an interpretation of that practice on which the assumption that the true answer to the Special Composition Question is necessary is just a mistake would be excessively uncharitable.[45]

14. Constraints on Metaphysical Analyticity

The notion of metaphysical necessity, then, seems to be too coarse-grained for our purposes, just as the notion of analyticity was too fine-grained. What we need is some notion intermediate in strength between the two. Fortunately, I think we can understand such a notion. Consider the sentence 'all water is H_2O' once again. Even though this sentence is not analytic—assuming that analyticity is supposed to be something that competent speakers of a language can in principle recognize, without need for further empirical evidence— there is a sense in which 'all water is H_2O' is true just in virtue of the meaning of its constituent expressions. 'Water' *expresses the same property* as 'H_2O'; in a natural sense, the *fact* that all water is H_2O is the same as the fact that all H_2O is H_2O. It is only because we do not have a *fully transparent* insight into the meaning of 'water' that we need empirical evidence to recognize this identity. Let me sum this up by saying that 'all water is H_2O' is *metaphysically analytic*. If you feel the need for a definition, perhaps you could say that a metaphys- ically analytic sentence is one that expresses the same fact as a logical truth— though this will of course help only if you have an antecedent grasp of the relevant sense of 'same fact'.

If I have succeeded in explaining this notion, the claim that all metaphys- ically necessary sentences are metaphysically analytic should seem conten- tious. And in fact, I think that many philosophers are implicitly committed to the claim that there are metaphysically necessary sentences that are not metaphysically analytic—what one might think of as 'laws of metaphysics'. For example, some philosophers think that it is metaphysically necessary that there is a God. It is hard to see how this could be metaphysically analytic (assuming that the ontological argument is unsuccessful): Surely no amount of penetration into the *meanings* of 'there is' or of 'God' will reveal this sentence to be a logical truth in disguise.

So suppose we revise Criterion 4 by replacing talk of metaphysical neces- sity with talk of metaphysical analyticity:

> *Criterion 5*: The language of ontology is one in which all *metaphysically analytic* truths can be transformed into logical truths by replacing non- logical expressions with their metaphysical analyses.

Does this new criterion fare better than its predecessors?

On the face of it, the counterfactual semantic theories entail that each tribe's central dogmas are not only metaphysically necessary but metaphysic- ally analytic. Consider for example the Universalists' claim:

(15) In Organicese, the sentence 'Everything is simple or living' expresses the proposition that if everything were simple or living, everything would be simple or living [alternatively: that every simple or living thing is simple or living].

This certainly *sounds* like it entails that a fully transparent grasp of the meaning of that Organicese sentence would suffice (together with logical acumen) for knowledge of its truth. But Criterion 5 entails that none of the answers to the Special Composition Question are metaphysically analytic, for the same reason that Criterion 4 entails that none of them are metaphysically necessary. So, if we take the counterfactual semantic theories at face value, Criterion 5 succeeds (like Criterion 4, and unlike Criterion 3), in distinguishing the language of ontology from all the languages of the tribes.

But do we really need to take the counterfactual semantics as seriously as this? Wouldn't it be enough to regard them instrumentally, as devices for systematically assigning possible-worlds truth-conditions to sentences in other languages? No it wouldn't—at least if there are metaphysically synthetic necessities. Suppose, again, that it is metaphysically necessary that God exists. Some people who found this fact hard to face might decide to speak a Theologically Impoverished English in which all quantifiers are restricted to things other than God. It could well turn out that the speakers of Theologically Impoverished English can state a compositional semantic theory for English which is adequate in the sense that it yields correct possible-worlds truth-conditions for every English sentence. It might, for example, entail that 'Something is a God' is true in English at a possible world iff at that world, something would have been a God, had God existed. But this fact does nothing to make us think that Theologically Impoverished English is 'just another way of talking'. Speakers of Theologically Impoverished English, just like speakers of Astronomically Impoverished English, would have a compelling reason to reform their language so as to render them capable of expressing the facts expressed by such English sentences as 'God exists'. Being able to express facts that are metaphysically necessarily equivalent to these facts is no consolation at all. So if we think that the languages of the tribes are not impoverished in this way, we should expect the tribespeople to be able to characterize the meanings of sentences in other tribes' languages in a way that is finer-grained than mere possible-worlds truth-conditions.

The problem with Criterion 4 was its lack of faithfulness: most foundational ontologists take it for granted that the true answer to the Special Composition Question is metaphysically necessary. Does Criterion 5 do any better in this respect? I think so. Although the expression 'metaphysically analytic' is new, I doubt the concept is. We have the somewhat inchoate idea that certain questions concern *substantive matters of fact* in a way in which others don't. And this distinction does not obviously line up with the distinction between the necessary and the contingent. If Moorean non-naturalism about goodness is true, then various conditionals of the form 'If something has such-and-such natural properties, it is good' are necessary but substantive. If God exists, then the claim that he exists is necessary but substantive. Characteristically, foundational ontologists regard existential sentences quite generally—even 'there are numbers'—as substantive. And even though the answers to the Special Composition Question are not existential, I think most foundational ontologists will agree that they are relevantly like existential sentences, so that they too must be counted as substantive even if they are necessary. What prompts these judgements? What is the relevant feature that the answers to the Special Composition Question share with existential sentences? I can't see what the answer could be if not something along the lines of Criterion 5: These sentences cannot be transformed into logical truths by metaphysical analysis of their constituent nonlogical expressions. The notion of substantiveness involved in these judgements seems at least to entail metaphysical syntheticity in my sense. So there is good reason to think that foundational ontologists are implicitly committed to Criterion 5 or something like it, on the grounds that this principle best explains and systematizes the judgements of substantiveness that are characteristic of foundational ontologists.[46]

We can also argue for the faithfulness of Criterion 5 in a more abstract way, by adapting the argument I presented in section 11 for the claim that any language in which the quantifiers were 'ultimate' and 'fundamental' would have to satisfy Criterion 3. When a quantifier-meaning generates distinctive, interesting metaphysically analytic truths—such as the answers to the Special Composition Question—that must be because it has some correspondingly distinctive and interesting internal structure, perhaps the sort of structure described by the counterfactual semantics. But the claim that a quantifier-meaning is ultimate and fundamental is surely inconsistent with the possibility that it has this sort of structure. Thus, a *fundamental* quantifier's role in generating metaphysically analytic truth would have to be exhausted by its role in generating *logical* truth in accordance with basic rules of inference. Since this is also true of other logical vocabulary, it follows that the metaphysical analyticity of any sentence in the language of ontology that is not a logical truth must be explained by the distinctive meanings of its constituent nonlogical expressions. But the capacity of a nonlogical expression, such as a predicate, for generating metaphysically analytic truths is revealed by meta-physical analysis. Thus, the only metaphysically analytic sentences in the language of ontology are those whose analyticity can be revealed by logic and the metaphysical analysis of nonlogical expressions.

This argument is at least as good as the corresponding argument for the faithfulness of Criterion 3.[47] And it is stronger than the corresponding argument for the faithfulness of Criterion 4. Believers in metaphysically synthetic necessities will want to resist the latter argument, on the grounds that the necessity of a sentence (e.g., 'there is a God') need not be explained by the distinctive meanings of any of its constituents, except in the trivial sense that the necessity of a sentence is *necessitated* by its meaning. But the whole point of the notion of metaphysical analyticity is that the metaphysical analyticity of a sentence is always 'rooted' in structural relations among the meanings of its constituents.

15. The Sceptic's Response

Although Criterion 5 is an improvement in several respects on its predecessors, no determined sceptic should accept it as an adequate explanation of the practice of ontology. For one thing, the sceptic might refuse to understand the notion of metaphysical analyticity that features in Criterion 5. This is not unlikely—as David Lewis (1986: 203) remarks, 'any competent philosopher who does not understand something will take care not to understand anything else whereby it might be explained'. Still, I would at least feel that I had made some progress if I could show that the only viable form of scepticism required rejection of a notion which, despite its unfamiliarity, is in my view clearer, and more important for many philosophical purposes, than the notion of metaphysical necessity, if these are two distinct notions.[48]

But in fact, even those sceptics who deign to understand Criterion 5 can and should deny that it is *satisfied* by any of the candidates to be the language of ontology. To get a sense for the plausibility of this response, consider an analogous move that might be made in a debate with a certain sort of sceptic about ethical disagreement. This sceptic claims that apparent ethical disagreement is spurious, arising from divergences in the meanings of words like 'good' and 'right'. For example, the proposition utilitarians express using the words 'Killing one to save five is right' is the same proposition that non-utilitarians express using 'Killing one to save five maximizes happiness.' The ethicists protest: 'As we ethicists understand them, claims of the form "An action is right iff it is F", where "F" is a non-normative predicate, are supposed to be substantive, metaphysically synthetic claims.' To which the sceptic will reply: 'I'm sure you'd *like* to be having a debate about the distribution of some mysterious nonnatural property. Unfortunately, naturalism is true. There just aren't any such properties; and you can't stipulate them into existence just by wishing that the predicate "right" would express one of them.'

The ontologist who insists that the language of ontology satisfies Criterion 5 is in an analogous position to the ethicist who insists that ethical predicates express non-natural properties. For if the language of ontology satisfies Criterion 5, we will have to admit that there is a whole domain of facts that can be expressed in the language of ontology, but not in any of the languages of the tribes. What metaphysically synthetic Universalese sentence, for example, could express the proposition expressed by the sentence 'Composition is universal' in the language of ontology, if, as Criterion 5 entails, that sentence is metaphysically synthetic? (Criterion 5 may, admittedly, be satisfied by possible languages in which 'Composition is universal' expresses the proposition expressed in Universalese by 'there are dogs', or 'snow is white', or 'the greatest philosopher of the twentieth century asserted that composition is universal'; but these languages are too crazy to be candidates to be the language of ontology.[49]) But the sceptic certainly shouldn't concede that the languages of the tribes are all impoverished in this sort of way. The plausibility of the sceptic's position depends largely on the thought that there *isn't* a whole domain of facts (or at least, a domain of facts to which ontologists have access) that are inexpressible in any of the tribes' languages, just as the plausibility of the sceptical view about ethical disagreement depends on the thought that there just isn't a whole domain of facts (to which ethicists have access) that are inexpressible in any language in which all predicates stand for natural properties. So the sceptic should deny that any of the candidate languages satisfies Criterion 5.

So if Criterion 5 is the best we can come up with in our attempt to initiate the sceptic into the practice of foundational ontology, the sceptic should remain unconvinced. However, as we shall see in the next section, there is an independently-motivated modification for Criterion 5 which will weaken the sceptic's dialectical position.

16. Semantically Defective Predicates

According to a theory held by many eighteenth-century chemists, burning and the calcination of metals both involved the emission of a substance called 'phlogiston'. In fact, these processes don't involve the emission of anything, but rather involve the absorption of oxygen. There is no phlogiston. Now consider the following question: what is it for something to be phlogiston? I can think of no answer to this question that is acceptable by ordinary standards. Someone might suggest an answer along the following lines:

(16)   To be phlogiston is to be an instance of a substance that is characteristically emitted in combustion and the calcination of metals.

But this claim seems problematic, in much the same way as the claim that to be oxygen is to be an instance of a substance that is characteristically absorbed in combustion and the calcination of metals. For one thing, it entails that it is necessary that any instance of a substance that is characteristically emitted in combustion and the calcination of metals is phlogiston. But this seems false: Couldn't a substance that was not phlogiston have played the characteristic 'phlogiston' role?[50]

If 'phlogiston' lacks a metaphysical analysis, then according to Criterion 5, the sentence 'there is no phlogiston' must be metaphysically synthetic in the language of ontology. If it is necessary that there is no phlogiston—as many philosophers now hold, following Kripke's (1979: 156–8) claim that it is necessary that there are no unicorns—this is a metaphysically synthetic necessity, like the alleged necessary existence of God. But there is good reason to think that this sentence is metaphysically analytic in ordinary English. 'Phlogiston' belongs to a distinctive class of what I will call *semantically defective* predicates. Besides false scientific theories, such predicates are to be met with in myth and legend ('unicorn'), fiction ('Snark'), and in false philosophical theories ('Form', 'substratum', 'emanates from' ...). Since these predicates' relation to other predicates is similar in some ways to the relation of empty names to ordinary referring names, we might want to think of them as failing to express properties. Be that as it may, the semantic defectiveness of a predicate F leads just as directly to the truth of 'Nothing is F' as the emptiness of a name a leads to the truth of 'Nothing is identical to a.' And the facts about which predicates are semantically defective (unlike the facts about which predicates simply happen not to apply to anything) are *semantic* facts: In the same sense in which a fully transparent grasp of the meaning of 'water' would reveal it to express the property of being H_2O, a fully transparent grasp of the meaning of 'phlogiston' would reveal it to be semantically defective. So if we can make sense of the idea that the truth of 'All water is H_2O' flows from its meaning, we should say the same thing about 'there is no phlogiston'.[51]

Here is a less impressionistic argument for the same conclusion. Suppose the Titanians developed chemistry without anyone's ever proposing a theory remotely similar to phlogiston theory. As a result, their language has no word that plays anything like the conceptual role of our word 'phlogiston'. They have no very good way to translate the sentence 'there is no phlogiston' into their language. But this difficulty is not worrying in the same way as the failure of Astronomically Impoverished English to translate English sentences. It would be absurd for the Titanians to advocate linguistic reform on the grounds that without a new word, they will be unable to express the fact about chemistry expressed in English by the sentence 'there is no phlogiston'. And their lack of any word equivalent to 'phlogiston' need not, intuitively, prevent them from stating a perfectly excellent semantic theory for English. But if 'there is no phlogiston' were a metaphysically synthetic sentence in English, it really would be impossible for the Titanians to give an adequate account of its semantics, given that 'phlogiston' lacks a metaphysical analysis. We would have to conclude that the Titanians' language really was impoverished, in much the same way as Theologically Impoverished English (section 14 above). Since the Titanians' language is *not* impoverished in this way, 'there is no phlogiston' must be metaphysically analytic.

All of these considerations apply just as much to the language of ontology as to ordinary English, since 'phlogiston' presumably means the same thing in both languages. Hence, if something along the lines of Criterion 5 is to be credible, it will need to be weakened so as to allow the universal quantifications of the negations of semantically defective predicates to be metaphysically analytic. Here is one way to do it:

> *Criterion 6*: The language of ontology is one in which all metaphysically analytic truths can be transformed into logical truths by replacing non-logical expressions with their metaphysical analyses, *and replacing semantically defective predicates with logically contradictory ones*.[52]

In section 14, I suggested that foundational ontologists were implicitly committed to Criterion 5, on the grounds that this explains their disposition to classify certain ontological claims, like the answers to the Special Composition Question, as 'substantive', and on the grounds that it partially articulates the meaning of the claim that the quantifiers in the language of ontology are 'ultimate' and 'fundamental'. Now that we are taking account of semantic defectiveness, we can now see that these claims should really have been made on behalf of Criterion 6 rather than Criterion 5.

17. Sceptics Unmasked as Nihilists

Criterion 6 opens up a new way in which an answer to the Special Composition Question might be metaphysically analytic in the language of ontology. For Criterion 6 is consistent with the claim that 'is part of' (i.e., 'is a proper part of') is semantically defective in the language of ontology, with the result that Nihilism—which is equivalent to the claim that nothing is part of anything—is metaphysically analytic. And Nihilism is unique in this respect: Criterion 6 still rules out the metaphysical analyticity of all the other answers to the Special Composition Question, just as Criterion 5 did.

The claim that 'part' is semantically defective is one that any Nihilist should find utterly natural. From the Nihilist's standpoint, 'is part of' looks just like the characteristic undefined predicates of other thoroughly false philosophical theories: it is a predicate that is supposed to carve reality at some very natural joint, but in fact there is no remotely natural relation that plays anything like the role parthood is supposed to play. So ontologists should not take it for granted that 'part' is not semantically defective, unless they are taking it for granted that Nihilism is false.

Because of this, it will be much harder for the sceptic to maintain that none of the candidate languages satisfies Criterion 6 than it was to maintain the corresponding view about Criterion 5. For nothing ontologists take for granted rules out an interpretation on which they speak a language in which 'part' is semantically defective, and Nihilism metaphysically analytic. And it seems that the sceptic has already told us about such a language: namely Nihilish, the language spoken by the imaginary tribe of Nihilists. For, given that 'Nothing is part of anything' is metaphysically analytic in Nihilish, and given that 'part' doesn't have a metaphysical analysis in Nihilish, it seems natural to conclude that 'part' is semantically defective in Nihilish. How could Nihilish fail to satisfy Criterion 6? I see four possibilities.

First, 'part', despite the metaphysical analyticity of 'Nothing is part of anything', and despite not having a metaphysical analysis, might somehow fail to be semantically defective in Nihilish. But even if we grant this, what reason could there be for the sceptic to deny that there is a language just like Nihilish except that 'part' was semantically defective in it is also one of the candidates to be the language of ontology? Not because making 'part' semantically defective would impoverish the Nihilists' language by depriving them of the ability to report such facts as the one they express using the sentence 'Nothing has any parts': for the sceptic shouldn't think that sentences like this are metaphysically synthetic in the way that would make such worries about expressive power appropriate.

Second, the conciliatory view could be false, as regards the Nihilists: The interpretation of the Nihilists as speaking a language in which Nihilism is true could be incorrect. But it seems unacceptably arbitrary for the *sceptic* to limit the scope of the conciliatory view in this way. If a conciliatory approach is appropriate for the Organicists (for example) but not for the Nihilists, wouldn't that have to be because organisms are 'ultimately real' in a sense in which nonliving composites are not? But the sceptic who refuses to understand talk of 'ultimate reality' can't give such an explanation.

Third, there could be some other ontological question as regards which a conciliatory attitude is appropriate, such that the Nihilists' answer to *that* question does not meet the requirement for metaphysical analyticity laid down in Criterion 6.[53] But we are free to flesh out our story about the Nihilists in any way we please. What happens if we make it part of the story that the Nihilists hold an 'eliminativist' view about this other question as well—for example, that they are Nominalists who deny the existence of sets, properties, etc.?[54] Wouldn't that make it appropriate to interpret them as speaking a language in which the eliminativist view in question was metaphysically analytic—as permitted by Criterion 6? If not, why isn't this limitation in the scope of the conciliatory view about the other question just as unacceptably arbitrary, from the sceptic's point of view, as the limitation in the scope of the conciliatory view about the Special Composition Question envisaged in the previous paragraph?

Fourth, there could be some class of sentences that pose the same sort of problem for Criterion 6 that sentences like 'there is no phlogiston' posed for Criterion 5. These would be sentences which cannot be transformed into logical truths by substitution of metaphysical analyses and substitution of logically contradictory predicates for semantically defective ones, but which nevertheless seem like they should be metaphysically analytic for reasons that apply not just in ordinary English, but in all the languages of the tribes, including Nihilish.[55] But it is hard to see how this could help the sceptic's case. If we find that we have overlooked some further sources of metaphysical analyticity, we can and should modify Criterion 6 so as to accommodate them; the modified principle will be satisfied by Nihilish, but not by any of the other tribes' languages.

Perhaps the sceptic will be able to make one of these avenues look more plausible than I have made it look. But for the moment, let us with due tentativeness conclude that the sceptic should agree that Criterion 6 is *satisfied*, by some version or variant of Nihilish.

The sceptic also has good reason to grant that Criterion 6 is *discriminating*. In section 15, I argued that the sceptic should think that all the candidates to be the language of ontology are languages, like the languages of the tribes, in which the answer to the Special Composition Question is metaphysically analytic. But Nihilism is the only answer to the Special Composition Question whose metaphysical analyticity is not ruled out by Criterion 6. Hence, the sceptic must conclude that Nihilism is metaphysically analytic, and hence true, in all candidate languages that satisfy Criterion 6.

Finally, I have already made the best case I can, in sections 14 and 16, for the *faithfulness* of Criterion 6 to the practice of foundational ontology.

So Criterion 6 seems to meet all three of our desiderata. I conclude that the sceptic should accept that foundational ontologists are properly interpreted as speaking a language that satisfies Criterion 6. The sceptic should also hold that this language is one in which 'part' is semantically defective, and Nihilism is metaphysically analytic. Sceptics should, in other words, cast off their scepticism, and announce themselves as what many of us suspected they really were beneath the surface all along: Nihilists.

If the language of ontology is a version of Nihilish, some semantic theory along the lines of (17) or (18) should be true in ordinary English:

(17) 'Something' in the language of ontology expresses the property of being a property that is instantiated by something simple.

(18) 'Something' in the language of ontology expresses the property of being a property that would be instantiated if everything were simple.

These claims would be easy to misunderstand. 'What?', I can imagine someone asking, 'So when ontologists say that there are no composite objects, they express the proposition that ordinary folk would express by saying that there are no simple composite objects, or that if everything were simple, there would be no composite objects? But aren't *those* propositions completely obvious? If that's all ontological questions amount to, how could reasonable people ever disagree about them?'

Quite easily! Propositions, in the sense in which we have been talking about them, are things which can be believed under one guise while simultaneously being disbelieved, or held in doubt, under another guise. For example, the proposition that all water is H_2O is the proposition that all H_2O is H_2O. If we think that the language of ontology is Nihilish, we will think that the proposition expressed by 'everything is simple' in the language of ontology has one guise on which it is obviously true; but it may have other guises under which it is far from obvious. There is a sense in which ontologists who are not Nihilists have contradictory beliefs; but this is a sense in which it happens all the time that perfectly reasonable people have contradictory beliefs. (We are not forced to adopt this coarse-grained way of talking about propositions; but if we adopt a finer-grained conception, the counterfactual semantics for Nihilish won't entail anything about the propositions expressed by Nihilish sentences.)

Of course, if it were *obvious* that the language of ontology was a version of Nihilish, it would be obvious that Nihilism was true. However, this claim is by no means obvious. I have just presented a rather complicated argument that the claim should be accepted by those who accept the intuition which, in my view, underlies the strongest case for scepticism: that ontological debate doesn't concern some *domain of facts* which are inexpressible in the languages of the tribes, as conceived by the conciliatory view. But many foundational ontologists will vehemently reject this intuition. They will claim that if Nihilish is supposed to be a language in which sentences like 'there are no chairs' and 'there are no people' are true, Nihilish must be a radically impoverished language, which stands to the language of ontology in the same sort of relation that Astronomically Impoverished English stands in to English. I have said nothing at all that could persuade these ontologists to change their minds. My argument for Nihilism has been addressed only to those whose first reaction to the Nihilist view was the conciliatory one: 'We could talk that way if we wanted to, but why should we, when there are many other ways of talking that are just as good?' I have tried to show that there is less distance than one might expect between the recognition of Nihilism as an option in this way, and the claim that it is—strictly, really, ultimately, in the most fundamental sense . . . —the truth.

Notes

Thanks to Adam Elga, John Hawthorne, Kathrin Koslicki, Edouard Machery, Jessica Moss, Jim Pryor, Kieran Setiya, Ted Sider, and Dean Zimmerman; to the participants in my Fall 2001 seminar, and John Hawthorne's Spring 2003 seminar, both at NYU; to audiences at North Carolina, Toronto, Notre Dame, Colorado, and Pittsburgh; and to the participants in the 2003 Bellingham Summer Philosophy Conference.

1. Cf. van Inwagen (1990).
2. According to a variant of the conciliatory view, the tribes all speak the same language, but this language is highly context-dependent. One of the contextual

parameters relevant to the interpretation of a great many sentences either is, or is generally coordinated with, the speaker's tribe. Thus, although the sentence 'there are chairs' has the same 'standing meaning' whether it is uttered by a Universalist or by an Organicist, the former utterances are true and the latter false, just as utterances of the English sentence 'It is raining' are sometimes true and sometimes false. I will generally ignore the difference between this version of the conciliatory view and the 'many languages' version described in the main text.

Other views about the tribes are of course possible. For example, one could be conciliatory towards only some of the tribes, holding perhaps that while the Universalists and Organicists are generally getting things right, the Nihilists' world-view is systematically mistaken. But hybrid views of this sort seem too arbitrary to be worth taking seriously, and fit much less naturally with the sceptical attitude towards ontological debate which is my ultimate target.

3. Alternatively, the differences in the meanings of sentences could be attributed not to differences in the meaning of any words, but to differences in the compositional rules by which the meanings of sentences are determined by the meanings of their constituent words.

4. Cf. Putnam (1987); Hirsch (2002).

5. How are we to explain the variation in the meaning of sentences like 'a chair is in the room' and 'donkeys bray'? One approach would be to posit variation in the meaning of expressions like 'a' and 'the', and of 'bare plurals' like 'donkeys'. This would be the natural approach if, as many philosophers of language hold, these expressions belong to the same distinctive semantic category as words like 'every' and complex expressions like 'all donkeys'. However, there is an alternative view, defended by Delia Graff (2001) and others, according to which the expressions 'a chair', 'the room', and 'donkeys' are *predicates*. Quantifiers are present in the 'logical form' of sentences like 'a chair is in the room', 'donkeys exist', and 'there are donkeys', but they don't correspond to any constituents in these sentences' surface form. (If this story works for 'a', 'the', and 'donkeys', it should probably be extended to many of the other expressions I characterized as quantifiers. 'Few' and 'ten,' for example, seem to be likely candidates, since they don't seem to be functioning as quantifiers in sentences like 'my friends are few' or 'those are ten long books'.) If Graff's proposal is correct, the variation in the meaning of these sentences should be attributed not to any variation in the meaning of words, but to variation in structural semantic rules, as envisaged in note 3 above.

6. This is not to say that *no* predicates are variable. Some predicates have meanings that are closely bound up with quantifiers, so that one would naturally expect them to inherit the variability of the quantifiers. For example, in English, 'father' means 'father of someone'; assuming that this is also true in each the tribes' languages, we will need to posit a variation in the meaning of 'father'. But I don't see that this sort of consideration will warrant us in positing variation in the meaning of a great many one-word predicates. Here I am disagreeing with

Hirsch (2002: 57), who suggests that 'Quantifier variance may be said to induce a certain kind of systematic difference of meaning in the word "touching" and, by the same token, virtually any other general word.'

7. Eklund (forthcoming) also points this out, and regards it as a deep problem for the conciliatory view. Substituting my example for his, his central argument appeals to the premise that if 'Mars' differs in meaning between Organicese and Universalese, this can only be because the Organicists cannot meaningfully use names that purport to refer to planets in their language. I agree with Eklund that we should be able to agree that Organicese *can* contain such meaningful names, since we will want to say that sentences like 'Mars doesn't exist' are true in Organicese. But I don't see why there couldn't be some other explanation for the variation in the meaning of the word 'Mars'.

8. I assume that the introducers of the language did not also change the meanings of expressions like 'true in ordinary English'.

9. There is a use of 'quantifier'—not mine!—on which it is part of what it is for an expression to be a quantifier that its semantic value should be extensional. If the Organicists use the word 'quantifier' in this way, they should say that 'some' in Universalese is not a quantifier. I see no reason for a conciliator to be dismayed by this result.

10. Even if for some reason we want to say that 'large', for example, has a different meaning in Universalese, we still won't want to say that there are things that don't belong to the extension of 'large' in our language—hence, things that are not large—that belong to the extension of 'large' in Universalese.

11. Thus the point about the predicate 'father' in note 6 also applies to the predicate 'extensional'.

12. Indeed, if 'It is metaphysically necessary that everything is simple or living' is true in Organicese, a parallel argument shows that, from the Organicists' point of view, 'some' in Universalese does not even count as an *intensional* connective, where an intensional connective is one that allows for substitution *salva veritate* of metaphysically necessarily coextensive arguments.

13. Including Universalese. Thus, if we are Universalists trying to give a semantics for the quantifiers in Organicese, we face a choice between the theory considered at the beginning of this section, according to which 'something' in Organicese expresses the property *being instantiated by something simple or living*, and a counterfactual theory, according to which it expresses the property *being a property which would have been instantiated if the only composite objects were living things*. But these properties are necessarily equivalent, so these two semantic theories will at least assign the same possible-worlds truth-conditions to Organicese sentences. Indeed, we might hope to find some even stronger sense in which we could think of these two theories as equivalent—the concept of 'metaphysical analyticity' which I introduce in section 14 below might be relevant here.

14. Thus, if our semantics assigns 'actually' in our own language (Organicese) a character which takes each context to the property of being a proposition that is true at the world index of that context, we should take the character of 'actually' in Universalese to be a function which takes each context c to the property of being a proposition p such that, at the world-index of c, the following holds: if composition were universal, p would be true.

15. This response leaves us with a residual worry. Suppose some Universalists say to themselves: 'Let's use "Organicese" as a name for the language spoken by the Organicists—the "language" in the sense of a formal system, a mapping from expressions to semantic values.' These Universalists then go on to utter the sentence 'All the central dogmas of the Organicists are true in Organicese.' How should the Organicists account for the truth of this sentence? If we take the quantifier to be the only relevant variable word, the counterfactual semantics entails that the sentence is true iff all the central dogmas of the Organicese would be true in Organicese, if composition were universal. But this is surely false—the fact that the Organicists would not have been speaking Organicese if composition had been universal is irrelevant in this case.

The only way I can see to avoid this problem to add the name 'Organicese' to the list of variable expressions. The Organicists should claim that the referent of 'Organicese' in Universalese is not Organicese, but the language the Organicists *would* have spoken had composition been universal. This may seem surprising: but in fact, it is only to be expected that names whose references are fixed by descriptions will vary in reference in this way. For example, Organicists and Universalists might both introduce the name 'Giganto' into their language by saying 'Let the biggest thing there is be called "Giganto".' Despite this similarity in use, the name can hardly have the same referent in both languages, given that in Universalese, the sentence 'Everything is part of Giganto' is true, whereas the Organicese can truly say 'Giganto is a large living being—perhaps a tree or a fungus.'

16. Here I am relying on the principle of *Centering*: a counterfactual with a true antecedent is true iff it has a true consequent $[P \rightarrow ((P \square\!\!\rightarrow Q) \leftrightarrow Q)]$ (Lewis, 1973: 26). Without this law, the counterfactual semantics would be in trouble. We would lose, for example, the logical equivalence between '$\exists x(Fx \,\&\, \exists y(Rxy))$' and '$\exists x \exists y(Fx \,\&\, Rxy).$'

This seems as good a place as any to mention another, much more controversial claim about the logic of counterfactuals without which the counterfactual semantics would be in even worse trouble: namely, *Conditional Excluded Middle* $[(P \square\!\!\rightarrow Q) \lor (P \square\!\!\rightarrow \sim Q)]$. Without the relevant instances of this law, we will (for example) lose the equivalence between 'It is not the case that all chairs are four-legged' and 'Some chairs are not four-legged.' Conditional Excluded Middle is defended by Stalnaker (1968, 1981), but denied by Lewis (1973: 79–83). However, it's not clear that we really need to take sides in this dispute. Even if Lewis is right about the counterfactuals of ordinary English, perhaps one could stipulatively introduce a related operator obeying Conditional Excluded Middle, in such a way that '$P \square\!\!\rightarrow Q$' would turn out indeterminate in truth-value whenever 'if P, it would be the case that Q' and 'if P, it would be the case that not-Q' are both false.

Given Centering, Counterfactual Excluded Middle, and the non-vacuity of the relevant counterfactuals, we can show that the result of applying the algorithm to any sentence 'Q' containing only quantifiers, variables, predicates, and truth-functional connectives is equivalent to 'if composition were universal, it would be the case that Q'. Centering lets us drop all iterated occurrences of counterfactuals with the same antecedent; Counterfactual Excluded Middle entails that any truth-functional complex of non-vacuous counterfactuals with the same antecedent is equivalent to a single counterfactual with a complex consequent.

17. Thanks to Kieran Setiya and Ted Sider for drawing this to my attention.

18. This move can be resisted. In recent unpublished work, Kit Fine has been advocating a 'semantic relationalism' in which failures of substitutivity are sometimes explained not by differences in semantic value but by appeal to semantic relations not grounded in semantic values.

19. I have presented this idea in a 'Fregean' form. The idea could also be worked out in a 'Millian' manner. On this version of the approach, we would deny that 'frozen water' expresses the property expressed by 'ice', viz. the conjunction of *being frozen* and *being water*. Instead, the property expressed by 'frozen water' is a more complex, though necessarily equivalent, property, constructed by existential quantification and predication from *being frozen*, *being water* and the relation *being the conjunction of*. This property is the one we might antecedently have expected to be the semantic value of the predicate 'has the property that is the conjunction of *being frozen* and *being water*', though if we adopt this view we will want to claim that *that* predicate too expresses an even more complex property than one might antecedently have expected. . . .

   Views reminiscent of this one have been defended by Bealer (1982) and Soames (2002: 276–8).

20. Thus, if some Organicists were to expand their language by stipulating that 'Mars*' is to mean whatever 'Mars' means in Universalese, sentences like 'Mars* is red' and probably also 'Mars* is larger than any living being' will be true in the expanded language, despite the fact that 'there are no red planets' and 'nothing is larger than any living being' are also true in that language. Hence the rule of existential generalization will fail in the expanded language (cf. Eklund, forthcoming).

21. To take just one example, David Braun (1993) defends a view which entails that any two empty names should be intersubstitutable *salva veritate* in all contexts.

22. At least, this will be true if we assume that 'possibly' doesn't vary in meaning between the two languages. This could be denied. Indeed, it would be quite

natural to deny it, in view of the equivalence of 'possibly' and 'in some possible world'. The idea would be that just as the Universalists 'recognize more objects' than the Organicists, so they 'recognize more possible worlds', such as one in which Mars has different parts.

23. This will only work, of course, if there is some property in which no essential reference is made to Mars or any other nonsimple, nonliving thing, of which we can truly say in Universalese that it is an individual essence of Mars. This will be denied by certain opponents of essentialism: for example, by those who maintain that it is possible for the particles that actually compose Mars to compose something other than Mars, even though they and all other simple and living things are arranged just as they actually are. Given that the Organicists can truly say 'Necessarily, if the simple and living things are arranged just as they actually are, then everything is just as it actually is', it is hard to see how the Organicists could accommodate the truth in Universalese of this sort of anti-essentialist view—unless they posit some sort of variation in the meaning of 'possibly', as contemplated in the previous note. However, this sort of anti-essentialism is not very popular: many philosophers think, for example, that all the facts about macroscopic objects, including facts about their identities, are determined by the facts about microscopic objects.

24. Hirsch (2002) endorses this argument. However, Hirsch seems to think that the mere *possibility* of languages in which different meanings for the quantifiers lead to different answers to the Special Composition Question being true is enough to establish this claim. He claims (2002: 68) that 'by any reasonable standards of interpretation' we should interpret people as speaking a language in which their claims about composite objects are generally true, if such a possible language exists. I disagree: since systematic error is possible, the principle of charity cannot be the whole of the theory of interpretation (cf. Lewis, 1984), and I see nothing 'unreasonable' about the claim that this is one of those cases where the principle of charity gives the wrong result.

25. Lewis claims that the notion of 'vague existence' (i.e., vagueness in unrestricted quantifiers) makes no sense. The kernel of the argument: 'Vagueness is semantic indecision.... But how could [unrestricted quantification] be vague? What would be the alternatives between which we haven't chosen?' (Lewis, 1986: 212; see also Sider, 2003) Advocates of vague existence may have felt obliged to reject this question as founded on a false theory of vagueness: but one lesson of the counterfactual semantics is that there is no need for them to do so.

26. Cf. Hirsch (2002: 62).

27. If talk of 'two languages' sounds odd, it might seem better to say that there is just one language involved, but that that language is context-sensitive, in such a way that the proposition expressed by 'there are chairs' in the context of the ontology room is distinct from the one it expresses in ordinary contexts. For my

purposes, this view is not importantly different from the 'two languages' view (see note 2 above).

The data also admit of a pragmatic style of explanation: although the sentence 'there are chairs' *semantically expresses* the same proposition no matter when it is uttered, either the ontologists or the folk typically use this sentence to *convey* some different proposition. Although I have chosen to give a central place to semantic idioms, my central points could be cast just as well in pragmatic terms.

28. Cf. Rorty (1982).

29. What features does a language have to have to be a candidate to be the language of ontology? For one thing, we certainly don't want to interpret the ontologists as speaking an *impoverished* language. For another thing, we want the language of ontology to be like ordinary English in the same way as the languages of the tribes: like ordinary English, that is, except for the difference in the interpretations of the quantifiers, together with correlative differences in the interpretations of predicates like 'father' whose meanings are closely bound up with the quantifiers, and of certain names and demonstratives. Beyond this, we should rule out intuitively *crazy* interpretations, such as one on which the proposition ontologists express with the sentence 'Composition is universal' is the same one ordinary folk express with 'There are dogs.' Moreover, if we accept that the members of the tribes should give counterfactual semantic theories for one another's languages, it would be very natural to require that these counterfactual semantic theories should also be true in the language of ontology.

30. Or as speaking the same context-sensitive language as everyone else, but occupying a special context relative to which that language satisfies the criterion. Or, at least, as using sentences about ontology in such a way as to *communicate* the propositions they express in a language that satisfies the criterion, even if the sentences have the *same semantic content* for them that they have in ordinary English. See note 27 above.

31. One could of course resist interpreting ontologists as speaking a language satisfying our criterion by finding *another* criterion, incompatible with ours, that is also satisfied, discriminating, and even more faithful than ours to the practice of foundational ontology. But this would not be a vindication of scepticism!

32. The pessimistic view that such disputes are merely terminological is defended by Unger (1984). King and Stanley (2005) provide a useful survey of the debate.

33. For arguments against Yablo's claims, see Stanley (2001).

34. More generally, we could say that a property of properties p_1 is a restriction of a property of properties p_2 iff there is some property r such that for any property q, the proposition that q instantiates p_1 is logically equivalent to the proposition that the conjunction of q and r instantiates p_2. Similar definitions could be given for the sorts of semantic values which we might assign to other sorts of

quantifiers—e.g., binary relations among properties, in the case of words like 'some' and 'all'.

35. This is not the only possible explanation. Stanley and Szabó (2000) argue, by appealing to certain facts about cross-sentential anaphora, that the context-dependence of these sentences has its source not in the quantifiers but in common nouns like 'bottle' and 'thing'.

36. We can certainly imagine languages that don't allow for any maximally unrestricted contexts. On the question whether a language of this sort could be anyone's native language, see Williamson (2003).

37. Of course, we might attempt to define an unrestricted quantifier as a maximally unrestricted member of some distinguished set of possible quantifier-meanings. But how is this distinguished set to be characterized? It won't do to say that the distinguished set comprises all those quantifier-meanings that are *extensional*. Since the meaning of 'extensional' varies in the same way as the meanings of the quantifiers (see section 3 above), we can truly say in any of the languages we're considering that the meaning of 'something' is a maximally unrestricted member of the set of extensional quantifier meanings.

38. David Lewis is perhaps an exception to this generalization. Although he doesn't use the word 'analytic'—the word hardly ever appears in his work—he does claim that Mereology (a theory of composition which entails Universalism) is 'certain' and 'ontologically innocent' (Lewis, 1991: 75–87)—features which one would naturally associate with analyticity. In conversation, he maintained that it was a mere historical accident that Mereology was not counted as part of 'logic'.

39. It doesn't matter much how we define 'logical truth', provided that the answers to the Special Composition Question don't themselves count as logical truths, even if they happen to be analytic. We could follow Tarski in defining a logical truth as a sentence that remains true no matter how the nonlogical vocabulary is interpreted: provided we count 'part' as a piece of nonlogical vocabulary, this will have the desired effect.

40. This last step in the argument might be resisted. Some philosophers think, for example, that the sentence 'Nothing is both green and red all over' is an analytic truth, despite the fact that there are no relevant conceptual analyses of 'green' and 'red,' and despite the fact that the analyticity in question clearly is due entirely to the meanings of the predicates, and not to anything distinctive about the meaning of the quantifier over and above its logical features. Those who hold this view will deny that Criterion 3 is satisfied by any of the candidate languages. For surely 'green' and 'red' have the same meaning in the language of ontology as in ordinary English: if so, then 'Nothing is both green and red all over' will be analytic in the language of ontology as well as in ordinary English.

41. It might be suggested that the Titanians should translate 'water' using some sort of descriptive phrase, like 'the stuff that actually falls from the sky of Earth as rain, fills the rivers and lakes of Earth, and is potable to Earthlings'. This

translation would doubtless be preferable for certain purposes. But unless Jackson (1998) and Chalmers (1996) are right that it is analytic that water, if there is any, actually does all these things, this translation will have exactly the same flaw of translating synthetic sentences into analytic ones.

42. And if you think that there's more to the semantics of 'water' to that—for instance, some sort of *mode of presentation* of the property of being H_2O—I don't see why the Titanians shouldn't be able to specify that as well.

43. A similar moral could be drawn from a real-world case discussed by Kripke (1979: 133). Kripke reports that Hebrew contains two words for Germany, 'Ashkenaz' and 'Germaniah', where English has only one. The best we can do in English to translate the Hebrew sentence 'If Ashkenaz exists, then Ashkenaz = Germaniah' is to use the sentence 'If Germany exists, then Germany = Germany.' This is not a perfect translation, since it translates a synthetic sentence into an analytic one. But the fact that we can do no better than this is no reason for us to regard our language as impoverished.

44. I haven't said what would be involved in giving a metaphysical analysis of a nonlogical expression other than a predicate, but I hope this can be understood by analogy. A metaphysical analysis of a *name* would be naturally reported using a sentence of the form 'to be a is to . . .'. For example, whenever 'a' and 'b' are directly referential names, 'to be a is to be b', will be true whenever '$a = b$' is; so Criterion 4 allows for the necessity of sentences like 'Hesperus is Phosphorus.' It is an interesting question whether there are any *interesting* metaphysical analyses of directly referential names—interesting truths about the *essences* of things, as Fine (1994) would put it. I find it hard to make sense of this idea. The direct referentialist's claim that there is an object such that to be a is just to be identical to that object seems to me to be inconsistent with the truth of any more interesting claim of the form 'to be a is to . . .'. At least, these claims seem inconsistent if the quantifiers we are using are the 'fundamental' ones of the language of ontology. In slogan form: The only objects that *ultimately* exist are *primitive* objects.

   The metaphysical analysis of a nonlogical expression that is not a predicate or name will most likely have to be a contextual analysis of some sort. I will set aside, as unlikely to be relevant in the present context, the question what such analyses might look like.

45. The answers to the Special Composition Question are not the only sentences whose necessity in the languages of the tribes follows from the counterfactual semantics. The semantics also entails that the sentence 'there is no gunk'—i.e., 'there are no objects all of whose proper parts have proper parts of their own'—is necessary in each tribe's language. For the Nihilists will interpret this sentence in any of the other tribes' languages as expressing the proposition that if there were just enough new objects to make true such-and-such principles about the circumstances under which some objects compose something, there would be

no gunk. And all these propositions are true, since the only objects one will ever need to add to make the antecedent of such a counterfactual true are objects composed of actual, simple objects.

Some ontologists report a strong intuition that 'there is no gunk' is not necessary (see, e.g., Armstrong, 1978: 32; Lewis, 1991: 70; Sider, 1993). So this is a respect in which the language of ontology, as conceived by some of its speakers, is unlike any of the languages of the tribes. However, I don't think we could rely on this as our criterion for explaining to the sceptic what is supposed to be distinctive about the language of ontology. For any sceptic who is serious about the claim that Nihilish is a possible, non-impoverished language will simply deny that this criterion is satisfied by any of the candidate languages.

46. What about those ontologists who (like Lewis) claim that their favoured theory of composition is a logical truth, or at least that it is like a logical truth in all philosophically significant respects? They certainly won't want to say that the theory in question is 'substantive'. Nevertheless, we might hope to make Criterion 5 acceptable even to them by explicitly defining metaphysically analytic sentences as those that 'express the same fact' as a truth of some *standard* logic that does not include any theory of composition. Of course these ontologists won't regard the notion of metaphysical analyticity, so explained, as a philosophically important one. But I don't see why this should prevent them from understanding and accepting Criterion 5. (Unless they think that all logical truths, and all sentences that are like logical truths in all philosophically significant respects, express the very same fact, in the relevant sense. But why would anyone think that?)

Proponents of Nihilism also have a special reason to regard their favoured answer to the Special Composition Question as metaphysically analytic, which I will discuss further in sections 16 and 17 below.

47. In fact, it is considerably better. In note 40 above, I considered a possible objection to the argument for the faithfulness of Criterion 3: since 'Nothing is both red and green all over' is analytic, despite the fact that it cannot be transformed into a logical truth by substitution of conceptual analyses, there must be more to a predicate's capacity for generating analytic truth than is revealed by conceptual analysis. The corresponding objection to the argument for the faithfulness of Criterion 5 is much weaker. Granted that 'Nothing is both red and green all over' is metaphysically analytic, why shouldn't we think that there must be some revealing account—perhaps a physicalist account—of what it is to be red all over and what it is to be green all over, from which the incompatibility of these predicates could be seen to flow, if only we knew it?

A natural moral one might draw from this case is that we sometimes have some a priori access to facts about the natures of properties—for example, the fact that the properties *being red all over* and *being green all over* are incompatible in virtue of their logical structure—even when we don't have a priori knowledge of *all* the facts about the natures of the properties in question. Whenever this happens, there will be analyticities that do not follow from conceptual analyses, even though they do follow from metaphysical analyses.

48. Given the sorts of things I said when I was trying to introduce the expression 'metaphysically analytic', outright refusal to understand the expression seems like an excessive reaction. It would be much more plausible for someone to claim not to see how 'metaphysical analyticity' could be anything other than another word for metaphysical necessity. Indeed, I myself am inclined to think that the two notions may be the same—at least, many of the things philosophers have said in trying to explain the expression 'metaphysically necessary' seem to point towards this interpretation. But this moderate claim need not undermine the explanatory power of Criterion 5. For Criterion 5 to succeed where Criterion 4 failed, in being faithful to the practice of foundational ontology, it needn't be the case that metaphysical analyticity and metaphysical necessity really *are* two different statuses. It suffices that those foundational ontologists who regard their preferred answers to the Special Composition Question as metaphysically necessary should, by and large, be disposed to *think* that they are two different statuses.

49. We can make this argument a bit more precise by making use of the assumption that all the candidate languages are ones in which a counterfactual semantics for the languages for the tribes is true (see note 29 above). If any language of this sort satisfies Criterion 5, the languages of the tribes—Universalese, for example— must be impoverished. For in any such language, we could state the following argument: 'The truth-values of Universalese sentences are determined entirely by the facts about what things *would* be like if composition were universal. But *these* facts do not determine whether composition is universal: they neither metaphysically analytically entail that composition is universal, nor that it isn't universal. Hence, no sentence of Universalese expresses any proposition metaphysically analytically equivalent to the proposition that composition is universal. The same goes for any other metaphysically synthetic general proposition about the ontology of composition. So Universalese is entirely blind to the facts expressed by general claims about composition in our language.'

50. What about the metaphysical analysis 'To be phlogiston is to be an instance of a substance that is *actually* characteristically emitted in combustion and the calcination of metals'? I take it that this metaphysical analysis is equivalent to the claim that to be phlogiston is to be an instance of a substance s such that necessarily, if things are thus-and-so [insert a complete description of the actual world here], s is characteristically emitted.... If this is right, the analysis is one on which 'there is no phlogiston' can be transformed into a logical truth, albeit an immensely complicated one. So there is no need to revise Criterion 5 to allow for the metaphysical analyticity of this sentence. If the same is true of all semantically defective predicates, the argument of the next section will work even if we leave Criterion 5 as it is.

51. This presentation makes it sound like semantic defectiveness is a feature possessed by a predicate once and for all, in virtue of its distinctive kind of meaning. But it might be better to think of semantic defectiveness as a relation between a predicate in a language and the quantifiers of that language. Consider, for example, a language just like ordinary English except that 'something' expresses the property of being a property which would be instantiated if everything that is actually an oxygen atom were a phlogiston atom instead. (Never mind whether anything could make it true that someone was speaking this language, as opposed to one in which 'phlogiston' meant what 'oxygen' actually means.) In this language, 'something is phlogiston' is true, despite the fact that 'phlogiston' means the same thing that it means in English. Is 'phlogiston' semantically defective in this language? We could say 'yes', but that would mean that we could no longer justify the claim that ordinary predicates like 'oxygen' are not semantically defective by appealing to the truth of sentences like 'something is oxygen'. Treating semantic defectiveness as a relation between predicate-meanings and quantifier-meanings would allow us to keep the entailment from '"F" is semantically defective' to '"Nothing is F" is true.'

52. A further weakening is called for to allow for the metaphysical analyticity of sentences involving empty names, like 'It is not the case that Vulcan is a planet.' But I have not thought it worthwhile to burden the reader with the question how such a weakening should best be expressed.

53. Peter van Inwagen pointed out to me that the question we get if we replace every occurrence of 'x is part of y' in the Special Composition Question with 'every point of space occupied by x is occupied by y' (or 'every point of spacetime occupied by x is occupied by y') might well be such a question.

54. As regards the question mentioned in the previous note, the relevant eliminativist view is the claim that nothing ever *occupies* anything. This view is held both by *relationalists*, who deny the existence of space[-time] points, and by *super-substantivalists*, who deny the existence of material objects that are not composed of space[-time] points.

55. Sentences involving modal operators are one potential source of such counterexamples. It seems quite plausible, for example, that 'it is possible that there should be exactly three simple things' is metaphysically analytic. But can this sentence be transformed into a logical truth by substitution of metaphysical analyses? Before we can answer this question, we will have to get clear on what it would mean to give a metaphysical analysis of an operator like 'it is possible that'.

Vague predicates are another potential source of counterexamples: 'No bald person is hirsute' seems to be metaphysically analytic, but who would venture to give a metaphysical analysis of 'bald' or 'hirsute'? If we wanted to accommodate this case without giving up Criterion 6, we might try saying that while it is indeterminate what the true metaphysical analyses of 'bald' and 'hirsute' are, it is determinate that they are logically incompatible.

REFERENCES

Armstrong, David M. (1978). *Universals and Scientific Realism*, 2: *A Theory of Universals*. Cambridge: Cambridge University Press.

Bealer, George (1982). *Quality and Concept*. Oxford: Clarendon Press.

Braun, David (1993). 'Empty Names.' *Noûs*, 27: 449–69.

Carnap, Rudolf (1950). 'Empiricism, Semantics and Ontology.' *Revue International de Philosophie*, 4: 20–40. Reprinted in *Meaning and Necessity: A Study in Semantics and Modal Logic*, second edition. Chicago: University of Chicago Press, 1956.

Chalmers, David (1996). *The Conscious Mind*. Oxford: Oxford University Press.

Eklund, Matti (forthcoming). 'The Deflationary Conception of Ontology.' In *Contemporary Debates in Metaphysics*. John Hawthorne, Theodore Sider, and Dean Zimmerman (eds.). Oxford: Basil Blackwell

Fine, Kit (1994). 'Essence and Modality.' In James Tomberlin (ed.), *Philosophical Perspectives*, 8: 1–16.

Graff, Delia (2001). 'Descriptions as Predicates.' *Philosophical Studies*, 102: 1–42.

Harper, William L., Robert Stalnaker, and Glenn Pearce (eds.) (1981). *Ifs: Conditionals, Belief, Decision, Chance, and Time*. Dordrecht: D. Reidel Publishing Company.

Hirsch, Eli (2002). 'Quantifier Variance and Realism.' *Philosophical Issues*, 12: 51–73.

Hume, David (1779/1997). *Dialogues Concerning Natural Religion*, J. C. A. Gaskin (ed.). Oxford: Oxford University Press.

Jackson, Frank (1998). *From Metaphysics to Ethics: A Defence of Conceptual Analysis*. Oxford: Oxford University Press.

Kant, Immanuel (1781/1965). *Critique of Pure Reason*, Norman Kemp Smith (ed.). New York: St. Martins.

King, Jeffrey C. and Jason Stanley (2005). 'Semantics, Pragmatics, and the Role of Semantic Content.' In Zoltán Gendler Szabó (ed.), *Semantics versus Pragmatics*. Oxford Clarendon Press.

Kripke, Saul A. (1979). 'A Puzzle About Belief.' In Avishai Margalit (ed.), *Meaning and Use*. Dordrecht: Reidel.

—— (1980). *Naming and Necessity*. Cambridge, MA: Harvard University Press.

Lewis, David (1973). *Counterfactuals*. Oxford: Basil Blackwell.

—— (1984). 'Putnam's Paradox.' *Australasian Journal of Philosophy*, 62: 221–36.

—— (1986). *On the Plurality of Worlds*. Oxford: Basil Blackwell.

—— (1991). *Parts of Classes*. Oxford: Basil Blackwell.

Nolan, Daniel (1997). 'Impossible Worlds: A Modest Approach.' *Notre Dame Journal of Formal Logic*, 38.4: 535–572.

Putnam, Hilary (1987). 'Truth and Convention: On Davidson's Refutation of Conceptual Relativism.' *Dialectica*, 41: 41–67.

Rorty, Richard (1982). *Consequences of Pragmatism*. Minneapolis: University of Minnesota Press.

Rosen, Gideon (1990). 'Modal Fictionalism.' *Mind* 99.395: 327–54.

Sider, Theodore (1993). 'Van Inwagen and the Possibility of Gunk.' *Analysis*, 53: 285–9.

—— (2003). 'Against Vague Existence.' *Philosophical Studies*, 114: 135–46.

—— (MS). 'Quantifiers and Temporal Ontology.' Available online at http://fas-philosophy.rutgers.edu/~sider/papers/quantifiers_and_presentism.pdf.

Soames, Scott (2002). *Beyond Rigidity: The Unfinished Semantic Agenda of Naming and Necessity.* New York: Oxford University Press.

Stalnaker, Robert (1968). 'A Theory of Conditionals.' In *Studies in Logical Theory: American Philosophical Quarterly Monograph Series*, No. 2. Oxford: Basil Blackwell. Reprinted in Harper *et al.* (1981: 41–56).

—— (1981). 'A Defense of Conditional Excluded Middle.' In Harper *et al.* (1981: 87–104).

Stanley, Jason (2001). 'Hermeneutic Fictionalism.' *Midwest Studies in Philosophy*, 25: 36–71.

Stanley, Jason and Zoltán Gendler Szabó (2000). 'On Quantifier Domain Restriction.' *Mind & Language*, 15: 219–61.

Unger, Peter (1984). *Philosophical Relativity.* Minneapolis: University of Minnesota Press.

van Inwagen, Peter (1990). *Material Beings.* Ithaca: Cornell University Press.

Williamson, Timothy (2003). 'Everything.' In John Hawthorne and Dean Zimmerman (eds.), Philosophical Perspectives, *17: 415–65.*

Yablo, Stephen (1998). 'Does Ontology Rest on a Mistake?' *Proceedings of the Aristotelian Society*, Supplementary Volume, 72: 229–61.

—— (2000b). 'A Paradox of Existence.' In Anthony Everett and Thomas Hofweber (eds.), *Empty Names, Fiction and the Puzzles of Existence*: 275–312. Stanford: CSLI Press.

Moral Fictionalism

RICHARD JOYCE

If there's Nothing that we Morally Ought to Do, then what Ought we to Do?

On the very last page of his book *Ethics: Inventing Right and Wrong*, John Mackie (1977) suggests that moral discourse—which he has argued is deeply error-laden—can continue with the status of a 'useful fiction'. I presume that most people will agree, for a variety of reasons, that morality is in some manner useful. The problem, though, is that its usefulness may depend upon its being *believed*, but if we have read the earlier stages of Mackie's book and have been convinced by his arguments, then surely the possibility of believing in morality is no longer an option. Even if we somehow *could* carry on believing in it, surely we should not, for any recommendation in favor of having false beliefs while, at some level, knowing that they are false, is unlikely to be good advice. So how useful can morality be if we don't believe any of it?

This chapter will assume without discussion that Mackie's arguments for a moral error theory are cogent (or, at least, that their conclusion is true). This amounts to assuming two things: first, that moral discourse typically is assertoric (that is, moral judgments express belief states); second, that moral assertions typically are untrue. Mackie's particular argument holds that the problems of morality revolve around its commitment to Kantian categorical imperatives: morality requires that there are actions that persons ought to perform regardless of their ends. But, Mackie argues, such imperatives are indefensible, and therefore morality is flawed. A moral error theorist must hold that the problematic element of morality (categorical imperatives, in Mackie's opinion) is *central* to the discourse, such that any 'tidied up' discourse, one with the defective elements extirpated, simply wouldn't count as a *moral* system at all.

There are rich and inventive arguments against Mackie, but here we will suppose them all to fail. The question that this chapter addresses is 'What, then, ought we to do?' Mackie's answer appears to be 'Carry on with morality as a fiction', and it is this possibility that I wish to examine closely. The aim is to understand what such an answer may mean, and to attempt a defense of it. I will call the view to be defended 'moral fictionalism'. Fictionalism promises to be a way by which we can avoid the situation that Quine so deplored, of employing 'philosophical double talk which would repudiate an ontology while simultaneously enjoying its benefits' (Quine, 1960: 242). Note that fictionalism is not being suggested as something that is true of our actual moral discourse; rather, it is presented as a stance that we could take towards a subject matter—morality, in this case—if we have become convinced that the subject is hopelessly flawed in some respect, such that we cannot in good conscience carry on as before. In the useful terminology of John Burgess, I am peddling a 'revolutionary' not a 'hermeneutic' fictionalism (Burgess, 1983).[1]

One might think that the question 'If a moral error theory is the case, what should we do?' is self-undermining. And so it would be, if it were asking what we *morally* ought to do, but that is not what is being asked. It is just a straightforward, common-or-garden, *practical* 'ought'. The answer that the question invites will be a hypothetical imperative, and we will assume that whatever arguments have led us to a moral error theory have not threatened hypothetical imperatives. (In other words, to hold a moral error theory is not to hold an error theory for practical normativity in general.) I do not want this issue to depend on any particular view of how we make such practical decisions. Let us just say that when morality is removed from the picture, what is practically called for is a matter of a cost-benefit analysis, where the costs and benefits can be understood liberally as preference satisfactions. By asking what *we* ought to do I am asking how a *group* of persons, who share a variety of broad interests, projects, ends—and who have come to the realization that morality is a bankrupt theory—might best carry on. (Two comments: (1) I wouldn't object if we decided to speak of *informed* rather than actual preferences; (2) no assumption is being made that preferences will be selfish in content.)

I will begin by discussing fictionalism in general, outlining how it might be that a person might carry on using a discourse that she has come to see as flawed. It will be useful if initially we avoid the distractions that the particular case of *moral* fictionalism might bring, and so I will begin by discussing an example that in some ways is less controversial: color fictionalism.

Critical Contexts

Suppose that after reading some eighteenth-century philosophers David comes to endorse an error theory about color. We needn't go into the arguments that might lead him to this conclusion, but they probably have something to do with the thought that one of the central platitudes about color is that it is a type of surface property of objects with which humans can have direct acquaintance (e.g., with normal eyesight on a sunny day), coupled with the thought that there simply aren't any properties like *that*. In other words, for philosophical reasons he ceases to believe that the world is colored in the way that it appears to be colored, which (further philosophical reasons lead him to think) implies that it is not colored at all. Maybe he is confused in coming to such a conclusion, but that is not the issue.

The issue is: given that he has come to have this philosophical belief (however confusedly) what happens to all his color discourse? Does he stop saying things like 'The grass is green'? If someone asks him what color his mother's eyes are, does he reply that they are no color at all? Does he cease to appreciate sunsets or Impressionist paintings? Does he wear clashing clothes (while denying that anything really clashes with anything)? Of course not. In 99 percent of his life he carries on the same as everyone else. His vision is the same, his utterances about the world are the same, and even what he is thinking while making these utterances is the same. It is only in the philosophy classroom—moreover, only when discussing sensory perception—that when pressed on the question of whether the grass is green David might look uncomfortable, squirm, and say 'Well, it's not *really* green—nothing is *really* green.' This may seem like an uneasy position for him to be in. Sometimes—99 percent of the time, let's say—he is willing to utter 'The grass is green', 'The sky is blue', etc., while at other times—one percent of the time—he is inclined to deny these very same propositions. Which does he believe?

It seems to me that in this case what he affirms one percent of the time determines his beliefs. Why? Because the circumstance in which he denies that the world is colored—the philosophy classroom—is the context within which he is at his most undistracted, reflective, and critical. When one thinks critically, one subjects one's attitudes to careful scrutiny ('Is my acceptance of *p* really justified?'); robust forms of skepticism are given serious consideration; one looks for connections and incoherencies amongst one's attitudes; one forms higher order attitudes towards one's first-order judgments. It is important to see that this distinction between more critical and less critical contexts is asymmetric. It's not merely that a person attends to *different* beliefs when doing philosophy than when, say, shopping; nor that she questions everyday thinking when doing philosophy, but equally questions philosophy when shopping. Critical thinking investigates and challenges the presuppositions of ordinary thinking in a way that ordinary thinking does not investigate and challenge the presuppositions of critical thinking. Critical thinking is characterized by a tendency to ask oneself questions like 'Am I really justified in accepting that things like shops exist?'—whereas the frame of mind one is in when shopping is *not* characterized by asking 'Am I justified in accepting that there is some doubt as to whether shops exist?'

This notion of what a person is disposed to assent to if placed in a critical context must not be read as involving any far-fetched counterfactual idealization. Who can judge what manner of bizarre things one would assent to if given *perfect* powers of reflection and critical thinking? A person's 'most critical context' must be fixed in actuality—and the obvious means of achieving this grounding is to stipulate that he must sometimes (at a minimum, at least once) have *actually inhabited* that context, and therein either assented to, or dissented from, the thesis in question. In other words, it would be too bizarre to hold that an individual, who has never given the issue any careful thought whatsoever, but thinks and acts in accordance with theory *T,* does not really believe *T* simply because if he *were* to think carefully about it, he would deny it. But if we add that at some point he *has* adopted a critical perspective and therein sincerely denied *T,* and remains disposed to deny *T* were he again to adopt that perspective, then he disbelieves *T,* regardless of how he may think, act, and speak in less critical perspectives. In David's case, his most critical context is philosophical thought—thus, though he occupies this position only one percent of the time, we're supposing, it is his pronouncements therein that reveal his beliefs. The rest of the time he still *has* this skeptical belief, but he is not attending to it. Nevertheless, *all* the time David remains disposed to deny that the world is colored if placed in his most undistracted, reflective, and critical context, thus *all* the time this is what he believes.

Fictive Judgments

This leaves us with the question of how we should describe David's color claims in that 99 percent of his life where he utters propositions (e.g., 'The grass is green') that he disbelieves. We can begin by reminding ourselves of a more familiar circumstance in which people utter propositions that they disbelieve: story-telling. When I utter the sentence 'There once was a goblin who liked jam' as part of telling a story, I am not expressing something that I really believe. If pressed in the appropriately serious way ('You don't *really* believe that there once was a goblin who liked jam, do you?') then I will 'step out' of the fiction and deny those very propositions that a moment ago I was apparently affirming.

Some people have argued that sentences concerning fiction ought to be interpreted as containing a tacit story operator, such that they maybe treated as true assertions; thus the sentence 'There once was a goblin who liked jam' may be used to express the true proposition 'According to Hans Christian Andersen's story, there once was a goblin who liked jam.' (See, for example, Lewis, 1978.) This is inadequate as a general claim, for it fails to distinguish two different things that we can do with a story: describing the story versus telling the story. When we tell a story we are pretending something: that we are a person who has access to a realm of facts that we are reporting. (We might also partially pretend to be characters in the story, which is why we will speak their parts in a gruff or squeaky voice.) But if every sentence of the story uttered contained an unpronounced fiction operator, then there is no sense to be made of the claim that the storyteller is pretending. (How would one *pretend* that according to Hans Christian Andersen's story, there once was a goblin who liked jam?)[2] This is not to deny that on occasions the proposition 'According to Hans Christian Andersen's story, there once was a goblin who liked jam' might be expressed elliptically, minus the prefix, but this is not what we are doing when we *tell* the story. On such occasions we are not asserting anything, but *pretending* to assert.

The same distinction can be made regarding skeptical David's color claims. When, in ordinary conversation, he utters the sentence 'The grass is green', we could interpret this as a kind of shorthand way of asserting something like 'According to the fiction of a colored world, the grass is green' *or* we could interpret him as not asserting anything at all, but rather doing something rather like engaging in a make-believe: pretending to assert that the grass is green. I prefer the latter interpretation. It is true that at the moment of making the utterance it doesn't *seem* to David as if he is participating in an act of pretence, but nor does it seem to him as if he's making an implicit reference to the content of a well-known fiction. The matter won't be settled by asking David what he takes himself to be doing. Unless we force him into the philosophical context where he denies the existence of colors altogether, then asking him in an ordinary context whether he is asserting that the grass is green is likely to meet with an affirmative answer. But *that* claim—'Yes, I am asserting that the grass is green'—may be just another part of the fiction. (A Roald Dahl story, recounting many fantastic events, contains an explicit declaration that the story is not a fiction, but it's *all true*. The declaration of truth is no less part of the make-believe than the rest of the story.)[3] The issue of whether David's everyday utterance 'The grass is green' is an assertion about a fiction or a fictional assertion is not an issue about how things feel to him—it is to be settled by philosophers providing an interpretation that construes David's linguistic practices most charitably.

The former interpretation—the 'tacit story operator view'—does him no favors. One problem is that it cannot account for the fact that when in a more critical context David will explicitly *overturn* what he earlier claimed—he might say 'What I said earlier was, strictly speaking, false.' But if what he said earlier concerned the content of the fiction of a colored world, then he does not think it was false at all. A second problem with this interpretation is that it fails to make sense of the ways David might employ a color claim in a logically complex context (see Vision, 1994). For example, he might endorse the following argument:

P1   Fresh grass is green.
P2   My lawn is made of fresh grass.
C   Therefore, my lawn is green.

But if the first premise is elliptical for 'According to the fiction of a colored world, fresh grass is green', then the argument is not valid at all. There is room for maintaining that the argument would be valid if all three claims were so prefixed, but the problem then would be that the revised second premise ('According to the fiction of a colored world, my lawn is made of fresh grass') seems so obviously false that it is surely not what David asserts when he utters P2. The fiction of a colored world, in so far as it has a determinate content at all, does not include claims about what anybody's lawn is made of (see comments by Lewis, 1978: 38-9).

To this it might be objected that the operator is being interpreted incorrectly. If 'according to...' means not 'it is claimed by...' but something more like 'it is true in the fiction of . . . ', then perhaps we might after all allow that according to the fiction of a colored world that my lawn is made of fresh grass. In much the same way we might allow (indeed, insist) that it is true in the fiction of the Conan Doyle stories that humans do not have long hairy tails, that $6 + 5 = 11$, that Ireland is to the west of Britain, and so on, despite the fact that one will not find such things *claimed* by the stories (nor even— with, perhaps, the exception of the arithmetical truth—*implied* by anything claimed by the stories).

But this objection leads to unsightly consequences. Suppose David just casually asserts 'My lawn is made of fresh grass.' Since this assertion may at any time be pressed into service as the premise of an argument (the other premises of which include color claims), if the resulting argument is to be valid we will have to interpret him as *really* having asserted 'It is true in the fiction of a colored world that my lawn is made of fresh grass.' But the very same assertion may be employed by David as a premise in another argument that involves no color claims and no obvious fictionalizing: he may combine it with 'Fresh grass is a type of vegetation', for example, to get the conclusion 'My lawn is made up of a type of vegetation.' In order for this new argument to be valid we had better interpret this new premise (and the new conclusion) as also bearing the prefix. In fact, any assertion that David makes might be combined with color claims as a premise of an apparently valid argument, and so if we're to maintain that apparent validity is real validity, we're going to have to interpret everything that he asserts about anything as having this unpronounced prefix. Things get worse still if we remind ourselves that color may not be the only fiction that David participates in. Eighteenth-century philosophy may also lead him to endorse an error theory for sound and smell, for causation, for virtue and vice, and thus in order for all his apparently unremarkable, apparently valid argumentative moves to be genuinely valid, we will have to interpret every claim issuing from his mouth as brimming with unspoken prefixes.

All such unpleasantness is avoided if we do away with tacit operators, and simply interpret David's utterance 'Fresh grass is green' as a kind of make-believe assertion. The content of the proposition doesn't change, any more than when I say (as part of telling a story) 'There once was a goblin who liked jam' I am using 'jam' with some special meaning. The sentence 'There once was a goblin who liked jam' has exactly the same content whether it is used as part of a fairy tale or to foolishly assert something false. What changes is the 'force' with which it is uttered. When asserting it I am presenting it as something that I believe, and putting it forward as something that my audience should believe. Linguistic conventions decree that when it has been preceded by 'Once upon a time . . . ,' all such expectations are lifted.

What are we to make of an argument when some of the premises are uttered as an act of make-believe (e.g., as lines in a play) while others are straightforward assertions? Since the presence or absence of assertoric force doesn't affect the content of the premises, then if the argument was valid with its components asserted, it will be valid with them unasserted, and remain valid if some of the components are asserted and some of them are not. For example, the following is a valid argument:

P1   It is cold tonight.
P2   It is the height of summer.
P3   A cold night in the height of summer is unusual weather.
C   Tonight is unusual weather.

If a logic teacher recited this argument to a group of incoming undergraduates as an example of validity, she would not be asserting any of the premises or the conclusion—but it would be no less valid for that. Alternatively, suppose that P1 is the line of a play, and the actor duly utters it while on stage, during a performance given on a hot summer's night. After the play, when pressed on climatic issues (curiously), he assents in all seriousness to P2 and P3. Clearly this person has not committed himself to the conclusion (which he may believe to be completely false), for the reason that he did not commit himself to P1. On the other hand, there is nothing to prevent him from 'going along' with the pretence if for some reason he wants to, combining P2 and P3 with the make-believe P1, and endorsing the conclusion as part of a fictional act. If he does so, there will be no need to reinterpret his attitude to P2 and P3. These were asserted, and in asserting them he has committed himself to certain other conclusions (e.g., 'If it were cold tonight, that would be unusual weather'), and may combine them with further asserted premises to yet further conclusions. In other words, unlike with the tacit operator account, we do not have to interpret David's ordinary claim 'My lawn is made of fresh grass' as anything other than it appears to be, let alone extravagantly reinterpreting all his other ordinary assertions that are not color claims.

Let us say, then, that David is not only an error theorist about color, but also a fictionalist. He does not believe in color, but he continues to employ color discourse. His color claims are fictive judgments, which we may think of as a kind of 'make-believe'—though one should be wary of the term, since the paradigm examples that it tends to bring to mind are of rather trivial activities (pretending that the puppet is talking, make-believing that the sofa is a boat, etc.). But there is no obvious reason to assume that make-believe is always a trivial business;[4] indeed, an important objective of this chapter is to convince you otherwise. We have not specified David's reasons for making these fictive color judgments—let us just say that he finds it convenient to do so. This practical value need be nothing more than the convenience of carrying on in the manner to which he has grown accustomed.

Since David is capable of overturning his everyday color discourse when-ever he enters a more critical frame of mind, we should hardly describe him as suffering from self-deception. He is no more self-deceived than is someone caught up in a good novel. I suppose that the term 'self-deception' *could* be applied to an ordinary person engaged in a novel, but (A) it would be an uncomfortable stretch, and (B) it would merely show that self-deception need not be in the least pernicious.[5] It is much better, I think, to distinguish being 'caught up' in a fiction from being 'deceived' by a fiction. A person deceived by a fiction is someone who might walk up and down Baker Street wondering where Holmes lived, or who tries to research Madame Bovary's ancestry, or who rushes on to the stage to save the princess. Fans of Sherlock Holmes do travel to Baker Street, of course, and they may well picture their hero there in the nineteenth century, but they know very well (most of them, I hope) what they're doing. At any time, if asked in all seriousness whether Holmes walked these streets, they will answer 'No'. They are not deceived and therefore not self-deceived; they are merely caught up in a fiction. It is the person who is incapable of dropping the fiction, who continues to speak of Holmes as a historical character even when in her most critical context, who is deceived (though further criteria would need to be met before we would describe such a person as *self*-deceived).

Noncognitivism and the Lone Fictionalist

If by 'noncognitivism' we mean the view that a certain discourse does not typically consist of assertions, despite normally coming in the indicative mood, then it would appear that we ought to be noncognitivists about David's fictive color claims. Remember that fictionalism is being considered here as something that we could *do* with a problematic discourse, not as an analysis of any actual discourse (problematic or otherwise), thus the same goes for the consequent noncognitive stance: it is a description of a discourse that we might choose to adopt, not a description of an actual discourse.

Another thing to note is that although over the years we have grown used to the idea of noncognitivists offering a 'translation' of allegedly problematic everyday sentences into some unproblematic idiom, that is not what is being suggested here. For example, we are familiar with moral noncognitivists telling us that a claim like 'Stealing is wrong' really amounts to 'Stealing: boo!' or 'I disapprove of stealing; do so as well!' One might misread the present noncognitivist proposal as suggesting in the same spirit that someone who claims 'Stealing is wrong' is really saying something like 'Let's pretend that stealing is wrong'—thus making it clear that the claim is not really an assertion. But this would be, as I say, a misreading. When playing a game of make-believe with children—say, crawling around on the floor pretending to be a bear—one might say, in a gruff voice, 'I am a bear; I am going to eat you!' It would be an odd theory that identified the true content of this utterance as 'Let's pretend that I am a bear; let's pretend that I am going to eat you.' Someone saying such things would hardly be 'playing a game' at all. He might as well start out saying (in an ordinary voice) 'Let's pretend that I am speaking in a gruff voice.' With noncognitivism defined as above, it is not incumbent on its proponents to provide a translation scheme from problematic language to unproblematic. For the moral fictionalist/noncognitivist, the content of 'Stealing is wrong' is exactly what it appears to be—with whatever erroneous implications she thinks that it has remaining in place. What is different about her utterance of the sentence is the force with which she utters it.

There is, however, a troubling consequence of this kind of noncognitivist proposal, for notice that I claimed that we should be noncognitivists about *David's* fictive color discourse, implying that we might not be noncognitivists about everyone else's color claims. Noncognitivism, thus, becomes a relativistic matter. There is nothing wrong with this *per se*, but it presents a problem. Does David communicate to other speakers his opinion about the nonexistence of color? Unless they discuss matters in a philosophical vein, we can assume not. Thus ordinary speakers will assume that when David utters the sentence 'The grass is green' he is expressing a belief. Of course, David could avoid this by employing some of the standard devices for indicating the withdrawal of assertoric force. He could precede his color claims by something equivalent to 'Once upon a time . . .'; he could utter them in a sarcastic tone of voice, or in the subjunctive mood; at a pinch, he could wear a T-shirt that declares 'I withhold assertoric force from color claims!' But if he does none of these things we can assume that his interlocutors will reasonably take his color utterances to be color assertions. And the possibility arises that if all listeners take an utterance to be an assertion, then, regardless of the speaker's true attitude, it *is* an assertion—in which case maybe we ought not be noncognitivists about David's color discourse after all.

If to assert *p* is to express one's belief that *p*, then it may seem impossible that David could assert 'The grass is green', given our assumption that he does not believe this. But this would reveal a misunderstanding of how 'express' is intended here: It indicates not a causal relation, but one established by linguistic convention. When one *lies*, for example, one expresses a belief that one does not have. That is to say, one exploits the linguistic conventions that decree that when 'Such-and-such' is uttered in certain circumstances (e.g., in a serious tone of voice, not as part of a play, not preceded by 'Once upon a time . . . ,' etc.) then the speaker is to be taken to believe that such-and-such. Since, we are assuming, David is not employing any of the well-entrenched devices to indicate withdrawal of assertoric force, then it might be argued that his utterance satisfies the criteria for being an assertion. And since David doesn't believe the proposition in question, then, according to this line of thinking, his alleged assertion that the grass is green looks suspiciously like a *lie*.

It would be nice to avoid the conclusion that fictionalists are liars. Let me offer two responses. First, the term 'lie' is a bit steep for the situation described. David, after all, doesn't intend to deceive anyone when he utters 'The grass is green.' He has no malevolent agenda. He remains disposed to admit his non-belief in colors if anyone wishes to pursue the philosophical point—it is just that such a cerebral turn is inappropriate for 99 percent of conversations. Though David and his interlocutors may not be on quite the same wavelength when they discuss the color of things, no harm comes of it. If 'the truth about David' were to become widely known, then ordinary people may be puzzled or amused at so esoteric an idea as that the world is not colored, but it seems unlikely that they would feel annoyed at having been duped. These comments can be interpreted in either of two ways—I don't mind which: (A) expressing the belief that *p* while not believing that *p* is a necessary but not sufficient condition for lying; or (B) expressing the belief that *p* while not believing that *p* may be a sufficient condition for lying, but lying need not warrant criticism.

The second response is to move attention away from the 'lone fictionalist', and remind ourselves that fictionalism is a proposed response to the question of what *we* could do if faced with an error theory concerning a hitherto fully endorsed discourse. Fictionalism may be a stable and viable strategy for a group, even if there are some unsettling aspects of it as an individual stance. A group may have a convention in place that when a certain subject matter is entered into, there is a withdrawal of ordinary conversational force. The question of how such conventions get established and passed on is an intriguing one. Consider the murky origins of the convention of sarcasm, for example. Who decided that a certain tone of voice would act as a kind of derogatory negation of manifest content? We employ the convention without even thinking of it as 'a convention'; we do not need to be explicitly taught sarcasm as children, we would have trouble articulating exactly how it works if asked to explain. The convention can also withstand the existence of a sizable number of people in the population who seem oblivious of its existence.

When fictionalism is presented in this light—as a proposal for how a *group* might respond to an error theory—we see just how 'revolutionary' are the theory's aspirations. Whether such a radically prescriptive spirit is seen as simply preposterous depends on how we conceive of our philosophical objectives. Do I really expect that ordinary speakers will adjust their attitude towards a problematic discourse? Of course not. Ordinary speakers will carry on doing whatever they please. Most of them believe in ghosts, miracles, astrology, and alien abductions. As philosophers writing against such silly beliefs we conceive of ourselves as correcting erroneous thought—of encouraging people to drop their false beliefs and adopt true ones—but we should not seriously expect to succeed! Revolutionary fictionalism is hardly more ambitious in its prescriptive spirit than this.

The Value of Morality

With a basic theory of fictionalism now on the table, we can turn, finally, to *moral* fictionalism. Suppose that a moral error theory is the case—or at least suppose that a group of people has become convinced of this—what should they do with their faulty moral talk? The conclusion that they should just abolish it, that it should go the way of witch discourse and phlogiston discourse, is certainly a tempting possibility, and may, for all I say here, turn out to be the correct response. But fictionalism shows us that it is not the *only* response; it is at least possible that they may reasonably elect to maintain moral discourse as a fiction. What they need to perform is a cost-benefit analysis. Let us suppose, firstly, that the option of carrying on *believing* in morality is closed to them. They have seen the cat out of the bag and they cannot believe otherwise. Even if they *could* somehow bring themselves sincerely to 'forget' that they ever read Mackie's book (for example), surely to embark on such a course is likely to bring negative consequences. I will

assume without presenting any arguments that these consequences are sufficiently detrimental as to place this option beyond contention.

Similarly, I will not give serious consideration to the proposal we might call
'propagandism': that *some* people may be 'in the know' about the moral error
theory while, for the greater good, keeping it quiet and encouraging the *hoi*
polloi to continue with their sincere (false) moral beliefs. Such a situation
really would amount to the promulgation of manipulative lies, which, I will
assume, leads ultimately to no good. Here I agree with Richard Garner,
commenting on Plato's state policy of deception in the *Republic*: 'If the
members of any society should come to believe Socrates' fable [the 'myth of
the metals'], *or any similarly fabricated radical fiction*, the result would be a
very confused group of people, unsure of what to believe, and unable to trust
their normal belief-producing mechanisms. It is not wise to risk having a
society of epistemological wrecks in order to achieve some projected good
through massive deception' (Garner, 1993: 96).

Two options remain as contenders in the cost-benefit analysis: abolitionism
(or we may call it 'eliminativism') and fictionalism. For moral fictionalism to
be viable it must win this pragmatic comparison. It is not required that taking
a fictional stance towards moral discourse will supply *all* the benefits that
came with sincere moral belief. It can be conceded up front that the pragmatically optimal situation for a group of people to be in is to have the
attitude of sincere belief towards moral matters. But it must also be grasped
that having a doxastic policy concordant with *critical inquiry* is almost
guaranteed to serve better in practical terms for a group than any other
policy. We are imagining a group of people whose careful pursuit of truth
has overthrown their moral beliefs. Perhaps such people correctly recognize
that they were happier and better off before the pursuit brought them so far,
but there is now no going back, and to sacrifice the value of critical inquiry
would be disastrous.

In order to assess who might win this two horse race, we must ask the
question 'What is the value of morality?' Unless we roughly know the answer
we can have no idea of what costs its abolition may incur. Let us at first put
fictionalism aside, and address the question of the value of morality *when it is*
believed. We may then assume that this is a benefit that, *ceteris paribus*, will be
lost if a group were to abolish morality, which puts us in a position to ask (in
the next section of this chapter) whether their adopting a fictionalist stance
would allow them to avoid some of those losses.

The popular thought that without morality all hell would break loose in
human society is a naive one. Across a vast range of situations we all have

perfectly good *prudential* reasons for continuing to act in cooperative ways with our fellow humans. In many situations reciprocal and cooperative relationships bring ongoing rewards to all parties, and do so *a fortiori* when defective behaviors are punished. When, in addition, we factor in the benefits of having a good reputation—a reputation that is based on past perform-ance—then cooperative dispositions can easily out-compete hurtful disposi-tions on purely egoistic grounds.

To an individual who asks why she should not cheat her fellows if she thinks that she can get away with it, Hobbes long ago provided one kind of answer: because the punishment-enforcing power is very powerful indeed.[6] This answer is developed and supplemented by Hume, who speaks of knaves 'betrayed by their own maxims; and while they purpose to cheat with moderation and secrecy, a tempting incident occurs, nature is frail, and they give into the snare; whence they can never extricate themselves, without a total loss of reputation, and the forfeiture of all trust and confidence with mankind' (Hume, 1751/1983: 82). First, the knave misses out on benefits that by their very nature cannot be gained through defection: 'Inward peace of mind, consciousness of integrity, a satisfactory review of [her] own conduct' (Hume, 1751/1983: 82)—advantages that are constituted by a disposition not to cheat one's fellows. Moreover, the knave will lose these benefits for comparatively trivial gains ('the feverish, empty amusements of luxury and expence'). Third, knaves will be epistemically fallible, and might think that they can get away with something when in fact they will be caught and punished. Fourth, since knaves have on their minds the possibility of cheating whenever they are confident of evading detection, they are likely to be tempted to cheat in situations where the chances of evading detection are less than certain, thus, again, risking severe punishment.

One result we can draw from Hobbes and Hume is that a person may have many reasons for acting in accordance with a moral requirement: the fear of punishment, the desire for an ongoing beneficial relationship, the motivation to maintain a good reputation, the simple fact that one on the whole *likes* one's fellows, that one has been brought up such that acting otherwise makes one feel rotten—all these being solid prudential reasons—plus the moral require-ment to act. To subtract the last one leaves the others still very much in play. But if this is so, then what useful role does the last kind of consideration play at all? To answer this it is worth underlining the reference to *temptation* in Hume's answer to the sensible knave. Merely to believe of some action 'This is the one that is in my long-term best interests' simply doesn't do the job. Most of us know this from personal experience, but there is abundant empirical evidence available for the dubious (see Ainslie, 1975; Schelling, 1980; Elster, 1984, 1985). Because short-term profit is tangible and present whereas long-term profit is distant and faint, the lure of the immediate may subvert the agent's ability to deliberate properly so as to obtain a valuable delayed benefit, leading him to 'rationalize' a poor choice. Hobbes lamented this 'perverse desire for present profit' (Hobbes, 1642/1983: 72)—something which Hume blamed for 'all dissoluteness and disorder, repentance and misery' (Hume, 1751/1983: 55), adding that a person should embrace 'any expedient, by which he may impose a restraint upon himself, and guard against this weakness' (Hume, 1739/1978: 536–7).[7] Let me hypothesize that an important value of moral beliefs is that they function as just such an expedient: supplementing and reinforcing the outputs of prudential reasoning. When a person believes that the valued action is *morally* required—that it *must* be performed whether he likes it or not—then the possibilities for rationalization diminish. If a person believes the action to be required by an authority from which he cannot escape, if he imbues it with a 'must-be-doneness' (the categorical element of morality that Mackie found so troublesome), if he believes that in not performing he will not merely frustrate himself, but will become reprehensible and deserving of disapprobation—then he is more likely to perform the action. The distinctive value of categorical imperatives is that they silence calculation, which is a valuable thing when interfering forces can so easily hijack our prudential calculations. In this manner, moral beliefs function to bolster self-control against practical irrationality.

I would not go so far as to claim that this is *the* value of moral belief, or even the most important benefit—but the argument requires only that we locate one general and reliable source of practical value. This suffices to show why a moral error theorist should hesitate before embracing abolitionism, for it reveals a practical cost that would be incurred on that path. (If there are other sources of practical benefit brought by moral beliefs, then the costs of abolitionism are even higher.) The crucial question, then, is whether some of the costs may be avoided by taking a fictionalist stance towards morality— whether the practical benefits of moral belief may still be gained by an attitude that falls short of belief. On the face of it, it seems unlikely. How can a fiction have the kind of practical impact—moreover, the kind of practical *authority*—that confers on moral belief its instrumental value? This is the major reason that moral fictionalism seems troubling in a way that color fictionalism does not: It seems implausible that a mere fiction could or should have such practical influence on important real-life decisions. In what remains of this chapter let me try to assuage this reasonable doubt.

Moral Fictionalism

First let me reiterate the caution already noted: that it is not incumbent on the moral fictionalist to argue that taking a fictional attitude towards morality makes *no* difference, or that morality as a fiction will supply *all* the practical benefits of a believed morality. A background assumption is that the arguments for moral error theory have put the option of a *believed* morality out of the running, so the only comparison in which we are interested is between fictionalism and abolitionism. The fictionalist wins the argument if she shows that there is *some* benefit to be had from keeping moral discourse as a fiction that would be lost (with no compensating gain) by eliminating moral discourse entirely.

In the previous section I argued that an important practical benefit to the individual of having moral beliefs is that they will serve as a bulwark against weakness of will—silencing certain kinds of vulnerable calculation, and thus blocking the temporary re-evaluation of outcomes that is characteristic of short-sighted rationalization. So our task is limited to addressing the question of whether a 'mere fiction' could also provide a similar benefit.

A quick argument to show that a positive answer is within reach begins by noting that engagement with fiction can affect our emotional states. This view is not without detractors: Kendall Walton, for example, has argued that fictions do not produce real emotions, but rather make-believe emotions (see his 1978, 1990).[8] But this is a terribly counter-intuitive view, which I am confident is incorrect. All the empirical evidence supports commonsense on this matter: watching movies, reading novels, or simply engaging one's imagination can produce real episodes of fear, sadness, disgust, anger, and so on. (One explanation is, in the words of two eminent psychologists, simply 'that the cognitive evaluations that engender emotions are sufficiently crude that they contain no reality check' (Johnson-Laird and Oatley, 2000: 465); alternatively, one may think that the human tendency to enjoy fictional engagement served some adaptive purpose in the ancestral environment.)[9] To this premise we can add the truism that emotional states can affect motivations, and thus behavior. Of course, the emotions arising from fictions do not necessarily affect behavior in the same manner as emotions arising in response to beliefs: the fear of fictional vampires is consistent with my sitting eating popcorn, whereas fear of vampires in which I *believed* would result in purchasing wooden stakes and a lot of garlic. But it does not follow that the emotions arising from engagement with fiction are 'motivationally inert'.

Reading *Anna Karenina* may encourage a person to abandon a doomed love affair; watching *The Blair Witch Project* may lead one to cancel the planned camping trip in the woods. Needless to say, these aren't the kind of beneficial behavioral responses that the moral fictionalist is seeking, but they at least show that the causal links between involvement with a fiction and action are undeniably in place.

Let us turn our sights more directly on the question of how a person combats weakness of will. Suppose I am determined to exercise regularly, after a lifetime of lethargy, but find myself succumbing to temptation. An effective strategy will be for me to lay down a strong and authoritative rule: *I must do fifty sit-ups every day, no less.* I am attempting to form a habit, and habits are formed—and, for the doggedly weak of will, maintained—by strictness and overcompensation. Perhaps in truth it doesn't much matter that I do fifty sit-ups every day, so long as I do more-or-less fifty on most days. But by allowing myself the occasional lapse, by giving myself permission *sometimes* to stray from the routine, I pave the way for akratic sabotage of my calculations—I threaten even my doing more-or-less fifty sit-ups on most days. I do better if I encourage myself to think in terms of fifty daily sit-ups as a non-negotiable value, as something I *must* do if I am ever to get fit.

However, to believe sincerely that fifty daily sit-ups are needed in order for me to achieve fitness is to have a false belief (we'll assume), the holding of which will require other compensating false beliefs. If it is true that *more-or-less* fifty sit-ups *nearly* every day is sufficient for health, then that is what I ought to believe. On the other hand, to *pay attention* to this belief exposes me to self-subversion—a slippery slope to inactivity. This is precisely a case where my best interests are served by rehearsing thoughts that are false, and that I know are false, in order to fend off my own weaknesses. But in order to get the benefit from this strategy there is no necessity that I *believe* the thoughts, or attempt to justify them as true when placed in a philosophically critical context. While doing my sit-ups I think to myself 'Must... do... fifty!' but if, on some other occasion, you ask me whether I really *must* do fifty, then I will say 'No, sometimes forty would suffice.'

Human motivation is often aroused more effectively by mental images than by careful calculation. Hume uses the example of a drunkard 'who has seen his companion die of a debauch, and dreads a like accident for himself: but as the memory of it decays away by degrees, his former security returns, and the danger seems less certain and real' (Hume, 1739/1978: 144). Hume's point is that humans put weight on near, recent, and concrete evidence, though there is no rational justification for our doing so. We can imagine the drunkard being presented with impressive statistics on the probabilities of alcoholics suffering an unpleasant end, but remaining quite unmoved; yet one friend dies and he becomes a teetotaler (at least for a while). It's not that he disbelieved the statistics, and the death of the friend need not alter his beliefs about how likely he is to suffer a similar fate, but the 'tangibility' of the one death has, in Hume's words, 'a superior influence on the judgment, as well as on the passions' (Hume, 1739/1978: 143–4).

If the drunkard has decided that his long-term interests are best served by abstinence, what strategy should he pursue to that end? He should read the statistics, yes, but—perhaps even more importantly—he should attempt to keep the image of his dying friend vivid. He does still better if he can relate that image to his own plight, if he thinks: 'If I drink, that's what will happen to me.' Now that proposition is false. What is true is something like 'If I drink, there's a 10 percent chance [say] of that happening to me.' But *that* thought looks dangerous. He does better with the stronger: 'If I drink, that's what *will* happen to me.' Yet does he, need he, *believe* this? No: he need not believe it in order for it to affect his actions in the desirable way, and, moreover, he *ought not* to believe it because it is false.

Hume's view that decisions are influenced by the 'tangibility' of how information is presented receives ample empirical support. In a large-scale survey conducted on doctors' attitudes towards smoking in the 1970s, it was noted that smoking had dropped most dramatically in chest physicians and radiologists—those who had been exposed to the effects of the activity—while other types of doctor, though no doubt aware of the statistics, were much less moved (Borgida and Nisbett, 1977). 'Tangibility' also affects the willingness of a person to enter into a mutually beneficial cooperative relationship. It has been shown that pairs of people playing iterated Prisoner Dilemma games will be much more likely to develop a cooperative strategy if the information concerning how the other player acted in the previous round is conveyed by a written note passed through a slot, as opposed to one of two small lights being activated (Enzle *et al.*, 1975). The same information is disclosed by either means, but one form is (in a way that's difficult to articulate) more 'concrete', more 'palpable', than the other, according it a greater influence in deliberations.

In another study of how people play Prisoner's Dilemma games it was shown that if, while sitting in the waiting room prior to playing the game, a person overhears a (fake) radio news item about an act of sacrifice (such as the donation of a kidney) then the person will be much more likely to adopt a cooperative strategy in the subsequent game (Hornstein *et al.*, 1975). By comparison, a radio story presenting violence and nastiness will encourage listeners subsequently to adopt a non-cooperative strategy. It is possible that a 'nice' news story affects the person's mood in a way conducive to cooperation, or perhaps it places in his short-term memory a kind of role model, or temporarily makes certain features of the real world appear more salient in deliberations. However it works, it is pretty clear that an engagement with a fictional story (as opposed to an apparent news item) may have a similar affect (though, to my knowledge, the obvious experiment has not been done).

Though these studies may be unfamiliar, what they reveal should hardly come as a surprise. The whole advertising industry (with which we are all far more familiar than we would wish) operates on the assumption that heavily exaggerated, idealized, and fictional images and narratives can influence real choice. We are shown an image of an absurdly happy family living in an eternally sunny world, and the basis of their rapture, we are encouraged to think, is the cereal that sits in the center of the breakfast table. Do we believe such garbage? Not for a second.[10] Do we, nevertheless, go out and spend our hard-earned money on that cereal? Much as we would like to deny it, masses of empirical research shows that we do.

One may object that choosing breakfast cereals hardly compares to moral decision-making, but it would be naive to deny that the same advertising strategies can encourage us to give to charity, vote for a president, support a bombing campaign, or sign up to join the armed forces. That engagement with fiction can influence our deliberations over the most weighty decisions is beyond question. What is perhaps unusual about the situation of the fiction-alist, and which requires more discussion, is the proposal that the action-guiding fiction be in some manner self-generated.

Moral Fictionalism as a Precommitment

Sometimes, when on a long airplane flight, I succumb to weakness of will and eat all the awful in-flight food that I had promised myself I wouldn't eat. It happens because I am trapped and bored with the food right in front of me for a long time. In order to avoid this I have developed a strategy for resisting my own imprudence. If I have decided that I really don't want to eat that slice of cheesecake, but suspect that I won't be able to resist picking at it until it's all gone (despite its tasting of plastic), I smear some gravy on top of it. (It raises the eyebrows of the person sitting next to me, but certainly ensures that I won't eat the cheesecake.) In doing this I am, in a very unglamorous way, following the example of Odysseus when he had himself bound to the mast of his ship so as not to give in to the song of the sirens. The circumstance in which he made that decision was one in which he was free of temptation, but he was shrewd enough to anticipate the overthrow of control. Such strategies for combating weakness of will John Elster calls 'precommitments' (Elster, 1984: 37ff).

The decision to adopt morality as a fiction is best thought of as a kind of precommitment. It is not being suggested that someone enters a shop, is tempted to steal, decides to adopt morality as a fiction, and thus sustains her prudent though faltering decision not to steal. Rather, the resolution to accept the moral point of view is something that occurred in the person's past, and is now an accustomed way of thinking. Its role is that when entering a shop the possibility of stealing doesn't even enter her mind. If a knave were to say to her 'Why not steal?' she would answer without hesitation 'No!— Stealing is wrong.' What goes through her mind may be exactly the same as what goes through the mind of the sincere moral believer—it need not 'feel' like make-believe at all (and thus it may have the same influence on behavior as a belief). The difference between the two need only be a *disposition* that the fictionalist has (though is not paying attention to): the disposition to deny that anything is really morally wrong, when placed in her most critical context.[11]

But what if the knave carries on: 'But in all seriousness, taking into account philosophical issues, bearing in mind John Mackie's arguments—*why not steal*?' Then, *ex hypothesi*, our fictionalist will 'step out' and admit that there is nothing morally wrong with stealing. So does she then stuff her pockets? No! For she still has all those Hobbesian and Humean reasons to refrain from stealing. It is no part of the argument of this chapter that moral thinking should be followed if it prescribes actions that we do not have good reasons for performing independently of moral considerations. One would deny this at the price of allowing that morality may serve no purpose to the individual at all. If we embrace the view that a believed morality is useful to the individual, then we must be employing some non-moral standard by which to make this assessment. If (as seems correct) an individual's believing that some available action is morally required increases the probability of his performing that action, then it seems plausible to assume that the usefulness to an individual of moral belief lies at least in part in its increasing the probability of his performing those actions that he judges he morally ought. From these assumptions it follows that such actions were useful to him anyway—i.e., that he had a non-moral reason for performing them.

The idea of the precommitment to the moral fiction being a conscious choice that someone makes is an artificial idealization. (In this it differs from pouring gravy on cheesecake.) It is more likely that a person is simply brought up to think in moral terms; the precommitment is put in place by parents. In childhood such prescriptions may be presented and accepted as items of belief (it is not implausible to hold that the best way to encourage prudent habits is to tell children a few white lies); thus thinking of certain types of action as 'morally right' and others as 'morally wrong' becomes natural and ingrained. Later, when a broader and more sophisticated understanding is possible, the person may come to see how philosophically troubling is the idea that there really are actions that people *must* perform, irrespective of whether they wish to, regardless of whether it suits their ends—and if convinced by such arguments she becomes a moral error theorist. But these patterns of thought might be now so deeply embedded that in everyday life she carries on employing them—she finds it convenient and effective to do so, and finds that dropping them leaves her feeling vulnerable to temptations which, if pursued, she judges likely to lead to regret. There is, besides, a practical value to be gained simply from the convenience of carrying on in the manner to which she has grown accustomed. She doesn't cease to be a moral error theorist, but she becomes, in addition, a moral fictionalist.

There are no doubt other ways of combating weakness of will. Perhaps some strategies are, taken alone, more effective than adopting a fictive attitude towards the 'must-be-doneness' of the optimal option. All that the present argument requires is that adopting a fictionalist stance would provide *some* help in strengthening resolve in addition to any other effective strategies. (Bear in mind also that I am not arguing that acting as a bulwark against temptation is the *only* value of morality, so even if my arguments concerning the contribution that a moral fiction may make in this respect fail to convince, moral fictionalism does not thereby fall flat.) In fact, the preceding argument entails that there is at least one other effective way of combating weakness of will. Why, one might start out wondering, isn't the decision to adopt morality as a fiction subject to weakness of will? If the presence of the shiny money within reach is likely to tempt one to grab it, ignoring the voice of prudence that is warning that this will lead to no good end, then why won't the same lure of short-term profit also incite the immediate abandonment of the moral fiction? The answer I gave is that the moral fiction is a precommitment that can exclude from practical deliberation the entertainment of certain options: all going well, the fictional attitude blocks the temptation to steal from even arising (just as does, all going well, sincere moral belief).

But if this answer is reasonable here, then isn't the same kind of answer, the same kind of prudence-reinforcing strategy, available without any fictionalizing entering the picture at all? Why can't a person simply have the precommitment not to steal (plus a precommitment to keep promises, to refrain from initiating violence, etc.)?

It is not clear what it means simply to have 'a precommitment not to steal (etc.).' Perhaps it means a *habit* of not stealing, such that a person is brought up so the thought of stealing simply doesn't enter his mind. Or perhaps it means a habit of feeling sympathy for fellow humans, such that the prospect of harming them by stealing from them motivates one to refrain from doing so. But though encouraging such habits may be a very good way of fortifying clear-headed instrumental reasoning (which, for Hobbesian and Humean reasons, generally comes down against stealing), my contention is that they would work even more effectively if supplemented with *moralized* thought.

Suppose that a person with no moralized thinking (neither as belief nor fiction) were, despite his voice of prudence properly counseling otherwise, for some reason to steal. Let's assume that he has in place a habit of not stealing, and a habit of feeling sympathy for others' suffering, but nevertheless these habits were not on this occasion strong enough to withstand the temptation of short-term profit. How does he now feel? The fact that he has broken a habit may surprise him. The fact that he has hurt someone that he didn't want to hurt may cause him disappointment and distress. But the important thing is that he can feel no *guilt*, for guilt requires the thought that one has done something *wrong*. With no moral concepts in play, this person does not have access to the thought that he *deserves* to be punished for his action; he regrets, but he cannot repent. His active sympathy may prompt in him a desire to alleviate the victim's suffering (he may even feel a desire to return the stolen goods), but since he has no thought that he *must* do something to make amends, were he to become distracted by other matters, such that his sympathy for the victim fades, then there is nothing to propel his deliberations back to the resolution that 'something must be done'. In the end, he has just done something out of character that he wishes he hadn't done. 'Sympathy', J. Q. Wilson once wrote, 'is a fragile and evanescent emotion. It is easily aroused but quickly forgotten; when remembered but not acted upon, its failure to produce action is easily rationalized. The sight of a lost dog or a wounded fledgling can upset us greatly even though we know that the woods are filled with lost and injured animals' (Wilson, 1993: 50).

By comparison, the person who can 'moralize' her thoughts (either as belief or fiction) will feel differently if on occasion she succumbs to temptation. She can tell herself that she has done something *wrong*, that her action was *unfair*, that she must make amends, that she not only has risked punishment, but also *deserves* it. (In addition, she can judge that other felons deserve punishment too—a thought that was unavailable to our previous non-moral agent.) The fact that these more robust forms of self-recrimination are available to the moral thinker when she does steal strongly suggests that when she is behaving herself her motivation not to steal is more reliable and steadfast than that of her non-moral counterpart. Her deliberations and justifications do not end in the thought 'Well, I just don't want to do that', but rather the more vivid and non-negotiable 'That would be wrong.'

Of course, what ultimately determines whether a person will refrain from stealing is the strength of the desire not to steal compared with the desire to do so. The claim is that the thought 'That would be wrong' plays a role in desire-formation and is likely to *strengthen* any desire against stealing that one has as the result of any 'non-moralized' habit. It is true that this thought as a fictive judgment may not play as robust a role in an agent's desiderative life as the thought as a belief, but so long as it reliably pulls *some* weight—so long, that is, as the fictionalist reliably has a pragmatic advantage over the moral eliminativist—then the error theorist is justified in keeping moral discourse as a 'useful fiction'.

Conclusion

The advice 'Maintain moral discourse as a fiction' is not intended to apply necessarily to any agent in any circumstances. It would be unreasonable to expect that it should, especially since the legitimacy of any more authoritative kind of prescription—for example, to the effect that one *must* adopt the moral fiction, irrespective of one's ends or interests—is likely to have been rejected in the prior argument for a moral error theory (the details of which argument this chapter has, for obvious reasons, skirted). It is enough if it turns out to be good advice for *us now*: people who are prone to temptation, epistemically fallible, and familiar with moral thinking. I have offered an argument in support of its being good advice, but of course ultimately it is an empirical matter which depends on the ability to assess far-fetched counterfactuals, and I am the first to admit that it may all turn out to be mistaken. It is possible that moral fictionalism deserves a place on the menu of metaethical options while the prescription urged by those of us on the 'revolutionary wing' of the theory remains poor advice.

Since this paper has presented no arguments in favor of a moral error theory, discussing the prospects of moral fictionalism may seem premature. I agree that the preferred strategy must always be to do our utmost to show that moral discourse is not really flawed at all—and I dare say that nearly all readers believe this battle still to be worth fighting. But the viability of moral fictionalism should be of more than academic interest even to those who are not error theorists, for I suspect that those eager to repudiate the error theoretic position often derive their concern in part from worries about what might *happen* if the theory were to become widely accepted as true. It is viewed not merely as counter-intuitive, but as a genuinely threatening and pernicious doctrine. David Brink, for example, once suggested that we should learn to live with whatever 'metaphysical queerness' is entailed by moral realism if the only alternative 'would undermine the nature of existing normative practices' (Brink, 1989: 173). But if this kind of concern is unjustified—as the possibility of moral fictionalism suggests it may be—then the motivation for resisting a moral error theory is in need of re-examination.[12]

NOTES

This chapter is a rewritten and condensed version of chapters 7 and 8 of *The Myth of Morality* (2001, Cambridge: Cambridge University Press). Some passages are taken straight from this book.

1. Burgess' original distinction was between two forms of nominalism: See also Burgess and Rosen (1997). For criticisms of hermeneutic fictionalism, see Stanley (2001).
2. Walton (1978) makes a similar point.
3. Dahl's story is 'The Wonderful Story of Henry Sugar', in case you're interested. Balzac's *Le Père Goriot* also famously claims of itself that it is neither a fiction nor a romance, but 'ALL IS TRUE'.
4. Autistic children fail to participate properly in games of make-believe, and this corresponds to, and arguably contributes to, a whole range of serious disabilities. See Baron-Cohen (1987); Jarrold *et al.* (1996). For discussion of the evolutionary importance of make-believe play in humans, see Steen and Owen (2001).
5. 'Self-deception' is a contested term. In this paper I avoid any theoretical commitment on the issue, though I should say that on other occasions I would object to the term being stretched to the extent considered.
6. Given that it is in an individual's interests to engage in mutually beneficial contracts, it will be in her interests to support a social system wherein contractual

compliance is enforced. Of course, for any individual the *optimal* scheme is if her neighbors are forced to comply and she alone is able to break contracts and evade punishment—but such an arrangement, we may assume, is not an available option. When the only options concern a *non-discriminating* police force, it will be to each individual's interests to choose the maximally vigilant sovereign power. That way a given individual will have to forego the benefits of cheating others, but stands the best chance of avoiding the proportionally greater costs of being cheated (bearing in mind that the disadvantages of having one's throat cut are far greater than any advantages that may accrue from cutting another's throat).

7. I have altered Hume's text from the first person to the second person singular.

8. Others who reject the view that we have genuine emotions in response to fiction include Kenny (1964) and Budd (1985).

9. The latter hypothesis gains support over the former when one considers that in fictional encounters people enjoy and seek out emotions that they otherwise generally avoid (fear, sadness, etc.). The evolutionary hypothesis holds that the capacity to engage with fiction and make-believe is a kind of 'safe training' for real life risks and opportunities. Natural selection makes the accompanying emotions enjoyable in order to motivate the activity (for the same reason as it makes eating and sex enjoyable). See Steen and Owen (2001).

10. In a study conducted in 1971, it was shown that only 12 percent of sixth graders believed that television commercials told the truth all or most of the time. Lyle and Hoffman (1971).

11. It is worth reminding ourselves that 'critical context' is a term of art, and in other vernacular senses of the phrase it is those times when the person is immersed in the fiction that involve more critical thinking. Working out the plot of a complex novel, for example, may involve a great deal of careful thinking, whereas the thought 'It's all just a fiction' is a simple matter. Nevertheless, in the sense defined, the latter is the more 'critical context' since it questions and challenges the world of the novel. In the same way, though a moral fictionalist will reject moral claims when doing metaethics, this is perfectly consistent with her employment of the moral fiction at other times involving an enormous amount of critical deliberation and careful calculation.

12. Thanks to Stuart Brock, Fred Kroon, and Jerry Vision for useful feedback.

REFERENCES

Ainslie, G. (1975). 'Impulsiveness and Impulse Control.' *Psychological Bulletin*, 82: 463–96.

Baron-Cohen, S. (1987). 'Autism and Symbolic Play.' *British Journal of Developmental Psychology*, 5: 139–48.

Borgida, E. and R. E. Nisbett (1977). 'The Differential Impact of Abstract vs. Concrete Information on Decisions.' *Journal of Applied Social Psychology*, 7: 258–71.

Brink, David (1989). *Moral Realism and the Foundations of Ethics*. Cambridge: Cambridge University Press.

Budd, Malcolm (1985). *Music and the Emotions*. London: Routledge and Kegan Paul.

Burgess, John P. (1983). 'Why I am Not a Nominalist.' *Notre Dame Journal of Formal Logic*, 24: 93–105.

Burgess, John P. and Gideon Rosen, (1997). *A Subject with No Object*. Oxford: Clarendon Press.

Elster, Jon (1984). *Ulysses and the Sirens*. Cambridge: Cambridge University Press.

—— (1985). 'Weakness of Will and the Free-Rider Problem.' *Economics and Philosophy*, 1: 231–65.

Enzle, M. E., R. D. Hansen, and C. A. Lowe (1975). 'Humanizing the Mixed-Motive Paradigm: Methodological Implications from Attribution Theory.' *Simulation and Games*, 6: 151–65.

Garner, R. (1993). 'Are Convenient Fictions Harmful to Your Health?' *Philosophy East and West*, 43: 87–106.

Hobbes, Thomas (1642/1983). *De Cive*. Oxford: Clarendon Press.

Hornstein, H.A., E. Lakind, E. Frankel, and S. Manne (1975).' Effects of Knowledge about Remote Social Events on Prosocial Behaviour, Social Conception, and Mood.' *Journal of Personality and Social Psychology*, 32: 1038–46.

Hume, David (1739/1978). *A Treatise of Human Nature*. Oxford: Clarendon Press.

—— (1751/1983). *Enquiry Concerning the Principles of Morals*. Cambridge, MA: Hackett Publishing Company.

Jarrold, C., J. Boucher, and P. K. Smith (1996). 'Generativity Deficits in Pretend Play in Autism.' *British Journal of Developmental Psychology*, 14: 275–300.

Johnson-Laird, P. and K. Oatley, (2000). 'Cognitive and Social Construction in Emotions.' In M. Lewis and J. Haviland-Jones (eds.), *Handbook of the Emotions*, second edition. New York: Guilford Press.

Kenny, Anthony (1964). *Action, Emotion and Will*. London: Routledge and Kegan Paul.

Lewis, David (1978). 'Truth in Fiction.' *American Philosophical Quarterly*, 15: 37–46.

Lyle, J. and H. Hoffman (1971). 'Children's Use of Television and Other Media.' In J. P. Murray, E. A. Robinson, and G. A. Comstock (eds.), *Television and Social Behavior*, 4. Rockville, MD: National Institutes of Health.

Mackie, John (1977). *Ethics: Inventing Right and Wrong*. New York: Penguin Books.

Quine, Willard Van Orman (1960). *Word and Object*. Cambridge, MA: MIT Press.

Schelling, Thomas (1980). 'The Intimate Contest for Self-Command.' *The Public Interest*, 60: 94–118.

Stanley, Jason (2001). 'Hermeneutic Fictionalism.' *Midwest Studies in Philosophy*, 25: 36–71.

Steen, F. F. and S. A. Owen, (2001). 'Evolution's Pedagogy: An Adaptationist Model of Pretense and Entertainment.' *Journal of Cognition and Culture*, 1: 289–321.

Vision, Gerald (1994). 'Fiction and Fictionalist Reductions.' *Pacific Philosophical Quarterly*, 74: 150–74.

Walton, Kendall L. (1978). 'Fearing Fictions.' *Journal of Philosophy*, 75.1: 5–27.

—— (1990). *Mimesis and Make-Believe*. Cambridge, MA: Harvard University Press.

Wilson, James Q. (1993). *The Moral Sense*. NY: Free Press.

10

Quasi-Realism is Fictionalism

David Lewis

Suppose that Simon Blackburn's quasi-realist program (1984, ch. 6, 1988) has succeeded perfectly on its own terms—something I think not unlikely. The quasi-realist has offered a special semantics for sentential expressions of moral attitudes; he has thereby earned the right to echo everything the moral realist says; and he has chosen to exercise that right. He even echoes all the realist says about moral psychology and metaethics, since those opinions are entangled with the realist's moralizing. Now he challenges us (1993b): wherefore am I a *quasi*-realist rather than a *queasy* realist? Once my agreement with the realist is exceptionless, why doesn't that prove that I'm a realist too?[1]

It's clear enough that the special quasi-realist semantics of assertibility conditions differs from the standard realist truth-conditional semantics. But that doesn't help if, once the quasi-realist semantics is perfected, it becomes inapplicable. It's plausible to think that a semantics is right for someone in virtue of best fitting his linguistic dispositions (and not, say, in virtue of fitting his philosophical predilections, making what he's disposed to say come out true by his own lights). Presumably the realist semantics is right for the realist. It best fits his linguistic dispositions. But once quasi-realism has been perfected, the quasi-realist's linguistic dispositions are exactly the same, so the realist semantics best fits them, so it's right for the quasi-realist too.

'Quietists' take Blackburn's challenge to be unanswerable. Others (for instance Fine, 2001) think it is answerable only if we help ourselves to a primitive distinction between truth *simpliciter* and *factual* truth. (Or between facts and **F*A*C*T*S**, or . . . .) I'd like to think there's an easier answer. We shouldn't look for something the realist says that the quasi-realist will not echo. *Ex hypothesi* there is no such thing. Rather, we look for something the quasi-realist says that the realist will not echo. And when that's what we look for, we find it. So the realist's and the quasi-realist's linguistic dispositions are not, after all, just alike.

There are prefixes or prefaces (explicit or implicit) that rob all that comes after of assertoric force. They disown or cancel what follows, no matter what that may be. Once the assertoric force is cancelled, no amount of tub-thumping will regain it. If you've disowned what follows, it doesn't matter whether you then say just that eating people is wrong, or whether you say it's true in the most robustly realist sense imaginable that eating people is wrong, or whether you say the wrongness of eating people is built into the very fabric of mind-independent reality—whichever you say, it comes pre-cancelled. Here are some examples of disowning prefixes and prefaces.

(1) According to the pack of lies my opponent has told you. . . .
(2) I shall say much that I do not believe, starting *now.*
(3) According to the Sherlock Holmes stories. . . .
(4) What follows is true according to the Holmes stories.
(5) Let's make believe the Holmes stories are true, though they aren't.

I classify (1), (3), and (4) as *prefixes*, (2) and (5) as *prefaces.* (So in view of (4), the distinction I'm drawing is not between complete sentences and mere phrases.) When the assertoric force of what follows is cancelled by a prefix, straightway some other assertion takes its place: an assertion, as it might be, about what my opponent's lies or the Holmes stories say or imply. Not so for prefaces. In the case of (5), a replacement is at least suggested, but it is not yet asserted. In the case of (2), no replacement assertion is even suggested.

I think that when the quasi-realist echoes everything the realist says, one sufficient reason why his 'assertions' are quasi-assertions is that they are preceded, explicitly or implicitly, by a disowning preface. That preface is to be found in the endorsement of projectivism that precedes and motivates his advocacy of quasi-realism (Blackburn, 1984, ch. 5). It is something the quasi-realist says that the realist will not echo.

There is a certain distinctive error that Blackburn takes to be characteristic of moral realism. Let us, for convenience, henceforth reserve the name 'moral realism' for a moral theory that is indeed committed to this error. (I myself think that some theories not guilty of the error deserve the name 'moral realism' equally well.) The distinctive error of 'moral realism' says that there are properties, perhaps non-natural properties, such that we can somehow detect them; and such that when we do detect them, that inevitably evokes in us pro- or con-attitudes toward the things that we have detected to have these properties. ('Inevitably' might mean 'necessarily', or it might mean 'as a matter of exceptionless psychological law'.) *Projectivism* is the view that this is indeed an error; our pro- and con-attitudes actually originate within us as a result of contingent aspects of our psychology and upbringing. Blackburn's quasi-realism is explicitly motivated by the wish to uphold projectivism and to avoid the error it rejects.

By now, morality has been accused of presupposing quite a variety of errors. Most simply, there is the error of supposing that the dictates of morality are divine commands when in truth God does not exist. There is the error of supposing that our moral attitudes are uniform, when in fact they differ widely (Burgess, unpublished). Surely this is indeed an error. To see that it is, we need not consider alien cultures living on remote islands—our friends and neighbors will suffice. Perhaps there is the error of supposing that our underlying dispositions to form moral attitudes are uniform. But it is not obvious that this is an error, since the diversity we observe might be due not to differences in our underlying dispositions but rather to the fact that different ones of us have actualized different ones of our shared dispositions (see Lewis, 1989: 125ff). There is the error of supposing that moral beliefs automatically motivate: one inevitably desires what he judges to be right or good. That is an error, sure enough, as witness the possibility of a sadist enamored of evil for its own sake (Rosen, unpublished). Perhaps there is the error of supposing that moral beliefs automatically motivate the rational: anyone rational inevitably desires what he judges to be right or good. If the rational are those who are good at logic, good at revising their beliefs in the way warranted by their total evidence, and good at serving their desires according to their beliefs, then this is an error, sure enough. But 'rationality' is an elastic notion. If someone sees fit to classify the pursuit of the right and good as an aspect of 'rationality', I am not as sure as I'd like to be that he has exceeded his linguistic rights; and under that usage it is trivially true that moral beliefs automatically motivate the rational. Perhaps there is the error of supposing that the dictates of morality give us reasons for acting regardless of our actual or potential desires (Joyce, 2001). But again I am not sure that this is yet an error, because I am not sure that someone who sees fit to use 'reason' in such an expansive way has exceeded his linguistic rights. I do agree, however, that it is an error to suppose that the dictates of morality give us reasons that are reasons in just the same non-disjunctive sense in which reasons based on serving our actual and potential desires are reasons, so that moral and desire-based reasons can compete for the status of reasons *simpliciter*.

The error Blackburn attributes to 'moral realism' is another error of which morality may stand accused. It overlaps several of the errors previously listed. If it were true, and if all of us were equally capable of detecting the moral properties of things, that would at least tend to make us alike in those of our moral attitudes that are evoked solely by the detection of moral properties; and it would make us still more alike in our dispositions to form such attitudes. If it were true, at least those of our moral beliefs that were evoked solely by the detection of moral properties would inevitably motivate us. If it were true, the question what to say about moral reasons unsupported by actual or potential desire would not arise, because all moral reasons would be supported at least by potential desire.

Morality as such *could* presuppose an error. It consists in part of a (rather ill-defined) system of alleged truths; in part of a practice of appealing to those alleged truths in order to guide one's own conduct or that of others; and maybe in part of other things, for instance a distinctive way of seeing-as. Whatever may be said about the rest of morality, at least the alleged truths might carry presuppositions, and those presuppositions might include one or more of the listed errors (those of them that really are errors). It could be so—but I don't think it is.[2] The system of alleged truths is just too ill-defined.

There are familiar examples of error-ridden theories that could not survive the correction of their errors. Phlogiston theory is one convincing example. The errors are so inextricably involved in the working of the theory that without them it just wouldn't be phlogiston theory (not even if it retained the word 'phlogiston'). Witchcraft theory is a second convincing example. Tapu theory (Joyce, 2001) is a third. Error theorists think that morality is in the same boat.

But other cases of error-ridden theories point in a different direction. The ancient theory of sunrise and sunset posited an absolute vertical: a uniform direction, parallel anywhere to what it is anywhere else, opposite to the uniform direction of gravitational motion. The erroneous ancients thought that when the sun rose, it moved in (approximately) the absolute vertical direction, and when it set it moved in (approximately) the opposite direction. (*How* ancient is this theory? Archaic antiquity. Educated medievals knew better, and so did educated Greeks of classical antiquity.) That was an error, sure enough. But it was not inextricably involved in the working of the theory. Another part of the theory says that when the sun rises its elevation over the horizon increases from zero to nearly a right angle, and when it sets its elevation decreases to zero again. That part (together with what's said about which plane perpendicular to the ground intersects the sun when) is free of error. The ancients believed it, and we believe it too. And this error-free part of the theory is the part that systematizes our observations, and that explains, for example, the behavior of shadows. Even if we suppose that the error-free part is deduced initially from the erroneous part—and by what right could we attribute that deductive order rather than its opposite to the erroneous ancients?—still the erroneous part soon retires and the derived error-free part does the work from then on. So correction of the error leaves most of the working of the theory intact.

I think that morality is more like the ancient theory of sunrise and sunset than it is like phlogiston theory. There may be errors in morality as such but correction of them is not tantamount to the abandonment of morality. Morality may be erroneous, but not essentially erroneous. I further think that the content of morality is sufficiently ill-defined that we cannot show that any errors are errors of morality as such, and not just the errors of some moralists.

But what should we do if, *contra* what I've just said, we become convinced that the error theorists are right and morality as such does indeed presuppose some error? We might abandon morality, as we have abandoned the error-ridden phlogiston theory. Or we might correct morality so that it no longer presupposes the error, unless correction would be tantamount to abandonment. These are the most straightforward responses, but they are not the only ones and they might not be the best. A more conservative alternative is *moral fictionalism*: we could retain morality, but treat it as a fiction. We could cease to hold it true, but we could make believe that it was true—errors and all. (Compare not holding the Holmes stories true while making believe that they are true, something we do quite often.) Joyce (2001) makes an unexpectedly strong case that moral fictionalism need not be either dishonest or irrational, and that it might be a better way to retain the practical benefits of morality than either abandonment or correction.

The same choice of responses is available if, like me, you think that not morality as such, but only some particular system of morality—as it might be, theistic morality or Moorean morality or Kantian morality or 'moral realism'—presupposes one or another of the errors. Again, you have three choices. You could abandon that system; or you could correct it, unless that would be tantamount to abandoning it; or you could treat it as a fiction, make-believedly believing it, errors and all, while at the same time really disbelieving it.

Now we focus our attention in particular on the error of 'moral realism'. I agree that it does indeed presuppose an error, and probably in such a way that correction would be tantamount to abandonment. We can see that quasi-realism and fictionalism are at least very much alike. They share a spirit of respectful, conservative debunking. They aim at avoiding the error of moral realism; but at the same time, they aim at retaining, unscathed, the error-ridden practice.

(You might take fictionalism or quasi-realism in two alternative ways: as possible revisions of our thinking in response to the discovery of an error, or as descriptions of how we are thinking already. Or there is an intermediate alternative: you might describe us—some or all of us—as being in a state of confusion such that fictionalism or quasi-realism would be the minimal unconfused revision of our present state. These alternatives cut across the purported difference between fictionalism and quasi-realism, so I shall not consider them further.)

Fictionalism is an easy way to achieve the avowed aim of the quasi-realist: to earn, and exercise, the right to echo the moral realist while avoiding his errors. The fictionalist is willing to say everything that the moral realist says, provided that he has first provided his disowning preface:

(6) Let's make believe that moral realism is true, though it isn't.

Thereafter he says just what the realist does, including whatever the realist may say about moral properties and facts, the objective truth of moral judgments, and so on and so forth. But the fictionalist is not asserting what he says, rather he is quasi-asserting it because of his disowning preface. So he is not making the errors he might appear to be making. And the reason why he is a kind of quasi-realist, not a queasy realist, is that he says more than the realist would: he provides his disowning preface, the realist never would.

But I think I can say more: Blackburn's quasi-realism *is* just this kind of moral fictionalism. For Blackburn's quasi-realism does not come out of thin air. (If it did, perfected quasi-realism might indeed be indistinguishable from realism.) It is motivated by the previous discussion of projectivism. One of Blackburn's avowed aims is to earn the right to say what the 'moral realist' does: that means either being or make-believedly being a realist. Another of his avowed aims is to avoid the realist's errors: that means not being a realist. Taking these aims together, he aims to make-believedly be a moral realist. So I think the fictionalist's disowning preface to all that comes after has in fact been provided in Blackburn's motivating discussion. When the quasi-realist goes on to exercise his newly earned linguistic rights, the disowning preface robs all he says of assertoric force. Like the explicit fictionalist, he is quasi-asserting what he seemingly asserts.

If this is on the right track, quasi-realism is a variety of moral fictionalism. It earns the right to agree with all the moral realist says in just the same way explicit fictionalism does, whether or not it goes on to earn that right twice over by offering its special semantics.

NOTES

Thanks to Stephanie Lewis for her kind permission to publish this chapter. [Editor].

1. A parallel situation arises in the metaphysics of time. It's famously difficult to distinguish a genuine presentist from a quasi-presentist: a four-dimensionalist who earns the right to echo all the presentist says by insisting that English grammar forbids any use of tenseless verbs. Both alike will deny, for instance, that there are any non-present things. The presentist denies it because he does not believe in non-present things; the quasi-presentist imposter denies it because he thinks—falsely—that it must mean that there are in the present non-present things. Likewise in the metaphysics of modality: we need to distinguish actualists from quasi-actualists.

2. I hope that I have given a fragment of a moral system (Lewis, 1989) that avoids all the listed errors (those of them that are errors) and yet is recognizably still a variety of morality. Values are those properties that we are, under certain ideal circumstances, disposed to value; valuing is an attitude that is connected, but only in a multifariously defeasible way, to desire. My view is a kind of analytic naturalism, though I admit that (like most interesting analyticity) it may be analytic under some and not all legitimate resolutions of semantic indeterminacy. It is a kind of subjectivism, though remote from simpler kinds of subjectivism. It is conditionally relativist: if we turned out to differ in our underlying dispositions to value, 'we' could refer not to everyone, but to as large a uniform population (including the speaker) as we could get away with. Whether my view is realist depends on whether 'realism' is deemed to be committed by definition to the errors that my view is built to avoid.

   What I've said so far is of course a very incomplete fragment of morality. For one thing, it needs completion in the light of empirical information about what we are in fact disposed to value under the appropriate circumstances. We can but guess. (An optimistic guess is that what we are disposed to value coincides fairly well with what some of us actually do value.) Settling the question properly must be left to empirical psychologists—presumably those of the distant future.

   For another thing, as it stands mine is a theory of the good—of values—and not yet of the right. Let us augment it as follows. When we are disposed to value a certain property, it may happen that having that property (or having it to the fullest possible extent) requires unconditional compliance with certain constraints on conduct. (It might even require unthinking compliance—compliance with no thought to the advantages of doing otherwise.) If so, I shall say that the constraints built into the value are the obligations associated with that value.

Since this is an account of obligations associated with particular values, it has the consequence that obligations can be as incommensurable as values themselves. That is an inconvenient predicament for us to be in, sure enough; but it is an advantage, not a drawback, of a theory that it finds us to be in that predicament.

Given obligations, we have much else besides. We have permissions: absences of obligations to refrain. And if we also help ourselves to a causal notion of 'seeing to it that' some proposition holds, we have several different varieties of rights (see Kanger and Kanger, 1966).

REFERENCES

Blackburn, Simon (1984). *Spreading the Word*. Oxford: Oxford University Press.
—— (1988). 'Attitudes and Contents.' *Ethics*, 98: 501–17.
—— (1993b). 'Realism, Quasi, or Queasy?' In John Haldane and Crispin Wright (eds.), *Reality, Representation and Projection*. Oxford: Oxford University Press.
Burgess, John P. (MS). 'Against Ethics.'
Fine, Kit (2001). 'The Question of Realism.' *Philosophers' Imprint*, 1: 1–32.
Joyce, Richard (2002). *The Myth of Morality*. Cambridge: Cambridge University Press.
Kanger, S., and Kanger, H. (1966). 'Rights and Parliamentarianism.' *Theoria*, 32: 85–116.
Lewis, David (1989). 'Dispositional Theories of Value.' *Proceedings of the Aristotelian Society*, Supplementary Volume, 63: 113–37.
Rosen, Gideon (MS). 'Internalism and Common Sense.'

11

Quasi-Realism no Fictionalism

SIMON BLACKBURN

I

David Lewis' chapter 'Quasi-Realism is Fictionalism' starts with a supposition and a comment upon it which are music to my ears:

Suppose that Simon Blackburn's quasi-realist program has succeeded perfectly on its own terms—something I think not unlikely.

Given the controversial nature of the program, this much endorsement from a philosopher and logician of Lewis' stature is pleasant indeed. And for the purpose of this chapter I am going to bask in its light. In other words, I am not going to say very much directly to defend my program, or render it more or less likely to be successful than it is already.

However Lewis goes on to suggest that quasi-realism is a kind of fictionalism, and it is here that our accord comes under strain. I do not think it is. This, of course, may be a merit, in quasi-realism, or may be a demerit. Fictionalism has long grumbled in the background of moral philosophy, with thinkers from Critias to Mandeville, Bentham, and Nietzsche as well as the more explicit Hans Vaihinger being cited as predecessors. And it has been gaining ground of late.[1] Maybe it would be better to be a fictionalist than to be a quasi-realist, or better to amalgamate the two approaches. Lewis himself thought that quasi-realism gained luster from being identified with fictionalism. But I believe on the contrary that my reluctance to be identified with fictionalism stems from a well-founded mistrust of fictionalism itself, at least in its application to the philosophy of evaluative thoughts and practices and discourses. I also believe that quasi-realism, properly understood, makes the deficiencies of fictionalism stand out. However, as we shall find, there may be various positions each claiming the title fictionalism, and some may be further from quasi-realism than others.

Years ago I recognized that the 'quasi' in quasi-realism might mislead people, and I took some care to distance myself from an 'as if' philosophy, holding that we talk 'as if' there are (for instance) rights and duties, although there are none really.[2] In my 1987 paper 'Morals and Modals' I asked:

What then is the mistake of describing such a philosophy [quasi-realism] as holding that 'we talk as if there are necessities when really there are none'? It is the failure to notice that the quasi-realist need allow no sense to what follows the 'as if' *except* one in which it is true. And conversely he need allow no sense to the contrasting proposition in which it in turn is true. He no more need allow such sense than (say) one holding Locke's theory of colour need accept the view that we talk as if there are colours, when there are actually none. This is doubly incorrect, because nothing in the Lockean view forces us to allow any sense to 'there are colours' except one in which it is true; conversely neither need it permit a sense to 'there are actually none' in which *that* is true.

I went on to say that if the words retain an uncorrupted, English, sense then the Lockean and similarly the quasi-realist, holds not just that we talk and think as if there are . . . but that there are.

I suspect that this apparently innocuous position has proved very puzzling to philosophers. What then, they ask, is the distinctive claim of quasi-realism? Is it, as Ronald Dworkin claimed, the Cheshire cat of moral theory?[3] It is very confusing for people when the quasi-realist comes upon the scene with his alarmingly large repertoire of confiscation orders, taking words that used to seem to be the private property of the realist, and giving them unashamedly to the putative anti-realist. But I thought then, and think now, that there is somewhere to stand from which to conduct these debates. As a package, both expressivism, and its ally the quasi-realist construction of various contexts, depend upon the functional distinction between belief and attitude, couched in terms of direction of fit. The package then aims to reconcile the superficial landscape of moral thought, what I call its 'propositional surface' with a genealogy of morals in the voicing of attitude and the demand for practical stances from others. Dworkin himself acknowledges that expressivism is a distinct theory of the nature of moral discourse—that is why he rails against it as he does. So there is something distinctive about expressivism, in which case there is something distinctive about combining it with an explanation and justification, a vindicatory genealogy, of forms of language that used to be thought inaccessible to expressivists.

Dworkin's reaction would be appropriate if expressivism had to stay forever in denial: identifying itself mainly by denying that in ethics we have truth or reason or objectivity. But it does not. It acknowledges these things, but tries to explain why they are appropriate. We dig one layer deeper, asking how it comes to be so that we have these things, and with a good conscience, in ethics. Those who dislike the exercise of digging may want to turn aside, although their plots are all too likely to become infested by worms of doubt. But it is not part of my purpose today to elaborate upon that side of the story.

Instead I want to elaborate upon the point which I took to be made by the comparison with Locke. So suppose someone did interpret Locke, not entirely implausibly, as holding that 'we talk as if there are colours, although there are none really'. It seems then that this Locke would owe us a number of explanations. One would be, that he would need to explain in what way this world is deficient in terms of colour—how does it differ from some other world in which there are colours, really? If we are told that ours is not, really, a coloured world, we cannot make much sense of what we are being asked to believe unless we can also make sense of the reverse property: what would it be for ours to be, really, a coloured world? Unless we understand the one, it is hard to see how we can understand the other. We consider possible modifications to this principle later, but on the face of it, for fictionalism to gain a foothold, we apparently know what it is to talk as if there are colours, although there are none, in which case we need an explanation of what the content of this saying might be.

The question might also be put to this Locke, motivated by the thought that fiction is parasitic on reality. The matter is especially clear if we put it in Lewis' own terms. In his paper 'Truth in Fiction' and its postscript Lewis gives us a number of progressively more sophisticated accounts of 'in the fiction f, F'. He starts with the simple idea that:

A sentence of the form 'in fiction f, F' is true iff F is true at every world where f is told as known fact rather than fiction.

Objections to this arise because we want to say that in the Holmes' stories Holmes has two nostrils. Yet there are distant worlds in which everything is such as it is told in the Holmes stories, but Holmes suffers from the peculiarity of having a third nostril. For Conan Doyle never explicitly enumerates Holmes' nasal cavities. Hence Lewis is led to consider those worlds that depart the least from the actual world, and where the story is told as known fact. Finally, there is some discounting in order to accommodate the world view of those writing the stories. So, for instance, it should not come out that in the Holmes' stories there was an atomic bomb detonated on Hiroshima within the next half century, although in the worlds closest to ours, but where the stories are told as known fact, there was such a bomb. After some gyrations, which need not concern us, the full-dress proposal is that:

A sentence of the form 'in fiction f, F' is non-vacuously true iff, whenever w is one of the collective belief worlds of the community of origin of f, then some world where f is told and known fact and F is true differs less from the world w, on balance, than does any world where f is told as known fact and F is not true.

The immediate consequence that does concern us is that this account requires us to understand the idea of the fiction being told as known fact.

In many cases, including the kinds of rather straightforward fictions on which Lewis concentrates, this requirement poses no problem. In the fiction, a knight called 'Don Quixote' tilts at windmills, and we can readily imagine it being told as known fact that a knight called 'Don Quixote' has tilted at windmills. We can imagine it being recounted as known fact that a blue carbuncle has been retrieved from a goose by a detective called 'Sherlock Holmes'.[4] But suppose we apply this account to the case in hand. To understand the Lockean theory of colour we are imagining, we would need to know what it would be for the fiction to be told as known fact. This implies that we know what it is both for it to be fact, and for that fact to be known. So consider 'canaries are yellow' which , on the account, in our world is told as if true, or should be told as if true, although it is actually just a fiction. Now we ask: is it true in the colour fiction, that canaries are yellow? To answer we need to understand what it is for 'canaries are yellow' to be fact, and to be known as such, although in our world it is not. This is a tall order. If it is neither a fact nor known to be such in our world, what is different in those worlds in which it is? Are canaries even more blazing yellow than they are here? But how does their not being so extremely yellow, if they are not, also disqualify them from being truly yellow as they are?

A similar reaction awaits moral fictionalism. I say that it is bad to neglect the needs of children. According to this version of moral fictionalism, I am taken to be saying that in the moral fiction, it is bad to neglect the needs of children, although it is not bad really. So: what would it be for it to be fact and to be known and told as such, that it is bad to neglect the needs of children? It is not so in this world, evidently, so what is different about worlds in which it is? Do children in that world suffer more? But why would that cast doubt on it being bad to neglect ours?

Lewis' own account of fiction can certainly be queried. Diane Proudfoot has urged that it fails to apply to 'postmodernist' fictions, in which things happen that are impossible, and hence cannot be told as known fact.[5] In the film *The Purple Rose of Cairo*, for example, a character in the audience of a film has an affair with a character on the screen (not the actor, the character). We cannot parse the plot in terms of it being told as known fact that this happened, because it could not have. I agree that this suggests that the problem of content is harder than Lewis' theory suggests, and it may also give some comfort to a fictionalist account of Locke, construed as holding that while colours are 'impossible' a fiction that they exist is not. But it does not itself solve the problem of understanding what the content of the fiction is.

Applied to ethics, it might be better to notice a distinction emphasized by Richard Joyce, between reporting on the content of a fiction, and oneself pretending or making-believe. Moral fictionalism, he says, should work in terms of the latter notion.[6] It is preferable to aim at an account whereby we make-believe that things are thus and so, rather than one in which we report, truly or falsely, on the content of some already given make-believe. This may well be right, for apart from anything else, moral fictionalism presented in Lewis' way needs to suppose that there is such a thing as *the* moral fiction. Whereas the painful facts of diversity suggest that there are as many moral fictions as there are forms of life that embody the values and obligations of which they talk. But once more, working in terms of make-believe does not avoid the problem that we have to have fixed a content for what we pretend to be true. If after reading some skeptic we only make-believe that there are colours or values or duties, we still need to know what it is that we are pretending, and that requires knowing the difference between worlds allegedly unlike ours, in which there are colours or values and duties, and worlds including ours in which there are not. We need to know how it is that our world fails to contain super canaries, which are truly yellow, and only contains poor facsimiles which are not.

II

Lewis' own chapter on fictionalism and quasi-realism is built around the notion of an error. His attachment to moral fictionalism is that it is a 'conservative alternative' to the idea that morality in and of itself is tainted with error, in something like the way in which phlogiston theory or witchcraft explanations are so tainted. If we come to believe in this error, one response is to abandon the whole thing: to cease to go in for morality, just as we have grown out of phlogiston and witchcraft theories. Another is to correct the error, retaining only whatever part of the practice kept free of it. But the fictionalist alternative is to continue as before, only prefacing our sayings with some indication that we are making believe that what follows is true. Lewis writes:

> You might take fictionalism or quasi-realism in two alternative ways: as possible revisions of our thinking in response to the discovery of an error, or as descriptions of how we are thinking already. Or there is an intermediate alternative: you might describe us—some or all of us—as being in a state of confusion such that fictionalism or quasi-realism would be the minimal unconfused revision of our present state.

And he goes on to claim that fictionalism is an easier way to gain the right to echo everything the realist says but without his mistakes. The fictionalist say everything the most doughty moral realist ever says, but only after a first, disowning preface: let's make believe that what's to come is true, though it isn't. After the disowning preface, the fictionalist is no longer asserting what he says, 'rather he is quasi-asserting it because of his disowning preface'.

By my lights, this raises rather a lot of questions. To explain them, we need to go through various possibilities, concerning the status of the hovering error. In particular, we need to ask whether the error, to which both fictionalists and quasi-realists are supposed to react, lies in the practice itself, or only in what some special theorists, misguided philosophers called realists, say about the practice, or yet again in some awkward amalgam or fusion of the two.[7]

The first alternative is that the error lies in the practice. That is, some first-order claims, the kind of things people come up with as they moralize in classrooms or parliaments, talk shows and tabloids are in themselves erroneous. They are erroneous enough that a clear-sighted person would not want to assert them, but would be content with something less, such as pretending or making-believe that they are true for some purpose or another.

There are two major problems with this alternative. The first is finding a reason for thinking that there is indeed an error just where this alternative places it. It is not so very clear how there can be. If the preacher says that it is bad to neglect children, he risks error if on the contrary it is good, or at worst indifferent, to neglect children. We can hold that he is in error but in everyday life only if we hold that one of these other positions, each of them moral, is not in error. But how is there scope for holding that all three are in error?

The answer must be that the error lay in picking up the vocabulary in the first place. Moralizing and evaluating, asserting any of the three options, is the culprit. Positions of this shape are certainly possible. If I am convinced, for example, that the everyday conception of free-will conceals metaphysical horrors such as Cartesian dualism, I will not respond to the assertion that we have free-will by saying that we do not, but by the kind of plea familiarly made by Richard Rorty, to junk the vocabulary, grow out of the discourse, change the subject. The whole conversation conceals too many presuppositions that I reject.

But if this is the model for ethical fictionalism, expressivism and its loyal ally quasi-realism stand foursquare in the way. For the combination undermines any obvious reason for imputing error to assertions made with the evaluative vocabulary in the first place. The diagnosis of error takes the form 'you wouldn't or shouldn't be asserting any of those things (bad, good, or indifferent to neglect children) unless you held M' where M represents some large scale, philosophical mistake. Examples might be: 'you wouldn't or shouldn't be asserting any of those things unless you held that there exists a timeless lawgiver in heaven, or unless you held that all human beings think alike on this, or unless you held that your opinion was the deliverance of pure rationality, or unless you held that some properties are in and of themselves magnetic, or...'

But quasi-realism shows us how to avoid any such thoughts. You can hold that it is bad to neglect children without being hostage to any of them. You assert it, thereby voicing your stance or attitude or prescription or desire. We thereby tell how the world would have to move to conform to your norms or standards, and we know what attitude to child neglect we need to have in order sincerely to echo you. Neither you nor we, your audience, need to care a jot about lawgivers, consensus, pure rationality, or magnetic properties. You presumably care about children's needs, and good for you.

Another kind of critique would be that it is somehow immature, bad form, to moralize and evaluate at all. We should grow out of saying 'should'. Apart from the self-referential trap into which this seems to have fallen, there is the insuperable difficulty of suggesting what life could be like without evaluation, grading, comparing, advising, esteeming and all the flux of prescriptions and attitudes, emotions and desires, that we would be being asked to give up. So we can safely ignore this kind of nihilism or braggadocio.

Here we must beware of a bad argument for fictionalism. Consider the inference:

We talk as if there are magnetic moral properties.
There are none really.
So: to retain respectability, we should see ourselves as only making-believe, pretending.

This argument fails because it is insufficiently generous with 'as if'. Perhaps it is right to say that we talk as if there are magnetic moral properties. But we also talk as if we are expressing practical attitudes in a language well-adapted for that purpose. Since that is what we are doing, we should not be seen as pretending anything at all. The coincidence between expressive language and metaphysically suspect, loaded language is merely epiphenomenal. That is, the actual phenomena of moral life may be 'as if' something metaphysically false is true. That would be one explanation of our adopting them. But they may also be as if some vindicatory genealogy is true. That would be a different explanation of our adopting them, and according to me the true one. A phenomenon can be 'as if' p, and also 'as if' some contrary, q. And q may be the true explanation and support of the practice, whereas p is not. By analogy, a nonogenarian who is unfailingly cheerful and hopeful might be said to behave as if she thinks she will live for ever. But she is also behaving as if she thinks that her remaining years, however many they are, will be better if she is unfailingly cheerful and hopeful, and since this thought is true and probably explains her attitude, any inclination to talk her as in the grip of error, or at best living out a fiction, is quite unjustified.

This means that fictionalism should not be presented simply as the philosophy that we talk as if something is true which is not. It should be the richer doctrine that the false content is integral to our practice, which must retreat to make-believe once this falsity is exposed. But the quasi-realist will dissent, because he will deny that a false content is integral to and explains our practice.

The second set of problems with this version of fictionalism arises if we turn to the positive proposal. Here, we are supposed to admit the diagnosis of error, right inside the first-order practice, but we are counseled to make-believedly assert the first order claim. We make believe that it is bad to neglect children. The quasi-realist, once more, finds this hard to understand, as a general proposal. Of course, we can play at moralizing; there are, one is given to understand, erotic games in which partners make-believe that one of them has been naughty, en route to further play-acting. But they hardly serve as representative specimens of practical life. Apart from anything else they seem parasitic on attitudes that have a life outside the game. Otherwise one might hazard that the erotic game would not work at all. It is no good pretending to attitudes that have no existence outside pretences.

So let us put aside games, and ask how else the make-believe works. Is the suggestion that we pretend to attitudes that we do not really have? Fie upon such hypocrisy. But if we do have the attitudes, perhaps campaigning for them, demanding them from others, putting our shoulders to the wheel of changing the world for the better, what false modesty prevents us from expressing them with all the force we can muster? On the face of it ethics is the last place in the world in which we are happy to preface our assertions and insistences with modest disclaiming prefaces. If I think that you are completely out of line, I am not only making-believe that you are completely out of line, even as I thump the table, go purple in the face, march you out of the door and forbid you to come back into my sight.

At this point I should enter a caveat. It might sound, from what I have said, that expressivism and quasi-realism are together morally conservative, protecting our everyday practices from any kind of thought that might seem to compel retreat. But this is not necessarily so. Attitudes vary with beliefs, and if relevant beliefs are shown to be false, the attitudes may have to change with them. It is especially the practices and attitudes associated with what Bernard Williams called 'the morality system' that excite philosophers in this direction. Thus Elizabeth Anscombe supposed that some considerable part of the attitudes and practices associated with the idea of moral obligation made no sense without the idea of a lawgiving God.[8] And it is often supposed that a lot of our practices of assigning or taking responsibility, or of succumbing to guilt, presuppose an untenable view of free will, and therefore represent ways of thinking about life or reacting to it that are defective. Thus Bernard Williams held that moral guilt involved the idea of responsibility 'all the way down', or in other words a complete immunity from all the 'moral luck' that is the inevitable bequest of our historical, contingent natures, and hence depends on a view of life that could only be fantastical.[9] I am not sure that his thought is true, but it might be, and if it is the attitudes and practices must retreat. Williams also lamented the tendency for the idea of moral obligation to take over the entire domain of the ethical, subjecting those of us in its grip to ever less realistic modes of self-consciousness.

Williams (and Nietzsche) may have over-interpreted the 'morality system', supposing that the fortuitous attitudes common to a certain culture and time go deeper than they do. But if their criticisms are right, then there is something unhealthy about the moral style that they diagnose. Change would be desirable, just as, I would say, it was desirable for us to stop thinking in terms of sin, with its concomitant ideas of pollution and abasement, corruption and disgust. But notice that these critiques suggest nothing at all in favour of a form of retreat that continues with the everyday-sounding assertions and verdicts, only prefacing them with a silent make-believe disclaimer. Fictionalism is by no means indicated. When Nietzsche mounted his attack on morality, partly because of its entanglement with just such responses to life as those that bothered Williams, I do not suppose he anticipated the response that yes, he was right, but an adequate response is to continue as before only with our fingers crossed. He wanted the attitudes to wither, not to continue only protected by a 'once upon a time,' or 'in the dream' preface. Insofar as Williams or Nietzsche or Anscombe convince us, this is what we should want as well. And to the extent that we cannot quite see how the improvements should go we are not finding ourselves quite convinced, either. Perhaps in our hearts we believe that even 'the morality system', let alone morality and ethics in general, are not quite as tainted as these critics think.

The idea that fictionalism is an adequate response to such writers as Nietzsche or Williams is especially ironic, given that it is the burden of their complaint that the attitudes they dislike are only kept afloat by fictions. According to them it is only because we lie to ourselves about who we are or what we might be that the practices and attitudes sustain themselves. Fiction is not part of the solution—it is the central core of the problem. Neither Nietzsche nor Williams think that we understand ourselves perfectly well, but then make up a fiction about obligation, so that everything would be in order once we recognized it as a fiction. They think we misunderstand ourselves, and that the aspects of morality which they deplore are the unfortunate children of that misunderstanding.

III

That was how the issue played out if the error was found in our first-order practices. What if it is placed more in the domain of the theorist? The idea now is not that there is anything erroneous in moral practice per se, but only in the things that some philosophers, realists, have said about it. One of the lessons of quasi-realism is that it is not easy to pinpoint this error, since even the realists favourite talk of truth, knowledge, and the rest can be sanitized. But let us suppose that there is an error. Suppose a philosopher does have a conception of how moral practice works, or what its aspirations are, that is defective on this count. He believes something very queer, for instance that there is literally a unique set of moral tablets stored up in a place called heaven, and that the truth of a moral opinion consists in its derivability from what is on the tablets. Let us call this theorist a 'Reealist'. The Reealist interpretation of what we say when we assert that it is bad to neglect children is that this proposition is derivable from what is on the tablets, and he can express this by saying that Reealy it is bad to neglect children.

Is fictionalism a good response to the Reealist? It might be. Suppose the Reealist is a bit of a brute. He does not just want you to agree that it is bad to neglect children, but also to assent to his theory. To save embarrassment you might want to say 'Reealy it is bad to neglect children' but you might also want to cross your fingers behind your back, saying it with what Catholics called a mental reservation, a private or concealed sign that in truth you only assent to the view that in the Reealist fiction, it is bad. You thus humour the brute, just as you might humour your devout mother by saying the words 'Jesus saves', privately holding that in the fiction Jesus saves.

But in the absence of emotional pressure or other threats, why would you want to humour the Reealist? Much better to say outright what you actually think, which is that this Reealist theory is untrue, and since much better accounts of moralizing are on the table, there is no point in pretending that it is true.

Perhaps that last remark needs qualifying. Perhaps humanity is so depraved that only myths and fictions keep us together. On pragmatic grounds, we may do better to assent to Reealist rubbish, because too much of the practice would fall to pieces if the people came to realize that Reealism is false. We need what Williams called a Government House attitude. There could be wisdom in this, but I very much doubt whether there is. Morality survived the loss of the religious myth without very much trouble, and I cannot but think it self-flattery for any philosopher to suppose that it needs an equivalent philosophical sustaining myth to supply its place. People will go on campaigning for children, or thumping the tables and showing each other the door without help from us. We need not disguise the truth, or play along with bad theory.

IV

The third location for the error lies in a combination of the other two. Perhaps there is an unholy fusion of first-order practice in the pulpit or the talk show, and some kind of other thoughts about the content of the practice or its empirical nature or its consequences. A bad philosophy has seeped out of the study and into the market place. And as a result our everyday moral practices are tainted. However, tainted though they are, we need them. Hence the recommendation that we go on, ruefully as it were, moralizing away, but all the time with our fingers crossed behind our backs, a silent disclaiming preface. We make-believe that all is well.

I can imagine situations that deserve this diagnosis. Here is one. Take the concept of a right, one of Bentham's own outstanding examples of a fiction. Suppose everyday practice shows us seamlessly supposing two things true of rights:

(1) Peoples' rights give even superpowers beyond the reach of their resentment, reasons to treat them decently;

(2) Peoples' rights ensure that whoever does not treat them decently will come to grief.

Now suppose I learn to my confusion that nothing satisfies both conditions. Whatever gives superpowers reasons to treat powerless people decently has nothing to do with whether they will come to grief if they do not. It turns out that we had injected a lot of wishful thinking into our conception of a right, confusing moral weight with actual weight. Rights are fictions.

Was our mistake first-order or second-order? It might be hard to say. On the one hand, we suppose rights are embedded in discourse about reasons for refraining from harm. On the other hand, we suppose they commonly crop up in arguments apparently designed to appeal to self-interest as a reason for respecting them. The first places them squarely within first-order discourse: Announcing a right is announcing a boundary to indecent conduct. The second seems more second-order, telling of one of the consequences of infringing rights. And each clause is adequate to one part of our practice, but they are not both true.

Here fictionalism might be a kind of remedy. It is, as Lewis says, more conservative than abandoning the notion of a right altogether. We might want to go on using the term as we talk to the superpower, but with our own mental reservation.

On the other hand, we might not. If the administration to whom we talk is not that much less insightful than ourselves, it too will have discovered the problem. It is then poised to dismiss rights talk with even more contempt than it instinctively does anyhow. Maybe it would be wise to shift our ground, deploying some set of moral concepts behind which we can put our shoulders more wholeheartedly—as Bentham thought.

I do not really believe that this model applies to our actual use of the concept of a right, which I see as centrally identified through the placing of boundaries, and only tangentially involved with predictions of harm. And if it does not apply to a culturally thick and supposedly Johnny-come-lately concept like that, it is much less to apply to the central concepts of reason for action, the good and the right.

As I read them, moral philosophers attracted to this model and to consequent fictionalism are perhaps over-impressed by the best-fit-to-the-platitudes model of reference fixing. At any rate, this makes us more likely to detect errors taken to be integral to practice, and more pessimistic about simply avoiding the errors and carrying on without them. So we trawl the market place and churches, to find what the folk sayings are. We find, for instance, that

good little girls don't suck their thumb
good people always know exactly what to do
the wicked shall be laid low and the good will inherit life everlasting

Earnestly writing these down, we become skeptical whether the 'folk-concept of the good' has any application at all, since there is unlikely to be any property that makes all of them true. But we have been taught that we cannot just excise bits of the folk concept without irreparably altering it. And then, if we do not want to do this, but we do want to carry on with a clean conscience, we need to keep our fingers crossed or enter a mental reservation. It is good not to neglect your kids becomes a fraught half-truth, and it is better intellectually if we only make-believe it is true.

Obviously, the quasi-realist does not believe a word of this. The folk may say as many weird things as they like about who is good, what follows from being good, or what are the consequences of being good. It does not affect in the least what they are doing when they say that something is good, nor our perfect right to go on and use the term as full-bloodedly as we wish, with no disclaimers, finger-crossing, make-believes, or mental reservations. Incidentally a staunch ally in this stance is Kant, who insisted so steadily on the autonomy of ethics, whose authority is dependent neither on external rewards nor on empirical convergence of opinion.

V

Much of what I have tried to say about moral fictionalism may transfer to other cases. Consider the modal case.

It is commonly thought, as Lewis himself thought, that modal realism has the virtue of taking possible worlds talk at face value. But does it? What value does such talk wear on its face?

It all depends what I am doing when I say that there is a possible world with a talking donkey, or that in all possible worlds, such-and-such is the case. Am I plunging carelessly into the most extravagant ontology? Or am I simply choosing a useful language for expressing things that intellectually or meta-physically I allow—talking donkeys, perhaps—and other things I forbid—$2 + 2$ being anything other than 4, or water being anything other than H_2O?

Once more, if Lewis' ontology makes us nervous, we might prefer to see ourselves as at best talking as if there Reeally are possible worlds. And we might go on to think we save our souls by only making-believe that there are Reeally possible worlds. But we might want to ditch the Reeally bit. When philosophers first became excited by using possible worlds as models, after their introduction by Kanger and Kripke, nobody seemed very worried about their status as fact or fiction. It seems to have been felt that they did the job, for instance of explaining various inference patterns in modal logic, regardless of how they were taken. So, for instance, take the fact that you cannot infer from 'possibly p' and 'possibly q' to 'possibly p & q'. It was felt to cast light on this to think of the modal operator *as if* it were a quantifier, and notice the parallel invalidity in first-order logic. Until Lewis forced the question, my impression is that most philosophers were happy to take the insight, and to ignore the nature of the *as if*.[10]

My strategy is to say that while we talk superficially as if there Reeally are possible worlds, we also talk as if we have found a neat way of tabulating modal commitments, policing our mental life and our sayings and keeping track of inferences and structures in what we allow and disallow. And in that case our commitments can be as full-blooded as we wish. We can put our hands on our hearts and assert. If we are met by dire Quinean threats of ontological overload and capsize, my lifejacket is simple security in what we are doing, the procedures we are adopting. Nobody with that lifejacket needs a metaphysical one as well.

VI

I should like to close by admitting that this chapter has proceeded in the light of one doubtful premise, and perhaps one which the case of possible worlds highlights. I have followed Lewis in supposing that when we talk of fictions, we know the contrast with fact. Now, just as Austin found himself inclined to play Old Harry with the distinction between constative or truth-orientated speech, and other kinds of speech, we might query whether all talk of fiction depends on understanding this contrast.[11] Might there be stories where the contrast is blurred or vague, or even impossible to make out? There might be a practice in which people just say these words, and then they have various consequences, but where it is not so much that there is a contrast with questions of truth or representation of known fact, as that interest in these things simply does not arise. Yet the words may be said with conviction, and they may have important practical consequences.

I have in mind here the situation exemplified by a certain kind of 'Wittgensteinian' modern theology. In a nutshell, there is a set of words, some of which sound to be telling a story, some of which sound to make claims on what exists, some of which sound like poetry or exhortations or requests. The story is told, the words are repeated with conviction, and often any variation is frowned upon. The words *pronounce* on apparent events and apparent hopes and fears, perhaps en route to pronouncing about human life in general. And these pronouncements are acted upon, unlike the sayings of an acknowledged storyteller. But the story does not admit of inquisition, in the way it would if we were in a more everyday context. For example, although the words to be said might include 'God's eye is all-seeing', as Wittgenstein said, it does not do to ask whether God has eyebrows, or what colour his pupils are.[12]

We can directly interrogate practitioners about truth, but if we do the answer is likely to be of little help. If the practitioner is asked whether what he is saying is intended to be true, the only answer is that indeed it is. The thing to say is that 'God's eye sees everything', and in familiar deflationist fashion, if it is right to say this, then it is right to tack 'it is true that' on the front.

Obviously there are serious problems of interpretation that arise here. What are the practitioners doing, what do they take themselves to be doing? The present question is whether it is right to construe them in fictionalist terms. I should say not, at least with the understandings of fiction so far before us. There is no retreat from full-blown commitment, no revealing moment when the participants cheerfully admit that it was all made up. Neither is there any tendency for practitioners to contrast what our world is like with a better one where the things they say are literally true. These trappings of story-telling are absent, while others, like indeterminacies of place (which direction does heaven lie in?) or time (perhaps these things happened in the dreamtime) are present.

Of course, those of us brought up as robust Enlightenment atheists will find plenty of moral reasons to dislike this story-telling practice. We may say that in their actions, which is where it counts, these people show that they believe what they are saying, but willfully blind themselves as to its improbability. And we will remark that if Wittgenstein has the status of one religion right, then he has the status of all of them right, leaving practitioners to worry about their tendencies to exclusivity and mutual accusations of heresy and error. I raise the issue here not to give comfort to theists, but to reflect further on issues of belief and commitment, truth and reality. Similar issues could be raised with, for instance, the place of metaphor and models in what is usually presented as strict scientific truth, with the associated contrast between different kinds of acceptance.[13] But that must be for another day.

NOTES

1. In parallel with fictionalism about scientific theories (constructive empiricism is the modern fountainhead, revealed in Bas van Fraassen (1980). Fictionalism about mathematics is found in Hartry Field (1980). Modal fictionalism was spearheaded by Gideon Rosen (1990).

2. This might be advanced as a *descriptive* thesis—this is how we do understand what we are doing. Or, it might be *prescriptive*—this is what we ought to understand ourselves as doing. For the moment, the difference is not important, although it becomes so below.

3. Ronald Dworkin (1996).

4. Some cases are harder: we could tell a fiction in which nobody knows that the treasure is in the cupboard, but it is not so easy to imagine it being told as known fact that nobody knows that the treasure is in the cupboard.

5. Diane Proudfoot (MS).

6. Richard Joyce (2001).

7. The same difficulty over locating the error has always seemed to me difficult for John Mackie. See especially my (1993c).

8. G. E. M. Anscombe (1981).

9. Williams' (1985: 195) critique of 'the morality system' makes other, subtle, charges as well. For comparison between Nietzsche and Williams, see Maudemarie Clark (2001).

10. I am grateful here to conversation with André Gallois.

11. J. L. Austin (1962).

12. I discuss this case further in my (2003).

13. For some initial puzzles, see my (2002).

REFERENCES

Anscombe, G. E. M. (1981). 'Modern Moral Philosophy.' In *Collected Philosophical Papers*, 3: 26–42. Minneapolis: Minneapolis University Press.

Austin, John L. (1962). *How to Do Things with Words*. Oxford: Oxford University Press.

Blackburn, Simon (1993c). 'Error and the Phenomenology of Value.' In *Essays in Quasi-Realism*. New York: Oxford University Press.

—— (2002). 'Realism: Deconstructing the Debate.' *Ratio*, 15: 111–34.

—— (2003). 'Fiction and Conviction.' In *Philosophical Papers*, 32: 243–60.

Clark, Maudemarie (2001). 'On the Rejection of Morality: Bernard Williams's Debt to Nietzsche.' In R. Schacht (ed.), *Nietzsche's Postmoralism: Essays on Nietzsche's Prelude to Philosophy's Future*: 100–22. Cambridge: Cambridge University Press.

Dworkin, Ronald (1996). 'Objectivity and Truth: You'd Better Believe It.' *Philosophy and Public Affairs*, 25: 27–139.

Field, Hartry (1980). *Science Without Numbers*. Princeton: Princeton University Press.

Joyce, Richard (2002). *The Myth of Morality*. Cambridge: Cambridge University Press.

Proudfoot, Diane (MS). 'Telling it as it Could Not Be.'

Rosen, Gideon (1990). 'Modal Fictionalism.' *Mind*, 99.395: 327–54.

van Fraassen, Bas C. (1980). *The Scientific Image*. Oxford: Oxford University Press.

Williams, Bernard (1985). *Ethics and the Limits of Philosophy*. Cambridge, MA: Harvard University Press.

References

Adams, Ernest W. (1975). *The Logic of Conditionals*. Dordrecht: D. Riedel.

Adams, Fred, Robert Stecker, and G. Fuller (1992). 'The Semantics of Thoughts.' *Pacific Philosophical Quarterly*, 73: 375–89.

Adams, Fred, and Robert Stecker (1993). 'Vacuous Singular Terms.' *Mind and Language*, 9: 387–401.

Ainslie, G. (1975). 'Impulsiveness and Impulse Control.' *Psychological Bulletin*, 82: 463–96.

Alston, William P. (1996). *A Realist Conception of Truth*. Ithaca, NY: Cornell University Press.

Anscombe, G. E. M. (1981). 'Modern Moral Philosophy.' In *Collected Philosophical Papers*, 3: 26–42. Minneapolis: Minneapolis University Press.

Armstrong, David M. (1978). *Universals and Scientific Realism*, 2: *A Theory of Universals*. Cambridge: Cambridge University Press.

Austin, John L. (1962). *How to Do Things with Words*. Oxford: Oxford University Press.

Ayer, Alfred J. (1946). *Language, Truth and Logic*. London: Gollancz.

Bach, Kent (1987). *Thought and Reference*. Oxford: Oxford University Press.

—— (1993). 'Sometimes a Great Notion: A Critical Notice of Crimmins' *Talk about Beliefs*.' *Mind and Language*, 8: 431–41.

—— (1997). 'Do Belief Reports Report Beliefs?' *Pacific Philosophical Quarterly*, 78: 215–41.

Balaguer, Mark (1996). 'A Fictionalist Account of the Indispensable Applications of Mathematics.' *Philosophical Studies*, 83: 291–314.

—— (2000). *Platonism and Anti-Platonism in Mathematics*. Oxford: Oxford University Press.

—— (2001). 'A Theory of Mathematical Correctness and Mathematical Truth.' *Pacific Philosophical Quarterly*, 82: 87–114

Baldwin, Thomas (1998). 'Modal Fictionalism and the Imagination.' *Analysis*, 58.2: 72–5.

Barker, Peter and Bernard Golstein (1998). 'Realism and Instrumentalism in Sixteenth Century Astronomy: A Reappraisal.' *Perspectives on Science*, 6.3: 232–57.

Barnes, Jonathan (1982). 'The Beliefs of a Pyrrhonist.' *Proceedings of the Cambridge Philological Society* NS., 28: 1–29. Reprinted in Burnyeat and Frede (1997).

Barnes, Julian (1984). *Flaubert's Parrot*. New York: McGraw Hill.

Baron-Cohen, S. (1987). 'Autism and Symbolic Play.' *British Journal of Developmental Psychology*, 5: 139–48.

Bealer, George (1982). *Quality and Concept*. Oxford: Clarendon Press.

Beaney, Michael (1997). *The Frege Reader*. Oxford: Basil Blackwell.

Bentham, Jeremy (1843). *The Complete Works of Jeremy Bentham*, 8, John Bowring and William Tait (eds.).

—— (1932). *The Theory of Fictions*. In Ogden (ed.), *Bentham's Theory of Fictions*. New York: Harcourt, Brace and Company

Blackburn, Simon (1984). *Spreading the Word*. Oxford: Oxford University Press

—— (1988). 'Attitudes and Contents.' *Ethics*, 98: 501–17. Reprinted in Blackburn (1993a).

—— (1993a). *Essays in Quasi-Realism*. New York: Oxford University Press.

—— (1993b). 'Realism, Quasi, or Queasy?' In John Haldane and Crispin Wright (eds.), *Reality, Representation and Projection*. Oxford: Oxford University Press.

—— (1993c). 'Error and the Phenomenology of Value.' Reprinted in Blackburn (1993a).

—— (2002). 'Realism: Deconstructing the Debate.' *Ratio*, 15: 111–34.

—— (2003). 'Fiction and Conviction.' In *Philosophical Papers*, 32: 243–60.

Blackwell, Richard J. (1991). *Galileo, Bellarmine, and the Bible: Including a Translation of Foscarini's Letter on the Motion of the Earth*. Notre Dame, Indiana: University of Notre Dame Press.

Boghossian, Paul (1990). 'The Status of Content.' *Philosophical Review*, 99: 157–84.

Borgida, E. and R. E. Nisbett (1977). 'The Differential Impact of Abstract vs. Concrete Information on Decisions.' *Journal of Applied Social Psychology*, 7: 258–71.

Brandom, Robert (1994). *Making It Explicit*. Cambridge, MA: Harvard University Press.

Braun, David (1993). 'Empty Names.' *Noûs*, 27: 449–69.

—— (2005). 'Empty Names, Fictional Names, Mythical Names.' *Noûs*, 39.

Brink, David (1989). *Moral Realism and the Foundations of Ethics*. Cambridge: Cambridge University Press.

Brock, Stuart (1993). 'Modal Fictionalism: A Response to Rosen.' *Mind*, 102: 147–50.

—— (2002). 'Fictionalism about Fictional Characters.' *Noûs*, 36.1: 1–21.

Budd, Malcolm (1985). *Music and the Emotions*. London: Routledge and Kegan Paul.

Burgess, John P. (MS). 'Against Ethics.'

—— (1983). 'Why I am Not a Nominalist.' *Notre Dame Journal of Formal Logic*, 24: 93–105.

Burgess, John P. and Gideon Rosen (1997). *A Subject with No Object*. Oxford: Clarendon Press.

Burnyeat, Miles (1980). 'Can the Sceptic Live his Scepticism?' In Richard Rorty, Quintin Skinner, and Jerome Schneewind (eds.), *Philosophy in History: Essays in the Historiography of Philosophy*. Cambridge: Cambridge University Press, 1984. Reprinted in Burnyeat and Frede (1997).

Burnyeat, Miles and Michael Frede (1997). *The Original Sceptics: A Controversy.* Cambridge, MA: Hackett Publishing.

Byrne, Alex (1993). 'Truth in Fiction: The Story Continued.' *Australasian Journal of Philosophy*, 71.1: 24–35.

Carnap, Rudolf (1950). 'Empiricism, Semantics and Ontology.' *Revue International de Philosophie*, 4: 20–40. Reprinted in *Meaning and Necessity: A Study in Semantics and Modal Logic*, second edition. Chicago: University of Chicago Press, 1956.

Chalmers, David (1996). *The Conscious Mind*. Oxford: Oxford University Press.

Chihara, Charles (1979). 'The Semantic Paradoxes: A Diagnostic Investigation.' *Philosophical Review*, 88: 590–618.

—— (1984). *Ontology and the Vicious-Circle Principle*. Ithaca, NY: Cornell University Press.

Churchland, Paul (1981). 'Eliminative Materialism and the Propositional Attitudes.' *Journal of Philosophy*, 78.2: 67–90.

Clark, Maudemarie (2001). 'On the Rejection of Morality: Bernard Williams's Debt to Nietzsche.' In R. Schacht (ed.), *Nietzsche's Postmoralism: Essays on Nietzsche's Prelude to Philosophy's Future*. Cambridge: Cambridge University Press.

Cohen, L. Jonathan (1992). *An Essay on Belief and Acceptance*. Oxford: Clarendon Press.

Copernicus, Nicholas (1995). *On the Revolutions of the Heavenly Spheres*. Charles Glenn Wallis (trans.). Prometheus Books.

Crimmins, Mark (1992). *Talk About Beliefs*. Cambridge, MA: MIT Press.

—— (1998). 'Hesperus and Phosphorus: Sense, Pretense and Reference.' *Philosophical Review*, 107.1: 1–47.

Currie, Gregory (1990). *The Nature of Fiction*. Cambridge: Cambridge University Press.

Danto, Arthur C. (1986). *The Philosophical Disenfranchisement of Art*. New York: Columbia University Press.

Davidson, Donald (1984). 'What Metaphors Mean.' In Davidson, *Inquiries into Truth and Interpretation*. Oxford: Clarendon Press.

Descartes, René (1960). *Discourse on the Method of Rightly Conducting the Reason and Seeking Truth in the Sciences,* 111. In *Descartes, Philosophical Essays,* Lawrence J. Lafleur (trans). Indianapolis: Bobbs-Merril.

Deutsch, Harry (1991). 'The Creation Problem.' *Topoi*, 10: 209–25.

Devitt, Michael (1995). *Coming to our Senses*. New York: Cambridge University Press.

de Zayas, M. (1912), 'The Sun Has Set.' *Camera Work*, 39: 17.

Divers, John (1995). 'Modal Fictionalism Cannot Deliver Possible Worlds Semantics.' *Analysis*, 55.2: 81–8.

—— (1999). 'A Modal Fictionalist Result.' *Noûs*, 33.3: 317–46

Dorr, Cian and Gideon Rosen (2002). 'Composition as Fiction.' In Richard M. Gale (ed.), *Blackwell Guide to Metaphysics*. Oxford: Basil Blackwell.

Duhem, Pierre (1969). *To Save the Phenomena: An Essay on the Idea of Physical Theory from Plato to Galileo*. E. Doland and C. Maschler (trans.). Chicago: University of Chicago Press.

Dummett, Michael (1993). 'Existence.' In *The Seas of Language*. Oxford: Oxford University Press.

Dworkin, Ronald (1996). 'Objectivity and Truth: You'd Better Believe It.' *Philosophy and Public Affairs*, 25: 27–139.

Eklund, Matti (forthcoming). 'The Deflationary Conception of Ontology.' In *Contemporary Debates in Metaphysics*. John Hawthorne, Theodore Sider, and Dean Zimmerman (eds.). Oxford: Basil Blackwell

Elster, Jon (1984). *Ulysses and the Sirens*. Cambridge: Cambridge University Press.

—— (1985). 'Weakness of Will and the Free-Rider Problem.' *Economics and Philosophy*, 1: 231–65.

Enzle, M. E., R. D. Hansen, and C. A. Lowe (1975). 'Humanizing the Mixed-Motive Paradigm: Methodological Implications from Attribution Theory.' *Simulation and Games*, 6: 151–65.

Evans, Gareth (1982). *The Varieties of Reference*. John McDowell (ed.). Oxford: Clarendon Press.

Field, Hartry (1980). *Science Without Numbers*. Princeton: Princeton University Press.

—— (1986). 'The Deflationary Conception of Truth.' In Graham McDonald and Crispin Wright (eds.), *Fact, Science and Morality*: 55–117. Oxford: Basil Blackwell.

—— (1989). *Realism, Mathematics and Modality*. Oxford: Basil Blackwell.

—— (1990). 'Mathematics Without Truth.' *Pacific Philosophical Quarterly*, 71: 206–22.

—— (1994) 'Deflationist Views of Meaning and Content.' *Mind*, 103: 249–85. Reprinted in Field (2001a: 104–40).

—— (1999). 'Deflating the Conservativeness Argument.' *Journal of Philosophy*, 96: 533–40.

—— (2001a). *Truth and the Absence of Fact*. Oxford: Clarendon Press.

—— (2001b). 'Postscript to "Deflationist Views of Meaning and Content".' In Field (2001a: 141–56).

—— (2001c). 'Attributions of Meaning and Content.' In Field (2001a: 157–74).

Fine, Arthur (1993). 'Fictionalism.' *Midwest Studies in Philosophy*, 18: 1–18.

Fine, Kit (1994). 'Essence and Modality.' *Philosophical Perspectives*, 8: 1–16.

—— (2001). 'The Question of Realism.' *Philosophers' Imprint*, 1: 1–32.

Frank, Philipp (1950). 'Metaphysical Interpretations of Science, II.' *British Journal for the Philosophy of Science*, 1: 2.

Frede, Michael (1979). 'Des Skeptikers Meinungen.' *Neue Heft für Philosophie*, Heft 15.16: 102–29. Translated as 'The Sceptic's Beliefs' in Burnyeat and Frede (1997).

Frege, Gottlob (1918/77). 'Thoughts.' In Peter T. Geach (ed.), *Logical Investigations*: 1–30. New Haven: Yale University Press.

Gardner, Michael (1983). 'Realism and Instrumentalism in Pre-Newtonian Astronomy.' In J. Earman (ed.), *Testing Scientific Theories, Minnesota Studies in the Philosophy of Science*, 10. University of Minnesota Press.

Garner, R. (1993). 'Are Convenient Fictions Harmful to Your Health?' *Philosophy East and West*, 43: 87–106.

Geach, Peter T. (1958). 'Imperative and Deontic Logic.' *Analysis*, 18: 49–56.

—— (1960). 'Ascriptivism.' *The Philosophical Review*, 69: 221–5.

—— (1965). 'Assertion.' *Philosophical Review*, 74: 449–65.

Geach, Peter T. and Max Black (1960). *Translations from the Philosophical Writings of Gottlob Frege*. Oxford: Basil Blackwell.

Gibbard, Allan (1990). *Wise Choices, Apt Feelings: A Theory of Normative Judgment*. Cambridge MA: Harvard University Press.

Gingerich, Owen (1973). 'The Role of Erasmus Rheinhold and the Prutenic Tables in the Dissemination of Copernican Theory.' *Studia Copernicana*, 6: 43–62.

Goodman, Nelson (1968). *Languages of Art*. Indianapolis, IN: Bobbs Merrill.

Graff, Delia (2001). 'Descriptions as Predicates.' *Philosophical Studies*, 102: 1–42.

Grover, Dorothy L. (1977). 'Inheritors and Paradox.' *Journal of Philosophy*, 74: 590–604.

Grover, Dorothy L., Joseph L. Camp, Jr., and Nuel D. Belnap, Jr. (1975). 'A Prosentential Theory of Truth.' *Philosophical Studies*, 27: 73–125.

Gupta, Anil (1993). 'A Critique of Deflationism.' *Philosophical Topics*, 21: 57–81.

Hahn, L. and P. Schilpp (eds.) (1986). *The Philosophy of W. V. Quine*. La Salle, IL: Open Court.

Hale, Bob (1995a). 'Modal Fictionalism: A Simple Dilemma.' *Analysis*, 55.2: 63–7.

—— (1995b). 'A Desparate Fix.' *Analysis*, 55.2: 74–81.

Harman, Gilbert (1986). *Change in View: Principles of Reasoning*. Cambridge, MA: MIT Press, Bradford Books.

Harper, William L., Robert Stalnaker, and Glenn Pearce (eds.) (1981). *Ifs: Conditionals, Belief, Decision, Chance, and Time*. Dordrecht: D. Reidel Publishing Company.

Harrison, Ross (1983). *Jeremy Bentham*. London: Routledge & Kegan Paul.

Heath, Thomas (1932). *Greek Astronomy*. and Kegen Paul J. M. Dent and Sons.

Henkin, Leon (1953). 'Some Notes on Nominalism.' *The Journal of Symbolic Logic*, 19.1: 19–29.

Hills, David (1997). 'Aptness and Truth in Verbal Metaphor.' *Philosophical Topics*, 25: 117–53.

Hinckfuss, I. (1993). 'Suppositions, Presuppositions and Ontology.' *Canadian Journal of Philosophy*, 23.4: 595–617.

Hinckfuss, I. (1996). 'Instrumental Theories: Possibilities and Space and Time.' In P. J. Riggs (ed.), *Natural Kinds, Laws of Nature and Scientific Methodology.* Dordrecht: Kluwer Academic Publishers.

Hirsch, Eli (2002). 'Quantifier Variance and Realism.' *Philosophical Issues*, 12: 51–73.

Hobbes, Thomas (1642/1983). *De Cive.* Oxford: Clarendon Press.

Horgan, Terrance (1984). 'Science Nominalized.' *Philosophy of Science*, 51: 529–49.

Hornstein, H.A., E. Lakind, E. Frankel, and S. Manne (1975). 'Effects of Knowledge about Remote Social Events on Prosocial Behaviour, Social Conception, and Mood.' *Journal of Personality and Social Psychology*, 32: 1038–46.

Horwich, Paul (1998). *Truth,* second edition. Oxford: Clarendon Press.

Hume, David (1739/1978). *A Treatise of Human Nature.* Oxford: Clarendon Press.

—— (1751/1983). *Enquiry Concerning the Principles of Morals.* Cambridge, MA: Hackett Publishing Company.

—— (1779/1997). *Dialogues Concerning Natural Religion*, J. C. A. Gaskin (ed.). Oxford: Oxford University Press, 1997.

Hutchins, Robert M. (ed.) (1952). *Ptolemy, Copernicus, Kepler, Great Books of the Western World*, 16. Encyclopedia Britannica, Inc.

Jackson, Frank (1996). 'Mental Causation.' *Mind*, 105: 377–413.

—— (1998). *From Metaphysics to Ethics: A Defence of Conceptual Analysis.* Oxford: Oxford University Press.

Jardine, Nicholas (1984). *The Birth of History and Philosophy of Science.* Cambridge: Cambridge University Press.

Jarrold, C., J. Boucher, and P. K. Smith, (1996). 'Generativity Deficits in Pretend Play in Autism.' *British Journal of Developmental Psychology*, 14: 275–300.

Johnson-Laird, P. and K. Oatley (2000). 'Cognitive and social construction in emotions.' In M. Lewis and J. Haviland-Jones (eds.), *Handbook of the Emotions*, second edition. New York: Guilford Press.

Johnston, Mark (1989). 'Dispositional Theories of Value.' *Proceedings of the Aristotelian Society*, Supplementary Volume, 63: 139–74.

Joyce, Richard (2002). *The Myth of Morality.* Cambridge: Cambridge University Press.

Kalderon, Mark Eli (2005). *Moral Fictionalism.* Oxford: Oxford University Press.

Kanger, S., and Kanger, H. (1966). 'Rights and Parliamentarianism.' *Theoria*, 32: 85–116.

Kant, Immanuel (1781/1965). *Critique of Pure Reason*, Norman Kemp Smith (ed.). New York: St. Martins.

Kaplan, David (1989). 'Demonstratives.' In Joseph Almog, John Perry, and Howard Wettstein (eds.), *Themes from Kaplan.* Oxford: Oxford University Press.

Kenny, Anthony (1964). *Action, Emotion and the Will.* London: Routledge Kegan & Paul.

Kim, Seahwa (2002). 'Modal Fictionalism Generalized and Defended.' *Philosophical Studies*, 111: 121–46.

King, Jeffrey C. and Jason Stanley (2005). 'Semantics, Pragmatics, and the Role of Semantic Content.' In Zoltán Gendler Szabó (ed.), *Semantics versus Pragmatics*. Oxford: Clarendon Press.

Kirkham, Richard (1992). *Theories of Truth*. Cambridge, MA: The MIT Press.

Kivy, Peter (1990). *Music Alone: Philosophical Reflections on the Purely Musical Experience*. Ithaca: Cornell University Press.

Kripke, Saul A. (1973). 'Reference and Existence.' John Locke Lectures (unpublished).

—— (1975). 'Outline of a Theory of Truth.' *Journal of Philosophy*, 72: 690–716.

—— (1979). 'A Puzzle About Belief.' In Avishai Margalit (ed.), *Meaning and Use*. Dordrecht: Reidel Publishing Company.

—— (1980). *Naming and Necessity*. Cambridge MA: Harvard University Press.

Kroon, Frederick (1992). 'Was Meinong Only Pretending?' *Philosophy and Phenomenological Research*, 52.3: 499–526.

—— (1996). 'Characterizing Non-Existents.' *Grazer Philosophische Studien*, 51: 163–93.

—— (2000). '"Disavowal through Commitment" Theories of Negative Existentials.' In Anthony Everett and Thomas Hofweber (eds.), *Empty Names, Fiction and the Puzzles of Existence*. Stanford: CSLI Publications.

—— (2001). 'Fictionalism and the Informativeness of Identity.' *Philosophical Studies*, 106: 197–225.

—— (2003). 'Quantified Negative Existentials.' *Dialectica*, 57: 149–64.

Lakoff, George and Mark Johnson (1980). *Metaphors We Live By*. Chicago: University of Chicago Press.

Lamarque, Peter and Stein Haugom Olsen (1994). *Truth, Fiction, and Literature: A Philosophical Perspective*. Oxford: Oxford University Press.

Lewis, David (1973). *Counterfactuals*. Oxford: Basil Blackwell.

—— (1978). 'Truth in Fiction.' *American Philosophical Quarterly*, 15.1: 37–46. Reprinted in Lewis (1981a: 261–75).

—— (1981a). *Philosophical Papers*, 1. Oxford: Oxford University Press.

—— (1981b). 'Postscripts to "Truth in Fiction".' In Lewis (1981a: 276–80).

—— (1984). 'Putnam's Paradox.' *Australasian Journal of Philosophy*, 62: 221–36.

—— (1986). *On the Plurality of Worlds*. Oxford: Basil Blackwell.

—— (1989). 'Dispositional Theories of Value.' *Proceedings of the Aristotelian Society*, Supplementary Volume, 63: 113–37.

—— (1991). *Parts of Classes*. Oxford: Basil Blackwell.

—— (1994). 'Reduction of Mind.' In Samuel Guttenplan (ed.), *A Companion to the Philosophy of Mind*. Oxford: Basil Blackwell.

Lindner, Robert M. (1954) 'The Jet-Propelled Couch.' In Lindner, *The Fifty Minute Hour: A Collection of True Psychoanalytic Tales*. New York: Holt, Rinehart, and Winston.

Lloyd, G. E. R. (1978). 'Saving the Appearances.' *Classical Quarterly*, 28: 202–22.

Lyle, J. and H. Hoffman, (1971). 'Children's Use of Television and Other Media.' In J. P. Murray, E. A. Robinson, and G. A. Comstock (eds.), *Television and Social Behavior*, 4. Rockville, MD: National Institutes of Health.

Mackie, John (1977). *Ethics: Inventing Right and Wrong*. New York: Penguin Books.

Maddy, Penelope (1990). 'Mathematics and Oliver Twist.' *Pacific Philosophical Quarterly*, 71: 189–205.

—— (1997). *Naturalism in Mathematics*. Oxford: Clarendon Press.

Maimonides, Moses (1963). *The Guide of the Perplexed*. Shlomo Pines (ed. and trans.). Chicago: University of Chicago Press.

Melia, Joseph (1995). 'On What There's Not.' *Analysis*, 55: 223–9.

—— (2000). 'Weaseling Away the Indispensability Argument.' *Mind*, 109: 455–79.

Menzies, Peter and Philip Pettit (1994). 'In Defence of Fictionalism about Possible Worlds.' *Analysis*, 54.1: 27–36.

Milne, A. A. (1928). *The House at Pooh Corner*. New York: Dutton.

Mishima, Yukio (1966). *Death in Midsummer*. New York: New Directions.

Moran, Richard (1989). 'Seeing and Believing: Metaphor, Image, and Force.' *Critical Inquiry*, 16: 87–112.

Moschovakis, Y. (1980). *Descriptive Set Theory*. Amsterdam: North Holland.

Nolan, Daniel (1997a). 'Three Problems for "Strong" Modal Fictionalism.' *Philosophical Studies*, 87.3: 259–75.

—— (1997b). 'Impossible Worlds: A Modest Approach.' *Notre Dame Journal of Formal Logic*, 38.4: 535–72.

—— (2002). 'Modal Fictionalism.' In Edward N. Zalta (ed.), *The Stanford Encyclopedia of Philosophy*, Summer 2002 Edition. http://plato.stanford.edu/archives/sum2002/entries/fictionalism-modal/.

Nolan, Daniel and John O'Leary-Hawthorne (1996). 'Reflexive Fictionalisms.' *Analysis*, 56.1: 26–32.

Nolan, Daniel, Gregory Restall, and Caroline West (forthcoming). 'Moral Fictionalism versus The Rest.' *Australasian Journal of Philosophy*.

Noonan, Harold (1994). 'In Defence of the Letter of Fictionalism.' *Analysis*, 54.3: 133–9.

Ogden, C. K. (1932). *Bentham's Theory of Fictions*. New York: Harcourt, Brace and Company.

Preminger, Alex and T. V. F. Brogan, *et al.* (1993). *The New Princeton Encyclopedia of Poetry and Poetics*. Princeton: Princeton University Press.

Price, Huw (2003). 'Truth as a Convenient Fiction,' *Journal of Philosophy*, 100: 167–90.

Priest, Graham (1979). 'The Logic of Paradox.' *Journal of Philosophical Logic*, 8: 219–41.

—— (1998). 'What is so bad about Contradictions?' *Journal of Philosophy*, 95: 410–26.

Proclus (1820). *The Commentaries of Proclus on the Timaeus of Plato*. Thomas Taylor (trans.). London: privately printed.

Proudfoot, Diane (MS). 'Telling it as it Could Not Be.'

Putnam, Hilary (1971). *Philosophy of Logic*. New York: Harper & Row.

—— (1975a). 'Philosophy of Logic.' Reprinted in *Mathematics, Matter and Method: Philosophical Papers, 1*. Cambridge, MA: Harvard University Press.

—— (1975b). 'The Meaning of "Meaning".' Reprinted in *Mind, Language, and Reality: Philosophical Papers, 2*. Cambridge: Cambridge University Press.

—— (1987). 'Truth and Convention: On Davidson's Refutation of Conceptual Relativism.' *Dialectica*, 41: 41–67.

Quine, Willard Van Orman (1951). 'Two Dogmas of Empiricism.' *Philosophical Review*, 60: 20–43. Reprinted in Quine (1961).

—— (1960). *Word and Object*. Cambridge, MA: MIT Press.

—— (1961). *From a Logical Point of View*, second edition. New York: Harper & Row.

—— (1986). 'Reply to Parsons.' In Hahn and Schilpp (1986).

—— (1992). *Pursuit of Truth*, revised edition. Cambridge: Harvard University Press.

Recanati, François (1993). *Direct Reference: From Language to Thought*. Oxford: Blackwell.

—— (2000). *Oratia Obliqua, Oratia Recta*. Cambridge, MA: MIT Press.

Reimer, Marga (2001). 'The Problem of Empty Names.' *Australasian Journal of Philosophy*, 79: 491–506.

Richard, Mark (1990). *Propositional Attitudes*. Cambridge: Cambridge University Press.

—— (2000). 'Semantic Pretense.' In Anthony Everett and Thomas Hofweber (eds.), *Empty Names, Fiction and the Puzzles of Existence* : 205–32. Stanford: CSLI Publications.

Richards, I. A. (1936). *The Philosophy of Rhetoric*. Oxford: Oxford University Press.

Rorty, Richard (1982). *Consequences of Pragmatism*. Minneapolis: University of Minnesota Press.

Rosen, Edward (1984). *Copernicus and the Scientific Revolution*. Malabar, Florida: Krieger.

Rosen, Gideon (MS). 'Internalism and Common Sense.'

—— (1990). 'Modal Fictionalism.' *Mind*, 99.395: 327–54.

—— (1993). 'A Problem for Fictionalism About Possible Worlds.' *Analysis*, 53.2: 71–81.

—— (1994). 'What is Constructive Empiricism?' *Philosophical Studies*, 74: 143–78.

—— (1995). 'Modal Fictionalism Fixed.' *Analysis*, 55.2: 67–73.

—— (2001). 'Nominalism, Naturalism, Epistemic Relativism.' *Philosophical Perspectives*, 15: 69–91.

Ross, David W. (1939). *Foundations of Ethics*. Oxford: Oxford University Press.

Rowling, J. K. (1998). *Harry Potter and the Sorcerer's Stone*. New York: Scholastic Press.

Russell, Bertrand (1956). 'The Philosophy of Logical Atomism.' In R. C. Marsh (ed.), *Logic and Knowledge*. London: George Allen & Unwin.

Sainsbury, Mark (1999). 'Names, Fictional Names, and "Really".' *Proceedings of the Aristotelian Society*, Supplementary Volume, 73: 243–69.

Salmon, Nathan (1986). *Frege's Puzzle*. Cambridge, MA: MIT Press.

—— (1998). 'Nonexistence.' *Noûs*, 32.3: 277–319.

Sambursky, Samuel (1962). *The Physical World of Late Antiquity*. Basic Books.

Schelling, Thomas (1980). 'The Intimate Contest for Self-Command.' *The Public Interest*, 60: 94–118.

Schiffer, Stephen (1995). 'Descriptions, Indexicals, and Belief Reports: Some Dilemmas (But Not the Ones You Expect).' *Mind*, 104: 107–31.

—— (1996). 'Language-Created, Language-Independent Entities.' *Philosophical Topics*, 24: 149–67.

Scruton, Roger (1983). 'Understanding Music.' In Scruton, *The Aesthetic Understanding: Essays in the Philosophy of Art and Culture*. London: Methuen.

Searle, John R. (1962). 'Meaning and Speech Acts.' *The Philosophical Review*, 71: 423–32.

—— (1969). *Speech Acts: An Essay in the Philosophy of Language*. Cambridge: Cambridge University Press.

—— (1979). *Expression and Meaning*. Cambridge: Cambridge University Press.

Sellars, Wilfrid (1997). *Empiricism and the Philosophy of Mind*. Cambridge, MA: Harvard University Press.

Sextus Empiricus (2000). *Outlines of Scepticism,* Julia Annas and Jonathan Barnes (eds.). Cambridge: Cambridge University Press.

Shier, David (1996). 'Direct Reference for the Narrow Minded.' *Pacific Philosophical Quarterly*, 77: 225–48.

Sider, Theodore (1993). 'Van Inwagen and the Possibility of Gunk.' *Analysis*, 53: 285–9.

—— (2003). 'Against Vague Existence.' *Philosophical Studies*, 114: 135–46.

—— (MS). 'Quantifiers and Temporal Ontology.' Available online at http://fas-philosophy.rutgers.edu/~sider/papers/quantifiers_and_presentism.pdf.

Siovoranes, Lucas (1996). *Proclus: Neo-Platonic Philosophy and Science*. Edinburgh: Edinburgh University Press.

Soames, Scott (1987). 'Direct Reference, Propositional Attitudes, and Semantic Content.' *Philosophical Topics*, 15: 47–87.

—— (1999). *Understanding Truth*. Oxford: Oxford University Press.

—— (2002). *Beyond Rigidity: The Unfinished Semantic Agenda of Naming and Necessity*. New York: Oxford University Press.

Stalnaker, Robert (1968). 'A Theory of Conditionals.' In *Studies in Logical Theory: American Philosophical Quarterly Monograph Series*, No. 2. Oxford: Basil Blackwell. Reprinted in Harper *et al.* (1981: 41–56).

—— (1981). 'A Defense of Conditional Excluded Middle.' In Harper *et al.* (1981: 87–104).

—— (2003). 'Conceptual Truth and Metaphysical Necessity.' In *Ways a World Might Be: Metaphysical and Anti-Metaphysical Essays*. Oxford: Oxford University Press.

Stanley, Jason (2001). 'Hermeneutic Fictionalism.' *Midwest Studies in Philosophy*, 25: 36–71.

Stanley, Jason and Zoltán Gendler Szabó (2000). 'On Quantifier Domain Restriction.' *Mind and Language*, 15: 219–61.

Steen, F. F. and S. A. Owen (2001). 'Evolution's Pedagogy: An Adaptationist Model of Pretense and Entertainment.' *Journal of Cognition and Culture*, 1: 289–321.

Steiner, Mark (2000). *The Applicability of Mathematics as a Philosophical Problem*. Cambridge, MA: Harvard University Press.

Szabó, Zoltán Gendler (2001). 'Fictionalism and Moore's Paradox.' *Canadian Journal of Philosophy*, 31: 293–308.

Tarski, Alfred (1944). 'The Semantic Conception of Truth.' *Philosophy and Phenomenological Research*, 4: 341–75.

Unger, Peter (1984). *Philosophical Relativity*. Minneapolis: University of Minnesota Press.

Vaihinger, Hans (1924). *The Philosophy of 'As If'*. C. K. Ogden (trans.). London: Kegan Paul.

van Fraassen, Bas C. (1980). *The Scientific Image*. Oxford: Oxford University Press.

—— (1994). 'Gideon Rosen on Constructive Empiricism.' *Philosophical Studies*, 74: 179–92.

van Inwagen, Peter (1985). 'Pretense and Paraphrase.' In Peter McCormick (ed.), *The Reasons of Art: Artworks and the Formations of Philosophy*. Ottowa: University of Ottowa Press.

—— (1990). *Material Beings*. Ithaca: Cornell University Press.

—— (2000). 'Quantification and Fictional Discourse.' In Anthony Everett and Thomas Hofweber (eds.), *Empty Names, Fiction and the Puzzles of Existence*. Stanford: CSLI Publications.

Velleman, J. David (2000). 'On the Aim of Belief.' Reprinted in *The Possibility of Practical Reason*: 244–81. Oxford: Clarendon Press.

Vision, Gerald (1994). 'Fiction and Fictionalist Reductions.' *Pacific Philosophical Quarterly*, 74: 150–74.

Walton, Kendall L. (1978). 'Fearing Fictions.' *Journal of Philosophy*, 75.1: 5–27.

—— (1990). *Mimesis as Make-Believe*. Cambridge, MA: Harvard University Press.

—— (1993). 'Metaphor and Prop Oriented Make-Believe.' *European Journal of Philosophy*, 1.1: 39–57.

—— (1997). 'Spelunking, Simulation, and Slime: On Being Moved by Fiction.' In *Emotion and the Arts*. Oxford: Oxford University Press.

—— (2000). 'Existence as Metaphor?' In Anthony Everett and Thomas Hofweber (eds.), *Empty Names, Fiction and the Puzzles of Existence*. Stanford: CSLI Publications

Westman, Robert S. (1975a). *The Copernican Achievement*. University of California Press.

—— (1975b). 'The Melanchthon Circle, Rheticus, and the Wittenberg Interpretation of the Copernican Theory.' *Isis*, 65: 165–93.

—— (1975c). 'Three Responses to the Copernican Theory: Johannes Praetorius, Tycho Brahe and Michael Maestlin.' In Westman (1975a).

Wiggins, David (1994). 'The Kant–Frege–Russell View of Existence.' In *Modality, Morality, and Belief: Essays in Honor of Ruth Barcan Marcus*. Cambridge: Cambridge University Press.

Wigner, Eugene, P. (1967). 'The Unreasonable Effectiveness of Mathematics in the Natural Sciences.' In *Symmetries and Reflections*. Bloomington, IN: Indiana University Press.

Williams, Bernard (1985). *Ethics and the Limits of Philosophy*. Cambridge, MA: Harvard University Press.

Williamson, Timothy (2003). 'Everything.' In John Hawthorne and Dean Zimmerman (eds.), *Philosophical Perspectives*, 17: 415–65.

Wilson, James Q. (1993). *The Moral Sense*. NY: Free Press.

Wittgenstein, Ludwig (1958). *The Philosophical Investigations*. New York: Macmillan Publishing Co., Ltd.

Woodbridge, James A. (MS). 'Propositions as Semantic Pretense.'

—— (2003). 'Deflationism and the Generalization Problem.' *Logica Yearbook 2003*: 285–97. Prague: Filosofia, Institute of Philosophy, Academy of Sciences of the Czech Republic.

Wrightman (1975). 'Andreas Osiander's Contribution to the Copernican Achievement.' In Westman (1975a).

Yablo, Stephen (1996). 'How in the World?' *Philosophical Topics*, 24.1: 255–86.

—— (1998). 'Does Ontology Rest on a Mistake?' *The Proceedings of the Aristotelian Society*, Supplementary Volume, 72: 229–61.

—— (2000a). 'Apriority and Existence.' In Paul Boghossian and Christopher Peacocke (eds.), *New Essays on the A Priori*: 197–228. Oxford: Oxford University Press: 197–228.

—— (2000b). 'A Paradox of Existence.' In Anthony Everett and Thomas Hofweber (eds.), *Empty Names, Fiction, and the Puzzles of Existence*: 275–312. Paolo Alto: CSLI Publications.

—— (2002a). 'Go Figure: A Path Through Fictionalism.' *Midwest Studies in Philosophy*, 25: 72–102.

—— (2002b). 'Abstract Objects: A Case Study.' *Philosophical Issues*, 12: 220–40.

—— (forthcoming). 'Content Carving, Some Ways.' *Philosophical Quarterly*.

Zalta, Edward (1983). *Abstract Objects*. Dordrecht: D. Reidel Publishing Company.

Index